❧ *Lafcadio Hearn*

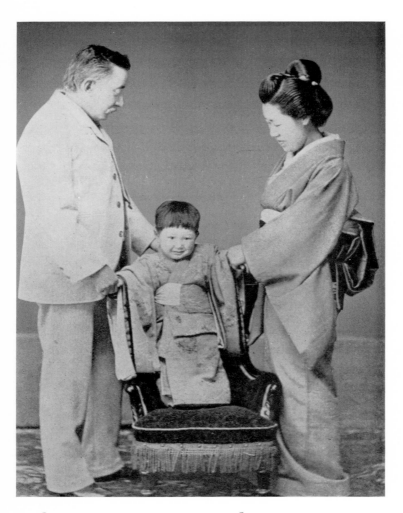

*Lafcadio Hearn with his wife
and son Kazuo at Kumamoto, 1895*

LAFCADIO HEARN

✣ *by Elizabeth Stevenson*

THE MACMILLAN COMPANY

New York 1961

First Printing

The frontispiece is reproduced from *Father and I,* by Kazuo Koizumi, published by Houghton Mifflin Company, Boston, 1935.

The Macmillan Company, New York
Brett-Macmillan Ltd., Galt, Ontario

Printed in the United States of America

Library of Congress catalog card number:
61-10337

For my sisters

JOAN STEVENSON WING

MARTHA STEVENSON FABIAN

For all this astonishment of beauty, all this majesty of light and form and color, will surely endure,—marvelous as now,—after we shall have lain down to sleep where no dreams come, and may never arise from the dust of our rest to look upon it.

No heart-beat is cheap, no gentleness despicable, no kindness is common . . .

Lafcadio Hearn
Two Years in the French West Indies

Acknowledgments

I owe my thanks to many persons and organizations who helped me find my way when I was searching for the traces of Lafcadio Hearn in the places where he lived and in the papers he left behind, scattered now in the manuscript collections of the libraries and private collections of two continents.

My editor, Cecil Scott, has, as always, shown patience and imagination, and an uncompromisingly high standard.

The John Simon Guggenheim Memorial Foundation made possible a year of work, a year which included a trip to Martinique. Jointly the Rockefeller Foundation and the John Simon Guggenheim Memorial Foundation made possible a trip to Japan.

The staff of the Public Library of Cincinnati and Hamilton County gave me access to the Hearn Collection and the files of the *Enquirer* and the *Commercial* of the 1870's. Yeatman Anderson III, Curator of Rare Books, was particularly helpful.

The staff of the Howard-Tilton Memorial Library of Tulane University in New Orleans put at my disposal the material of the Lafcadio Hearn Room and the resources of the Lafcadio Hearn Collection, as well as the files of the *Item,* the *Democrat,* and the *Times-Democrat* of the 1880's.

In Fort de France, Martinique, a staff member of the Schoelcher Library showed me that Martinique still reads Lafcadio Hearn—in French.

Tokyo University, through the courtesy of Iyoji Aono, Associate Librarian, allowed me to explore the holdings of the Hearn Collection housed in the Department of Literature.

Tenri Central Library of Tenri College, Tenri, Japan, gave me access to the Hearn Collection through the courtesy of the Chief Librarian, Mr. M. Tominaga, and the Keeper of the Hearn Collection, Mr. Tadanobu Kawai.

The Hearn papers in the C. Waller Barrett Collection in the Alderman

Library of the University of Virginia were put at my disposal by the staff. I should like to thank particularly John Cook Wyllie, Librarian, and Francis L. Berkeley, Jr., Associate Librarian.

The Librarian of the Houghton Library, Harvard University, William A. Jackson, made available to me the resources of the library's Hearn Collection.

The Century Association of New York City, through its Librarian, Theodore Bolton, allowed me to read Hearn's manuscript letters to Ellwood Hendrick. The New York Public Library's Manuscript Room, and its head, Robert W. Hill, Keeper of Manuscripts, allowed me to read the other half of Hearn's letters to Hendrick.

Herbert Cahoon, Curator of Autograph Manuscripts of the Pierpont Morgan Library of New York City, showed me four important Hearn letters recently acquired in the Harper Collection.

David C. Mearns and the staff of the Manuscript Division of the Reference Department of the Library of Congress gave me access to the Hearn papers the Library holds in various collections, particularly the large George M. Gould Collection of Hearniana.

Alice H. Bonnell, of Special Collections, Columbia University libraries, sent me on microfilm Hearn's letters to Dr. Gould, from the Stedman Collection. Lyle H. Wright, Head of the Reference Department of the Huntington Library, San Marino, California, sent me on microfilm Hearn's letters to Henry Mills Alden.

The staff of the McCain Library of Agnes Scott College, Decatur, Georgia, has, as usual, helped me in many ways on numberless occasions. I thank again the Librarian, Mrs. N. E. Byers, Miss Lillian Newman, and the other members of the staff.

Lee Allen, who has made Hearn's Cincinnati life his field, gave me the benefit of his research.

N. I. Ludwig of Grand Isle told me about his father's recollection of Hearn on the island and showed me where Hearn's vacation place, Krantz's Hotel, once stood.

My only professional guide in Japan was a gentle scholar named Ikeda who showed me Hearn's grave in the Zoshigaya Cemetery and the campus of Waseda University.

In Tokyo Professor Ichiro Nishizaki showed me the sites of Hearn's two houses in the city as well as the remnants of the Kobudera Temple, and gave me the benefit of his many years of research and editing as a Hearn scholar.

In Kyoto, P. D. Perkins, the scholarly book dealer and editor of a monumental bibliography of Hearn, talked with me knowledgeably about Hearn material and where to find it. He shared generously both his insights into Hearn scholarship and his personal enthusiasm on the subject.

In Matsue, Yasuyuki Kajitani, Professor at Shimane University and adviser to the Lafcadio Hearn Museum of Matsue, helped me to see Hearn's city, not only the Museum, the Hearn house, the school where he taught, but the city and its countryside as it existed for Hearn. In making charts and outlines of Hearn's activities in Izumo, in drawing maps of his journeys, in conducting our joint expeditions to Yaegaki, Mionoseki, and Taisha, Professor Kajitani was an unselfish sharer of everything he had learned of Hearn in many years of scholarship and firsthand exploration of Hearn's Izumo terrain.

The administrative staff of Kumamoto University in Kumamoto, Japan, were gracious in showing me the building and one of the classrooms where Hearn taught. Professor Masayuki Kawarabata of the Faculty of Law and Literature shared with me his considered judgment on Hearn's career in Kumamoto, and delighted in showing me that Hearn's "Stone Buddha" on the hill above the school still existed.

Alan Priest, Curator of the Department of Far Eastern Art of the Metropolitan Museum, gave me generously the benefit of his experience and knowledge of Japan, as well as the stimulus of his enthusiasm.

Mrs. Charles Hartshorne of Atlanta gave me good advice on living and working in Japan.

For all my Hearn travels I had the invaluable aid of Dorothy T. Joyner, both in her professional advice and in her personal encouragement.

On first arriving in Japan I had the advantage of the gifted staff of the International House to help acclimate me in a strange land. I thank particularly John E. Howes, then Associate Director, for his advice and encouragement.

I appreciate the kindness of Professor O. W. Frost of Willamette University in letting me use some of the material in his "Two Unpublished Hearn Letters," which appeared in the fifth anniversary issue, January 1960, of *Today's Japan*, material which Kazuo Koizumi first gave permission to be used. I thank Professor Frost also for his interest and stimulation given a worker in a field in which he has done pioneer work. I thank also, for a similar encouragement, Albert Mordell of Philadelphia, who was an initiator of scholarly research on Hearn in America. I thank also all the other Hearn scholars upon whose work I have built: Elizabeth Bisland, Charles W. Hutson, John Erskine, Nina H. Kennard, Oscar Lewis, Vera McWilliams, Edward L. Tinker, Marcel Robert, and others. I want also to record my respect for three acute critics of Hearn's writing: Edward Thomas, Paul Elmer More, and Malcolm Cowley.

Preface

He was an unimportant person. He was a minor writer. His struggle for life went on almost unnoticed. His heroism was private, his pathos unseen, his small victories unheard and unannounced. He has been forgotten or almost forgotten today.

Only the Japanese make a positive claim to Lafcadio Hearn. But they are in an awkward position in relation to their fading national hero. They must read him in English, or in translation, and in the last fifty years Japanese admiration for Hearn has deteriorated. He is a vivid name now only in Matsue, the small unchanging city Hearn made known to the outside world. Even here the tradition of affectionate reverence for Hearn has stiffened into something official. Most Japanese read Hearn in fragments in school text-books. Only a handful of writers and teachers scattered through the islands stubbornly defend his name and try to enhance it by modest jobs of editing and republishing. The fierce, uncritical energies of the young follow new fashions and adore new names. Among these ardent, impatient ones who do not read him, Hearn is pushed back into the storehouse of national memory. He is one more museum piece belonging to the older Japan that failed. It is concluded on insufficient evidence that Hearn presented a soft image of Japan to the world, and must be damned.

Making a related mistake, the contemporary Western interpreters of Japan blame Hearn, as the most noted interpreter of Japan to the West, for the West's incomprehension of that complex land. They shoulder on Hearn a whole half-century's failure of understanding. Not knowing him—his range, his development, the slow, painful change of opinion he underwent in Japan, and the faithful reflection there was of this broad movement of his spirit in his work—they make his name stand for all the superficial misinterpretations of Japan in his own time and in the time since his death in 1904.

They commit another grave fault. Writing from the viewpoint of history or the social sciences, they ignore or miss the point of the artist's kind of work. They dismiss as beneath their notice the small, self-contained, and self-sustaining wholes which Hearn's stories and sketches sometimes were, and the enduringness of them which has nothing to do with either false or true views of history.

Since Hearn during the last part of his life was peculiarly identified with Japan, the literary historians and critics of the West have never been anything but halfhearted in claiming him for the West. Yet they might well do so. He wrote a considerable body of mature work before he ever saw Japan. The case for the British is thinner than for the Americans, if they should ever wish to add him to their list of writers, but it is not altogether hopeless. Hearn spent his formative years in Dublin. He went to college in England. He retained his British citizenship to the age of forty-five. He was the most noted teacher of English literature ever to hold a position in the Japanese schools.

The American case for claiming Hearn is considerably better than that of the British, but it has not been exercised. Catapulted by misfortune to the American side of the Atlantic at an immature and frightened nineteen, Hearn survived, and adapted himself handily to the American scene in the decade of the 1870's in Cincinnati and during the 1880's in New Orleans. During these twenty years he was a newspaperman of unusual energy and imagination, and in each of his American cities he was considered the best man in his profession. At the very end of his time in New Orleans he was beginning to be accepted as a considerable figure of the New South. But Hearn went first to Martinique and then to Japan, and his American places forgot him.

Hearn's youthful and mistimed romanticism was another reason for Western critics hesitating to place him. He came to the lagging movement late, and labeled himself romantic just when romanticism disguised itself and began to call itself by other names. Yet Hearn's romanticism was genuine. It gave him a push toward his first good work. It gave him a pride in his solitude. It gave him confidence in what a single individual could do in an indifferent community.

It has been carelessly assumed that Hearn's explorations of Japan were only those of an undisciplined romantic whoring after exotic novelties. Some of his own terminology aided this misconception. It was not noticed that both in his thinking and in his living the older Hearn modified his youthful ideas. He enlarged himself through his amateur studies of science and religion. He enlarged himself by living in Japan. There he discovered a beautifully ordered society which was not inimical to the artist's work, but which had no use for individualism. It was this push and pull of opposing forces in Hearn's development that matured him. It was this molding work of opposites that gave to his last best writing the flavor, economy, and force it had in its small chosen field.

Hearn was widely read during his lifetime, and praised, often for wrong reasons. After his death serious criticism dropped him. He was quarreled over for a generation by friends and enemies, the partisans of love and hate. Only within the last decade has there stirred the beginning of a new, objective appraisal of Hearn. And even yet he is not seen whole, or in proper relation to his background.

Yet Hearn could bear scrutiny. To read him again is to discover a person of resistant value and a writer of solid virtue. It is this substantiality in his writing that his contemporaries overlooked. They granted him color but not solidity. It has taken fifty years for the real shape and weight of these slight pieces to be apparent.

His output was more limited than comprehensive. He was not a poet, although he achieved some small bits of poetry in translation. He was not a novelist, although he wrote a kind of novel in *Chita* and in *Youma*. He was not a thinker, although his writing was aquiver with ideas. He earned his living for many years as a newspaper reporter. When he escaped from this daily drudgery, he chose to write travel essays, and to retell folk tales. The body of his work is therefore special.

Yet these essays and tales—aside from the art that is in them—have a weight not to be expected. A bias of his mind organized his vivid impressions into a shape of some significance. That significance was not primarily the color and the exotic flavor for which he was celebrated during his own lifetime. In addition to his childlike delight in bright surfaces, he was concerned with basic human motives. He saw these motives moving most nakedly in the harried lives of the poor. Without a trace of condescension, without any wounding pity, he entered into the life of the dock workers of Cincinnati, the French-speaking Negroes of New Orleans and Martinique, and the unimportant townspeople and villagers of Japan. He came to know, even to the very ache of it in him, the way these people worked, how they named things, what they believed.

He was distinguished in these unselfconscious acts of discrimination by an attribute of the temperament. What was remarkable in Hearn, wrote Paul Elmer More, in one of the first serious appraisals of the writer, was his emotional tact, "the peculiar sympathies of his mind." [1] Hearn excelled in bending the intellect in the direction of understanding and acceptance. And necessarily as he moved from west to east, carrying with him his native gifts, Hearn picked up a few of the ideas of his time, ideas which may be labeled conveniently the romanticism of his youth, the evolutionism of his maturity, the "Buddhism" of his last years. These ideas gave a sort of fiber to the impressionism of the senses and the temperament.

His writings are not just aids for understanding various odd cultures. They are an end in themselves. Hearn served an apprenticeship in the art of literal translation, but in his best work he did not just translate stories from other cultures: he re-created them. Finding, rescuing, remaking—Hearn left behind a group of irreplaceable tales which give the pure pleasure of art. His essays too—of discovery, description, conclusion—are often creations; facts in them are laced together by art.

The biography of a man who snatched a small achievement out of much waste must not scant the deformities of character and the accidents of circumstance. This life, set twisting upon its eccentric course by birth upon the Greek island of Leucadia, and finished by death upon the Japanese island of Honshu, functioned within an unusually limiting set of conditions. Brought up upon a diet of great expectations, the child was betrayed of them and grew up shy, suspicious, and touchy. Deprived of the sight of one eye and disfigured in appearance, the adolescent redoubled his childish faults. Abandoned by his family to suffer some direness of poverty, the young man chewed bitterly upon his misfortunes, and childish and youthful flaws hardened into mature traits. Hearn led always a life that was somewhat strange and occasionally, by the standards of respectability, scandalous. Yet he had the courage of the unencouraged man. He lived to his ultimate fifty-fourth year in a succession of disasters; but he made his way, and he held onto his honesty. As native to him as his faults were his unbudgable virtues: personal bravery, a stiff integrity, a childlike love of beauty, a naïve sympathy for all that lived. He drifted, but in the end he halted the drift and made a pattern of his life as he had made patterns of the disorganized impressions of his senses. An awkward and touching mixture of circumstance and essence—Lafcadio Hearn—and worthy of meditation.

Contents

1 ✂ Entrance

There walked the streets of Cincinnati in the year 1869 a new inhabitant of that gross and prosperous city upon the Ohio River. He was a slight boy of nineteen, blind in one eye, half starved, raggedly dressed, dirty from sleeping in stables and streets and industrial dump yards. He betrayed his origin by the faintest touch of Irish in his speech.

He had come into the city—busy and big to him in his smallness—on a train from the east crowded with immigrants. A Norwegian girl had impulsively handed him a sandwich on the long voyage westward from New York City. It was his only meal on the train. In the strange city he looked up the gentleman whose name had been given to him. A few dollars were doled out to him grudgingly. He realized that this, and a little more, was all the help he was going to be given here. Soon cast off and told, as he remembered, "to go to the devil and take care of myself," [1] he did both.

He picked up a bit of work here, a bit there, not holding any job for long. He carried mirrors to sell for a peddler, clumsily broke his consignment on the street, and fled. He lettered placards. He tried to sell books from door to door. He carried handbills. He became, for one day only, a telegraph messenger boy, and gave up because he was older and odder than the other boys, and they laughed at him. He slept one night in a boiler in a back lot. He slept another in the loft of a stable, and was grateful in his straw nest for the warm breath of the horses steaming upward in the cold night. He lost very early his father's picture, and his luggage, when he was thrown out of a lodging place.

His telling of this time was always disconnected, and he never unraveled the proper sequence, only blurting out to friends bits and pieces of this experience of earliest maturity. But at last, in the worst period of hungriness and raggedness, he found a friend.

Henry Watkin, who kept a printing shop, into which for some reason Lafcadio Hearn stumbled, saw something to save in the thin, pale face, and something worth listening to in the cultivated, eloquent words that at last poured out in return for kindness. Devilishly proud, touchy, consumed with resentments, the boy was soothed and fed and given a bed of paper shavings in the back of the shop. To clean the floor, to run errands, perhaps to learn how to set up type, for these good reasons Watkin took him in, but also because he himself was a lonely person.

Thus, on the edge of falling off into nothingness, of being finally and completely lost, Lafcadio Hearn, nineteen years old, found a foothold. The tattered young drifter of the streets washed himself, smoothed his hair, filled his stomach, and composed his tired bones to rest. Awakening to the security of the shop, he began awkwardly to learn to work and to live again.

2 ❧ Patrick Lafcadio

The child was begotten by accident, or almost so. Only a chance of military movement caused the meeting of his father and mother. The father,
Charles Bush Hearn, was a surgeon and officer in one of Queen Victoria's
regiments. He was an Anglo-Irishman out of Dublin, the son and grand-
son of army officers whose father and uncles had all served under Wellington in Spain. He was a graduate of Trinity College, Dublin, and the
Royal College of Surgeons, Dublin, and a nominal Anglican. The
mother, Rosa Antonia Cassimati, the daughter of Anthony Cassimati,
was a native of the small island of Cerigo, the ancient Cythera, the most
southern of the Ionian Islands off the west coast of Greece, and the
most desolate and barren, the most wind-swept and sea-dominated of
those islands. Her people were honorable people of the island, of noble
Ionian rank, consequential in their small world.[2] As was customary
among the people of these islands, it was not thought proper for a
woman, even of gentle family, to be taught to read or write, and Rosa
could do neither. Her faith was a passionate adherence to the Greek
Orthodox Church. These two unlike people met in 1848, when Charles
was thirty and Rosa was twenty-five, because British troops, to which
Charles Hearn as Assistant Surgeon was attached, happened during a
time of trouble to be transferred from Corfu to Cerigo.

The people of Rosa's island had seen an almost numberless series of
invasions and occupations. There had been since the Middle Ages the

Turks, the Venetians, the French, the Russians, and now, the British. The French had taken the islands from Venice when the Venetian Republic fell in 1797. The British had taken them from the French when Napoleon fell in 1815. There had been a Russian interlude between 1798 and 1807. Emperor Paul had fed the islanders' already latent nationalism during these nine years by calling the seven Ionian Islands the Septinsular Republic.

The national temper, roused by the mere concept of entity, fretted under British rule. In 1848 a rebellion broke out on Cephalonia, one of the islands of the group. The Ionian Parliament, a shadow parliament, passed a resolution that the islands should belong, not to England, but to Greece. More troops were needed, for Britain was not prepared to give up the islands, and would not till 1864. Troops already stationed on the islands were moved about from one island to another according to military necessity. Charles Hearn, who had served already on the islands of Zante, Ithaca, and Corfu, was sent in April 1848 to Cerigo. It was on Cerigo that Charles Hearn met Rosa Cassimati.

Assistant Surgeon Hearn was prepossessing and not shy. It was not difficult for him to become acquainted with a girl of the islands. He had the self-confidence of his rank, class, and nationality, and not much imagination. It was more difficult for the girl. Her people did not like the sight of Rosa walking out with a member of the hated foreign army. What brought this casual romance to the stage of defiance and self-assertion was some extra push of pressure from one side or the other, some reaction against a prohibition of meeting. The child of that union remembered having been told a story, which may have been an embroidery or an exaggeration:

My father was attacked by mother's brother, terribly stabbed, and left for dead. He recovered, and eloped with mother when the regiment was ordered away.[3]

The known facts show a sequence of some pathos. Charles Hearn was transferred from Cerigo to another island of the group, Leucadia (the British called it Santa Maura), in June 1849. There, in the following month, on July 24th, a child was born to the young and as yet unmarried pair, a boy —George Robert Hearn. On November 16, 1849, Charles Hearn was promoted to Staff Surgeon, Second Class, the equivalent of Captain, and within a month ordered to return to England for reassignment. Nine days after his promotion, on November 25, 1849, Charles Hearn and Rosa Cassimati were married in the ritual of the Greek Orthodox Church. On February 27, 1850, Charles left Leucadia for England, and Rosa, in the fifth month of her second pregnancy, remained behind.

On June 27, 1850, the second child of the oddly mismatched parents was born. The birth of Patrick Lafcadio, the name a witness to his divided heritage, was recorded in the ceremony of baptism in the parish church of Santa Paraskevi. Irish in his first name, Greek in his second, it was by the second name that he would be known. Rosa had named the child for the island that was his birthplace. Leucadia in modern Greek is pronounced Lafcadia, or Lefcadia. Today it is called Levkas.

Two months after Lafcadio's birth, on August 17, 1850, the first child, George Robert, died. For the next two years Rosa's absent husband served in the British West Indies, first on the island of Dominica, and then on the island of Grenada. He did not during this time find a place for his wife and remaining child. He came close to behaving as if they did not exist. He had not told his army superiors of the marriage, fearing the scandal that might arise because of the temporary irregularity of the union. But in a letter signed July 30, 1852, written from Grenada, Charles Hearn formally notified the War Office in London of his marriage and the birth of his children, and at about this time recalled Rosa and Patrick Lafcadio into his life. They were told to come north to Dublin to live with his family.

At the time that Rosa was bidden to make this long journey away from her homeland, Charles was still in the West Indies. The arrangements were taken care of by a younger Hearn brother, Richard Holmes Hearn, who lived in Paris. Whether he came south to Greece is not known, but through the haze of very belated researches one can see Rosa, the child, Richard Holmes Hearn, and an attendant Englishwoman who served Rosa as interpreter, a Miss Butcher, arrive at last in Dublin after a trip that may have taken them by way of Malta where Robert, another brother of Charles, was stationed. When the mother and child arrived in Dublin on August 1, 1852, Lafcadio was slightly more than two years and one month old.

Hearn remembered very little of his earliest Greek environment. Only childish and fragmented bits of color and light teased his memory, and a recollection of a time of uncomplicated happiness. These broken bits of memory were not much, but they were to be very precious to him, and were purified and manipulated by his imagination. Handling these memories, he made a claim upon a Mediterranean past. He wished, under gray Irish skies, to be Greek, to be pagan, to be even "Oriental." Therefore the island Leucadia was important to him. He gave this remote Greek past a passionate allegiance he always withheld from the settled Irish upper-class respectability of his Dublin upbringing.

His mother soon vanished out of his life in a haze of unhappiness. He never knew very much about her or her people, but he willed her to have been happy in those lost days of his infancy.

I have memory of a place and a magical time in which the Sun and the Moon were larger and brighter than now. Whether it was of this life or of some life before I cannot tell. But I know the sky was very much more blue, and nearer to the world,— . . . The sea was alive, and used to talk,—and the Wind made me cry out for joy when it touched me. . . . And all that country and time were softly ruled by One who thought only of ways to make me happy.[4]

The lost earthly paradise always glimmered southward thereafter to Lafcadio. Perhaps this might not have been so, perhaps he might have wandered in another direction, but for the fact that his mother failed to be happy in the north and returned at last southward.

When in August 1852 the mother and child appeared upon the doorstep of No. 48, Lower Gardiner Street, Dublin, where Charles' mother, Elizabeth Holmes Hearn, was then living with her daughter Jane, and her son-in-law, Henry Clocough Stephens, they could not have seemed more outlandish. In their clothes, their manners, their talk—a mixture of Romaic and Italian— and in the oddly demonstrative faith to which Rosa clung, as if it were all she had of her own, the pair were utterly foreign.

It was the beginning of an unsuccessful sojourn for Rosa. She could not adjust and did not try to. And the tightly knit clan into which she had been dropped was not pliable. Not much has been learned about Rosa's family, but something is known about Charles' family. To begin with, it was two families, united into one through Charles' widowed mother, Elizabeth Holmes Hearn. Although in Dublin a slight difference of tone might have been seen between a Hearn and a Holmes, the difference would not have been noticeable to a Greek girl, speaking no English. Both families belonged solidly and unthinkingly to the ruling class of the Ireland of the 1850's. They were not important members of the dominant group, but they belonged to it in all their thinking and acting. Their ways were so set as never to be considered at all. Anglo-Irish, in a sea of Irish Catholicism, they did not know even the Irish very well. Greek ways were beyond their comprehension. Lafcadio wrote later, "Skepticism is hereditary on my father's side," [5] but the skepticism of his father's family was safely wrapped in outward conformity. The mother who crossed herself publicly, the child who looked so odd with little gold earrings in his ears seemed very strange and difficult. Rosa was very unadaptable too. She was both passionate and careless of the suitability of her passions. And the child who had come to Ireland with his black hair hanging long to his shoulders, clutching a doll tightly as if afraid it might be snatched from him, was of a hypersensitive temperament, with perceptions of the keenest, nerves quickly jangled, and an imagination of alarming growth.

The Hearns had been in Ireland at least since the seventeenth century.

Charles Hearn's great-grandfather, the Venerable Daniel Hearn, 1693 to 1766, had a distinguished ecclesiastical career after earning the B.A. and M.A. degrees at Trinity College, Dublin, becoming Archdeacon of Cashel and Rector of St. Anne's, Dublin, as well as serving as chaplain to Lionel Sackville, the Duke of Dorset, who was Lord Lieutenant of Ireland. There had been Hearns of their own line in Ireland ever since that time, and perhaps before, first in the County of Westmeath where they held property granted by the crown, and then scattering and multiplying, in various other corners of Ireland. The Hearns were useful, responsible people who had furnished an unusual number of clergymen for the Church of England and soldiers for the army of England. They had one crotchet. They cherished the innocent and unverifiable belief that they had gypsy blood in their veins. They held to this belief in the midst of an ungypsy-like solidity of living. To Lafcadio this notion would mean more. It would be another justification for differentness.

Charles' mother, Elizabeth Holmes Hearn, came of a somewhat more lively and varied family than the Hearns. Her mother was the great-niece of Dr. John Arbuthnot, physician to Queen Anne, the Dr. Arbuthnot of Pope's *Epistle to Dr. Arbuthnot.* The Holmeses of her own and preceding generations were lawyers, writers, and artists of middling ability. Mrs. Hearn's daughter, Mrs. Thomas Elwood, was musical. Mrs. Hearn's son Richard was a painter, a popular if rather dilettantish figure among the French and American painters at Barbizon. The latent artistic ability showed even in the impervious Charles. He sketched rather well. But there was nothing demoniac or possessed about these gentle artistic people. They dabbled in art; they domesticated art.

Charles Hearn was fulfilling family tradition by his soldier's career. He had betrayed family tradition by his marriage. If the family could have made over Rosa, there might have been an adjusted sort of happiness for the couple, but this was impossible. Nina Kennard, who talked with members of the Hearn-Holmes family who remembered Charles' Greek wife, set down their reminiscences from her notes:

She was handsome, report says, with beautiful eyes, but ill-tempered and unrestrained, sometimes even violent. Musical, but too indolent to cultivate the gift, clever, but absolutely uneducated, she lived the life of an oriental woman, lying all day long on a sofa, complaining of the dulness of her surroundings, of the climate of Ireland, of the impossibility of learning the language. To her children she was capricious and tyrannical . . .[6]

The unhappy face of his mother who fitted so ill among the Hearns and the Holmeses—the face, tender, petulant, frightened—was the center of

the little boy's universe. It became an obsession later that all he remembered
of his mother was her face.

He wrote once in a letter to a half sister whom he never met:

My mother's face only I remember, and I remember it for this reason. One day
it bent over me caressingly. It was delicate and dark, with large black eyes—very
large. A childish impulse came to me to slap it. I slapped it—simply to see the result,
perhaps. The result was immediate and severe castigation, and I remember both
crying and feeling I deserved what I got. I felt no resentment, although the aggressor
in such cases is usually the most indignant at consequences.[7]

He wrote to a full brother whom he also never met, trying to pull memories out of the dark for both of them:

And you do not remember that dark and beautiful face—with large, brown eyes
like a wild deer's—that used to bend above your cradle? You do not remember the
voice which told you each night to cross your fingers after the old Greek orthodox
fashion, and utter the words— "In the name of the Father, and of the Son, and of
the Holy Ghost"? She made, or had made, three little wounds upon you when a
baby—to place, you, according to her childish faith, under the protection of those
three powers, but especially that of Him for whom alone the Nineteenth Century
still feels some reverence—*the Lord and Giver of Life* . . . We were all [he was
thinking of the three of them, the first child who had died, as well as of himself and
the younger brother to whom he was writing] very dark as children, very passionate,
very odd-looking, and wore gold rings in our ears. Have you not the marks yet? [8]

Rosa's manners and Rosa's beliefs, and even Rosa's unhappiness, could
only exasperate the Hearns. She made little effort to communicate with her
husband's relatives across the piled-up barrier of misunderstanding. Only
one of the Irish kin penetrated her awkward pride and became her friend.
This more sympathetic relative was Charles' Aunt Sarah, Mrs. Justin Brenane, who had been a Holmes, a sister of Mrs. Hearn. She was a widow now,
alone and lonely.

Sarah Holmes had done the unthinkable and stepped outside the im-
pregnable circle of Anglo-Irishdom, and married a Catholic. She was better
able than the others to understand the loneliness of outsiders in the closed
world of the Hearns and the Holmeses. She befriended Rosa and Lafcadio
first out of a naïve and simple goodness. But another motive began to work
powerfully upon her at the continued sight of the child. She was childless,
and she wanted an heir. So she took Rosa out for an occasional airing in her
grand carriage; she invited the young Greek woman to her house at 21
Leinster Square in the Rathmines suburb; she began to make plans for the
child's future.

The family recalled Aunt Sarah Brenane as a perfected Victorian widow, very like the Queen herself. All in black silk or satin, impeccable, upright, wrapping herself and the seat of her carriage in a holland sheet to withstand any least speck of dust; alert, in control behind her footman, a rich aunt, an eccentric aunt—she might do much for Lafcadio. Her giving Rosa a resource was a relief not only for the Greek girl but for the Hearns too. They did not know what to do with Charles' wife and Charles' child.

On October 8, 1853, three years and four months after the birth of the little boy he had never seen, Charles Hearn came home to Dublin. His presence brought moments of color and fun into the child's life:

> I remember my father taking me upon horseback when coming into town with his regiment. I remember being at dinner with a number of men in red coats and striped trousers, and crawling about under the table and pinching their legs.[9]

His father's presence brought also constraint and a vague sense of trouble to the child. Something of hindsight colored his memory, but the crisis was sharp enough to be felt by a sensitive child. On the evening of Charles' return, Rosa fell ill, an illness of the mind.[10] During her husband's absence she had suffered a sense of uprootedness. When he returned she discovered he no longer loved her. The nervous disorder was at this time temporary, but the aggravation caused by a suffering renewal of relations with her husband was not. The image of the father with the set stern face and unyielding manners stayed with Lafcadio the rest of his life. To the unseen younger brother Lafcadio wrote in late 1889 or early 1890:

> I can remember seeing father only four times—no, five. He never caressed me; I always felt afraid of him. He was rather taciturn, I think. . . . When I look on the portrait of father (I lost mine about '72 or '73; I thank you very much for yours), with the rigid grim face and still-steady eyes, I can not feel much in my life common with his. I suspect I do not love him.[11]

Charles Hearn left Dublin in March 1854 to join a regiment in the Crimea. Rosa Hearn left Dublin early in the summer, pregnant with Charles' third son, but also stricken with homesickness, setting her course blindly toward Greece. Aunt Sarah Brenane, with whom she left Lafcadio, paid for what was planned to be only a visit to her family, and saw that a nurse went with Rosa, to look after her and the child that was soon to be born. Daniel James was born on the island of Cephalonia and was brought home to Cerigo by his mother.

Charles Hearn survived the Crimean War to return to Dublin on July 23, 1856, a more portly and determined man. A photograph shows a settled, hardened, substantial figure, in stiff dark civilian wear. He decided to terminate his marriage to the Greek girl and in her absence did so easily. He found out, either upon his return voyage from the Crimea, or earlier on his return from the West Indies, that the Irish woman he had wanted to marry years before he met Rosa was now free again.[12] Before Charles Hearn ever left Ireland to go to the Greek islands, he had been in love with Alicia Goslin, a girl of his own kind and his own world. He was not then sufficiently advanced in his career, or the girl well enough off for them to marry against family pressures. He was persuaded to go to Greece single; she, to marry a wealthier suitor, a judge, George John Crawford.

Alicia was now free. Her husband had died and left her with two small children. She had brought them back to Dublin from Australia where she had gone at the time of her marriage. Charles went to see her, and in his cavalier way, took little Lafcadio with him.

One day my father came to my aunt's house to take me out for a walk. He took me into some quiet street, where the houses were very high—with long flights of steps going up to the front door. Then a lady came down to meet us, all white-robed, with very bright hair—quite slender. I thought her beautiful as an angel, perhaps partly because she kissed me and petted me, and gave me a beautiful book and a toy gun. But my aunt found it out, and took away the book and the gun, and said that was a very wicked woman and my father a very wicked man. She was the woman who afterward became my father's second wife and died in India . . .[13]

The father's disloyalty to his mother did not penetrate to the child's mind till later. When it did, his emotion was strengthened and directed by the words and acts of his aunt who disinherited her nephew and upheld the part of the foreign wife. Never in later years did Lafcadio grant to his father even his considerable good qualities. Never would he acknowledge that he inherited anything from him. His darkness was as much a trait of the "gypsy" Hearns as of the Cassimatis, but he denied one-half his blood and his background. He reconstructed his ancestry in his imagination until it was completely Greek.

But in 1856 the six-year-old child was separated completely from his absent Greek mother. Without giving Rosa a chance to return and speak for herself, Charles secured an annulment of the marriage based apparently on a dubious technicality: one party to the marriage—Rosa—had not signed the contract (she could not, she could not write). His aunt told the child that his father "had got a divorce from my mother without just cause." And she informed the child that she had forced his father "to pay back all the money she had advanced him," and that she had "disinherited" him.[14] The following year, when Lafcadio was seven, on July 18, 1857, Alicia Goslin Crawford and Charles Bush Hearn were married in Dublin. On August 4th the father, whom Lafcadio was never to see again, departed for army duty in

India and took with him Alicia and Alicia's children. He gave up the care of his own children.

The younger brother, Daniel James, was sent back to Ireland when Rosa married again in Cerigo. Her second husband, Giovanni Cavallini,[15] an islander of Italian descent, made a condition of the marriage his refusal to care for the other man's children. The Hearn family promised to care for both children. Charles and Rosa both gave up their rights and responsibilities toward Lafcadio and Daniel James.

As Rosa Cavallini, Lafcadio Hearn's mother bore four children. Her husband became a man of some consequence. He served as a governor under the British at Cerigotto, a small island near Cerigo. In Cerigo he was Vice-Consul for Austria-Hungary. He collected archaeological relics for his own amusement. Rosa, according to an unproved but much repeated story, returned once to Ireland to see her children, but was not allowed to do so. Her mental illness returned. She finished her life, at the age of fifty-nine, on December 12, 1882, at the National Mental Asylum at Corfu, having been there ten years. Of this sequence Lafcadio knew nothing except a vague story of his mother's second marriage.

Whatever the sequence of events just preceding his mother's flight from Dublin, the effect of quarrels, ugliness, upset, and insecurity upon a sensitive child was permanent. Years later, Lafcadio, writing to the younger brother, defended with passion and partiality the fragment of memory he owned:

With regard to what you say about mother's treatment of us—I must tell you that, even as a child, I used to wonder at it. But my old grandaunt and others, the family servants especially, would say to me: "Don't believe anything unkind about your mother; she loved you all as much as any mother could do; she could not help herself."

Afterward I heard that the man whom she married had made this condition with her: "I will go with you anywhere; I will give up everything for you; but I will not bring up the children of that man."

Mother was in a strange country, without means, unable to speak a word of English; then again, the boys seemed well provided for. I was to be grandaunt's heir and she was quite rich; my father had made some promises regarding you. As for her never making inquiries afterwards, I doubt it. . . . She must have hated father's memory. Neither could I blame her, nor cease to love her, were I to hear she had committed any fault. Her circumstances were very peculiar and cruel, and her nature probably intensely confiding and impulsive, with him. We heard nothing of her from 1858.[16]

Rosa's face began to recede into the past of memory. The image, soon forgotten, of a little brother, smoothed out to blankness. During all the time he was growing up, Lafcadio thought that Daniel James was with his

Uncle Richard, and no one in the family took the trouble to correct his assumption. The family, as soon as the younger child was old enough, sent him away permanently to a school in England. There he lived until he was almost grown, and then Lafcadio's younger brother emigrated to America.

It is not clear whether Lafcadio's own permanent settling at Aunt Sarah Brenane's took place before or after his mother left Ireland. When he was left parentless, Mrs. Brenane wanted him, and no one else did. Apparently without ever making the adoption legal, she assumed care of the child, and behaved as if she planned to make him her heir.

Thus in his sixth year Lafcadio became the object of an aging woman's peculiar and exclusive hopes. (When the child arrived in Ireland at the age of two, Aunt Sarah was sixty; in 1856, when Charles Hearn turned over his son to her, she was sixty-four.) There was tragedy inherent in the situation: she interested herself in Lafcadio not for his own sake, but for the sake of a dead husband's dying wish—for an heir, and a proper Catholic heir. Lafcadio was to be a dedication to a dead man's last words.

It is only at this time that Lafcadio in his own consciousness comes into view. His memories of childhood and adolescence were never fully expressed, but he wrote some interesting fragments of confession in his later years. These fragments show a small but intense consciousness beginning in Aunt Sarah's house to live and react in his own emotions and nerves, and to undergo experiences that would echo down his life. From this point on, we can examine his memories, and not just those of the Hearn family.

There was to be no more of Rosa, no more of his father, except in the receiving of a letter: "The one kind act I remember on his part was a long letter written to me from India, all about serpents and tigers and elephants, printed in Roman with a pen so that I could read it easily." [17]

The tenuous thread of connection frayed out. Aunt Sarah held to a strong disapproval of her nephew. "I never wrote to him, I think Auntie used to say something like this: 'I do not forbid you to write to your father, child,' but she did not look as though she wished me to, and I was lazy." [18]

Charles Hearn, preoccupied with his career and a new young family, never saw again his two boys of his first marriage.[19] His second wife died of fever in India in 1861. Charles returned from India on sick leave during the next year but did not see Lafcadio, nor did the child even know of this visit of his father. When, in his sixteenth year, his father once more sailed for home on the ship _Mula,_ no happy climax came as a result of this voyage. Charles Bush Hearn died of malaria in the Gulf of Suez on November 21, 1866.[20] What had gone before between the child and his father was all there was to be.

The house in which Lafcadio began to grow up was a prosperous one. It sat in a pleasant suburb. Rathmines was a carriage drive from Dublin, southward away from the coast and toward the mountains. Large high houses owned pleasant gardens. Carriages rolled their owners smoothly to and from town for shopping, or to the cathedral for mass.

Scattered words from Hearn's few references identify the kind of house it was. It was a tall house: he spoke of landings on the stairs, and of a third, infrequently visited floor. It was a formal and heavy house: he spoke of a lobby to the third floor. It was a dark house: shadows in its corners and on remote ceilings frightened him. It had a library: he found forbidden books there. It had soft carpets on its stairways, it had four-poster beds in its bedrooms, it had a parlormaid, it had footmen. It had all the other appurtenances of the well-being of the British upper middle class of the 1860's. The house and all who were in it centered an anxious attention on the child Lafcadio. He was its focal point, expensively and carefully fed, clothed, and schooled.

When the small boy came into her care, Aunt Sarah was filled with a terrible desire to do right. From the beginning she did not know how. "At that time I was scarcely ever mentioned by name, but only referred to as 'the Child.'" [21] Writing these words forty years later, he still felt the sting of having been in childhood a category rather than a person.

The aunt thought it would be good for him to sleep in a room alone and learn to get over his fear of the dark. From the age of five, the Big People nightly shut him up—light out, door locked—in a room to himself. Put there to get over a fear, the fear redoubled. He screamed when he discovered screaming would bring punishment and a light and company. When his elders found out his ruse, they simply did not come. He learned then to be quiet and listen for those others who came in dreams, melting through the door, pulling back his covers, tossing him in the air, or from one to the other. The vividness of the nightmare came to life again in the retelling that must have wrung out of him some of the old pain.

In this fragment of autobiography he recreated the room, the **Child's Room**: ". . . narrow, but very high, and, in spite of one tall window, very gloomy. It contained a fire-place wherein no fire was ever kindled; and the child suspected that the chimney was haunted." [22] And he recreated the Child, precocious, passionate, persuasive, and disregarded, telling the older people by whom he was surrounded of his dreams, repeating and repeating to them that he saw the shapes in the corners of the room. They told him his sight was mistaken, and locked the door again.

And they came again, "shadowy dark-robed figures, capable of atrocious self-distortion—capable, for instance, of growing up to the ceiling, and then across it, and then lengthening themselves, head-downwards, along the opposite wall." [23] Sometimes, and this was more horrible, they were felt: "the bolted door would open—slowly, slowly—and the thing would enter, gibbering soundlessly—and put out hands—and clutch me—and toss me to the black ceiling—and catch me descending to toss me up again, and again, and again." [24]

He slept for years in the locked Child's Room. His life of the time before the Room seemed very far away. Only his mother's face remained. A little trick of self-deception saved that memory. In his room was an icon, a darkfaced virgin and child looking out at him from a black frame. He thought the Virgin's face was his mother's, and the child's, his own.

His aunt took him to church in Dublin. He caught something of the atmosphere of her own anxious belief, and the place became horrible to him. "The wizened and pointed shapes of the windows immediately terrified me. In their outline I found the form of apparitions that tormented me in sleep;—and at once I began to imagine some dreadful affinity between goblins and Gothic churches." [25]

The flavor of Aunt Sarah's faith was the flavor of Lafcadio's youngest years. She had been a convert at the time of her marriage. Her faith was not Catholicism in its expansive, consecrative, humanist form, but it was rather anxious, puritanical, and concerned almost entirely with sin and death. It was in this darkness of belief that the little boy grew up. Even her kindness was sometimes mistaken. She thought the child too nervous to be taught the dogmas of the religion just yet. He must be taught only to feel it. The effect was dire. The overwrought atmosphere in which he lived was causeless, reasonless, and all-pervading.

Aunt Sarah herself was not frightening. She was kind. Only her house, her surroundings, the people who were attracted to it, were fearful. There was Cousin Jane who came every year. She was not really a cousin, but a protégée of the older woman, "a tall girl who looked like some of the long angels in my French pictures," [26] as Lafcadio recalled. And this recollection of her added: "She seldom smiled; and I never heard her laugh; she had some secret grief . . ." [27] Like the other members of the great-aunt's circle, she was overserious in her faith. She found out one day that Lafcadio did not really know who God was, and did not care. "I boldly asked Cousin Jane to tell me why I should try to please God more than to please anybody else." [28]

The little boy was seated on a stool at her feet. She grasped him to her, frightened him by the intensity of her gaze, and began, hardly breathing herself, to tell him who God was, or who her God was. "You do not know about Heaven and Hell?" [29] she asked.

I do not remember all the rest of her words; I can recall with distinctness only the following:

"—and send you down to Hell to burn alive in fire for ever and ever! . . . Think of it!—always burning, burning, burning!—screaming and burning! screaming and burning!—never to be saved from that pain of fire! . . . You remember when you burned your finger at the lamp?—Think of your whole body burning—always, always, always burning!—for ever and ever!" [30]

The beautiful face of the tall girl became terrible. The face became indeed the subject of a daytime nightmare, a childhood memory never to be forgotten, never to be explained, perhaps at last to be exorcised in the telling of it in an essay and the transforming of it in a Japanese ghost story.

Cousin Jane had gone away from the house in Rathmines for a time. But one day Lafcadio saw her in the lonely third-floor hallway of the house. She walked past him, very tall, her face turned upward and away from him. He called out to her and followed her into a bedroom. At last she turned her head toward him.

"She had no face. There was only a pale blur instead of a face. And even as I stared, the figure vanished." [31]

The little boy scrambled frantically out of the room "and fell—rolling over and over down to the next lobby. I do not remember being hurt; the stair-carpets were soft and very thick. The noise of my tumble brought immediate succor and sympathy. But I did not say a word about what I had seen; I knew that I should be punished if I spoke of it." [32]

Later the real and not the ghostly Cousin Jane came back to the house and was kind to him. But he wished she were dead. Soon, mysteriously, she grew ill and died. She left her books to Lafcadio, with not a religious one among them, books to open the world to him.

Out of the darkness, the confusion, the dissensions that raged around him, he began to grow into himself. The stages of that development are like flashes of light and dark. There is no detailed knowledge of that time to make a continuous smooth blending of one element into another. What is known comes from family hearsay, recollected a generation or two later, and from Hearn's own fragmentary memories.

A steady background was the house itself, its comfort, as well as its darkness, its stolidity becoming more important than its menace as the child outgrew some of his earlier mindless fears. It was a proper house of a proper mistress. But kind Aunt Sarah's goodness was not really available. She could not quite reach the child. His lost parents' faces intervened. His resentments toward them kept him emotionally too busy for another elemental tie. Yet on the level of everyday living he grew attached to her. She poured all her attention upon him. He tagged after her, as the family remembered, like a little dog.

As Lafcadio grew out of childhood, certain pressures lessened. The memory of wrangling parents faded. The terror of sudden abandonment yielded to a nagging ache of half-forgotten loss. Other people, other places, came between him and those faces that floated far away. There were many hospitable houses of relatives and friends to visit. There were trips to be made to various corners of Ireland, trips to Wales, and before long, trips to England too.

The boy had quick responses and emotions like quicksilver. He heard a Welsh harper sing, a rough harsh man whose appearance frightened him, and the wringing quality of the trite song made him burst into tears he could not understand.[33] He heard at night the sound of the sea, and was afraid. It seemed the sound of something alive. Both the singer and the sea may have belonged to his summers on the Welsh coast near Bangor. Or the sea sound of his earliest memory was more likely a recollection of a visit to the south Irish coast at Tramore, near Waterford.

It was to Tramore that the family went, year after year. It was probably there that the little boy learned to swim. It was on Tramore's wide sands, with a broad sky full of clouds and winds, that he learned to love the sea. The fear that had come to him from hearing the growl of the tides and the waves, the fear that had invaded his dreams and smothered him, changed into another quality when he learned to cope with the water and stay upon its surface. The sea became a tremendous playmate to him.

Summers were escapes into wildness and into light and air. Going back to town was a diving down into darkness, strictness, unnaturalness. Writing about his own first-born son he was to say, "He will have what I never had as a child—natural physical freedom." [34] In saying this he forgot for a moment Tramore and Bangor, where as a child he was sometimes sent with the maid, Kate. Her company—away from Aunt Sarah—meant fairy stories and folk sayings, a preposterous thick medium of superstition and ritual, all forbidden at home, but richly indulged in once well away from the house in Rathmines. The child, listening to these Irish sayings and stories, had a mind ready for all wonders, queernesses, all the exultations of the impossible.

After these summer seaside escapes, there came again each autumn the dark restoration to the tall house in Dublin. But as Lafcadio grew older, there was more of boredom and less of terror in the house. His active mind was caught and held by multiplying interests. A tutor was installed to teach the boy the dogmas and creeds of the Church, and to give him the rudiments of early schooling. Reading and writing seemed a natural kind of activity to him. Counting and adding and subtracting did not seem so.

Reading set him free. There was a disregarded dusty library in the house. No one bothered him there. The act of reading was at first not thought subversive upon the part of the slender boy, stretching up in inches now. In the large room lined with books he got away from all supervision. He read books by the shelf-ful. Books gave him a world to wander in, a place to liberate his dreams, vast rooms for his imagination. The nightmares of early childhood diminished into daydreams. In an ingenuous way he began to reach out and to make discoveries.

He found a book one day, a wonderful book full of pictures of Greek gods and goddesses, of fauns and satyrs, dryads and nymphs. He grasped at once that these creatures signified something different from the etherealized saints on the French religious cards he had for years been given to play with. And he exercised a preference. These were his, he was theirs. He exulted in their good looks, their health, their bold, free self-sufficiency. But his tutor found out what had absorbed the attention of the boy. The book disappeared from the library, and the conscientious man exercised his censor's function. When the book appeared again on its shelf—without a word of caution, explanation, or reproval—Lafcadio found that the beautiful gods and goddesses had been clothed, or partially clothed. Most inimitably the tutor had directed young Lafcadio to what he thought was censorable:

Evidently "the breasts of the nymphs in the brake" had been found too charming; dryads, naiads, graces and muses—all had been rendered breastless. And, in most cases, *drawers* had been put upon the gods—even upon the tiny Loves—large baggy bathing-drawers, woven with cross-strokes of a quill-pen, so designed as to conceal all curves of beauty—especially the lines of the long fine thighs. . . . However in my case, this barbarism proved of some educational value. It furnished me with many problems of restoration; and I often tried very hard to reproduce in pencil-drawing the obliterated or the hidden line.[35]

The older Hearn, in writing this recollection, smiled back at the earnest restorer, but he could fix the moment as important in his life:

Now after I had learned to know and to love the elder gods, the world again began to glow about me. Glooms that had brooded over it slowly thinned away. The terror was not yet gone; but I now wanted only reasons to disbelieve all that I feared and hated. In the sunshine, in the green of the fields, in the blue of the sky, I found a gladness before unknown. Within myself new thoughts, new imaginings, dim longings for I knew not what were quickening and thrilling. I looked for beauty, and everywhere found it; in passing faces—in attitudes and motions—in the poise of plants and trees—in long white clouds—in faint-blue lines of far-off hills. At moments the simple pleasure of life would frighten me. But at other times there would come to me a new and strange sadness—a shadowy and inexplicable pain.

I had entered into my Renaissance.[36]

The odd little boy was growing into an impetuous, joy-loving adolescent. But he had no goals for his hot young desires. Any normal expression of thought or emotion was thought wicked. His old fears had seemed unnatural; now his new emotions seemed actively dangerous. He was a strange growth in Mrs. Brenane's sad and careful house. He puzzled as well as alarmed his aunt. He seemed completely careless of her shy, deeply cherished idea of what he was to be, the fit Catholic heir of Mr. Brenane. One can only surmise the seesaw of their relationship: dependence and then revolt upon his part; tenderness, uneasiness, and finally resentment upon her part. In all his later years Hearn never wrote of Mrs. Brenane with more than moderate feeling. He never spoke one word of real affection for the ghost of Aunt Sarah. One must infer, in that earlier time, a tragic holding back of love. She was to be pitied, as well as the boy.

As Lafcadio grew into the restless questioning age, Mrs. Brenane was less able to help him. She was older. All her prejudices were stiffening, as her old bones stiffened, and the set of her spine grew harsher. The tight bond that had held the old woman and the little boy together was not adjustable. It could not be made easier; it could only be broken. There was not lacking another person to take advantage of the brittleness of the tie between Mrs. Brenane and Lafcadio.

Mr. Henry Hearn Molyneux now entered the scene. Molyneux, a well educated, personable young man, only thirteen years older than Lafcadio, was the son of a good friend, Elizabeth Hearn Molyneux, of Tramore.[37] He was distantly related to the Hearns, and probably to Aunt Sarah's dead husband too. The clever young man was at first only an adviser to Mrs. Brenane in money matters, but since these matters were at the center of her life he became more and more important to her. The disposal of her dead husband's legacy was the most serious problem of her old age. It had led her to adopt the strange little boy whom her nephew Charles had willingly given to her. It now engrossed her in a new relationship with a young financial adviser who pleased her in the rightness of his moral and religious judgments. Molyneux was almost ostentatiously Catholic. He was soon almost a son to Sarah Brenane, at least a favorite nephew, and firmly centered in her existence—shouldering the boy Lafcadio out of his aunt's attention.

It did not strike Mrs. Brenane as at all out of order that Henry Molyneux was almost immediately the principal beneficiary of her own investments. Molyneux had a job in the Admiralty in London, but he was restive of clerk's hours. He wanted to go into business for himself. He persuaded Mrs. Brenane to help him. Through a loan from her, he became an importer of goods from the East.

The young man planned to be married. He introduced his young woman to Mrs. Brenane, who was charmed with Agnes Eliza Keogh. With characteristic generosity the childless woman set aside a large part of her landed property to be held in trust for the young couple. After the marriage, Mr. and Mrs. Molyneux became a kind of family for the aging Mrs. Brenane. She visited them in England for longer and longer stays, and at last gave up having her own house in order to move in with them. It was now the coltish young Lafcadio who seemed an odd member of the small circle. But the problem of his fitting in did not have to be solved at once. He was old enough to be sent away to school, and upon Henry Molyneux' advice, he was dispatched first to France and then to England, to remain away from home for a number of years, often spending vacations at his school as well as terms.

At the immature age of twelve or thirteen, Lafcadio found himself a lonely and foreign boy among the schoolyard of French boys in the grounds of Institution Ecclésiastique, at Yvetot near Rouen.[38] It was a church school well known and well thought of among British Catholics, but to Lafcadio it seemed only overpoweringly solemn, rigid, and ugly. His attendance at this school in 1862 and possibly in the early part of 1863 explains how he missed his father's visit during the year 1862. It explains also how he learned the rudiments of French, a knowledge he somehow held onto in other surroundings.

But the good of learning French was gained only in enduring an experience the boy loathed. The place caused a continual ache in him; the ache remained with him, tied to the memory all the rest of his life. He seldom spoke of having been there, but when he did, it was in derogatory terms.

From Lafcadio Hearn one can learn about the school only through indirection. Fortunately, one can gain a more direct bearing upon the place through the eyes of another writer who happened also to have attended the school. By a teasing coincidence the writer whom Hearn translated with so much care in the 1880's, Guy de Maupassant, was another victim and rebel at the Institution Ecclésiastique. The two boys were the same age, but apparently missed each other narrowly. Young Guy attended the school just after Hearn left, in 1863–1864, and again in 1866–1867, and then succeeded in having himself thrown out.

Later, with some bitter relish, Maupassant described the school in a story, "Une Surprise": [39]

I can never think of the place even now without a shudder. It smelled of prayers the way a fish-market smells of fish. Oh! That dreary school, with its eternal religious ceremonies, its freezing Mass every morning, its periods of meditation, its gospel recitations, and the reading from pious books during meals! Oh! Those dreary days passed within those cloistering walls! . . . We lived there in narrow, contemplative, unnatural piety—and also in a truly meritorious state of filth, for I well remember that the boys were made to wash their feet but three times a year, the night before each vacation. As for baths, they were as unknown as the name of Victor Hugo. Our masters apparently held them in the greatest contempt.[40]

The adolescent Guy, during his second stay, was just as explicit in a letter:

I don't know whether you know that barrack, that gloomy monastery, home of curés, hypocrisy, boredom, etc., etc., out of which rises such an odor of priests' robes that it permeates the whole town of Yvetot and permeates one's self, too . . .[41]

How long the Institution's Irish boy remained is not known. Perhaps one year, perhaps part of two, but by the fall of 1863 he was being sent away to another school, this time to a substantial Catholic school in England. It is a gauge of how deeply Mrs. Brenane was tied to Henry Molyneux that when Lafcadio went away to school a second time his leave-taking was from the Molyneux house, Linkfield Lodge, at Redhill, Surrey, and not from the house in Rathmines. At about this time Mrs. Brenane gave up her independent residence and went to England to live with Henry and Agnes Molyneux.

It was on September 9, 1863, that young P. L. Hearn, thirteen years old, had his first sight of the prosperous boys' school, St. Cuthbert's, at Ushaw, near Durham. Under the capable direction of Monsignor Robert Tate, St. Cuthbert's trained boys for the university and for the priesthood. It was a preparatory school, a college, and a seminary. His aunt knew that there could be no question of the priesthood for Lafcadio, but she thought that at least at St. Cuthbert's the boy would be protected from bad influences in rigorously Catholic surroundings. It was a school rich in liturgical celebration, where the whole body of students and teachers took part in celebration, in song and procession, of each Church season in turn. And it was a school rich in the number of churchmen it turned out. Cardinal Wiseman had been a graduate. Within a few years of Hearn's leaving, Francis Thompson would be a St. Cuthbert's boy. There would be some boys and some teachers who would remember both students.

What Hearn recollected from the school was the staleness of its formal teaching, the brutality of its manners, a few friendships, and one horrible accident. What he learned was privately learned; what he did not want to learn, he skipped. He had rebelled silently at home. He rebelled openly at St. Cuthbert's.

P. L. Hearn became Paddy Hearn. He would admit to Patrick, but the L. was his own affair. He discerned from the start that it would be easier to be Irish Paddy than Greek Lafcadio. "In an English school the life is rough, very rough, and a sensitive boy is likely to suffer a great deal before he learns to submit himself to this strange order of existence." [42] His form of submission did not look like submission, but in fact it was.

In displeasing the masters, he pleased the boys. The masters were tainted, as he thought, with the belief that had poisoned life at home. So he became a nuisance to them, and the school rebel. His gaiety in the face of punishment, and his ingenuity in provoking it, dazzled the rough boys into granting him the license to be himself. He was Paddy, and therefore he did not play games. He was Paddy, therefore he could write poems, tell ghost stories, and be odd in any way he chose. A future Bishop of Salford, Dr. Casartelli, recalled Paddy "letting the nail of the index-finger of the right hand grow to a great length, then cutting it into the form of a quill pen and trying to write with it." [43]

He was wild and conspicuous, full of pranks and notions, known to all the boys and the masters, thus safe to escape when he wished into his own private world of the imagination. His tricks were not ugly, but full of a winning charm. In the end he was liked even by the teachers who shook their heads at him.

He did not become all at once a rebel from the faith in which he had been so prayerfully brought up. He was even at first anxious to perform his devotions to the last elaborate nuance. He questioned very closely a visitor one day, a young cousin who, being an Anglican, did not genuflect before the Blessed Virgin's image. And he got into trouble with his confessor for being embarrassingly honest:

One day I told the ghostly father that I had been guilty of desiring with unspeakable desire that the devil would come to me in the shapes he came to those anchorites of the desert,—so that I could yield to any and all temptations offered. He was a grim man who rarely showed emotion, my confessor; but on that occasion he actually rose to his feet in anger. "Let me warn you!" he cried:—"let me warn you of all things!— never wish that! You might be more sorry for it than you can possibly believe!" Now, when he thus spoke, his earnestness filled me with a fearful joy;—for I thought all that I wished for might be realized—so serious he looked. And, after that, oh! how I prayed for some pretty gracious devil to come to me, and take my soul in exchange for—! But the merciless succubi all continued to remain in hell! [44]

That Lafcadio eventually became an outright rebel against the religion as well as the dull routine of the school was not surprising. What had happened to him at home in the name of religion made him immune even to its taking qualities, in such a good and devoted atmosphere as St. Cuthbert's.

Yet the school was negatively good for a wayward imagination. There were fields nearby for walks. There was a room with books where he was left alone to read while other boys played soccer outside in the sunlight. Games were not compulsory. Activities were not organized. There was enough unregarded time to form an individuality.

Lafcadio's time at St. Cuthbert's lasted four years, from September 1863 to October 1867. He was thirteen when he went in, seventeen when he left. The school engrossed him during these impressionable years, and the Molyneux house was not hospitable to him as a place to come away to. In the last part of his time at St. Cuthbert's he did not go home at all, but spent his vacations at school. His best school friends remembered that Patrick never spoke of his relatives. He began in these years to understand that he was losing his place in his aunt's concerns. He began to resent Mr. Henry Molyneux.

During these years Sarah Brenane fondly and generously gave over to Molyneux more and more of her property to invest. Not only her business investments, but her investments of affection, interest, and zeal—these were in his hands too. Lafcadio (he was still Greek Lafcadio inside, and not Paddy at all) resented what he understood of Molyneux's domination of his aunt.

In his private life of reading and dreaming at school—and he had fortunately much time for both—he identified himself more and more with the non-Irish side of his inheritance. School work, except for something known as "high figures," was easy for him, and only a minor interruption of his real life. Pranks were only for show, and for disguise. He liked the courses in English and easily won a prize, and was appalled to find himself standing up before the whole school to receive it. Classes were something to get through. Before and after them there was time to lie on the grass and dream. There was time to stroll in the spacious school grounds with a friend, Achilles Daunt, who remembered Hearn, and years later, ventured to write to him in Martinique.

All his flaunting of wildness and differentness hid and protected a serious young love of life and the beautiful things of the world to which he was just opening his eyes. It seemed to him that all life must tremble, as he trembled, with love. He found out by accident that there was a name for the way he felt:

I remember, when a boy lying on my back in the grass, gazing into the summer blue above me, and wishing that I could melt into it—become a part of it. For these fancies I believe that a religious tutor was innocently responsible; he had tried to explain to me, because of certain dreamy questions, what he termed "the folly and wickedness of pantheism"—with the result that I immediately became a pantheist, at the tender age of fifteen. And my imaginings presently led me not only to want the sky for a playground, but also to become the sky! [45]

In the adolescent years at Ushaw he began to enjoy, in reading, some of the very fears and terrors which had made his childhood miserable. Transformed by some magic in fiction, ghosts, magic, horror delighted him. One story by Bulwer Lytton, "The Haunted and the Haunters," appealed particularly to his imagination, although its psychological horror was only rudimentary and almost mechanical. He discovered in this story, and in others like it, how books of terror could be an easement to literal terrors. It was the first step he took toward creation.

Nina Kennard sought out and found valuable remembrances of the person youthful Lafcadio Hearn was in his school days. His former friends of St. Cuthbert's, when she wrote to them, or talked to them, had gone smoothly on their way after their years of guidance at Ushaw. Not one of them had led the disturbed kind of life their friend had led. Yet from their great distance, and difference, they recalled a remarkably unified picture of Paddy Hearn at school.

"I can see his face now," one wrote, "beaming with delight at some of his many mischievous plots with which he disturbed the College and usually was flogged for. . . . He was always considered 'wild as a March hare,' full of escapades, and the terror of his masters, but always most kind and good-natured, and I fancy very popular with his schoolmates . . . He laughed at his many whippings, wrote poetry about them and the birth, [Virgin birth] etc., and was, in fact, quite irresponsible." [46]

Another said: ". . . No one could be in the College without knowing him. He was always very much in evidence, very popular among his schoolfellows. He played pranks of a very peculiar and imaginative kind. He was full of fun, wrote very respectable verses for a boy, was an omnivorous reader, worshipped muscle, had his note-book full of brawny arms, etc. . . . He was not altogether a desirable boy, from the Superior's point of view, yet his playfulness of manner and brightness, disarmed any feeling of anger for his many escapades . . . He was so very curious a boy, so wild in the tumult of his thought, that you felt he might do anything in different surroundings." [47]

Wrote another: "Naturally of a skeptical turn of mind, he once rather shocked some of us by demanding evidence of beliefs which we had never dreamt of questioning. He loved nature in her exterior aspects, and his conversation, for a lad of his age, was highly picturesque . . . I believe he was regarded as slightly off his mental balance." [48]

At sixteen this odd, ebullient boy suffered a piece of bad luck that affected him for life.

In a game called Giant's Stride, a boy holding a knotted rope let slip this instrument of play and struck Paddy Hearn in the left eye. The blow caused a severe inflammation. There was an operation, apparently performed in Dublin, and consultations with doctors in London, but the sight of the eye was not saved. Scar tissue formed and whitened the surface of the cornea. The eyeball was not removed.

The physical effect of this accident was very serious. Lafcadio had been nearsighted from birth. From this time on, he abused his one good eye in reading and writing and several times endangered what vision he had left after the accident. Punishing use of his good eye caused it to become enlarged and to protrude out of its socket in a fashion that people meeting him for the first time never failed to notice, and to find both alarming and ludicrous.

The emotional effect of the accident was more hurtful than the physical result, permanent and limiting as that was. It was as if the blow to the eye had struck inwardly and damaged the essential person.

When Lafcadio returned to the school after the operation, it was noted by his former comrades in mischief, and by those who had simply admired his dangerous, wild spirits, that he was not the same boy. The gaiety and ease of manner for which he was noted had changed into a suffering quietness. Proud and sensitive, he believed now that he was repulsive, and had his intuition confirmed by starts of surprise and alarm upon the part of those meeting him for the first time in his new condition. Threatened, sometimes with teasing, and sometimes with pity, he stiffened into a self-protective unresponsiveness.

The loss of his eye had an incalculably harmful effect upon Hearn's emotional balance for the rest of his life. It added a specific, justifying cause to the morbidity his disturbed childhood had implanted in him. Friends, more often than he would have credited the fact, simply forgot the disfigurement in the face that was otherwise well shaped. "He seemed always beautiful to me!" [49] said his friend Mitchell McDonald, when someone commented to him on Hearn's disfigured eye. If his friends did not remember, finding his expression a kindling one, and his talk illuminating, Hearn always remembered: ". . . He never forgot that he was deformed," [50] said his son.

With men, after trying them out, waiting to see if they jeered at him, he could establish comfortable relations. With women, he found it very difficult to do so. He was certain he was personally and sexually unattractive, yet at the same time he was filled with the most ardent susceptibilities to charm and refinement, to the delicacy or robustness of physical beauty. His ugly eye was not the sole cause of this lack of ease, but it was a major one. Loss of all trust in his family, the falling away from him of all background, early youthful poverty made him touchy, shy, difficult, ugly of mood himself. The fact that he had a hideous eye, as he thought, added the last impossibility. He could not be quite normal in his relations with those of the other sex whom he thought his equals and whom he was most desperately anxious to please. He was sure he could not please, so his practice was to back off like an awkward crab or to exaggerate deference to the point of caricature. It was only sometimes with women of an entirely different background that he could forget that he was not acceptable. (It was in his own mind that a voice cried out passionately that he was not acceptable.)

A portrait photograph taken of Lafcadio in his sixteenth year, just when he was setting out on his course of complicated suffering, caught him in the moment when he ceased to be a boy.

He sits upon an ornate straight chair in the photographer's studio. The floor is of tiles, the background dark. The slender boy arranged so stiffly seems particularly defenseless. He rests his left elbow rather awkwardly, and as if posed, upon a damask-draped round table. He wears painful black, black clothes, black shoes. His dark shining hair is brushed back with superlative neatness. Only his slender hands and sad young face are white. The hurt eye is turned only slightly away from the camera. It is blind but not deformed. The other eye is well shaped, with a smooth straight brow above it. The good eye is only slightly prominent. (The enlargement came later with the consistent abuse of overuse.) The expression is quiet, sad, repressed.

This child of sixteen, of a disposition naturally exuberant and gay, not yet of an age to bear misfortune well, experienced one stunning misfortune after another until at the age of nineteen he was a haggard, old young man.

In 1867 Mr. Molyneux suffered business losses. Mrs. Brenane, being involved in her investments in all his dealings, suffered losses too. At seventy-five Aunt Sarah was now a dependent of Henry Molyneux. She was much enfeebled both mentally and physically. To retrench and recover, the

Molyneux family and Mrs. Brenane moved to Tramore to live. There was now no money for Lafcadio's school fees. He was not to finish at St. Cuthbert's. He was not to go to a university. On October 28, 1867, he was withdrawn from school.[61]

Lafcadio's own curt description of Henry Molyneux' career—written many years later, and still in hot anger—may not have been accurate in every detail, but it held the emotion of the earlier time intact:

> Mr. Henry succeeded in having himself declared heir in Aunty's will; I to be provided for by an annuity of (I think, but am not sure) £500. Henry, who had "made himself the darling" was not satisfied. He desired to get the property into his hands during Aunty's life. This he was able to do to his own, as well as Aunty's, ruin. He failed in London. The estate was put into the hands of receivers. I was withdrawn from college . . . [52]

Lafcadio had to be disposed of. Henry Molyneux remembered a former maid of Mrs. Brenane's, Catherine Ronane, now Catherine Delaney. She had often visited Redhill with Aunt Sarah, and was presumably the maid sent to Bangor with Lafcadio when he was a little boy. She had left Mrs. Brenane's employ, married a dockworker in London, and lived in that city now. Lafcadio could go to live with her. What an eighteen-year-old boy was to do with himself there was not asked. He was to go, and be quiet. A little money could be sent to Catherine from time to time, enough to board him.

It was a miserable time Lafcadio spent in London. His own absolute aloneness made the boy quite wild. He thought he looked hideous. He had no real home. He had no aim. In the ugly, unending present of walking London's streets he saw only misery, his own misery, in the poor around him. Later he told wild stories of poverty, hunger, of a session in a London workhouse. Apparently he ran away from Catherine Delaney's house for weeks at a time, and came back only because he had to. In these wanderings he learned his first hatred of great cities.

He found a refuge only in books, and in fugitive glimpses of the happiness of passers-by. This was the year he read Swinburne and murmured the long swinging lines of the hypnotic ballads to himself in filthy alleys and in the room in Catherine's house where the Delaneys let him sleep. Swinburne was his bridge between the ancients and the rebellious moderns. He showed the scornful young Hearn how it was possible to be "Greek" in 1868. He gave Lafcadio's gearless rebellion a reference, a background, a banner.

Hate and anger were softened into wistfulness only transiently when he witnessed a happiness which excluded himself:

One summer evening, twenty-five years ago, in a London park, I heard a girl say "Good-night" to somebody passing by. Nothing but those two little words—"Good-night." Who she was I do not know: I never even saw her face; and I never heard that voice again. But still, after the passing of one hundred seasons the memory of her "Good-night" brings a double thrill incomprehensible of pleasure and pain,— pain and pleasure, doubtless, not of me, not of my own existence, but of pre-existence and dead suns.[53]

He had not the consolation of philosophy when he heard the "Good-night"—only the pain.

At this point, Henry Molyneux determined to complete his responsibility toward Lafcadio. Mrs. Brenane, older and feebler, was out of reach of any appeal from her nephew. Molyneux sent Lafcadio passage money to America and curt instructions to make his way to the city of Cincinnati, and there seek out Mr. Thomas Cullinan, the husband of Molyneux's sister, for help in getting himself established.

Sometime in the spring of 1869 another immigrant from the Old World, Lafcadio Hearn, almost nineteen years old, journeyed across the Atlantic, traveled by railroad across the eastern states, and arrived at the city on the Ohio. He had nothing to bring to Cincinnati but the little luggage he carried and soon lost, and a talent with words he had not discovered he owned. Though he was filled with numerous resentments, hates, and fears, he owned also some pride, ambition, and a yearning, rudderless love.

3 ⚘ Cincinnati Streets

The city to which Lafcadio Hearn was dispatched, and in which he soon
lost himself, was in 1869 a growing, noisy, dirty, busy, and prosperous
city. Cincinnati thought of itself as western, and therefore young, energetic, and progressive. The end of the Civil War had brought a spurt of
good times to the great Ohio Valley region of which Cincinnati was the
center. The explosion of new things brought also pain, corruption, and
filth as part of the general, northern, haphazard postwar prosperity.
Cincinnati had been the greatest city of the area for many decades. Its
citizens hardly realized that they had been left behind by Chicago and
would inevitably be passed by Cleveland. They thought in terms of
never ending growth, expansion, and a bigness becoming bigger. There
was latent in the confused bustle of the place a desire for consolidation,
for relaxation into a more reasonable and cultivated life, of a hungry
yearning after knowledge and beauty. But the explosive bigness and
busyness hid these mitigations.

Cincinnati seemed at that time an ugly place to newcomers, even a
stinking place, a city of pork-packing, of soap-making, of tanning. Every
part of the city's prosperity had grown up without order or plan, in a
sort of joyous confusion of money-making. Yet the physical scene was a
splendid one: great bluffs standing up from the basin in which the city
had consolidated itself; a turgid, living river flowing across its front; a
rich greenness escaping where it could from the blight of settlement

and covering heights and valleys, softening slums as well as suburbs.

The city's peoples were as rich a confusion as the city's activities. There were Cincinnatians of older American descent stemming from New England or Pennsylvania, or vaguely from upriver. There were others, more than one-fifth in 1870, of German descent, speaking for the most part two languages instead of one, reading their daily news in German-language papers. There were the Irish too, not long from the old country. And, almost buried under newer influxes, there was a small element of the French society of the river valley. More apart, more alien, there were thousands of Negroes packed together near the river in sections that the earliest settlers had thought salubrious, now crowded, dirty, yet teeming with the vitality of hopeful life and careless crime. Cincinnati had been a magnet for escaping slaves before the war. Here Kentucky heaved its southernness straight into the North, with only the river separating the ways of the North and the South. The scene had been mythologized already, in *Uncle Tom's Cabin,* which came into being through Harriet Beecher Stowe's residence in the city.

Now, with the war over, slavery done for, the rootless Negroes of the near South beyond the river crossed over in their thousands to Cincinnati. They came out of hope—for freedom and for work. In reward for hope the city gave them many small, footling opportunities, restrictions, and hurts. Yet among themselves, in spite of disease and casual death, they thrived. They held onto their songs, their stories, their own racketing, colorful way of life. They gave something to the city, as the French had done, and the Germans, and the mass of upriver Americans.

The presence of the troubling thousands of Negroes was only one sign of the intimate way the Civil War had affected the life of the city. The war had been close to Cincinnati as it had never been close to New York City. But, like New York, Cincinnati wanted now to put the war resolutely behind her. With the breath upon them of a newer, bigger, and different kind of prosperity, the city's ambitious, acute citizens put behind them the old troubles and shames of the war years. They wanted passionately to forget the sick South. They wanted passionately to make money. Everything would heal itself, cure itself, and be all right. Let be, and let us be. The city began to whir—a noisy, energetic center of trade and industry. It was a whirlpool of opportunity, for death, for disease, neglect, as well as for success in the most blatant and obvious forms. Fortunately all sorts of little opportunities lurked in the shade of the big vulgar ones. In spite of the improbability of Patrick Lafcadio Hearn's succeeding here, given his meager equipment for success, Cincinnati in the 1870's was just the kind of place where he might, as he surprisingly did, become within a few years a person of some local fame.

But in 1869 there was no promise offered. He arrived hungry of belly and mind. To the city's more than two hundred thousand competing inhabitants one more was added. Lafcadio sought out at once the one person whose name he had been given, Mr. Thomas Cullinan. From him he received a few driblets of money from Ireland, but no encouragement, or even any ready toleration. He kept up this link just long enough to receive a letter from Molyneux informing him of his Aunt Sarah's death on January 13, 1871. Lafcadio answered the letter, which was probably not a friendly one, in a highhanded manner, and broke off his communications with Molyneux and with Cullinan too. He never heard again from Dublin, never knew if anything had been saved out of the wreck of Mrs. Brenane's fortune, never knew actually if he had been cheated or not. But he assumed the cheat, and nourished the bitterness of it for the rest of his life.

The ugliness of want seemed to get inside him, as well as to thrive outside in the dirty streets which were all he knew of the city. Writing later to his half sister, a child of his father's second marriage, from whom he never heard until he was prosperous and well known, he said:

My dear little sister has been very, very lucky, she has not seen the wolf's side of life, the ravening side, the apish side; the ugly facets of the monkey puzzle.

I found myself dropped into the enormous machinery of life I knew nothing about, friends tried to get me work after I had been turned out of my first boarding-house through inability to pay. I lost father's photograph at that time by seizure of all my earthly possessions. I had to sleep for nights in the street, for which the police scolded me . . .[2]

He stumbled from day to day, scratching and biting in his attempt to survive. He found refuge one night in the hayloft of stables where some English coachmen "fed me by stealth from victuals stolen from the house." [3] To his half sister, years later, he catalogued attempts to find work:

I endeavored later to go as accountant in a business office, but it was soon found that I was incapable of filling the situation, defective in mathematical ability, and even in ordinary calculation power. I was entered into a Telegraph Office as Telegraph Messenger Boy, but I was nineteen and the other boys were young; I looked ridiculously out of place and was laughed at. I was touchy—went off without asking for my wages. Enraged friends refused to do anything further for me. Boarding-houses warned me out of doors. At last I became a Boarding-house servant, lighted fires, shovelled coals, etc., in exchange for food and privilege of sleeping on the floor of the smoking-room. I worked thus for about one and a half years, finding time to read and write stories. The stories were published in cheap Weekly Papers, long extinct;

but I was never paid for them. I tried other occupations also—canvassing, show-card writing, etc. These brought enough to buy smoking tobacco and second-hand clothes—nothing more.[4]

Nothing of the stories for the weeklies has been found. But his recollections of this early try at writing puts that movement of his being very far back into the bad days of his first coming to America. It would seem that storytelling, and the writing down of stories, must have grown very naturally out of his school-time scribbling and tall taletelling, and that there was not one moment of his grown young life, even when most deprived, that he did not already think of himself as some kind of a writer.

In all these earliest experiences there was no fixed center to his existence. He was jerked from one horror to another. Mr. Henry Watkin was the first friend he made in the city. His print shop was his first resting place. Just where Henry Watkin enters, in this series of embarrassments and disasters, is not known, but it is probable that Lafcadio met the older man within a few months of his first coming into the city. He told his own version of the meeting to his half sister, three decades later:

I asked him to help me. He took a fancy to me, and said, "You do not know anything; but I will teach you. You can sleep in my office. I cannot pay you, because you are of no use to me, except as a companion, but I can feed you." He made me a paper-bed (paper-shavings from the book-trimming department); it was nice and warm. I did errand boy in the intervals of tidying the papers, sweeping the floor of the shop, and sharing Mr. Watkin's frugal meals.[5]

The paper-shavings bed was only a temporary resting place. The job as errand boy was temporary too. But working around the print shop, Lafcadio picked up some little knowledge of printing that he never lost. He never got far away after this from activities connected with the printed word. Watkin helped him to one little job after another. Lafcadio was able precariously to support himself and sleep in a bed. But the cheerless rooms where he slept were not the home that the print shop became to him. He returned evening after evening from whatever kind of work he could find to Watkin's place. When all the customers had gone, the two of them, Watkin and young Lafcadio, would sit in chairs tilted back against the counter and talk or read or be congenially silent together.

In Watkin, Lafcadio had stumbled upon an authentic figure of an America almost gone. The older Englishman belonged to those Americans, native and immigrant, who held to naïve faiths in various contradictory schemes of a better life to be established on the American earth. Henry Watkin was old-fashioned, out of place, in the America of the 1870's, when individualism was crumbling, and when individuals were being tied to the schemes of industry, and losing their opportunities for naïve action.

Hearn looked back at Watkin more than twenty years later, and wrote:

I had a dear old friend in America, who taught me printing. He had a great big silent office, and every evening for two years, it was our delight to have such reading. [Reading aloud] I read nearly all the old *Atlantic* stories to him—at that time, you know, the *Atlantic* was the medium of Emerson, of Holmes, of every man distinguished in American letters. The old man was something of a Fourierist. In his office I made acquaintance first with hosts of fantastic heterodoxies, Of Fourier himself, Hepworth Dixon ("Spiritual Wives"), the Spiritualists, the Freelovers, and the Mormons,—the founders of phalansteries and the founders of freelove societies.[6]

Watkin was a slow-spoken, thoughtful man, self-educated, holding to many curious ideas tenaciously, having worked each one out for himself. He was skeptical of revealed religions, but ingenuous, even gullible, in the hopes he had for science, or the claims of any self-styled scientist. He sat quietly by and let Lafcadio talk. The rebellious thoughts and the angry moods of the nineteen-year-old boy did not shock him. As for Lafcadio, who had had no friendship, no love for so long, Watkin's listening to him, humoring him, sympathizing with him—this was salvation. The shape of Watkin's shop-room, and some of its fittings, remained vividly in his mind the rest of his life. There was an odd little Sphinx upon one shelf. There was a grandfather clock whose tick was like the stride of a long-legged man. The hesitant stride of the slow-ticking clock measured off hour after hour of easy companionship.

What did Watkin see in Lafcadio Hearn? What did the boardinghouse keepers see, both those who turned him out and those who kept him on against their better interest? It was not a very imposing figure that met judgment day in their decisions. He was only five feet three in height, would never be taller, but would be considerably broader. In the early Cincinnati days he was as slender as a pole, and looked even younger than his age. His clothes were nondescript, but somber, the leavings of sober school dress, and the patched-up suits he found in secondhand shops. The face was memorable. The left eye was blind, its cornea scarred with dead white tissue. The right eye was enlarged through too much use. Both eyes were covered at this time by thick lenses which distorted the intelligent gaze of what was left of his sight. The eyes were thick lashed. They had been beautiful in childhood, large, dark, and well formed. The thick hair above the ruined eyes was black, falling in a shock over the pale forehead. The nose was thin and aquiline, the mouth and chin well shaped and sensitive.

It might have been an attractive face. It could be a sympathetic one to those who got beyond the mask of indifference and pride Lafcadio put on, and behind which were a kindling emotion, a fugitive quiet humor, and a wayward imagination. But to casual viewers, the eyes were queer. And Hearn was very self-conscious of the oddity of his appearance. In talk he raised a hand for self-protection, and, hardly knowing what he did, hid the blind eye from view. Doing so, he emphasized and exaggerated the importance of the damaged sight. When he could forget himself, the quick movement of his mind shone through the natural white pallor of his olive skin. The face was animated by a lightning dexterity of thought and mood flickering one upon the other. He was quick and quiet on his feet, graceful and animal-like in his movements, getting about almost without notice. He was rather strongly built, with the good swimmer's supple frame. The hardships of the early months in Cincinnati had thinned him down and obscured the latent strength of the body.

The mind had been starved more drastically than the body. It hungered for something to fill it. Looking for jobs, holding them, losing them, he found his way very soon out of the poorer and meaner streets near the river northward to the more prosperous part of town, and came upon the Public Library. He must have entered it first when it was located (before 1870) in the Ohio Mechanics' Institute, at Sixth and Vine. Then in 1870, when the library moved into a new building a few doors away on the west side of Vine, a generous large place, it became a palace of refuge for him. He had only troubles outside on the streets of the city. Inside, there were worlds at command. He could rest, he could breathe, he could fill his mind with something more than the wretched struggle to live. In this generous space, wasteful of convenience, restful in that waste and bigness, he had peace. And he began to cultivate some of the real interests of his mind.

He had not lost the rudimentary French he had acquired at the Institution Ecclésiastique in Yvetot. Somehow, improbably, in Cincinnati he cultivated a taste for the French romantic writers. He read Gautier for his enameled luxuries, Baudelaire for his intelligent despairs, Gérard de Nerval for his dreams, Flaubert for his anguished perfections. Aside from these French creators of his own century, he wandered into a reading of folklore and anthropology. More of his reading was in French than in English, but he read omnivorously. Among English writers, nothing pleased him more at this time than Tennyson, and the brooding modern doubt netted in his idyls.

Libraries have strange habitués, but Cincinnati's Public Library had none stranger than the ragged young reader who was Lafcadio Hearn. His intentness compelled respect. He soon had the freedom of the library. He learned to ask for the library's curiosities, and was given the privilege of looking at its treasures. Cincinnati's library in the 1870's was a good one for the time. By 1872 (when Hearn was a constant reader there) it had a collection of almost fifty thousand books, and its staff numbered nineteen. An art room, which Hearn soon explored, opened in November of that year. He had at his fingertips all the French books of the period in which he was developing a passionate interest.[7] What mattered most: he had the freedom of the word. He knew by this time what that freedom meant to him. He felt that in the world of books he could handle anything his unleashed curiosity led him to discover: the tortuous thread of logical argument, the complex statement of poetry, the teasing intricacy of French which he soon began to try to put into English. Outside the library, he stumbled from job to job—incompetent, odd, unhappy. Inside, he was serene.

Words might be his business, but how live by them? When he came out into Vine Street from the library, he faced again the crisis of his existence. He grasped a tenuous thread: it must be something to do with words.

He had the good luck of encountering another established citizen of Cincinnati who became his friend. Thomas Vickers was a minister of the Unitarian Church. Vickers saw something remarkable in the boy, and gave him clerical and secretarial work to do for him from time to time.[8] After 1874 Thomas Vickers became Librarian of the Public Library. In this position he continued to encourage Lafcadio and take an interest in his career, although by then Hearn no longer needed his financial help.

Henry Watkin also continued to help Lafcadio, most practically by helping him to find work. Lafcadio's first substantial job in Cincinnati came to him through Watkin's recommendation. Through Watkin, Lafcadio was taken on by the editor of the trade journal the *Trade List,* and with some humor given the title of Assistant Editor. Captain Leonard Barney sent young Hearn out to solicit advertisements, and used him in the office in every kind of job done on a small paper. Hearn found the work dull, but he learned publishing and editorial practices. Somewhat unreasonably he had an ambition far beyond the modest job he had on the *Trade List.*

He was aware of another editorial world more favored than this one, the arena of the big dailies. The reporters of those papers were virtuosos of the word, men who went out proudly and gaily into the city, looked at all the wickedness it held, and came back to their offices to splash and splatter that wickedness across the pages of their papers. He intended to be one of those privileged men.

Meanwhile he lived, and that was more than he had done when, for so many months, he had barely existed. The Cincinnati City Directory of 1872 reflected his more settled status. He had an address, 215 Plum Street; he had a profession, Assistant Editor, the *Trade List*.

His coming to the address on Plum Street preceded any rise in his fortunes. Without money, without baggage, without clothes except the poor ones on his back, Lafcadio had arrived at Kate Haslam's boardinghouse. Having fallen in with printers through knowing Henry Watkin, it was likely that he would turn up at the Haslam. It was the haunt of down-on-their-luck printers. Its keeper and guiding spirit, Kate Haslam—Mrs. J. W. Haslam [9]—was a widow of a printer. A young friend in the business, John Bean, whom Hearn had met through Watkin, recommended the place to him, and took him there to introduce him to Mrs. Haslam. Bean promised to be good for his board till Hearn found a job.

It is probable that Lafcadio worked as a servant in the Haslam boardinghouse at the beginning of his time there. But he did not remain one long, for in the year 1872 he secured his job on Captain Barney's *Trade List*. He was never again in a completely desperate condition in Cincinnati, in so far as money was concerned. If he had arrived at the Haslam down and out, he was not much worse off than the other regulars there. It was a cheap place where meanly dressed men came and went without exciting much notice. The neighborhood was a near slum.

Hearn had been so constantly rebuffed by respectability that he wanted to be in a place where he would not be noticed. He was not even Lafcadio there. The boarders could not manage Lafcadio. He was Pat at the Haslam. He shared with the others only a common experience of trouble. He lived his real life in private.

Even after his luck improved, and he might have moved on, he remained. He had now another reason to stay. He had made a friend in this dismal house. Her name was Mattie Foley. She was the young cook in the harassed kitchen of the boardinghouse, a pretty young woman with a four-year-old son, and a story as rueful as Lafcadio's.

Hearn described Mattie, but did not identify her, in a newspaper sketch he wrote three years later:

She was a healthy, well built country girl, whom the most critical must have called good looking, robust and ruddy, despite the toil in a boarding-house kitchen, but with a strangely thoughtful expression in her large dark eyes, as though she were ever watching the motions of Somebody who cast no shadow, and was invisible to others. Spiritualists were wont to regard her as a strong "medium," although she had a peculiar dislike of being so regarded. She had never learned to read or write, but possessed naturally a wonderful wealth of verbal description, a more than ordinarily vivid memory, and a gift of conversation which would have charmed an Italian *improvisatore*. These things we learned during an idle half hour passed one sum-mer's evening in her company on the kitchen stairs; while the boarders lounged on the porch in the moonlight, and the hall lamp created flickering shadows along the varnished corridors, and the hungry rats held a squeaking carnival in the dark dining-room. To the weird earnestness of the story-teller, the melody of her low, soft voice, and the enthralling charm of her conversation, we cannot attempt to do jus-tice . . .[10]

In this piece, he let her speak in her own voice, as she must have spoken to him, before they had entangled themselves in a relationship which was hard and binding and not idyllic at all. She had described to him a farm in Kentucky, the place where she had grown up:

I was a very little girl then and had a little boy-playmate, who used to run about with me all over the farm, digging in the blue clay, running after the fowls, watching the great snakes that glided about the noisome well, climbing the strangled apple trees in search of withered and shrunken apples, and throwing pebbles at the great, ugly horned owls that used to sit there among the creepers, blinking with their great yellow eyes.[11]

The country girl was kind to Lafcadio, who, when he first knew her, was a servant of Mrs. Haslam too. The kitchen was a refuge for him. She was someone to whom he could tell his unendurable story. She did not under-stand everything he told her, and retained into her later years a garbled version of his story of a Greek mother and an Irish father, of Leucadia, Dublin, and France. It was quite necessary for Lafcadio to romanticize his past to someone. That she would furbish up her own story was to be ex-pected too.

This teller of tales who looked white had been a slave child on a Ken-tucky farm. Her father was the white owner of the plantation, her mother, a slave. When the proper white daughter of the plantation owner married, the illegitimate slave daughter was given to the first as a wedding present. To the foreign boy this story was romance. He had not been bred within the border region's code of what was done and what was not done. Made conscious of this tradition, he damned it. It seemed to him that the two of them had a bond: they had both been mistreated by this proud, indifferent society in which they had struggled and barely made their way to this place. They might help each other. But his turning to Mattie was not all generosity and sympathy. His senses were stirred—and they had been starved. She offered warmth, vitality, fulfillment.

He was inexperienced and perhaps mistaken in judging Mattie. But he was hungry for affection on any terms. And Mattie was good looking. Even thirty-four years later, when Mattie was interviewed by the press, and made much of by reporters who wanted the story of her claim upon the estate of Lafcadio Hearn, even then Mattie impressed with her native and ineradicable good looks. When Lafcadio first knew her, he did not care what she lacked. He found out only in the bitterness of a shared life that she was not only ignorant, but without a trace of sympathy or understanding. At twenty-two he felt only the force which drew him to the girl (she was four years younger than he was), and anger at the social order which said they should hold apart. It was not a casual or a light relationship he entered into in the dingy address on Plum Street.

The rather desperate solidity of this union was the only surety in his life. His job on the *Trade List* did not last. The owner quarreled with him, or more likely he quarreled with the owner. Again Watkin helped him by recommending him to the Robert Clarke Company, book dealers and publishers, as a proofreader. The fact that Pat Hearn worked with words was set and settled. But the new job was mechanical and tedious, and the work hurt his eye. His ambitions were not so little as his situation. He read, he thought, he criticized. It was not rewarding to the ego encased in the inoffensive shy body to be merely an underpaid, unimportant, and exceedingly bored proofreader.

Haltingly he went one day in October 1872 to the office of the Cincinnati *Enquirer*. Accosting the managing editor, John A. Cockerill, he asked him to read something he had written. Cockerill retold the story in the 1890's:

Some twenty years ago I was the editor in charge of the daily newspaper in a Western city. One day there came to my office a quaint dark skinned little fellow strangely diffident, wearing glasses of great magnifying power, and bearing with him evidence that Fortune and he were scarce on nodding terms.

In a soft, shrinking voice he asked if I ever paid for outside contributions. I informed him that I was somewhat restricted in the matter of expenditures, but that I would give consideration to whatever he had to offer. He drew from under his coat a manuscript, and tremblingly laid it upon my table. Then he stole away like a distorted brownie, leaving behind him an impression that was uncanny and indescribable.

Later in the day I looked over the contribution which he had left. I was astonished to find it charmingly written and full of ideas that were bright and forceful.[12]

The article the editor surveyed with some surprise was probably Hearn's review of a lately published part of Tennyson's *Idyls of the King*. Cockerill did him the inestimable favor of printing it—Hearn's first work in print that has been saved—in two issues of the Cincinnati *Enquirer,* on November 24 and December 1, 1872:

It is a pity that Tennyson ever wrote *Gareth and Lynette* [wrote Cincinnati's new critic, fond enough of Tennyson to be somewhat impudent with him] . . . The subject of the narrative—the adventures of a promoted scullion in charge of a pert snub-nosed Miss—is not romantic, and is related in language so completely complicated that it all seems like a first-class parody on *The Idyls of the King*.[13]

When Cockerill accepted this piece, he paid Hearn out of his own pocket. Yet he did not know quite what to do with him. Hearn asked for regular employment, but the editor advised him to hold to his small steady job with the Robert Clarke Company. Not willing to lose sight of him, Cockerill told him he would consider other contributions, and he let Hearn use a desk in his office for his writing.

Something in the intensity of his new employee's manner engaged Cockerill's sympathy as well as support. He kept an eye on Hearn, who came promptly—day after day—to work at the desk set up for him. The material that came out of that corner of his office compelled Cockerill's respect. Hearn soon quit the Robert Clarke Company and subsisted upon what the *Enquirer* paid him. He was a regular member of the staff by the early part of 1874. Hearn had many difficulties with editors in the future, but they were all extracurricular. None of them doubted he could write.

Hearn had no style of his own yet, but the fact did not hurt him in the newspaper world. Cockerill, who struggled day by day to get out a readable paper, was interested in approximate results, and he saw that what Hearn wrote was colorful and conscientiously complete. It was Hearn's private problem to work out his own way of writing: to cut down on the crudeness of being colloquial in one paragraph and overly literary in the next, of being objective on one page and subjective on the next.

Cockerill thought he had a book reviewer on his hands at first and let him review Aldrich's *Marjorie Daw* and praise an almost unknown writer, Henry James. "H. James, Jr. [wrote the twenty-three-year-old Hearn], is certainly a first class word-painter. It is hoped that he will not show this to be his last effort in the peculiar line of imaginative literature in which he has proved himself so fully capable of success." [14] The story praised was James' "The Last of the Valerii" in an omnibus article by Hearn on "The January Magazines," on December 21, 1873. If the new man could do literary things, he might do artistic things too: so Cockerill sent Hearn to interview the local painters. Out of this experience Hearn gained a friend in H. F. Farny, and gave Farny top billing in his report on "Our Artists."

Even in his first year on the staff Hearn wrote some of the pieces about people at which he became a specialist later. He described a street scene of peculiar and low-life vividness in "Almost a Riot," on August 24, 1873. On August 31st he investigated "Grave-Digger Baldwin." On November 9th, in "The Golden Balls," he considered the city's pawnshops. On the same date he wrote "The Hebrews of Cincinnati," an early attempt to depict a cohesive cultural group living its own life within the larger American life. On December 14th he admired ironically the "Wonders of Assassination."

Hearn began writing about the Negroes of Cincinnati soon after becoming a regular staff member. His early interest in this group got into print on January 25, 1874, in "Mr. Handy's Life," a quietly phrased biography of an ex-slave. On August 9, 1874, came "Swarthy Beauty," a lively and humorous, but unpatronizing, write-up of the good-looking girls of the Negro community. On August 17th came "Blue Blood," a satirical sketch upon social climbing in that community. He was beginning to find an interest and exercise a flair.

Hearn's well developed sense of the injustice of things was the basis for another series, about people working long hours for little money. On February 15, 1874, he wrote about the seamstresses of the city in "Slow Starvation." In a piece that followed in the next month, he wrote about the barbers whose wages were held down by a Barber Ring. One should not think of Hearn as developing into a writer of protest. The protest was there, but subordinated to a contemplative enjoyment of life itself. The display of personality, the revelation of setting, the humor, or the pathos, of human nature: these things were beginning to afford a satisfaction beyond his reporter's pay.

By midsummer of 1874 Hearn's pieces on picturesque poverty were being printed regularly and displayed with picturesque headlines (probably of Hearn's coinage) to catch the eye of the daily reader. A typical story was headlined in the following manner:

LES CHIFFONIERS
RAGS, WRETCHEDNESS AND RASCALITY
THE GNOMES OF THE DUMP
HOW THEY LIVE, WORK & HAVE THEIR BEING

He combined prosaic detail with a fine horror in final effect. He listed first and very carefully a dozen actual ragpickers by name and habit. He told how they worked, how much they made, how they lived. One woman made as much as two or three dollars a week and hired two boys to help. Some ragpickers were neat and clean and saving; others were filthy and disorderly.

On September 27, 1874, Hearn celebrated:

CARRIERS
MERCURIES OF THE DAILY PRESS

In this piece he set the stage of the empty news office at the hour of dawn when the boys went forth with the papers. An unnamed reporter was the viewer of this aftermath of the weary hours of work, of this quietness when all the presses had stopped, of this loneliness in which the coming and going of the carriers was the only punctuation. He did not use his own name but gave a sense of an ego looking on, and of a viewpoint.

The most widely read series he produced in his early months of work was one on the city's popular mediums and spiritualists. The purpose was exposure, but it was an exposure designed to wring all the titillation possible out of the process. Cockerill thought well enough of the series to display them prominently from the beginning. Number one, "Modern Spiritualism," appeared on January 4, 1874, "Occult Science" on January 11th, and "Among the Spirits" on January 25th. These articles were cheerfully contemptuous, but in the last one Hearn got beyond his depth.

It began in a light vein, showing an easy scorn of mediums and their patently phony processes. Hearn described a seedy room and an ordinary woman who called herself a medium. He reported a stupid rigmarole of conversation with the "spirits."

But a corner was turned—either in the actual experience or in the writing of it. Hearn found himself through this obvious charlatan of a medium speaking with the spirit of his dead father:

"I am your father, P—."
"Have you any word for me?"
"Yes."
"What is it?"
"Forgive me"—in a long whisper.
"I have nothing to forgive."
"You have, indeed"—very faintly.
"What is it?"
"You know well"—distinctly. . . .
"I wronged you: forgive me"—a loud, distinct whisper.
"I do not consider that you have."
"It would be better not to contradict the spirit," interrupted the medium, "until it has explained matters."
"I do not wish to contradict the spirit in the sense you imply," answered the reporter. "*I thoroughly understand the circumstances alluded to;* but I wish to explain that I have long ceased to consider it as a wrong done me." [15]

This was very odd, both the manner of it and the substance of it. He was trying to lay the ghost of his father. Never given to public confession, this fragment was somehow wrung out of him without his caring how little the public would understand. If they got from it only a tickling of their nerves of susceptibility, so much the better, and he would be fulfilling his job; but the passage meant obviously much more to him. In it, he looked

back toward childhood and said goodbye to it. He never completely succeeded in exorcising the past, but this was an almost unconscious attempt
to do so. From this moment he began to belong to Cincinnati, and to be
no longer an alien walker in her streets.

4 ✂ *Sensational Reporter*

He had been a starveling on the streets, he had been a half-paid helper
in shops and offices; as "your *Enquirer* reporter" Hearn gained place
and position as well as regularity of pay. Cockerill found out that the
young man he had hired on a dubious hunch was capable of bringing
back quick-witted and entertaining news. He began to use him merci-
lessly. Hearn, in the harsh world of the daily reporter, fitted in surprisingly well. His hours grew longer, his stories better. Shy of conventional circumstances, he was not shy of unconventional ones in which
he was only an observer. Sometimes the beginnings of his stories, or the
ends of them, were awkwardly literary; he dropped his bookishness bit
by bit, and acquired a racy everyday language to describe Cincinnati's
everyday lives.

His oddity of appearance did not awaken a prejudice among the
people of the streets who made news for him. Strange, small, apparently
unimportant, like water he made his way wherever there was an opening. He never pushed, he never patronized. He was quiet and receptive.
People talked to him readily. His loneliness, his differentness, his apartness were assets. Because he was alone, unplaced, and unassimilated in
this restless, straining community, essentially and not just accidentally
a foreigner, he was able to look at the city's life with a clear, innocent
childlike gaze. He saw things in Cincinnati that no one had seen before. He was the best possible *Enquirer* reporter of that day when the
reporter was required to entertain as well as report.

In this arena of civic entertainment the *Enquirer*'s editor was a formidable man. Hearn recalled Cockerill, and the atmosphere of work under him, in a letter written in 1895:

I began daily newspaper work in 1874, in the city of Cincinnati, on a paper called "Enquirer" edited by a sort of furious young man named Cockerill. He was a hard master, a tremendous worker, and a born journalist. I think none of us liked him, but we all admired his ability to run things. He used to swear at us, work us half to death (never sparing himself), and he had a rough skill in sarcasm that we were all afraid of. He was fresh from the army, and full of army talk. In a few years he had forced up the circulation of the paper to a very large figure.[2]

Cockerill went on to larger jobs in St. Louis and New York, but he was never more full of drive than when he bossed among others an unlikely little Greek-Irish reporter named Hearn, and sent him out to interview the Cincinnati saints and sinners.

There were very many more of the sinners than the saints who qualified for newspaper space. Up on the bluffs, down in the Basin, Hearn trudged tirelessly, summer and winter, to talk to murderers and ministers, saloon-keepers, stevedores, actresses, artists, coroners, police officers, prostitutes. On the steep hills above the city he could look out to the green fields of Kentucky. Down in the crowded bowl of the old city, he made his way in mean streets through dirt and smoke. Hearn became a familiar figure to the waterfront region, known to policemen, riverboat men, barmen. The police talked Irish to him and called him Paddy. Two particular officers of the force, Knox and Brazil, became his special sources. He named them again and again in his sketches about the misadventures or crimes of the waterfront. They became recurring characters in these hastily written dramas.

"Beastly Cincinnati," [3] "practical, pork-packing Cincinnati," [4] were epithets Hearn hurled at the place. But in the dirty, ugly, beastly side of the city he found an element of stubborn, unflattened-out life. The best stories came out of the grimiest streets, or the dirtiest faces, or the ghastliest actions. There was news value in the low. But more than news value drove Hearn to these alleys and alley people. He discerned a thing he could do with this dark, noisome side of the great, disorderly city. He began to bring back from this field of action all sorts of reeking and enthralling news for the worthy citizen who, with his clean napkin spread, his smoking egg and sausage held in mid-air, thrilled to the latest racy report of what his less respectable neighbor was up to, and what new thing the *Enquirer* reporter had uncovered.

On the morning of November 9, 1874, the worthy reader had a dish to make him forget his breakfast or, if he remembered it, to abstain from eat-

ing it. Hearn that morning attained a kind of fame among his fellow reporters.

A tanyard worker named Herman Schilling had been set upon, beaten,
stabbed with a pitchfork, stuffed into the furnace of the tannery where he
worked, and there cremated. His suspected murderers were quickly found
and arrested. They were three men: a father and son, Andreas and Frederick
Egner, and George Rufer, a fellow worker from the tannery.

The piece is as readable today as when Hearn very hastily and breath-
lessly put it together, his hurry showing—"the murderers laid in wait." Before analyzing its lasting appeal to the taste for sensation, one should note
first that it was firm and clear in its presentation of the facts. The order of
events was laid out, visualized, and made easy for the reader to grasp. The
victim, the gross murderers, the weak-kneed witness who failed to call for
help, were all rapidly characterized and set moving through the rapid course
of fatal action. The motive of each actor was suggested.

Some time before the murder, Andreas Egner, a saloonkeeper and boardinghouse operator in whose house Herman Schilling lived,

. . . claimed that Schilling had seduced his daughter, which charge was denied by the
accused, who, while admitting his criminal connection with the girl, alleged that he
was not the first or only one so favored. At all events the girl became pregnant and
died at the Hospital on the 6th of August last from cancer of the vulva, being seven
months advanced in pregnancy at the time.[5]

Rufer, who had joined forces with the two Egners in their attack upon
Schilling, had a simpler motive for revenge than they: he had claimed that
his fellow worker Schilling had cost him his job at the tannery.

There were two parts to the piece: first, the narration of the events set
in motion by the discovery of the body, and second, the imaginative narration of the killing. As police reporter, Hearn was all business, listing
names, places, times, very carefully, and for their own edification, the names
of the investigating officers. In the other role he was more original. He put
in motion for the benefit of the breakfast-table reader a hauntingly lively
re-creation of the struggle, the torture, the death in the stable where next
day the horse, who had been a witness to Herman Schilling's death, still
trembled.

The reporter accompanied the coroner to the funeral establishment. He
saw and made the reader see the fragments of the burned body laid out
upon the "clean white lining of the coffin," [6] and which

. . . rather resembled great shapeless lumps of half-burnt bituminous coal than
aught else at the first hurried glance: and only a closer investigation could enable a

strong-stomached observer to detect their ghastly character—masses of crumbling human bones, strung together by half-burnt sinews, or glued one upon another by a hideous adhesion of half-molten flesh, boiled brains and jellied blood mingled with coal. The skull had burst like a shell in the fierce furnace-heat; and the whole upper portion seemed as though it had been *blown out* by the steam from the boiling and bubbling brains.[7]

The ineffable touch was that:

The brain had all boiled away, save a small wasted lump at the base of the skull about the size of a lemon. It was crisped and still warm to the touch. On pushing the finger through the crisp, the interior felt about the consistency of human fruit, and the yellow fibers seemed to writhe like worms in the coroner's hands. The eyes were cooked to bubbled crisps in the blackened sockets, and the bones of the nose were gone, leaving a hideous hole.[8]

The climax of agony was the relentless presentation of the victim's feelings upon finding himself being stuffed alive into the furnace.

His teeth were so terribly clenched that more than one spectator of the hideous skull declared that only the most frightful agony could have set those jaws together. Perhaps, stunned and disabled by the murderous blows of his assailants, the unconscious body of the poor German was forced into the furnace. Perhaps the thrusts of the assassin's pitchfork, wedging him still further into the fiery hell, or the first agony of burning when his bloody garments took fire, revived him to meet the death of flame. Fancy the shrieks for mercy, the mad expostulation, the frightful fight for life, the superhuman struggles for existence—a century of agony crowded into a moment—the shrieks growing feebler—the desperate struggles dying into feeble writhings. And through all the grim murderers, demoniacally pitiless, devilishly desperate, gasping with their exertions to destroy a poor human life, looking on in silent triumph! Peering into the furnace until the skull exploded and the steaming body burst, and the fiery flue hissed like a hundred snakes! [9]

There were three elements wound round each other in this affront to the breakfast-table reader. There was first the ordinary newspaperman's desire to catch the reader's attention with sensation. There was in addition Hearn's own reaching out from the darkness within him to the darkness outside: to violence, pain, death—out of a surfeit of hate, fear, and something like a desire for revenge. Mixed with these two elements was a perfectly true and pure agony of sympathy for the victim; he would make the reader die a little as he had died in telling the story.

The *Enquirer's* circulation soared in the sale of the story of the Tanyard Case. Writing of Schilling's death, Hearn was confirmed in his role, to which he had been tending before this date, as the *Enquirer's* particular sensational reporter. It was a title he gave himself. He was quite canny and cool about the gain to himself. Yet his nerves did not let him off lightly. The infernal way he had treated death in the Schilling story was exploitation. The other reporters admired him but were not quite easy with him.

Loneliness, lostness, suffering had put upon him an intolerable weight. Ridding himself of this emotional burden in crude stories, he gave expressive shape to his own fears. He began, in this coarsely limited métier, to be a writer. And he began to create and to live a particular role as the *Enquirer*'s "sensational reporter." He was himself most alive, and found the most life to report, in the city's nighttime streets. He often wrote his stories just before dawn in the darkened quiet of the newspaper offices—"those huge human-owls'-nests"—with only the carrier boys coming and going about his still, bent figure. After he had done his stint of work and stretched, he looked about and in such a lonely setting assessed himself and his work. Cockerill had thought Hearn shy. But Hearn's inarticulateness was only in his relations with others. With himself he was bold and irreverent. He knew already how well he filled the shoes of the *Enquirer*'s "sensational reporter," and he knew too how little a thing this job was to which he had raised himself from the streets. Outside the vivid area of work he was lonely. He postponed his going home to a mean boardinghouse room to the last possible moment. Finished with the nervous excitement of his work, tired from walking, weary from interrogating, overwrought from experiencing vicarious violence and death, he faced a kind of nothingness in his empty room. In later years he recited, with a sense of identification, the lines of Goethe:

> Who ne'er his bread in sorrow ate,—
> Who ne'er the lonely midnight hours
> Weeping upon his bed has sat,—
> He knows ye not, ye Heavenly powers.

"Of course it is only the young man who sits upon his bed at midnight and weeps; he is weak only for want of experience." [10] So spoke the professor to his classes in the 1890's. But he remembered an inexperienced weeper.

Work was an alleviation, and the companionship of other men who did his same kind of work was another. The reporters of the various city dailies, the German-language papers as well as the English-language papers, banded together, not only in looking for stories in the dangerous dark streets near the waterfront, but in their moments of leisure. They ate together, talked interminably about personalities, prospects, jobs, and even ambitions. The relationship was casual but strong.

Hearn was odd, but these men were used to curiosities. He could write,

and so won their respect. And his talk, a strange outpouring pried loose
from such a silent man, won their interest. With encouragement Hearn
quickly gained self-confidence and even a sort of jaunty insouciance. He,
and these others, who worked sixteen hours a day, and lived in an upside-
down world where bad news was more important than good news, knew
what was important for Cincinnati before the city knew. He recalled the
Cincinnati fellowship of hard-pressed night reporters after he had moved
away and before he had begun to like his situation in New Orleans: "No
literary circle here; no jovial coterie of journalists." [11] The statement was
to be modified in time, but it shows that later there was something to remember, and something to regret, of Cincinnati.

Included in the fellowship of newspapermen were Feldwisch, Johnson,
Tunison, Farny, Krehbiel, and others more shadowy. Of Feldwisch there
is left only a reminiscent glance of appreciation. In New Orleans years later
Hearn thanked Krehbiel for sending on a letter from Feldwisch: "sharp,
fresh, breezy." [12] Johnson was Charley Johnson. He persisted as an occasion into the New Orleans days, for he came down from Cincinnati like a
healthy whirlwind to visit Hearn in a mildewing French Quarter room and
then jogged him into going with him on a vacation to Florida. Hearn admired Johnson and his undauntable air, "his Rabelaisian mirth, and his
Gargantuesque laughter." [13] Johnson wrote for a German-language paper.
Some years later he became American consul in Hamburg, Germany.

Tunison meant even more. Joseph S. Tunison was the man with whom
Hearn spent his last days in America almost two decades later in an apart-
ment in Greenwich Village. By that time Tunison was working for the
New York *Tribune*. Later he became editor of the Dayton, Ohio, *Journal*.
Joe Tunison was quiet and literary, and yet owned a rude brusqueness on
occasion. He was to be the author, in 1904, of *The Graal Problem from
Walter Map to Richard Wagner*.

Henry F. Farny was the careless and talented center of their group, not a
newspaperman proper like the rest of them, although he did illustrations
for the papers. Grandly and impecuniously he upheld the bohemian tradition in his studio in the Pike Opera House building, pulling into the orbit
of the coterie his friend and fellow painter Frank Duveneck. Hearn had
given Farny a boost in his article "Our Artists." He was soon an intimate
of Farny's famous cheese-and-wine suppers arranged impromptu in the
midst of a cheerful insubstantiality of means.

It was probably to Farny's studio that Hearn was invited to see a pretty
model, locally famous among Cincinnati painters, and it was from this
viewing that the *Enquirer*'s man brought back another sensation:

BEAUTY UNDRAPED
WHAT A WICKED REPORTER SAW
IN AN ARTIST'S STUDIO

A curious *Enquirer* reporter whose wicked and ever wide-open ears these stories had reached, became finally convinced that this model must be a very extraordinary person indeed . . .[14]

The beginning deliberately teased his readers. The middle lapsed into pure reverence for the nude:

She lay at full length upon a long sofa, unclad and unadorned save by the matchless gifts of nature, her white limbs lightly crossed, both hands clasped over her graceful little head, and her luxurious blonde hair streaming loose beneath her in a river of tawny gold.[15]

Farny in his studio led a disorganized, lazy, talented existence. He was an honest, likable man. Soon after meeting each other, he and Hearn were deep together in the fun and trouble of a crackbrained partnership.

The other serious friend of this group was H. E. Krehbiel, a man who took himself much more solemnly than Henry Farny. Honest, ambitious, learned, Henry Krehbiel kindled Hearn to concurrent dreams of attainment. Krehbiel dreamed music, as Hearn dreamed writing. They talked about their ambitions as they went together on their nightly rounds of police courts, saloon brawls, riots, shootings, arrests. They would slough off this night-reporter life one day and do more than talk art. They would create.

Four years younger in years than Hearn, Henry Krehbiel was a soberer and cooler young man, a brake on Hearn's effervescence. He reasoned where Hearn romanced. The two of them might stand together transfixed to listen to a stevedore's song. The emotion of the wavering chant pierced Hearn without any interference of cerebration. Krehbiel, sensitive to mood too, began at once to analyze the scale system.

By 1874 Krehbiel graduated from night reporting to music criticism. His paper, the Cincinnati *Gazette,* gave him his start in the career of musicologist he pursued for the rest of a long, industrious, scholarly life. After his promotion he was a member by curtesy only of the night crew, but the interests he and Hearn shared kept them close. They went to an occasional concert together, they talked music and books, and they saw something akin in their two independent desires: one to be a scholar in music, the other to write—he hardly knew what. Both saw a horizon beyond newspaper work and beyond Cincinnati. Hearn deferred to Krehbiel. His talk and his letters to Krehbiel had always the tone of the younger to the older brother—until he exploded in Krehbiel's face like a firecracker.

Feldwisch, Johnson, Tunison, Farny, Krehbiel, and Hearn: they entertained themselves. All stopped to listen when Hearn could be enticed to
talk. His melodious low voice, his restrained chuckle, his infrequent high
yell of laughter became a familiar part of their circle of responses. In his
soft voice Hearn loosed among them all sorts of fantastic theories, made
acute points, or let himself dream aloud reveries of luxury or imaginative
richness. He lifted them out of their everyday work and life.

Hearn became a light of the Cincinnati newspaper world with comparative ease. He was crammed with ideas picked up along the way he had come
from one trouble to another, and needed desperately to express himself.
He had had no formal education since he was stopped short of graduation
at St. Cuthbert's College, but the outpouring of eager words in Cincinnati
testified to the variety and liveliness of the informal learning he had acquired along the way.

The summer of 1874 was full of a particular activity for the twenty-four-
year-old Hearn. During the hot months of that year he tried to attain independence in the newspaper business, and failed. He tried also to legalize
his relationship with Mattie Foley, and failed in that venture too.

His professional career took a detour into penniless self-sufficiency when
H. F. Farny persuaded him into a partnership in editing a new weekly
newspaper. It was backed but not sustained by the publishers of a German-
language paper already in existence, *Kladderadatsch*. Although one or two
other newspapermen worked with them from time to time, the short lively
career of the new weekly belonged principally to Farny and Hearn. They
endured the troubles, the quarrels, the successes, and the final breakdown.
Between June 21 and August 16, 1874, they brought out nine issues of
Ye Giglampz.[16]

The name was a joke flung at a hypothetical reader. "The name pleases
us," the editors announced in issue Number 1. "We look upon it in the
light of a conundrum, calculated to induce reflection in simple minds. We
hope someone may solve it, as we have incontinently given it up." Apparently Farny, in a fit of abstraction, gazing at the flashing surfaces of
Hearn's thick eyeglasses, had the inspiration. Just before the demise of the
paper, Hearn, back at his post in the *Enquirer* city room, explained: "The
name needs interpretation to the polite-spoken American nation. It sig-
nifieth 'spectacles'—spectacles of a huge and owlish description—just such
spectacles as sat upon the intellectual nose of the myopic editor (No. 1)
who furnished the newborn paper with literary fodder." Designating himself as the No. 1 editor was a jibe at his ally Farny, for they fought furiously
all through the life of the paper.

Given a little luck the two might have made the paper what they proclaimed it: "A Weekly Illustrated Journal Devoted to Art, Literature, and Satire (Published Daily, Except Weekdays)," but they did not have the luck. Times were bad in the mid-seventies. There was not any spare money in the city to be spent on an irreverent little sheet that made fun of temperance, doctors, the YMCA, Henry Ward Beecher, and solicited its few ads from breweries and saloons.

The two young men fell into their adventure easily. It cost them only their savings and their security. Hearn tried at first to work his *Enquirer* assignments and his *Giglampz* assignments at the same time but found he could not do it. But it was only after some persistent arguing that he could make the city editor of the *Enquirer* take seriously his resignation:

> Our City Editor sat down and laughed until his ribs threatened to burst asunder, and the tears rolled down his cheeks in torrents. [So wrote Hearn in the *Enquirer* in a piece marking the passing of the *Giglampz*.] The idea of an *Enquirer* man resigning his position in order to accept an interest in *The Giglampz* was too much for him. When he recovered the use of articulate speech, however, he ironically congratulated the Ghoul [one of Hearn's self-applied epithets] on his extraordinary good fortune. Then all the *Enquirer* boys went down to Jake Aug's, and gave the Ghoul an ovation. And the resignation of the Ghoul was accepted.[17]

In their joint work Hearn and Farny quarreled not once but many times. Hearn began soon desperately trying to resign from the *Giglampz*, but his interest in the crazy venture held him to his unpaid editorship. It was only after Farny attempted to censor his writing that Hearn formally quit, asked forgiveness at the *Enquirer,* and was taken back on the staff. "It was bad enough," he wrote in his mock-solemn account of the affair in the *Enquirer,* "to live on air, but he said he could not stand having his English mangled . . ."[18] Going back to the *Enquirer* did not at first rid him of his concern with *Ye Giglampz.* He worked on it spasmodically till its end.

It was not Hearn's writing, but Farny's cartoons and drawings, which were the best of *Giglampz.* For the Number 2 issue he drew a lumpish Henry Ward Beecher (who had lived in Cincinnati) haled up to the scaffold for adultery with a scarlet letter on his front—Beecher's troubles at law being much in the news at that time. His cartoon for the Number 4 issue showed the rulers of Europe cowering under the glare of the comet *Communism.* Number 5 showed a sketch of a slum family sitting dejectedly on the charred ruins of their house, burned out by the Chicago Fire. Underneath was the caption:

> The Chicago Fire—"only the Plebs"
> "The Fire Took Only Tenement Houses, and was rather a Blessing."
> —Chicago Telegram

Farny finished himself, Hearn, and the paper with his best work in the eighth issue, a set of drawings of a river disaster, the sinking of the steamer *Pat Rogers*. The unimportant *Giglampz* scooped the big daily papers and brought back moving and exciting firsthand pictures of the wreck. But there was no modulation from satire to seriousness, and the public took offense, thinking that a comic paper was trying to make fun of the dead and dying. Hearn and Farny apologized in issue Number 9, but they were finished. The little circulation they had had among antitemperance people dropped to almost nothing. Number 9 was the last issue.

Hearn's huddled writing for *Ye Giglampz* was for the most part only a faint prefiguring of better work he would do working for other editors in Cincinnati and New Orleans. He wrote two early fantasies: "Fantasies for Sultry Seasons," on July 12th, and "Fantasy of a Fan," on July 26th. His "Eddaic Fragments" on August 9th was a practice piece for such a book as *Stray Leaves from Strange Literature*. Yet these essays lacked the polish or the quality to make them memorable. The best of Hearn in *Ye Giglampz* was similar to his contemporary best work on the *Enquirer:* paragraphs descriptive or critical of daily Cincinnati life.

He wrote about conscienceless doctors in Number 2, June 28, 1874:

A Cincinnati empiric, recently amused himself by torturing a wretched woman with obstetrical instruments for fifteen hours, at the expiration of which she died in agony; while he coolly washed his hands, pocketed his fee, went home, and ate a hearty dinner. Another murderer in Lawrenceburg, who lately performed a similar surgical operation gratuitously, has actually been arrested, and will probably be condemned to have his neck dislocated. The former individual had been shrewd enough, however, to procure a license to kill; the latter foolishly went to work without a diploma.

He carried on a running fight with the "temperance lunacy." In Number 3 he made fun of the new YMCA which proposed "chequers" to replace "the opera, the ballet, the beer-garden, the wine-house." "What is there like unto chequers?"

He jeered at the quality of the city paving and the quality of Cincinnati police protection in his squib on slum streets in Number 5, July 19:

Persons desiring information regarding the condition of Constantinopolitan streets after dark, should take a midnight stroll in the east end of Cincinnati during the sultry season, armed with a heavy club, and observe the fierce loves and ruthless wars of the wolfish dogs, innumerable, that infest the quarter alluded to.

There was not much of Hearn, the writer, in the nine papers, but there was a vivid reflection of the place he lived in as a harassed reporter who stumbled into one adventure after another, and casually pulled himself out again. Although Hearn made light of the failure of *Ye Giglampz,* the failure hurt.

> *The Giglampz* died of inanition and the bad taste of the great American people, at the age of nine weeks, on the 16th day of August, 1874. . . .
> A complete file of *The Giglampz*—nine numbers—is for sale cheap at this office.[19]

In 1874 Hearn was as harassed in his private life as he was in his career. He could dismiss the misadventures of attempted independence with a rueful grin. He could not so easily shrug off the suffering he endured or made another endure in trying to make something correct out of his relationship with Mattie Foley. He was blind and stubborn in his desire to make some kind of retribution. He decided to regularize the union. He decided that he and Mattie must be married. He found out first that the act would be a legal fraud, but determined to go through with it anyway. An Ohio law, valid only between 1861 and 1877, prohibited the performance of a marriage between a white person and a Negro. Mattie stated later, probably with truth, that she warned Hearn that he would be ostracized if he married her, and that she tried to prevent his insisting on the performance of the ceremony. But he could not be stopped.

Apparently he lied to secure a license. He broke with one friend who refused to be a witness. He was turned down by one minister before he secured the services of a second one. Presumably all the participants of the ceremony knew that according to the letter of the law the marriage could not be a legal one. Yet Hearn bullied and pushed and persuaded and saw to it that the ceremony took place in proper form. An Episcopalian minister, a Negro, John King, married Lafcadio, almost twenty-four, and Mattie, aged twenty-one, in the house of a Negro woman, Mrs. Lottie Cleneay, probably on the night of June 14, 1874. The second witness was another Negro woman, Mrs. Mary Field. Lafcadio and Mattie removed with her child Willie from the Haslam boardinghouse to lodgings at 114 Longworth Street, next door to the Adams Express Stables.

Hearn's closest friends knew of the act. They shrugged it off, or ceased to be his friends. A low whisper of gossip began, but did not crackle into public attention for many months.

After the alarms of the summer of 1874—the fantasy of being professionally independent, the fantasy of marriage—Hearn lost himself more and more in hard work. The *Enquirer* had taken him back after the fiasco of *Giglampz.* The paper was brilliantly justified of him when in November 1874 he wrote the notorious and profitable Tanyard Case story.

"In our great cities, beauty is for the rich; bare walls and foul pavements and smoky skies for our poor, and the tumult of hideous machinery—a hell of eternal ugliness and joylessness invented by our civilization to punish the atrocious crime of being unfortunate, or weak, or stupid, or overconfident in the morality of one's fellow-man." [1]

LH: *Gleanings in Buddha-Fields*

5 ❧ *Low Life and Romanticism*

The darkness and wetness and dirtiness of winter in Cincinnati, the slipperiness of the hill roads, the somberness of the idle, iced-up waterfront, all this was as it had been; but there was a new eye to see. And Hearn's inner vision was of a corresponding blackness to the mucky horrors he was encouraged to view. After the success of the Tanyard Case on November 9, 1874, Hearn was given his head in searching for sensations. On November 15th he painted word pictures of "The Quarter of Shambles":

Mammoth slaughter-houses, enormous rendering establishments, vast soap and candle factories, immense hog-pens and gigantic tanneries loom up through the miasmatic atmosphere for blocks and blocks in every direction. Narrow alleys, dark and filthy, traverse this quarter in every direction. The main streets here lose their width and straightness in tortuous curves and narrow twists and labyrinthine perplexity—so that the stranger who loses his way in this region of nastiness must wander wildly and long ere he may cease to inhale the ghoulish aroma of stink-factories and the sickening smell of hog-pens fouler than the stables of Augeas.[2]

The "tortuous curves" and the "labyrinthine perplexity" could stand for a state of mind. The filthiness of the shambles, the ugliness of death without dignity—these were in him as well as around him. Caught in a trap he had carefully fashioned for himself, not daring to break away, Hearn came and went daily through the door of a relationship that had become meaningless and bitter.

On November 29th his congenial subject was:

Golgotha
A Pilgrimage to Potter's Field

To potter's field went the coroner, a friend, and "the *Enquirer*'s Dismal Man, whose rueful countenance was flushed with the hope of hearing or seeing something more than usually horrible." At the burying ground they pretended they wanted bodies, and a careless sexton let them know it would be all right so long as they kept out of his sight. It shook the sexton's nerves considerably to find out that one of the visitors was the coroner, another, an *Enquirer* reporter, making notes for a front-page story.

In early January 1875, pursuing what had been found profitable, Hearn described:

Mad-House Horrors
The Inferno of the Insane

But it was not the superficial, but the inherent horror he uncovered:

The mad know they are mad, and there can be no mental torture more horrible than their intervals of lucid consciousness, which only find expression in the thought, "I am mad!" [3]

By the spring of 1875, Hearn was writing about opium and its addicts. He recurred to the subject again before another year had gone by. The substance of both pieces was sober rather than sensational. His conclusion was cool and clinical: "Its consumption is a disease." [4]

He continued to haunt slaughterhouses and "stink-factories." Butcheries, both animal and human, occupied his attention. He wrote ceaselessly, almost without pause, in a relentless practice of the word. Much of it was hack work. Yet some quality began to show.

In the summer of 1875 he lost his job. And almost for a moment he gave up. Some wind of scandal reached his employers: Hearn was living with a Negro woman. Cockerill was forced to act, not so much because of the scandal itself, but because the scandal was used by a group of city politicians to attempt to silence a critic. Probably against his own desire, he rid himself of his best reporter. Hearn, coming into the city room one day, to receive an assignment, received instead a peremptory dismissal. He thought that his world had come to an end. He rushed out in a suicidal mood and was held back from jumping into the Miami Canal only by the forcible interference of his friend Charley Johnson.

But Hearn could hardly have drowned himself. He was too good a swimmer. The joint recollection of his friends softens the seriousness of the act, if not the misery of the gesture. When, after his death, all his acquaintances were remembering stories about Hearn, H. E. Krehbiel recalled his attempted suicide in a letter to Joseph Tunison:

> Charley Johnson was in Cincinnati on a visit from his home in Berlin when I was there, and reminded me that he had once caught Hearn in the act, or on the verge of jumping into the canal,—possibly one of his frequent theatrical exhibitions. I can't honestly say that I ever saw Hearn really miserable or profoundly unhappy. Did you? Yet he often talked about suicide, as you know. He would have liked to kill himself spectacularly if he could have written the story for his newspaper.[5]

All the possible variations upon Hearn's relationship with Mattie Foley were by this time, July 1875, circulating briskly from lip to lip. Sensation had caught up with the *Enquirer*'s sensational reporter.

Cockerill bore no grudge against Hearn for having been his victim. In 1896 he wrote a column of recollection of his reporter:

> His eyes troubled him greatly in those days. He was as sensitive as a flower. An unkind word from anybody was as serious to him as a cut from a whiplash, but I do not believe he was in any sense resentful. The classics were at his fingers' ends. He was poetic, and his whole nature seemed attuned to the beautiful, and he wrote beautifully of things that were neither wholesome nor inspiring.[6]

Cockerill's Hearn and Krehbiel's were both true. Each man saw Hearn in a perspective colored by his own temperament. He was both excessively sensitive, and efficiently capable of exploiting that sensitiveness. Hearn could feel suicidal for only one indecisive moment. He was too interested to die. As a person he suffered, but as a writer just beginning to grasp firmly his instrument of expression he was willing to make use of his suffering.

"Had he been then on a New York daily," wrote Joseph Tunison, remembering Hearn's situation in 1875, "his articles would have attracted bidding from rival managements, but in Cincinnati there was little, if any encouragement for such brilliant powers as his. The 'Commercial' took him on at twenty dollars a week." [7]

Edwin Henderson, who hired Lafcadio Hearn for the *Commercial*, was sure enough of his own position to resist the pressures of gossip. He justly estimated the talent housed in the troublesome reporter. The *Commercial* scrupled only in using soberer headlines than the *Enquirer*. It demanded the same substance of sensation.

It was the sensational reporter who demanded more of himself. Shielded by Henderson's indifference to pressure, assigned again and again to violent scenes of action, Hearn moved swiftly toward a more trenchant expressiveness and toward greater depth of feeling.

He focused a mild gleam of humor in "Bones":

"Are you gathering rags, young man?" we inquired.

"Bones," was his laconic answer.

"And what on earth do you do with bones?"

"Sell 'em down to the bone factory; half a cent a pound. They grind 'em up down there."

"What do they grind them up for?" we asked.

"Dun-no," he replied, with a suspicious grin. " 'Spect they sell 'em for flour." [8]

His reporter's work proliferated during 1874, 1875, 1876, and 1877. He wrote a certain number of self-consciously literary pieces. He did a number of researches into curious, morbid, and erudite lore. He tried his hand at prose poems. But his best work was still concerned with the raw life of Cincinnati. Paradoxically, there was more art in his "horrible" pieces and in his low-life sketches than in his consciously artistic and literary essays. His purposely artful pieces were indicative of new interests, but in achievement they were pale, faint, and tentative. His report of life itself was sure.

Shock value was not abandoned, but it was enriched by other values. John Cockerill had sold papers with Hearn's sensational pieces. Edwin Henderson would do so too. And an obscure hurt still worked in Hearn: he would show those others—those worthies who lived so fine and clean—what life was like below. Let them pay their pennies to be shocked. He would thrust under their genteel noses the throbbing, vagrant life of the poor.

In "Gibbeted" he gave them—terribly—the hanging of James Murphy, a hanging so badly mismanaged that it had to be done twice. The rope having broken in the first attempt, the boy, who was only slightly injured, awoke to whisper, "Why, I ain't dead—I ain't dead." [9]

He gave them in pure naked misery the mismanaged death of an animal, in "Halcedama." The outrage of resistance to its fate brought the animal only an outrage of suffering in its dying:

Wheedling and coaxing were in vain; and the butchers loudly cursed the poor cow. But at last the noose was flung about her neck, and they laid on the rope while she braced herself to resist. Then a great, yellow-haired brute of a man, with very large calves and very ugly feet, seized a pritch, and put out the poor cow's left eye.[10]

He led the reader through the stench of the halls of the poor in "Some Pictures of Poverty" where the horror was not just that of hunger, but of the ultimate disarrangement and degradation of lives lived too close to each other. The Overseer of the Poor, and the reporter who accompanied him on his rounds, heard a noise of crying and beating in a room below the one they were visiting:

"Why, she must be killing her children," muttered the Overseer.

"To be sure she is," whispered the Aged Woman, looking awfully at the hole in the floor as though fearing lest the "Divil" might suddenly rise up through it.

"But how often does this thing go on?"

"How often, is it? Shure there's no ind to it at all, at all. Ah, she bates the childher whinever she takes a dhrap too much, bad cess to her! an' may God forgive me fur spakin' that word—an' she's dhrunk all the time, so she is, night and day. Thin, if I wor to spake a word to the Divil, she breaks up the flure undher us wid a pole; an' many's the night I've stud over the hole, thryin' to kape the flure down, an' she a-breaking it up betune me feet." [11]

Moving alone and isolated in his orbit of horrors, never knowing his reader, almost forgetting him, he went far beyond his superficial motive of showing them. In the end he showed only himself. He stripped away excrescences of motive as well as of style. Honesty was what he hungered for: honesty of seeing and honesty of saying. Therefore, he looked unflinchingly at James Murphy's death. He even felt with his own finger for the dying man's pulse. He did not excuse, condemn, or even explain. He simply showed what was so:

But the facts in the case, as they appeared to the writer, were simply that a poor, ignorant passionate boy, with a fair, coarse face, had in the heat of drunken anger taken away the life of a fellow-being, and paid the penalty of his brief crime, by a hundred days of mental torture, and a hideous death.[12]

Yet honesty, though necessary, was not enough. Something besides was needed, a kind of perspective to make honesty itself endurable. Sometimes a fugitive humor made a margin around horror. Sometimes imagination served the same purpose. Certain facts haunted the mind like a vision. In retrospect his round of visits with the Overseer of the Poor seemed a kind of dream:

. . . a dream of reeling buildings of black plank, with devious corridors and deformed stairways; with interminable suites of crooked rooms, having sloping floors and curving walls; with crazy stoves and heavy smells; with long rags and ragged gowns haunting the pale walls like phantom visitors or elfish mockeries of the dead; and all the chambers haunted by sharp shadows and sharp faces that made them piteous with the bitterness of withered hopes, or weird by fearful waiting for the coming of the dreamless slumber, as a great Shadow, which silently falling over lesser darknesses, absorbs them into Itself.[13]

He had one bedrock belief: that these miseries mattered. His vision was as unshaded and glaring as the raw material on which it shone its small bright beam. Excluded from the center of society, rejecting the middle values acceptable to that center, he concentrated his attentions upon the extravagances and extremities of the fringes of society. One extremity of Cincinnati life—beyond the ken of the average citizen—was the life that was led by the people of the river. To this group Hearn devoted more and more of his time.

There was in their world not only a fearfulness of poverty to report, but a color and a vitality and even a kind of beauty he had found nowhere else in the city. The qualities which attracted him were embedded hopelessly in disorder, dirt, violence, and death. But Hearn had the instinctive wisdom of the artist. He did not separate or blame or excuse; he merely accepted all that his imagination told him was good. The luck of his profession made him free of the community of the levee people. It was a world small enough to walk through from front to back in thirty minutes, yet a world complete, a world stuffed full of sins and virtues, darkness and light. It was a world for him to claim and possess for himself alone, for he had no rival either in the ambition or the imagination of making something out of the Cincinnati levee.

Deliberately he turned his face away from the city proper and toward the human frontier of the river:

Along the river-banks on either side of the levee slope, where the brown water year after year climbs up the ruined sidewalks, and pours into the warehouse cellars, and paints their grimy walls with streaks of water-weed green, may be studied a most curious and interesting phase of life—the life of a community within a community,—a society of wanderers who have haunts but not homes, and who are only connected with the static society surrounding them by the common bond of State and municipal law. It is a very primitive kind of life; its lights and shadows are alike characterized by a half savage simplicity; its happiness or misery is almost purely animal; its pleasures are wholly of the hour, neither enhanced nor lessened by anticipations of the morrow. It is always pitiful rather than shocking; and it is not without some little charm of its own—the charm of a thoughtless existence, whose virtues are all original, and whose vices are for the most part foreign to it.[14]

The river timed and tempered all this life of the levee. For the dwellers in the Rows—Rat Row and Sausage Row—for the inhabitants of the "ranches" and the bars, the comers and goers from the boats, the dwellers in the soiled tenements, for all the shifting population of longshoremen, saloonkeepers, and their women who brought them quarrels and consolations, a touch of color or a touch of gall, there was no life without a reference to the river. Boat arrivals and departures, floods and freeze-ups, inspired the celebrations and dirge-songs of the levee. Hearn kept this presence of the river in all his levee pieces.

Sometimes in his bright, crude laying on of color he seemed to see only surface. Sometimes in the stinking somberness of night vistas, he seemed to see only ugliness. Some of the essays were mere fragments; a few were developed at some length. In some, Hearn sketched the levee people carelessly and haphazardly, more interested in the stream of life than in the characters who enlivened it. In others he examined certain figures of the landing more carefully.

It was a rich broth of life, attracting, repelling, alluring, disgusting. No part could be separated from any other part. For a man of Hearn's incurable sensitiveness, it was an exhausting, if exciting, experience. He went everywhere, his senses assailed, caressed, stimulated. He saw everything, took part in every kind of scene. What he did not see he keenly and intelligently imagined.

He became a familiar at Butler's, and knowledgeable in the litany of its smells:

> Suppose we take a peep into "Butler's."
> On opening the door you are saluted with a whiff of hot air, redolent of multifarious foulnesses—the stench of saliva squirted upon a red-hot stove, the odor of villainous tobacco, the familiar smell of salt fish, the sickening aroma of bad breaths qualified with forty-rod whisky, and one or two other stinks which it would not be decorous to name.[15]

He was known at Pickett's, where he paused to talk to Pickett himself— "through the rattling of tinware, the strains from a cracked violin, a dismal guitar, and a wheezy bass viol, together with the jingling of glasses, and the calls of 'Swing partners; forward & back, first fo' right and left.' "[16] He was one of an audience in a crude little theater improvised in a bar where "the screams of laughter and futile stuffing of handkerchiefs in laughing mouths, the tears of merriment, the innocent appreciation of the most trivial joke, the stamping of feet and leaping, and clapping of hands —a very extravagance of cachination" [17]—held him with a sympathetic grimace of enjoyment. The people on the benches were more touching and more interesting than the performance upon the boards of the miniature theater.

He pushed his way into the half-buried dwelling of Jot, the Obi-Man, and saw the spiders richly festooning a dark and sooty ceiling, and believed by the superstitious to be reared there for use in Jot's incantations. He searched out Auntie Porter's house for a story about her adoption of the orphans of the Rows. He went on an all-night search with the police through dangerous tenements, a hunt for a criminal in hiding. He sat, relaxed and attentive, with the police officers of the Hammond Street Station when there was brought in, half drowned, Albert Jones, who had fallen drunk into the river. Recovered, he entertained them all with a concert of river-boat whistles.

Hearn was down on the river the morning the ice broke up and the spring flood rose above the wharves, above the basements, above the sidewalks. Jot had to move out of his sepulchral room, old Maggie Sperlock had to move, and others, but an abandon of joy seized them all. The river was open, they could live again, and Pickett would have to feed them no more:

. . . When the ice broke, and the steamboats whistled once more, and the river surface became alive with the heaving and gliding of the pale ice, the Row gave vent to a burst of noisy joy which must have been plainly heard on the Kentucky shore. Women and men all rushed out of doors, cheered, shouted, waved hats and turbans, and danced with delight; for the crashing and booming of the broken ice promised work for all, money, and the merriment of dancing and drinking. Some even cried with joy, and wandered about with tears on their cheeks.[18]

The mood of these little newspaper pieces, rapidly written, read care-lessly, thrown away with each day's paper, shifted kaleidoscopically to re-flect the joy and grief, the lightness and heaviness of the levee life. Nothing of color or emotion was scanted. The tough, the ignorant, the stupid, the shrewd—all who lived their careless lives along the river were the writer's dials of feeling.

Pickett, a former slave, and an accessory it seemed of many criminals, the keeper of bars and "ranches," was the benefactor of the whole community. He could neither read nor write, and hired a man to keep his simple book, to set down in it the name of those who fed or drank or slept under his roof. When the river froze and the people starved, Pickett laughed, and gave away food, drink, and shelter. More efficient than the organized charity of the city, he cared for the levee people when they were hard up; when they were flush he prospered. Old Man Pickett was well worth the time the reporter took to talk to him:

He is crafty and curious and frank . . . He is now laid up with what he calls "busted veins," his lower limbs being constantly swollen, and he is therefore ready to converse upon death, hell, judgment, and other cheerful subjects.[19]

Dolly West, or "Detroit Dolly," Belle Bailey and Pocahontas, old Maggie Sperlock, Auntie Porter—these were women of the Rows, and variously gifted or cursed. It was about another Dolly that he wrote his best piece about the landing. Her living and dying, in "Dolly, an Idyl of the Levee," was like the casting of craps from a skilled hand, a gesture of savage finality. When she died,

. . . there boomed up from below the furious thrumming of banjos and bass viols, and the wild thunder of the dancers' feet. Downstairs the musicians were playing the tune, *Big Ball Up Town;* upstairs the women were chanting to a weirdly sweet air, *My Jesus Arose.*

> *Oh, ain't I mighty glad my Jesus arose,*
> *Oh, ain't I mighty glad my Jesus arose,*
> *Oh, ain't I mighty glad my Jesus arose*
> *To send me up on high.*[20]

There was one girl he remembered who did not even have a name, a girl made drunk and raped and abandoned in the gutter of the street: "Here she failed to attract attention while the officers passed down the other side . . ." But they stumbled on her, on their way back, and took her to shelter "at a neighboring shanty, Kate Miller's. Kate agreed to take care of her, but expressed fears that the rowdies would return for their victim!" [21]

The gaiety of the levee was as hearty and disproportionate as the misery of the place. The songs and dances which startled Hearn with delight found him ready with pencil and paper. Almost the first writer of the North to take them seriously (Stephen Foster excepted, but Foster softened and mellowed them), he took them down as literally as he could, and reported them in the newspaper as closely as possible, regretting— "A great part of 'Limber Jim' is very profane, and some of it not quite fit to print": [22]

> *Way beyond de sun and de moon,*
> *White gal tole me I were too soon.*
> *White gal tole me I come too soon,*
> *An' nigger gal called me an ole d——d fool.*
> > *Limber Jim,*
> > *Shiloh!*
> > *Talk it agin,*
> > *Shiloh!*
> > *Walk back in love,*
> > *Shiloh!*
> > *You turtle-dove,*
> > *Shiloh!* [23]

It was as natural to kick up the heels in dancing as to open wide the mouth in singing, and Hearn was as aware of the dances as of the songs of the river people. Reels, quadrilles, breakdowns, eighteenth century colonial forms, and African forms were mixed together. But the patterns melted into one in the heat of participation.

The dancers danced a double quadrille, at first, silently and rapidly; but warming with the wild spirit of the music, leaped and shouted, swinging each other off the floor, and keeping time with a precision which shook the building in time to the music. The women, we noticed, almost invariably embraced the men about the neck in swinging, the men clasping them about the waist. Sometimes the men advanced leaping and crossed legs with a double shuffle, and with almost sightless rapidity. Then the music changed to an old Virginia reel, and the dancing changing likewise, presented the most grotesque spectacle imaginable. The dancing became wild; men patted juba and shouted, and negro women danced with the most fantastic grace, their bodies describing almost incredible curves forward and backward; limbs intertwined rapidly in a wrestle with each other and with the music; the room presented a tide of swaying bodies and tossing arms, and flying hair. . . . Even the curious spectators involuntarily kept time with their feet; it was the very drunkenness of music, the intoxication of the dance.[24]

In these essays Hearn tried always beyond the effect of immediacy to attain a kind of perspective. Sometimes he overreached himself and arrived only at sentimentality. More often, he succeeded and showed a shadow of time and nature behind these dancing, singing, gesticulating figures. In this soiled district, both time and nature could be spoken for only by the river. The voice of the river was the whistle of the steamboats. This voice was made to sound again and again through the levee stories, calling to the heart that was in these people, to their adventurousness, their wildness, and their longing for something they could never have. Its call was a warning, an entreaty, a solace. It was life in abundance and release into death.

The steamboat whistles were the only kind of music Albert Jones knew. He did not play the banjo, he did not care for the fiddle, he cared only for riverboat whistles. ". . . He imitated the whistle of the Andy Baum, of the Bostona, Potomac, Charles Morgan, Mary Miller, Thompson Dean, Arkansas Belle, the old Robert E. Lee, and numerous deep-snorting towboats." [25] ". . . Their voices come to his ear," Hearn mused, the night he heard Albert display his virtuosity, "as mighty living cries." [26] The steamboats whistled, in Hearn's story, for Auntie Porter's children. They whistled for the rising of the waters, and for the death of Dolly. The voice of the boats was a vivid part of the whole impression made upon him by the rude river life. He wrote about these people:

Their whole existence is one vision of anticipated animal pleasure or of animal misery; of giant toil under the fervid summer sun; of toil under the icy glare of the winter moon; of fiery drinks and drunken dreams; of the madness of music and the intoxication of fantastic dances; of white and dark mistresses awaiting their coming at the levees, with waving of brightly colored garments; of the deep music of the great steam whistles; of the torch-basket fires redly dancing upon the purple water, the white stars sailing overhead, the passing lights of well-known cabins along the dark river banks, and the mighty panting of the iron heart of the great vessel, bearing them day after day and night after night to fresh scenes of human frailty, and nearer to that Dim Levee slope, where weird boats ever discharge ghostly freight, and depart empty.[27]

Although Hearn achieved a kind of distinction in his daily work, he was constrained to reach out for something more. He fed his imagination on a different kind of matter in his private time. After fourteen to sixteen hours of newspaper work, delaying his return home as long as possible, he often pulled out a book and read in the almost empty newspaper building. His principal reading of this time was French romanticism from Théophile Gautier to the contemporary publications of Gustave Flaubert.

The conditions of his newspaper work did not encourage independent writing. "In Cincinnati such work was much harder than now," wrote Tunison, who shared these conditions with Hearn, "because more and better work was demanded of a man for his weekly stipend than at present . . . Though he worked hard for a pittance he never slighted anything he had to do. He was never known to shirk hardship or danger in filling an assignment. . . . His employers kept him at the most arduous work of a daily morning paper—the night stations—for in that field developed the most sensational events, and he was strongest in the unusual and startling." [28]

Although the *Commercial*'s publisher, Murat Halsted, and its editor, Edwin Henderson, were well disposed toward Hearn, they did not try to make it easier for the city feature writer to do extracurricular work for his own amusement. They simply liked him, and to a certain extent appreciated and encouraged him. Henderson remembered, after the fact of Hearn's fame, something of the strain Hearn endured under his own relentless editorial regime:

More robust and less intellectual men would have declared themselves worked to death in positions like his and thought it preposterous to attempt study. I have seen him, after the hard work of the night rounds of police stations and the swift handwriting of a couple of columns in his inimitable style, with his one poor eye glued down to the French of Theodore Gautier's [sic] "One of Cleopatra's Nights," and to the paper to which he was transmitting his translation of that fascinating work.[29]

With such rigor did Hearn accomplish his own private work in the 1870's. He was not ready for original work, except in his newspaper stories, which he thought little of. But he was ambitious, and to test himself he tried translation. He was as exact as possible in the technique of putting certain French paragraphs into English. In the matter of these paragraphs he lost himself in dreaming. He, of the dark streets, the dingy house, the insoluble problem, became a walker in the unreal and gorgeous realms that Gautier and Flaubert spread out before him.

Sneering at Cincinnati, his thought as well as words echoed Gautier in his story "One of Cleopatra's Nights": "With our miserable habits we find it difficult to conceive of those enormous existences, realizing everything vast, strange, and most monstrously impossible that imagination could devise." [30] ". . . réalisant tout ce que l'imagination peut inventer de hardi, d'étrange et plus monstrueusement en dehors de possible." [31] Lafcadio's feet might stumble in the potholes of Rat Row, and his eyes peer short-sightedly at the roundup of prisoners at the Hammond Street Station, but his head swayed to a strange music, his eyes saw in city darkness strange processions of ancient splendor. He gazed out at the Nile, not the Ohio: "The banks were desolate, a solemn and mighty sadness weighed upon this land, which was never aught else than a vast tomb . . ." [32] "Les rives étaient désertes; une tristesse immense et solennelle pesait sur cette terre, qui ne fut jamais qu'un grand tombeau . . ." Lafcadio's haunts might be the dirty tenements. He saw in his mind's eye a landscape of artificial and perfect beauty: ". . . The stars, fair night-flowers of heaven, opened their chalices of gold in the azure of the firmament." [33] ". . . leur calice d'or dans l'azur du firmament."

In his sorely spared marginal time Hearn translated six stories from Gautier, in addition to the lost "Avatar." The six which survived and were later published as his first book were: "One of Cleopatra's Nights" from "Une Nuit de Cléopâtre," "King Candaules" from "Le Roi Candaule," "Arria Marcella," "Clarimonde" from "La Morte Amoureuse," "The Mummy's Foot," and "Omphale." The stories he chose from two volumes by Gautier—*Nouvelles* and *Romans et Contes*—were consistently remote in time, opulent in circumstance, and consecrated a particular attitude toward physical passion. Passion was exalted, worshiped, but never satisfied. First aroused, then caressed, it was left always unassuaged. It was a kind of teasing of the exasperated senses.

Gautier appealed almost altogether to Hearn's senses. In Flaubert it was a quality of mind that attracted him. In *The Temptation of Saint Anthony* Hearn saw justified and glorified his own instinctive rebellion against the ponderous vested and respectable institutions which had seemed to unite to make his young life miserable. In Flaubert revolt led onward, at least in this book, to a tentative new faith, a belief in the vague and marvelous new entity of Science. Hearn followed Flaubert enraptured through the scenery of the book and in the direction of the book's imperative. Temptation speaks through Hilarion, and is approved by writer and translator:

My kingdom is vast as the universe; and my desire knows no limits. I go on forever,—freeing minds, weighing worlds,—without hatred, without fear, without pity, without love, and without God. Men call me *Science!* [34]

This was a larger release than his unburdening of himself in juvenile tirades in Henry Watkin's shop. He had been stinted of light and warmth and space. Here were generous rhythms and golden images to which he eagerly gave assent. Here was a delicate sensuality in which to bathe his starved susceptibilities. Here were superb postures to mirror his own scorns and desires. In words rather than in human relations he eased an aching mind.

Whereas in French literature he discovered models in style and attitude, in American literature he found a companion for his dream world. Edgar Allan Poe became for Lafcadio Hearn, in his twenties, a kind of older brother in misfortune. He saw the parallel to his own case and his own troubles in Poe's life. This American orphan and outcast of society had journeyed through an inimical society with a superb if tragic composure. It made a profound difference to Hearn in identifying himself with Poe that he could invest his deprivations and sufferings with a literary coloring and meaning. He began, early in his friendship with Watkin, to leave at the print shop impudent and impromptu notes decorated with caricatures and signed The Raven.

It was a long infatuation which influenced his writing in many ways. He copied Poe even in the use of certain words, as in the awkward adjective "psychal," or in his finical style in punctuation. Like Poe, he played games with his reader in order to give a specious scientific backing to tales of pure fantasy. Like Poe he loved words for their sounding alone, and like Poe sometimes wandered over the line of the rational and wrote passages which were musical but inane.

He thought he accomplished two completely different kinds of work in Cincinnati: his hack work for the newspapers and his careful literary work. But these two kinds of writing were more alike than he suspected. The low-life sketches and the translations were only two aspects of his romantic aspiration. They were both parts of the lonely effort he made to reconstruct a personal universe in a dirty shambles of a world.

Before he could blend the separate elements of his expression into one, he had to endure many more experiences than even Cincinnati could offer him. But the future of his work was latent in what he did here: the obsession with people and the obsession with words. The two interests were at this time forcibly and awkwardly separated. Time would anneal the two elements into one harmonious expression of a life.

"Tenantless warehouses, with shattered windows; poverty-stricken hotels that vainly strive to keep up appearances; rows of once splendid buildings, from whose façades the paint has almost all scaled off; mock 'stone fronts,' whence the stucco has fallen in patches, exposing the humble brick reality underneath; dinginess, dirt and dismal dilapidation greet the eye at every turn." [1]

Memphis as seen by LH in 1877

6 ✕✕ Flight Southward

In 1876 and 1877, the last years of his residence in Cincinnati, Lafcadio Hearn squeezed the city hard for material. He wrote the best of his low-life and river-landing stories as he came almost to loathe the place of their origin. The dark corners of the city gave him material for "The Leech," "Bones, Rags, Iron, Stoves!" and "A Slaughter-House Story"—all in the single month of January 1876. Police reporting put him on the scene for murder in "Horror on Alison Street," on August 29th, and placed him in the police station for the contemplative "Friends of the Prisoners," on November 19th. In the same vein of nosing about where no one else would go, he uncovered the material for "Some Pictures of Poverty," on January 7, 1877, and for "The City Dumps," on May 6th. There were vivid pictures of the waterfront in "Levee Life," on March 17, 1876, "Black Varieties," on April 9th, "A Child of the Levee," on June 27th, "Mrs. Lucy Porter," on July 14th, "Dolly," on August 27th, "Banjo Jim's Story," on October 1st, "Jot," on October 22nd, "The Rising of the Waters," on January 18, 1877. "Gibbeted," on August 26, 1876, held as full a cup of horror as the Tanyard Case; it was much better written. The *Commercial* published his second most notorious piece, written in Cincinnati on May 26, 1876: "Steeple Climbers."

For the sake of this piece, he allowed his shrinking and high-strung little body to be hauled by a steeplejack to the top of the Cathedral of

St. Peter-in-Chains, and to be perched, birdlike and gasping, on the arm of the cross, the climax of the loftiest structure of Cincinnati. With cool economy, he exploited his own jittering fear and brief exultation at being above and beyond the city. There was a bitterness in his exultation which he eradicated from the newspaper piece but which he confided to a friend. The delight of the occasion, as Krehbiel recalled Hearn told him, was "the Mephistophelian delight he felt when he 'piddled on the universe.' " [2]

Each succeeding piece of the last two years showed an intensification. "Gibbeted," his most exquisite work of sensation and pure horror, immaculately built on fact, was followed in one day by "Dolly," his richest Negro piece. The first appeared on August 26, 1876, the second on the 27th. At the cost of the total involvement of himself, his work went well.

Although his life had not moved as surely as his work through its intricate and self-made complexities, it seemed probable to his friends that patience would overcome local prejudice, and that Hearn might have a solid future in Cincinnati. But Hearn was not only unhappy in his private life, he no longer found satisfaction in his newspaper work at which he was so furiously adept. He was weary. The strain of long hours, and of dirty, dangerous work, told on him. The way in which he abused his good eye, after hours, for the sake of translation showed how little tolerance he felt for his better-known role as Cincinnati's sensational reporter.

Yet when he stopped to think, Hearn could see that he had risen high. From living in the gutters he had moved up to reporting upon the life in them. He had in fact reached the journalistic eminence barely descried from below by Henry Watkin's errand boy.

For sympathy he still turned steadfastly to Henry Watkin, who had been his first rescuer and first friend in Cincinnati. It did not matter that Hearn no longer followed the older man's lead in intellectual matters. He teased Watkin a little for being one of "The Friends of the Inquiry," an obscure little club for which Hearn wrote cryptic and humorous notices in the paper. He hunted up his ingenuous, eccentric friend for companionship. Watkin was unshockable and staunch. Whatever Hearn did, he was his friend still. Watkin hesitated on one point only: he failed to invite his young friend home where there must have existed a lesser tolerance upon the part of his wife. But in his shop Watkin was the same. Here the two men talked together, read to each other, argued genially as they had during the first months after the thin nineteen-year-old arrived in Cincinnati.

Hearn clung too to the rougher companionship of his newspaper friends. He grasped particularly at what Krehbiel could teach him, for Krehbiel was the dogged scholar among them. Hearn was one of the company Krehbiel organized for a concert of Chinese musical instruments played by

Chinese laundrymen scoured up from obscure neighborhoods. He listened wistfully to these voices of the East and wrote an article about the experience, "A Romantic Episode at the Music Club." It was to the memory of this experience and his friendship with Krehbiel, that he dedicated his book *Some Chinese Ghosts:*

> To My Friend
> Henry Edward Krehbiel
> The Musician
> Who, Speaking the Speech of melody unto the
> Children of Tien-Hia,—
> Unto the wandering Tsing-Jin, whose skins
> Have the color of gold,—
> Moved them to make strange sounds upon the
> Serpent-bellied San-Hien;
> Persuaded them to play for me upon the
> Shrieking ya-Hien;

Distractions did not help much. A pervading trouble filled all of Hearn's thoughts. His relationship with Mattie Foley had turned disheveled, despairing, and ugly. There was no bond of congeniality left. He hardly ever saw her. There were a few shreds of regard between them, but no common ground of understanding. A recently published letter of Hearn's to Henry Watkin, in which he tried to work out his own thoughts and purge his emotions, shows how the case stood during the last two years of his life in Cincinnati. Mattie was heedless, careless, would not stay in one place, look after herself, her clothes, her reputation. Hearn's letter shows him trying to nerve himself for a final break, but considering ways to help the girl. He had, apparently, sent her to the country, but she had not stayed. She had come back to town, got in bad company, become destitute, asked his help again, and when he had given her money, once more disappeared into the worst streets of the city.

Hearn's letter to Watkin, undated, but written on the letterhead of the Cincinnati *Commercial,* must have been written between July 1875 and the fall of 1877. In part he said:

Friend Watkin,—I have been much too miserable within the past forty-eight hours to converse with you pleasantly: and as you were more than usually busy I could not speak to you of what I wished. I write to you partly because I can best express myself on paper and partly because I know that it will occupy much less of your time to read a letter than to hold a conversation. . . . I have no one else to whom I can speak freely. Moreover I promise never to worry you in a similar maneuver again.

I have been much more troubled about Mattie than you have any idea of; and

the prospect of leaving her to ruin herself is something I can scarcely bear. Whatever I may have said or done, I love her,—more I fancy than I will ever love
any woman; and somehow the lower she falls, the fonder I feel of her. I think I
have been unjust to her—unjust in marrying her at all—lifting her up only to let
her fall lower than ever. Had I never taken her, she would suffer far less in going
to the devil. She has latterly been doing very badly. I have been told that she is
living where she ought not to live; and has been quarreling with all her former
friends; has drawn a razor upon a woman near the Grand Hotel; and has been
visiting the offices of worthless lawyers with a view to getting into further trouble.
I don't know if she has been keeping company with anyone else; but that does
not trouble me, so that she does not sell herself.

No one here will board her that knows her; she has got the reputation of being
violent and vicious. Several I speak to say that Mattie owes her money. . . .

. . . All the little things I get for her are lost, or destroyed, or stolen from
her. She left her valise with her clothes and things long ago in the house of a
woman on Front street; and quarreled with the woman at the same time about a
debt. Consequently she cannot get her things. She leaves a dress in one place and
another dress in another. . . .

She is so utterly helpless, and yet so proud and wilful; that I don't know what
to do, except to cry about her. I was very foolish to have done anything for her
when she refused to stay in the country. I ought to have made her go back there
by leaving her without resources. I fear she has been lying to me in order to hide
other things she has done. . . .

Of course I fear that I cannot prevent her following the sad path which her
nature worked out for her. But I could not endure to think of her doing it here
in this city;—of finding her a prisoner in the station-house;—of hearing that every
drunken brute could buy or beat her;—of learning that she was broken down with
disease or ill-treatment;—or perhaps (it is quite possible) of being told that some
ruffian had beat her to death.

There is so much innocent childish goodness in her after all . . .[3]

Talking out his troubles on paper, trying to decide how to help Mattie,
Hearn reached no possible conclusion. He proposed something he knew to
be hopeless: another offer of the country for Mattie, with a guaranteed sum
from him coming to her every week. Watkin was to tell Mattie this, and,
"that she must not look to me for any help or recognition while she remains
here against my will. Her stay here is destroying her, and making me
miserable . . ."[4]

When Mattie Foley (calling herself Alethea Foley then) broke silence in
1906 to make a claim upon the dead Lafcadio Hearn's estate, she said nothing of the desperate circumstances of those years long gone, but revealed
her own turning away from Hearn. "She states [she was interviewed by
Hearn's first Cincinnati paper, the *Enquirer*] that she wearied of his pe-
culiarities. Hers was not the morose, silent disposition that was his. Nothing
ever suited him, she says."[5] Forgetting for a moment what kind of impres-

sion she was making on the newspaper reporter, Mattie cast a long backward glance at this remembered relationship and regarded the distant figure
of young Lafcadio Hearn with only a cold attention.

After he left Cincinnati, Hearn never spoke of Mattie again except to
Henry Watkin. These few references, in letters written from Memphis and
New Orleans, have a tone of complete severance, and yet of continuing pity,
as well as a troubled sense of responsibility. But in speaking or writing of
other subjects, he sometimes gave away the motives and emotions of that
other time. To a Japanese student who had done something to make himself ostracized by his own people, Hearn wrote:

> When I was a young man in my twenties, I had an experience very like yours.
> I resolved to take the part of some people who were much disliked in the place
> where I lived. I thought that those who disliked them were morally wrong—so I
> argued boldly for them and went over to their side. Then all the rest of the people
> stopped speaking to me, and I hated them for it.[6]

In a late letter to Henry Watkin, Hearn marveled at his own youthful
foolishness, his "extraordinary, superhuman foolishness," as he phrased it:

> When I think of all the naughty, mean, absurd, detestable things I did to vex
> you and to scandalize you, I can't for the life of me understand why you didn't
> want to kill me,—as a sacrifice to the Gods. What an idiot I was!—and how could
> you be so good?—and why do men change so? I think of my old self as of some-
> thing which ought not to have been allowed to exist on the face of the earth,—
> and yet, in my present self, I sometimes feel ghostly reminders that the old self
> was very real indeed.[7]

The most revealing words he spoke later—in another context—were
these: "This is very foolish, to marry a woman out of pity." [8] They were
words he spoke in a university lecture on Shelley.

When someone from beyond the sterile cage in which he found himself
offered him a hand, he eagerly responded. Even a foolish and frivolous new
relationship was welcome. One day at a party to which he had been sent
by the *Commercial* as a reporter—both awkward and critical—Hearn was
engaged in conversation by the hostess. Something in his talk stopped her
attention. The wife of a local Cincinnati physician, a woman of some social
pretension and activity, Ellen Freeman saw in Lafcadio Hearn, the eccentric
and clever young reporter, someone to take up and to show off. Hearn
found himself courted: invited to parties, taken for drives, given books and
flowers. It was a situation grateful to one starving for appreciation. He
seldom went to see her, but wrote her many letters in which he gave away
his ideas but not himself:

I love everything beautiful . . .[9]
I do not believe in God . . .[10]
I do indeed revere Woman as the creator . . .[11]

He told her foolish small things about himself: "My love for things Oriental need not surprise you, as I happen to be Oriental by birth and half by blood." [12] He told her about his reporter's work, about his reading, about his ambitions. But it was all a matter of words. He was extremely circumspect, and wanted only the soothing flattery of her attentions without the entanglement of a serious relationship. He excused himself from nearly all the occasions she contrived for their meeting:

I have not visited out since I was sixteen,—nine years ago; have led a very hard and extraordinary life previous to my connection with the press,—became a species of clumsy barbarian,—and in short for various reasons considered myself ostracized, tabooed, outlawed.[13]

Wriggling out of an invitation, he wrote:

I am very anxious to be able to write that I have a week's freedom or a fortnight's holiday; and I promise to let you know as soon as possible. But as yet I cannot leave my dull office . . .[14]

One time only in writing to her he strayed into an allusive warmth:

And talking of little roses. I like them because of the fancies they evoke; their leaves and odor seem of kinship to the lips of a woman humid with fresh kisses . . .[15]

Whether he offended by being too cool or too warm, whether the physician's wife discovered the existence of Mattie Foley, the bundle of letters was returned, and the flattering attention was at an end. Hearn was vain about these letters which had little personal feeling in them but some straining toward the literary. He gave them to Henry Watkin when he left Cincinnati. Watkin carried them with him to his last destination, the Old Men's Home of Cincinnati, and it was there that Milton Bronner found them. He pried them loose from the proud, childish old man and, after Hearn's death, published them with the more honest letters to Watkin in *Letters from the Raven*.

William Anderson, Mattie's son, told Albert Mordell, the first editor of Hearn's newspaper writings, that his mother had suffered because of Hearn's relations with Mrs. Freeman. She need not have done so, for all his feelings of that time were bound up with Mattie. Only one of the two or both of them could break the bond that linked them in obscurity and suffering but was not hardy enough to survive the differences growing between them.

They parted finally, after many separations, in the fall of 1877. They never met again. In her story, told thirty years after the event, Mattie related a sequence saving to her pride: that of her own will she left Hearn and the city. When she returned after nine months' absence, she found him gone, and later had word by a roundabout route that he had died in the South.

Hearn's letters to Watkin—in those portions hitherto unpublished [16]—make clear another sequence of events, one painful to himself, and for which he acknowledged a disturbed sense of responsibility. His first reference to Mattie after he left Cincinnati was written in Memphis on October 31, 1877. In it he spoke of "her despairing efforts just to speak to me once more, and my only answer being to have her arrested and locked up all night in the police station." And he continued: "Yet I could not be of much use to her now, as I am perfectly helpless. I hope I am not going blind." (His eyes tortured him during this period of his journey to the South.) In another passage excised from the published letters he wrote from New Orleans: "I am glad you saw Mattie—I hope she will do well—of course let her have her trunk." At another time he referred to her: "I am glad Mattie came to see you. I wish I could help her, but I do not know how. If she had a good place she would do well." In the spring of his first full year in New Orleans, on April 18, 1878, he wrote of the unexorcised subject: "Glad to hear good news of Mattie. I don't know, however, whether it would do her or me much good to write. I wish I had something to make her comfortable; but I am afraid she is better off left to herself. Don't you think so." Two months later, in June 1878, he wrote again obsessively: ". . . I am very happy to hear such good news of Mattie; for I have been horribly tormented by remorse down here. It is one thing to be right in the sight of others; but a very different thing to be right in one's own consciousness of right."

However the separation took place, Hearn took on himself the burden of guilt. His leaving Cincinnati was more a flight than a planned and sensible migration. He could no longer breathe an atmosphere of disapproval, an echo of which, for a different cause, he found in himself and carried with him. That Hearn's belief in this disapproval was not altogether imaginary could be tested in the Cincinnati of eighty years after the event. One could hear again the remark: "Hearn left Cincinnati under a dark cloud." [17]

Edwin Henderson, Hearn's managing editor on the *Commercial*, believed later that he might have been responsible for Hearn's having chosen New Orleans as the goal of his flight. One night the two of them, editor and reporter, sat late in the *Commercial* office and talked comfortably of many things. There were such islands of friendliness in the midst of the city's displeasure with Hearn. Henderson, experienced, tolerant, rather inclined to admire the man he worked so hard, fell into a mood of reminiscence, and described to Hearn a place he loved: the rich, tattered fringe of southern America. His picture of the Gulf Coast caught and held the attention of Hearn, who hated cold and loved warmth, who enjoyed color and detested drabness, who was sick of the near scene and hungry for the far-off and strange. The South became, in the mood of 2:00 A.M., a place all softness, brightness, and warmth.

Henderson could hardly have been surprised when his harassed reporter told him rather abruptly one day in October 1877 that he was leaving Cincinnati, and going south. Henderson was aware of the stresses working on Hearn. He was reasonably sympathetic to him as a person, but there was a little exasperation in his sympathy. Neither he nor Murat Halsted, the owner of the paper, could have seen this action as anything but somewhat ungrateful to them. They had sheltered and protected Hearn and given him scope. He was one of the *Commercial's* most valued men. No one in Cincinnati could replace him.

Hearn was adamant. Nothing could stop him from going. He had saved a little money, but not enough to assure many days' security in New Orleans. But he hoped to get a job on a newspaper in that city. He proposed also to Henderson that he would supply the *Commercial* with articles on the South. Henderson agreed to consider the articles but did not promise to take them. No money was advanced, no contract was signed. On the basis of this dubious agreement, Hearn set out for a new life in the South.

Halsted, Henderson, and Watkin saw Hearn off at the railroad station. Henderson carried his bag. The editor remembered years later the substance of what Hearn said to them on this occasion, that he had lost his feeling of loyalty to Cincinnati and thought he would do better in the South.

The train carried Hearn, shorn of his few friends, shorn of his Cincinnati past, all too quickly to the midpoint of his journey, the shabby city of Memphis, on the Mississippi River. His not very grand progress southward came to a stop here, for the riverboat he had expected to meet at this point had not yet left New Orleans on its Memphis run. He determined to wait for its coming.

Memphis became a limbo between two worlds. He had cut himself off from Cincinnati: he did not know what to expect in New Orleans. All the misery and confusion he had felt in his last two years rolled over him and almost foundered him. From Memphis he wrote frequent notes to Henry Watkin, notes that were full of unhappiness:

I am terribly tired of this dirty, dusty, ugly town,—a city only forty years old, but looking old as the ragged, fissured bluffs on which it stands. . . . I suppose you will not laugh if I tell you that I have been crying a good deal of nights,— just like I used to do when a college boy returned from vacation. It is a lonely feeling, this of finding oneself alone in a strange city, where you never meet a face that you know; and when all the faces you did know seem to have been dead faces, disappeared for an indefinite time. I must not have travelled enough the last eight years, I suppose; it does not do to become attached insensibly to places and persons.[18]

Being unable to read without pain or indeed to find anything to while the time away, I cannot succeed in keeping away one fancy that is always trying to haunt me. I never dwelt much upon it even to you latterly, but it has become an absolute torture recently. I feel all the time as if I saw Mattie looking at me or following me and the thought comes to me of the little present she made me and a little woolly lock of hair she sent me, and her despairing effort to speak to me once more.[19]

He suffered with his eyes in addition to having a bad conscience and a sense of dislocation. His fear of going blind frightened him. On October 29th he scribbled a postcard to Watkin which ended: "New Orleans far off. Five hundred miles to Vicksburg. Board two dollars per day. Trouble and confusion. Flabbergasted. Mixed up. Knocked into a cocked hat."[20]

He hunted a cheaper room. He found one for a dollar a night, and then another for twenty-five cents. In his chill despair he found enough spirit to describe the room to Watkin with some appreciation for its picturesque quality:

My room is carpetless and much larger than your office. Old blocked-up stairways come up here and there through the floor or down through the ceiling, and they suddenly disappear. There is a great red daub on one wall as though made by a bloody hand when somebody was staggering down the stairway. There are only a few panes of glass in the windows. I am the first tenant of the room for fifteen years. Spiders are busy spinning their dusty tapestries in every corner, and between the bannisters of the old stairways. The planks of the room are sprung, and when I walk along the room at night it sounds as though Something or Somebody was following me in the dark.[21]

He dealt with a surly, dirty landlord and kept his money under his pillow at night. He acquired a pistol and kept it with his money. When he went out to walk—to survey the river and the Arkansas shore, or to follow a rutted country road out of town—he took the pistol with him.

One day without warning an outrage sprang up before his nearsighted gaze, and caused him to fumble for the gun he did not know how to use. Out of nowhere, into the range of his vision, stumbled a man, drunk or furiously angry, who kicked at a kitten that got in his way, reached down a brutal hand to snatch it up, and gouged out its eyes in one horrible, visible moment, and threw the animal away from him. The shaking Hearn got out his gun, cocked it, and fired at the man—meaning to kill. He fired more than once, but each time the shot went wild. But he remembered all the rest of his life how he had willed death for that moment. Nothing is known of how Hearn got out of the situation, whether the man became angry, or simply wandered off, hardly conscious of the livid anger he had roused in the small, trembling figure in his path. (Hearn told the story to his family, and to Ellwood Hendrick.) [22]

This exceptional outrage seemed only a sample of the general sense of outrage in which he lived at this time. Many years later Hearn stated in letters to his friends that he had once suffered a nervous breakdown. He located the breakdown vaguely but approximately as having occurred at the time of his leaving Cincinnati and arriving in New Orleans. No one else testified to knowing of such a breakdown. If he exaggerated the memory of nervous disability, the exaggeration testified to the anguish of this time of transition. It was the most serious dislocation of his entire life. The physical hardship of his early days in Cincinnati had been extreme, and the general uncertainty of his first days in Japan would be hard to bear; yet in that earlier time, and in the time to come, there were buffers to despair. In 1869 in coming to Cincinnati he was of an extreme youthfulness and lack of prepossession: he kicked and fought and survived without thinking. In 1890 in going to Japan he would have the conscious weight of good work to sustain him. But in 1877 he had neither the first strength of youth to buoy him up nor the consciousness of achievement. He might, at this point, have let go, given up, gone down—never to try again, or even to remember an ambition. But he did not. Something sustained him to search through the streets of Memphis for a story.

He found the story in the funeral of a dead Confederate general, celebrated with all the emotion and display that the battered city could muster. Just as Hearn had come into Memphis, Nathan Bedford Forrest had died. Hearn's first article sent back to the *Commercial* was an account not only of the funeral procession but a rough, quick, living sketch of the man who had just died, a man whom the town loved and loathed in about equal measure.

Forrest was a man:

Rough, rugged, desperate, uncultured, his character fitted him rather for the life of the borderer than the planter; he seemed by nature a typical pioneer, one of those fierce and terrible men, who form in themselves a kind of protecting fringe to the borders of white civilization.[23]

His funeral, in a wild rainstorm, seemed to Hearn a comment upon the lostness of the South.

From the same room whence I had watched the funeral I saw the Northern mists crossing the Mississippi into Arkansas, like an invading army; then came gray rain, and at last a fierce wind, making wild charges through it all. Somehow or other the queer fancy came to me that the dead Confederate cavalrymen, rejoined by their desperate leader, were fighting ghostly battles with the men who died for the Union.[24]

This was the first of the articles Hearn signed *Ozias Midwinter,* and sent north to the Cincinnati *Commercial.* Others were to follow in succession from New Orleans. The name he used was a private joke. He had found it in Wilkie Collins' novel *Armadale* where it belonged to a queer rapscallion of a character who "had evidently lived a wild and varied life," [25] and whose talk "showed a strange mixture of sense and absurdity—of vehement earnestness at one time, and fantastic humor at another." [26]

Hearn, experiencing a tremor of hope when the *Thompson Dean* from New Orleans docked in Memphis in the second week in November, went on board as a passenger for the return downstream. He assumed that Henderson had received his article, but he had heard nothing from him. As the ship turned ponderously southward, he forgot eye trouble, remorse, uneasiness. The *Dean* had been one of the riverboats Hearn had often enviously watched leave its berth on the levee at Cincinnati. Its whistle was one of the riverboat whistles Albert Jones had imitated in the police-station concert which Hearn had turned into an article. So now, he too, following the way the rivermen went, was slipping southward through the unresisting water.

As the river widened and the sky rolled back, a sense of spaciousness wrapped him round. Here were the warmth and color he had craved. Here was the beauty he had expected. The living brown of the river which floated the *Dean*—a smaller and smaller object upon its surface—the green-gold of the cane fields spread out beneath the piled-up cotton clouds and hazed blue of the sky, the jungle dark of the woods glimpsed on the banks: these were, so far, absolute rewards. Nothing he would ever suffer southward could take away from him the benediction of this first fulfillment.[27]

He blessed the careless landscape which so lived up to the promise of his preconceptions. These overgrown fields, crumbling docks, and neglected houses were what he had expected. This giant land did not care whether he loved it or not. He had never been native to the North; perhaps he could be native here where, from the beginning, he felt no need to bristle and react, or to hold back, as from an enemy. The desolation was endearing. He wrote shortly from New Orleans:

The wealth of a world is here,—unworked gold in the ore, one might say; the paradise of the South is here, deserted and half in ruins. I never beheld anything so beautiful and so sad. When I saw it first—sunrise over Louisiana—the tears sprang to my eyes. It was like young death,—a dead bride crowned with orange flowers,—a dead face that asked for a kiss.[28]

7 ❧ *Poverty in the Sunshine*

Lafcadio Hearn came into New Orleans by way of the river. The city,
after that introduction, seemed always water-surrounded, water-soaked,
and water-loving. That it was a port reawakened preferences and prejudices that he had thought laid by in his adolescence. To be near the
ocean again meant more than he had imagined. From these wharves
along the Mississippi one could voyage to anywhere.

He voyaged first into the interior of the old city, into a revery upon
its sun and soil, its stained bricks and plaster. It was a place as prone to
warmth as himself. Quiet and sad, it lazed away the long southern fall
which was prolonging itself as if for his benefit into November.

He had little money and a load of trouble. His head ached from his
suffering eyes. What he called a "congestion of the retina" [2] had damaged
his good eye so acutely that he could see only in patches for a number
of weeks. But New Orleans greeted him so kindly on his arrival that he
let a rash hope stir his imagination. He was busy almost at once telling
his readers in the Cincinnati *Commercial* what it was like to hunt for
a room in the French Quarter. He found very sweet the sound of the
soft French spoken by the quadroons who at this date were the quiet,
well mannered keepers of *chambres garnies* for gentlemen: "The day
after my arrival in the city I must have examined twenty-five or thirty
furnished rooms offered for rent by colored housekeepers, and it was very
pleasant to hear them speaking the speech of their old masters." [3]

"Raven liveth at 228 Baronne St., care Mrs. Bustellos," wrote Hearn to Watkin on a post card which he enlivened with two sketches of himself as the anxious, big-eyed bird. "Indite him an epistle. Don't give him particular H—." [4] Baronne Street was to be only the first stop on an erratic, zigzagging course he would pursue through ten years of living in the city, both in the old quarter and in other nearby streets. Through these early years he moved from one bare room to another, existing soldier-like indoors, living luxuriantly outdoors in the plenitude of his senses and his imagination.

When he had settled upon his first stopping place, he gave all his money away into the hands of his landlady, and so freed himself for a space of days from all necessity for practicality. Until he heard from the *Commercial* he would live upon the excitements of the street.

As he found his way to Canal, to Royal, to Bourbon, to Toulouse, his "Letters from New Orleans" began concocting themselves in his head. He concerned himself conscientiously about tourist sights—the Cathedral, the French Market, the wharves along the brown river, the balconied houses— for the sake of the hypothetical Cincinnati reader. But he soon lost himself in looking, and forgot the practical reason for his rambles. He wrote for himself, and not for the Cincinnati reader, when he began to put down on paper what he had seen and felt. What he sent to Henderson was uncompromisingly personal in its interest. He discussed the corrupted French of the Creoles. He recommended a brilliant Creole newspaper, *Le Carillon*, recently dead. He explained who the true Creoles were. He gave the *Commercial* reader exquisite little lessons in Creole grammar. He began translating, almost as soon as he grasped the forms, little street songs in Creole:

> Since first I beheld you, Adèle,
> While dancing the *calinda*,
> I have remained faithful to the thought of you;
> My freedom has departed from me.
>   . . . .
> I love you too much, my beautiful one;—
> I am not able to help it.
> My heart has become just like a grasshopper,—
> It does nothing but leap.
>   . . . .
> Ah, you are so like the serpent-of-the-rattles
> Who knows how to charm the little bird,
> And who has a mouth ever ready for it
> To serve it for a tomb!
> I have never known any negress
> Who could walk with such grace as you can.

Or who could make such beautiful gestures:
Your body is a beautiful doll.[5]

In wandering along the waterfront where many interesting songs were
sung and brief impromptu dances shuffled along the rough boards, he was
startled into remembrance by the smell of salt blown off the surface of the
river. It needed only that pungent odor of the past to remind him of all that
the sea had meant to him as a boy on the sands at Tramore. He composed
a spontaneous rhapsody to the sea. It began:

If you, O reader, chance to be a child of the sea, if you once breathed as your
native air the divine breath of the ocean, and learned the swimmer's art from the
hoary breakers, and received from the Ocean-god's christening, the glorious baptism
of salt . . .

And it ended:

Have you forgotten the mighty measure of that mighty song?—have you forgotten the divine saltiness of that unfettered wind? Is not the spell of the sea strong
upon you still? [6]

If Hearn turned away from his personal reactions and concerned himself
from time to time with the South's immediate political and economic problems, he did not try to temper his tone particularly for the North. He had
become interested in southern attitudes, and in "A Southern Prophet," [7]
basing himself upon an article by Charles Gayarré, he presented to northern
stomachs a full and fair report of the mood of the South of that moment.
But the small personal and social things of the life of the street were more
to his interest. He continued, not knowing yet what reception his pieces
were having, to write about the things that hit the eye and ear in this French-
flavored southern city.

He continued to try to put into English the queer French of the street
songs. He set down, side by side:

Si to té 'tit zozo	If thou wert a little bird,
Et moi-meme mo té fusil	And I were a little gun,
Mo sré tchoué toi,—*Boum!*	I would shoot thee—*bang!*
Ah, cher bijou	Ah, dear little
D'acajou,	Mahogany jewel,
Mol 'aimin vous	I love thee as a little pig
Comme cochon aimin la boue!	loves the mud.[8]

He searched out the overgrown grave of the first American governor of
Louisiana. He mourned the extravagant past of the city, even the part
played in it by the unliked and unlikable Claiborne. Tactlessly he told the
North that the South, in becoming like the North, would lose all its lovable

qualities: "The old Southern hospitality has been starved to death, and leaves no trace of its former being save the thin ghost of a romance." When the South had become thoroughly sensible in northern style and regained prosperity without picturesqueness, then it would be, "quite practical and quite unromantic. This period of decay seems to me the close of the romantic era of Southern history." [9]

Still he did not receive any money from the *Commercial*, although Henderson was printing his pieces. The period of grace lent him by the twenty dollars he had brought with him came to an end. He wrote to Watkin for help, sorely sparing even the few cents he had to spend to put a stamp on the letter. But at the moment Watkin too was pinched and could not help him. The unpaid correspondent of the *Commercial* was soon in a plight as desperate as anything he had endured before. Only a gift of twenty dollars from Charley Johnson carried him along. "Saved me from starving," [10] commented Hearn to Watkin two months later.

At last and in driblets, with long pauses, an inadequate recompense—quite unlike his regular salary in Cincinnati—began to come to him. Hearn continued writing his pieces; he had no other prospects, but he was angry with Henderson. He had become a special correspondent at an unlucky time. There was some doubt in Cincinnati that the *Commercial* would survive. But of this, Hearn in New Orleans knew little or nothing. He felt only a personal anger and sense of outrage. Still he continued to send articles north. With a shaken composure he made his own scrimping the subject of one of his pieces:

Now, one may live comfortably at the market-houses for the small sum of twenty-five cents a day.

Each market-house has its own long, marble-topped coffee-stand, with a dozen fat-bellied sugar-bowls marshaled in shining rows. Here, for five cents you may purchase an excellent cup of coffee, with a plate of doughnuts; and for five cents more a long loaf of sweet and milky-white French bread. That makes a good ten-cent breakfast. Then for dinner fifteen cents will purchase you meat, vegetables, coffee and bread *ad libitum*. If you are a smoker you must have a good cigar with each light meal; and these two cigars will cost you two and a half cents each. So that your daily expenses for eating and smoking need not exceed thirty cents a day.[11]

Eating his thirty cents of food a day (twenty cents, he told Watkin more candidly), growing thinner, darker from the sun, his clothes more ragged week by week, with no prospects of anything solid, he picked up odd jobs which allowed him barely to survive in between irregular checks from Cincinnati. He fooled himself into thinking that he could go on in this manner. "I am determined," he wrote to Krehbiel, "never to resume local work on a newspaper. I could not stand the gaslight; and then you know what a horrid life it is. While acting as correspondent I shall have time to study, study . . ." [12]

He treated himself to the privilege of being a student when he could not afford it. Letters to Watkin and Krehbiel of this period show him, hungry or not, pursuing his Creole interests, reading, writing, studying, even when he did not have the means to pay for full meals or a soft bed. The intense unselfconsciousness of his scholarly interest in the city won him friends. The ragged young man could be convincing to anyone who shared one of his enthusiasms. One friend of this early time was Alexander Dimitry, a Greek-American professor, and the head of the Board of Education. He was a scholar himself, and recognized the genuineness of Hearn's student's passion. Dimitry led Hearn to Major William M. Robinson, the editor of the New Orleans *Republican,* and the author of a volume of verse, *Forest Pilgrims and Other Poems,* published in 1867.[13] The major had no job to give Hearn, but turned him loose in his library. Books were a great luxury to Hearn, and he returned again and again to the major's house to read.

Robinson soon learned of the unpublished Gautier translations Hearn had brought with him to New Orleans. He begged to hear them read. Hearn carried them to the major's house and sat down to the first of many sessions. While the major sat admiringly across the table from Hearn and listened, his wife lingered in the distance to look on with some disapproval. John S. Kendall recalled:

I have often heard Major Robinson describe Hearn's visits to his home, to read the manuscript as it progressed [his work was probably revision], and of Mrs. Robinson's intense displeasure with the forlorn, unkempt, dilapidated individual who occupied so much of her husband's scanty leisure . . .[14]

How Hearn lived in this lean time he never told. He was even more silent, in later years, about his bad days in New Orleans than about bad days in Cincinnati. Memories of such times cast a chill over the rest of his life. Many years later, in Japan, when there was a chance that he might return to America, he wrote:

I dream of old ugly things—things that happened long ago. I am alone in an American city; and I have only ten cents in my pocket—and to send off a letter that I must send will take three cents. That leaves me seven cents for the day's food. . . . the horror of being without employ in an American city appalls me—because I remember.[15]

Finally the Cincinnati *Commercial* decided that it could not afford a New Orleans correspondent. After fourteen articles Ozias Midwinter was cut off.

Hearn's own telling of the end of his relationship with the newspaper was bitter:

Did you read my *Commercial* correspondence? [Hearn wrote to Watkin.] Paper treated me quite shabbily, left me sometimes two months and more without a cent,—then would send me $25. when I wrote them frenzied letters. Finally after vainly waiting for money due, wrote sharply, receiving an insulting letter about "charity" and "newspaper value" and "impertinence," resented it by a much more insulting letter, got paid off, and, very happily, discharged.[16]

This was only the first of a long series of unhappy conclusions with other publishers. Hearn's anger on this and the other occasions always went beyond a just wrath. It blazed illogically into fury. In such a case, he acted out of the center of pure uncontrolled emotion, and cut off all chances of compromise.

Innocently Henderson wondered, when Hearn came back to Cincinnati on the way to New York in 1887, why his former employee acted as if he— Henderson—did not exist; and why, in the following years when the writer began to be famous, Hearn behaved as if he had never known his former editor, or worked closely and well under his direction. Hearn had a harsh way of cutting off a relationship completely, or at least the outward signs of friendship. Sometimes he spoke well of such a man in private, but the link of communication between them was broken.

Hearn wrote his final article for the Cincinnati *Commercial* in January 1878. His last pay came possibly as late as February or March of that year. From that time till June he had no regular income. In the same period not only his own situation but the situation of everyone in New Orleans became uncertain. With the first warmth of spring the city experienced an outbreak of yellow fever. Hearn had arrived in New Orleans in time to witness the last of the city's major yellow-fever epidemics. To his imagination he seemed to be in a medieval city in plague time.

Smudge fires in pots smoked and streaked the bricks of the narrow streets. Cannon, on prominent corners, boomed from time to time. Both smoke and shot were thought to clear the air of the miasma of fever that hung over the city. It was the air from the swamps that brought the fever, the inhabitants thought, or perhaps an infection from rotting wood. There was a shuddering fear of the clothes and bedding of the infected. Bonfires were heaped with these stinking remnants of the dead. The dead themselves were hustled off to a common grave without ceremony or care. Whole families perished. Whole households of boarders died. The disease worked so quickly that a man might seem well one day and dying or dead the next. Nothing was understood about the cause of the disease, and so it was terrible in its quickness. To one with the dark imagination of Hearn the spectacle had an extra dimension: it seemed to him that the shuddering fears of his own mind had infected a whole population. The city performed an elaborate dance of death.

Newcomers were said to fall ill more easily than permanent residents. Without understanding the immunizing effect of a mild or undetected case, old-timers who had endured other epidemics believed themselves somehow acclimated to the disease. It was the drifter like Hearn who lived in a boardinghouse, and who had not yet spent a hot summer in the city, who succumbed most easily. When Hearn, weakened by months of poor living, fell ill himself, he thought he had yellow fever and that he was going to die. His joints ached, his eyeballs hurt, fever burned him: he had the taste of death in his mouth.

But it was soon apparent that he had dengue, or breakbone fever, and not yellow fever, which it resembled, especially in its initial symptoms. The lesser of two evils, it was considered a sort of substitute for yellow jack. It incapacitated its victim for as much as a week, but it did not kill. (The virus which carries dengue lives in the same mosquito, *Aëdes aegypti,* as the virus which carried yellow fever. Today authorities say circumspectly: "Recovery [from dengue] confers considerable immunity to the homologous strain of the virus.") [17]

Hearn tottered back to his feet again, probably from the bed of a charity hospital—he wrote an essay about such a place shortly. However, he may have been nursed haphazardly by a casual friend, or by a landlady in one of the many boardinghouses of the darker streets of the city where he was at this time almost fatally transient. "You would scarcely know me now," he wrote to Watkin, "for my face is thinner than a knife and my skin is very dark. The Southern sun has turned me into a mulatto. I have ceased to wear my spectacles, and my hair is wild and ghastly." [18]

Although he slowly got better, he did not rejoice: a specific lingering effect of dengue was a period of mental depression. It was perhaps of this period, and this effect, that Hearn referred to as his "breakdown."

He announced, in the same letter to Henry Watkin, a miraculous deliverance: "Somehow or other, when a man gets right down in the dirt he jumps up again." [19] In a lucky moment, while he was still shaky from his attack of breakbone fever, and as unsure as ever about his next meal, he stumbled again upon his friend Major Robinson. Robinson saw the uncertainty of survival in the face and hunger in the thin body. He remembered a circumstance which might help Hearn. He had a friend who needed help in the running of a little newspaper. The future of the paper was as unsure as the future of the young man before him.

Robinson took Hearn to meet Mark Bigney at 39 Natchez Alley. Here Bigney was editing singlehandedly the four-page sheet called *The Item* which had been in precarious existence for less than a year. It had a curious history. It was the creation of a number of unemployed printers who thought they might own and edit, as well as set the type, of the paper for which they worked. They had started the *Item* as a cooperative enterprise, but it had failed to be profitable and they had sold their forlorn hope to Colonel John Fairfax. He thought he might make the *Item* into a more conventional type of newspaper. Fairfax had put Bigney in charge as managing editor, and every other kind of editor.

Apparently Bigney approved at once of Hearn, for he needed help, and the tattered young man's qualifications seemed surprisingly good. But Hearn had first, before going to work, to pass the test of an interview with the owner, Colonel John Fairfax. The owner of the paper surveyed Robinson's protégé without any disposition to favor him. He disliked the taint of a supposed radical Republicanism in the young man from Cincinnati. Apparently some hint of his views about the Negro question had reached Fairfax and hardened him somewhat against this newcomer to New Orleans. It is possible, but not probable, that he knew of Hearn's notorious common-law marriage. And to Fairfax the young man was not reassuring in appearance. "That odd, rolling eye of his was the only thing you could see at first —enormous, protruding. After you got used to that eye, you saw that his other features were good, and his face refined. But, in addition, when he first presented himself here he was miserably dressed, and even his hands were grimy and his nails black." [20] Thus Fairfax remembered his first sight of Lafcadio Hearn.

The mark of dirt on him speaks more eloquently than anything else of Hearn's situation at that moment. Many of his friends spoke later of the meticulous cleanliness and spotlessness of his person and wearing apparel. Clean as a wild animal, was to be Elizabeth Bisland's phrase.[21]

But Fairfax was kind as well as keen. He discerned a person who needed help, as well as a person who might conceivably help him and the suffering *Item.* He not only hired Hearn; he invited him again and again for a good meal at his own house.[22] He and his wife had the delicacy—when Hearn sat shy and strange at their table, desperately crumbling his bread, unable even to eat—to go on with their conversation, and to ignore him, till he lost his tension, uttered a few opinions of his own, and at last forgot himself in a teasing, laughing relationship with their daughter.

Hearn only gradually realized his good luck: to be alive at all while thousands continued to die during the summer; to be working again, and making a living, at something he could do not only easily but brilliantly; to find that his daily work left him time for study. His editor and publisher quickly realized their extraordinary luck in having Hearn on their staff. Bigney was interested in writing only the political news. He was glad to leave the other columns of the paper, which were undistinguished and uninteresting when Hearn came to work, to someone else. From the day Hearn was hired, June 15, 1878, the drab little paper began to change. The dry columns of local items and exchanges developed a kind of sparkle and unpredictability. The paper began to be noticed in the city.

After June 15, 1878, there were no more hungry days for Hearn in New Orleans. Although he worked at first for ten dollars a week, there was no need in the deflated economy of the South, except out of pure carelessness, to eat too little, to sleep under an inadequate roof. But Hearn could not at first rid himself of his habit of uneasiness. The trouble had got into his bones. For several months he saved fantastically out of this pittance. And in addition he cast about for some sure way of making money, some scheme, some plot, even if crackbrained and not quite respectable.

Although the office of the newspaper was a quiet, dusty, tranquil place, Hearn could not rid himself of restlessness. He thought of going to England or to Texas, of taking up ship life, of wandering as a deck hand from port to port. He changed rooms frequently. He bought a collection of pots and pans so that he could cook for himself and so save more money for security. More dangerously, he found a partner.

This was a man as insecure as Hearn, but less scrupulous, and with the look of being capable in many dubious ways. Hearn never gave his name to anyone. Even as late as a year after being hired by the *Item,* Hearn was still pursuing the delusion of schemes to make money, the most ambitious and the last of which was setting up with his partner in the eating-house business. Hearn called the place indifferently the "5 Cent Restaurant" or "The Hard Times Restaurant." He wrote and placed advertisements for it in the *Item* and he had a handbill printed pointing out its virtues. He sent a copy of the handbill to Watkin. Watkin—wondering what Hearn could be up to down in New Orleans—read the following paragraph:

The 5 Cent Restaurant
160 Dryades Street

This is the cheapest eating-house in the South. It is neat, orderly, and respectable as any other in New Orleans. You can get a good meal for a couple of nickels. All dishes 5 cents. A large cup of pure Coffee, with Rolls, only 5 cents. Everything half the price of the markets.[23]

Hearn was both proud and ashamed of this enterprise. He had written earlier to Watkin, "Money can be made here out of the poor." [24] He wrote to Krehbiel:

I have become a restaurant proprietor. Doling out coffee and hot rolls; beefsteak and soup; cold tongue and stew. It is the cheapest restaurant in New Orleans. We have one room for coloured folks in the back part; one for white folks in the front part, opening on the street with a swing door. Profits are about 300 percent. But the tax collector has not been around yet.[25]

He spent his spare time away from the newspaper sitting in a back corner of the room, observing his partner operate the place with a suspicious and awesome efficiency. The business was begun on one hundred dollars supplied by Hearn. How things would work out Hearn could only guess as he watched the man. An impression of his watching him, and wondering, can be gleaned from a letter to Watkin which he interpolated with drawings of himself as the Raven.

The business has already cost about one hundred dollars to set up. May pay well; may not. The Raven has a partner,—a large and ferocious man, who kills people that disagree with their coffee. The Raven expects to settle in Cuba before long. . . . The Raven may succeed right off. He may not. But he is going to succeed sooner or later, even if he has to start an eating-house in Hell.[26]

Hearn at least honorably failed. His partner scooped up the considerable profits of the first month's running of the eating house and walked out of New Orleans with them. The assistant editor of the *Item* was left with empty pockets and an experience to get over. The end of the Hard Times Restaurant was the end of Hearn's casting about for a way other than words by which to earn a living.

8 ❧ A Creole City

Lafcadio Hearn went to work for the New Orleans *Item* in June 1878. He was twenty-eight that month. He stayed with the *Item* for three and a half years, holding a not very important job on a not very important newspaper. "The *Item*," he wrote to Krehbiel, "is only a poor little sheet." [2] But, as assistant editor of a dubious four-page daily that might cease printing at any time, Hearn began to recover his balance and to percolate with a quiet efficiency. He maligned the *Item* to Henry Watkin too, but shared with him a growing cheerfulness about his situation. "I'm only making about ten dollars a week, but that is better than making twenty-five dollars and being a slave to a newspaper. I write what I please, go when I please, and quit work when I please. I have really only three hours a day office duty,—mostly consumed in waiting for proofs." [3]

Somewhat later, in a good mood with himself and his place in life, Hearn wrote even more expansively to Watkin (substituting for the personal pronoun his usual familiar, droll sketch of the worried little Raven):

The Raven passeth Its time thusly: In the morning It ariseth with the Sun and drinketh a cup of coffee and devoureth a piece of bread. Then It proceedeth to the office and concocteth devilment for the *Item*. Then It returneth to Its room, whose windows are shadowed by creeping plants and clouds of mosquitoes, and receiveth Its Spanish tutor. Then It goeth to a Chinese restaurant, where It eateth an amazing dinner,—Its bump of ALIMENTATIVENESS being enormously developed. Then It spendeth two hours among the secondhand bookstores. It then goeth to bed,—to arise in the dead vast and middle of the night and smoke Its pipe. For a year It hath not smoked a cigar; and Its morals are exemplary. It sendeth you Its affectionate good-will and proceedeth forthwith to smoke Its pipe.[4]

The fact that Hearn could thus pleasantly dramatize himself showed that life had become at least tolerable to him. The grosser fears of his early months in the city lightened, if they did not entirely disperse. The experience of being hungry in New Orleans was added to the experience of being hungry in Cincinnati and hoisted upward to add to the load he carried— of fears, dreads, hates. But the thin dark young man coming and going through the door of the *Item* office lived and looked forward to life; he did not suffer it merely to roll over him.

He would have liked, above all things, to have been ignored, but his very thoughtlessness of self caused his appearance to seem very odd indeed and to attract a keen attention. Coming into Mark Bigney's sight every morning through the door opening upon the alley was a short, slight person, his naturally clear olive complexion burned harshly dark by the sun of the streets where he had recently spent so many desperate hours. He was thin from near starvation and recent illness. His clothes, to which he never paid any particular attention, were ragged. They improved only slowly and haphazardly with better fortune. The difficulty he had with his sight (and which he never mentioned, or to close friends made little of—saying he saw better with his one good eye than others did with their two) could not be hid. He worked with his right eye close to the level of his desk. In the street, if Bigney or Fairfax or Robinson passed him, Hearn went by them, not seeing them at all. An exasperation with ill-fitting glasses made him, at this time of his life, give up the wearing of glasses altogether. He went his way in a world of shifting, shimmering shapes and colors. As foolish and as proud as he was in giving up help, he cunningly helped himself. Like the shrewd deaf man who uses a hearing aid to hear only what he wishes to hear, Hearn wore and used an attachment for his eye: a magnifying glass fastened to the button of his overlong dark suit coat, and hidden in a pocket. When he needed help, he pulled out the glass and used it swiftly and unobtrusively. Later, he added another aid to his sight, a collapsible telescope close to his hand in his pocket, which gave him at the necessary moment a quick, minute, all-seeing glance at something far away, an instrument he could use in a flash and put quickly away.

Thus Hearn could be in the thick of the world, and yet be coolly outside it when he wished. He walked the world with his own impregnability wrapped round him in his lack of sight. Yet the maiming of his eyes was an anguish and a torment to him in the privacy of his own thought. He was free hardly for a day or night of the fear that he would some day be altogether blind. But partially he fooled himself in the broad light of day. He wrote several small, self-confident essays upon the good of myopia, saying how much nearer to the artist's true perspective, with the doing away of all niggling, haggling littleness of detail, was the nearsighted man's sight than a normal man's.

With his damaged, shortsighted gaze, Hearn surveyed the city, and found more and more matter for his private interest and for the blank spaces of the *Item,* which from day to day he must fill up. Before the advent of its new assistant editor, the *Item* was a tedious little paper filled mostly with excerpts from other newspapers. Hearn handled the routine side of his job with skill and expedition. He got such things out of the way so he could have time for things that were his own. On his second day with the paper, June 16, 1878, he began running one of his stories from Gautier, "The Mummy's Foot." A week later he printed the concluding part. There may have been some holding back upon the part of the management in the matter of Hearn's translations. He did only a scattered few for the *Item:* two from Gautier, one from Daudet, one from Zola during the next months. But he wrote essays on the art of translating, and essays on the French writers whom he translated. It was only later, when he went to work for the *Democrat,* that he was allowed to translate what he wished. Otherwise, with space to be filled, the *Item* management allowed the new assistant editor to write what he pleased.

What he pleased was often a dreamy, imaginative comment on the day's news. On June 24, 1878, Hearn wrote, not facts, but his own musings upon recent discoveries at Pompeii. "It is not impossible that the lost works of Pindar, Menander, Sappho, and other Greek poets—of whom we possess fragments—might be recovered in the debris of some Pompeiian library . . ." [5] On June 25th his fancy colored the future in a piece called "Fantastic Possibilities of Invention": "The armies and navies of the world may substitute lightning for gunpowder in the course of the next century." [6] On "Insect Politics" Hearn drew anthropocentric parallels. "They have an architecture . . . Their builders construct subterranean cities . . . Certain ants who hoard too much golden honey, or other wealth, are occasionally the victims of communistic riots. The poor and starving ants strike against the tyranny of capital, slay the millionaires, and distribute their hoards throughout the community." [7] When a specific and local social question stirred his imagination, he wrote less fancifully. "Louisiana needs all the Jewish emigrants she can obtain . . ." [8]

The *Item* gave Hearn the freedom of print. He was limited only by scrappy space, a minute circulation, and the unstated iron boundary of what could be said in the South on certain issues. He did not at first much feel the limitation. He was in possession of a license to say what he wanted to say. He was often foolish but never ordinary. Even in delusion the twist of his mind was ingenuous. He had no false modesty about being indifferent or uninteresting to others. He assumed a reader although he had no desire to meet one. (And he had readers: as in Cincinnati, so in New Orleans, the newspapers of the time were the entertainers and the instructors of the literate.)

He was free to indulge his crotchets. His largest crotchet was the city. On November 26, 1878, he wrote an early piece (aside from those he had done for the Cincinnati *Commercial*) about New Orleans, "The Glamour of New Orleans." He had now got beyond a first interest in the architecture of the streets—ironwork and cobblestoning—to an interest in the human nature of the streets: the animated passers-by who called out to each other, the hawkers who announced their wares in song, the quarrelers, the lovers, the slow lazy talkers of the narrow sidewalks.

He was particularly fascinated by the *gumbo,* the language of the poorer streets. It was not a proper French, but a bastard sublanguage, a dialect of slaves who had adapted their masters' language to their own tempo and to their own emotional pitch. It was a sort of second language for the educated whites too, something used in careless or intimate pungencies, for they had learned it from their Negro nurses in childhood and never forgotten it.

The dark side of life in the alleys was as faithfully reflected in this language as the bright, sunward side. Hearn was as concerned with these little darknesses of belief as he was with the singing, dancing, banjo-strumming side of the city's life. He traced curiosities of practice—in food, in medicine, in the vestiges of voodoo—which grew out of the same climate which brought forth each spring the camellias, the azaleas, and the beautiful, poisonous oleanders in their proper order.

The person to whom Hearn poured out his new interests was his former companion of the Cincinnati pavements, the scholar and critic of music, Henry Edward Krehbiel. The music critic of the Cincinnati *Gazette*, who in 1880 moved to New York to hold the same job for the New York *Tribune,* was an enthusiastic collector of folk music. But he liked exact knowledge and he disapproved of the amateur in Hearn. After Hearn's death Krehbiel acknowledged, with some grudging of his qualifications, Hearn's help to him in his own special scholarly study. He quoted Hearn in his book *Afro-American Folksongs*. The juster verdict of this book

Hearn was musically illiterate, but his powers of observation were keen and his intuitions quick and penetrating. He felt what I have described as the imposition of French and Spanish melody on African rhythm.[9]

should be set over against the harsher verdict he made in a letter to Joseph Tunison: "Hearn could not tell one tune from another." [10]

Incautious, enthusiastic, and unsystematic, Hearn plunged helter-skelter into his amateur study of Creole dialect and song for the sake of the quick life he found in it. He discerned with the intuition Krehbiel granted him that he could get into Creole thought and feeling most expeditiously from the street speech which went lilting easily from talk into song. Hearn read Creole, talked it, wrote it, almost before he could understand it. And he sent pell-mell to Krehbiel copies of songs, examples of different methods of taking down the dialect in phonetics, attempts to get at the rhythm of the Negro singers, notes about the strangeness of the ways they played the fiddle, the banjo, and the piano. "Did you ever hear negroes play the piano by ear? There are several curiosities here, Creole negroes. Sometimes we pay them a bottle of wine to come here and play for us. They use the piano exactly like a banjo." [11]

He reported that he had even reached the stage of arguing with a native white New Orleanian that a Negro song was a remarkable thing, worth listening to, almost impossible to set down. He began to mention what his friend Cable said, or his friend Rouquette. His interest in the French and African layers of New Orleans had gained him new friends. The city began to be a warmer place, animated by conversation, enlivened by excursions to see things and do things with these others.

In making the acquaintance of the writer George Washington Cable, Hearn had done a bold thing for him—he had initiated a friendship himself. When Hearn came to New Orleans, Cable's was the one name he knew. Cable had even in a way helped him to decide to come to New Orleans. Several years earlier, in Cincinnati, Hearn had happened upon Cable's story "Jean-ah Poquelin," in the May 1875 issue of *Scribner's Magazine*. It fixed an image of Louisiana in his mind. So, hesitantly, admiringly, he sought out the man who had written the story.

He found in Cable a young man only a few years older than himself, small, delicate, keen in appearance. His youthfulness could not be hid behind the dark, drooping mustache or the extravagant beard. No more than Hearn could Cable at this time make his way by independent writing. He was preparing his stories to be published in book form, but the book, *Old Creole Days,* would not appear for another year.

Cable supported his family and his writing by working as a valued clerk in the firm of a cotton factor. He had written for the New Orleans *Picayune* several years earlier but had found little satisfaction in it and had quit. The daily requirements of the press irked him: he refused flatly, out of an iron Presbyterian scruple, to report theatrical events. Very queerly there lived in him the sensuous susceptibilities of an artist and the scruples of a self-limiting moralist.

Cable's responsibilities were heavy. His family was growing. He was a devoted husband and father with no trace of bohemian temperament. The recent yellow-fever epidemic had killed a small son. Almost his entire household had been dangerously ill, and during this time he had served them as nurse.

Hearn's kindling interest in Cable's native city ignited a friendliness between the two very different men. They were soon roaming the streets together, streets Cable had known since childhood. Cable, who had an amateur training in music, delighted almost as much in the order of musical notes as in the order of words. It was he who took down by ear the curious quavering Negro melodies of the street songs the two men paused to hear, while Hearn took down the words.

Cable generously invited Hearn to his house and there fed him and coaxed him, not always successfully, to talk. The house, at 229 Eight Street, was a modest bungalow, its living quarters raised up the height of one story from the damp ground. Steps in the center of the front took one up to the veranda. The house was in the spacious Garden District, outside the pent-up French Quarter. The comfortable English-speaking section of the city was less picturesque, but more open, than the Vieux Carré, with a generous spread of green and spangled by the inconsequence of flowers. Here Cable lived happily and domestically in the middle of his family and attracted to him writers, talkers, and other genial appreciators of their own city. In chill weather the group would gather in Cable's study, its tall windows giving on the garden. In warming weather they adjourned to the veranda where about them in the dark, mockingbirds (whose melodies Cable tried to write down on music paper) sang from the orange trees screening the talkers, fencing them together in a fragrant, comfortable unity of feeling. Cable would be begged to take up his guitar. Hearn, having retreated to the darkest, farthest corner, listened while Cable easily and fluently picked out African-Creole melodies or swung into old Scottish and English ballads.

The upright, independent Cable, cheerful under the weight of heavy responsibilities—a large family to support, an imperious destiny in writing —was both a native and an alien in his own city. As native, he was bone-close to the physical scene and could describe a New Orleans street or courtyard or conversation with easy familiarity. As alien, he lived by ideas intrusive and unwanted in the place.

He had fought in the Confederate Army while still a boy in years. His father was altogether a Southerner by inheritance, but he had married in Indiana. His mother, although a proud New Orleanian (she had refused the oath of allegiance to the United States during the occupation) was also, through inheritance, a product of New England and of abolitionism. There-fore, although George Cable was himself a child of the South, he entertained ideas which were anything but welcome in his own city and among his own people. The slight difference of viewpoint which at first separated him from his neighbors grew into a wider divergence with the passing of years of consideration and experience. He found he could not think that the freed Negroes were getting justice in the South. He was a man uncomfortable to himself until he had made his thought clear to his own people. He then became a person so uncomfortable to New Orleans that the city and its people at last repudiated him and drove him into exile. This happened just at the moment when his stories and novels were creating a new interest and sympathy for the South in all the other parts of the United States.

But all this inevitable consequence of the stiff rectitude of George Wash-ington Cable was reserved for the future. When Hearn and Cable first came to know each other, nothing had yet spoiled the idyl of Cable's house or his sense of communion with his native place.

Lafcadio Hearn assented to George Cable's ideas, but he was not greatly interested in them. Perhaps he found this out to his own surprise, for he had suffered for similar ideas in Cincinnati. But ideas of another kind were jostling one another in his head. He found he did not have room enough for every kind of interest. What drew him to Cable was the artist in the man. It was only later that he discovered that the artist in Cable was bound up with a Sunday-school teacher. The element of religious rigidity and stiffness of practice spoiled the character of the man for him. The perfect sweetness and sincerity of Cable could not mitigate for Hearn the smell of puritanism. The personal atmosphere in which Cable lived, of sureness of right, of narrowness of expression of that rightness, repelled Hearn. His and Cable's natures were totally different. Cable, seized on by an idea, let the idea partially sink the artist in him. Hearn, played on by many ideas, subordinated ideas to the uncommitted openness of the artist.

But Cable's early work—his first stories and articles about Creole New Orleans—was more artistic than reforming. As long as the two young men—when they met Hearn was twenty-eight and Cable was thirty-four—could be simply searchers through the streets for Creole songs and dances and character, they could be happy together. Hearn could ignore Cable's strict Sundays and visit the house on other days. Hearn warmly reviewed Cable's early work and acted as his advocate. His notice of Cable's first novel, *The Grandissimes,* appeared in the *Item* on September 27, 1880.

Hearn's own Creole studies printed in the pages of the *Item* soon won him another friend, the missionary priest, Père Adrien Rouquette. This elderly man (he was sixty-seven in 1880), who came and went like a ghost out of the past of New Orleans, was a missionary priest who had lived most of his life among the Choctaw Indian remnant in the pine woods of the north shore of Lake Ponchartrain. To the Indians he was perhaps more a helper and a friend than a priest. He had possibly conformed his own life more to the Indian way than theirs toward his.

Born into a family which was pure French on his father's side and New Orleanian French on his mother's, Rouquette had submitted to various influences in his native Louisiana and in France, but he had never lost his New Orleanian interest in Creole speech. He wrote verse in Creole and had invented his own phonetic system for writing it down. When he came upon the ingenuous efforts of an unnamed writer in the *Item* to concern himself with the Creole, he sought him out in a roundabout fashion by printing some verses of his own where he knew the writer in the *Item* would see them.

Hearn noticed the curious verses and sent them to Krehbiel: "'The 'Chant d'un jeune Creole' was simply a personal compliment. The author gives something of a sketch of his own life in it. It was published in 'Le Propagateur' a French Catholic paper, for the purpose of attracting my attention, as the old man wanted to see me, and thought the paper might fall under my observation." [12]

Hearn did not like Rouquette's phonetic system nor did he think much of his versification. "The Creole rhymes I sent you are unintelligible chiefly because they were written phonetically after a fashion which I hold to be an abomination. . . . There is nothing remarkable about his poetry, except for its eccentricity." [13]

But Hearn was delighted with Rouquette himself. "The author, Adrien Rouquette, is the last living Indian missionary of the South—last of the

Blackrobe Fathers, and is known to the Choctaws by the name of Charitah-Ima. You may find him mentioned in the American Encyclopaedia published by the firm of Lippincott & Co." [14]

In the blindness of his recoil from Roman Catholicism it would have been logical for Hearn to have repulsed the offer of friendship from a priest. But he was not logical. The unworldly, dreaming old man did not seem at all orthodox, and he shared two of Hearn's enthusiasms—one for folk language, the other for French romanticism.

In fact, Adrien Rouquette had poured his whole life into a mold determined by what he had absorbed of romanticism during his youth, which he had spent studying in France. As an impressionable young law student in Paris, where the university classes of the 1830's echoed to the battle strokes of the young romantics, he had first read *Atala*. In 1841 he published in France his own verses of a romantic New World, *Les Savanes*. He had been preceded in almost exactly the same emotional sequence by a brother Dominique, who had studied in France, drunk the excitement of the new movement, and published in 1839 a book of verse, *Meschacébéennes*.

Adrien Rouquette became almost immediately famous. Sainte-Beuve praised him. Thomas Moore called him "the Lamartine of America." Dominique, too, excited attention. Going home to a small parochial New Orleans, neither brother found at first any scope for romantic aspiration. Dominique never found any end or aim and deteriorated into a picturesque tramp, walking the streets of New Orleans wrapped in a dirty Indian blanket and reciting his verses to any listener he could buttonhole.

Adrien was luckier. Returning to Louisiana as to a place of romantic inspiration, to luxuriant forests and primitive peoples, he was persuaded in time, after the death of an Indian girl he loved, to become a priest. He gave up a career as an eloquent preacher in the St. Louis Cathedral to go into the woods to live with the Indians. He did not lose his belief that he was another René.

"If the columns of a good periodical were open to me," Hearn said to Krehbiel, "I should write the romance of his life—such a wild strange life —inspired by the magical writings of Chateaubriand in the commencement; and latterly devoted to a strangely beautiful religion of his own—not only the poetic religion of 'Atala' and 'Les Natchez,' but that religion of the wilderness which flies to solitude, and hath no other temple than the vault of Heaven itself, painted with the frescoes of the clouds, and illuminated by the trembling tapers of God's everlasting altar, the stars of the firmament . . ." [15]

Hearn's nature worship, what he had called his pantheism, stirred in him again after it had been quiet for years. The chance meeting with Père Rouquette brought to life again much that had been lost to him in Cincinnati. He saw with an awakening sympathy the beauty of the mild, deep forests of the countryside pressing in about New Orleans.

On February 25, 1879, Hearn wrote a notice for the *Item* of the older man's narrative poem *La Nouvelle Atala*. He called his review "A Louisiana Idyl." Later in the year, when the father's poem was published, it was bound in one cover with Hearn's review. The book was issued by the Imprimerie du Propagateur Catholique. Hearn's first appearance in book form was thus ironically through the courtesy of a Catholic publishing firm.

Lafcadio Hearn, making new friends, was finding New Orleans, in its defeat and poverty, his first romantic place. Cable helped make him free of the streets of the city, Rouquette, of the wildness still pressing close to and shadowing the city. Hearn needed no further urging to drink deep of all his impressions, which came to him colored with the fresh, naïve hues of romanticism.

Hearn's whole work in the early *Item* days, with the exception of reviews and editorial comment, was built upon the awareness of a new place. This was his way wherever he went, to let beat upon him, and to miss nothing of, the sights, sounds, smells, and tastes of a place, and then in repose to find out just how and in what way these impressions settled into the designs of his imagination. In each succeeding scene of his life a portion of his writing would belong to the first rush of impressions, and a portion to the composition of those impressions into a pattern. This had been his way in patrolling the broken, dirty, colorful Rows of Cincinnati. This was his way presently in New Orleans, and would be, in Martinique and Japan.

As these impressions of New Orleans battered him, everything to which his imagination paid attention became personal to himself. When on a trash-littered street he paused to watch hungry little street dancers singing or jigging untaught to the music of a barrel organ, a tune of Verdi or something new from Bizet, he appropriated this precarious moment of the poor as something belonging to him too. When he heard emphatic talk in the newspaper office of imminent change in the city, talk of remarkable revolutions in drainage, in paving, in sanitation, he felt in his own nerves the tremor of change not particularly desired. New Orleans was to him at this time only Creole New Orleans.

He understood the correct uses of the word. Creole was first a noun or an adjective denoting a people: the present-day white descendants of the colonial settlers, mostly French and Spanish, but possibly Swedish, German, or any other strain that had come in before the Yankee invasion at the time of the Louisiana Purchase by the United States. Creole was in the second place a noun or adjective denoting a kind of bastard French patois: the language of the Negroes who had learned French from their masters but mixed it well with African and molded it in grammar and sense into something of their own. Practically speaking, Hearn, like many others, used the word Creole also as a descriptive term with a wide application. There could be Creole houses, Creole manners, Creole food, Creole Negroes. In fact, anything that was indigenous to the old French-flavored New Orleans was in some manner Creole.

Hearn described to Krehbiel his own Creole day. "Early in the morning I visit a restaurant, where I devour a plate of figs, a cup of black coffee, a dish of cream-cheese—not the Northern stuff, but a delightful cake of pressed milk floating in cream—a couple of corn muffins, and an egg. This is a heavy breakfast here, but costs only about twenty-five cents." [16] He knew that Krehbiel remembered the harsh cold nights when they walked the streets of Cincinnati. He underlined the ease of his New Orleans routine, after his exotic southern breakfast:

Then I slip down to the office, and rattle off a couple of leaders on literary or European matters and a few paragraphs based on telegraphic news. This occupies about an hour. Then the country papers—half French, half English—altogether barbarous, come in from all the wild, untamed parishes of Louisiana. Madly I seize the scissors and the paste-pot and construct a column of crop-notes. This occupies about half an hour. Then the New York dailies make their appearance. I devour their substance and take notes for the ensuing day's expression of opinion. And then the work is over, and the long golden afternoon welcomes me forth to enjoy its perfume and its laziness. It would be a delightful existence for one without ambition or hope of better things. On Sunday the brackish Lake Ponchartrain offers the attraction of a long swim, and I like to avail myself of it.[17]

Although Krehbiel was interested in the Creole matter Hearn sent him, he disapproved of Lafcadio's new southern, Latin life where long afternoons of freedom let him dabble in what seemed to his friend an alarming relaxation of attitude. He did not approve either of the small original pieces Hearn began writing soon for the *Item*, pieces he called his "fantastics." Hearn's cheerful easiness he thought of as a too pliant and too complaisant surrender to a corrupting and unprogressive atmosphere.

"You cannot make a Goth out of a Greek," Hearn replied to Krehbiel's disapproval:

Now I am with the Latin; I live in a Latin city;—I seldom hear the English tongue except when I enter the office for a few brief hours. I eat and drink and converse with members of the races you detest like the son of Odin that you are. I see beauty here all around me—a strange, tropical, intoxicating beauty. I consider it my artistic duty to let myself be absorbed into this new life, and study its form and colour and passion. And my impressions I occasionally put into the form of the little fantastics which disgust you so much, because they are not of the Aesir and Jotunheim. Were I able to live in Norway, I should try also to intoxicate myself with the Spirit of the Land, and I might write of the Saga singers—

> From whose lips in music rolled
> the Hamavel of Odin old . . .[18]

Hearn did not yet know who he was but he knew already how he had to work. He gave himself up to the impressions of Creole New Orleans as he had given himself up to those of the river landing of Cincinnati, and wrote what his instincts told him to. There was more material in this city than he could possibly use in the columns of the *Item*. He collected notes on proverbs, songs, street calls; he read old Creole newspapers, he studied Creole dictionaries.

Writing his daily newspaper copy, compiling ambitious notes, he soaked himself in the flavor of the city, so different from the puritanical Catholicism of his childhood in Dublin, from the stern righteousness of the school in France, from the business bustle of Cincinnati. New Orleans, rounded by the brown Mississippi, threatened by the river, cherished by it, had long ago relaxed into an equable acceptance of life. Hearn's mood of these years was acceptance too, acceptance of the most fugitive thoughts, feelings, sensations. It was random life which was his subject matter. He stood aside and let flow into words and images the very talk of the streets. The *Item* of September 27, 1879, carried the "Complaint of the Boarding-House Keeper":

Den I have a sick man. He fall on de banquette in face of my house, and I take him in to nurse. When dat he get well he tell me he vas one professor of langedge. He eat and sleep here four mont; and first he pay a little. He complain much from noise. He vas what you call nerveux—so like I was oblige to make my daughter walk without shoes in naked foots; and we to speak in dumb and deaf language by fear of make him trouble. He smoke in de bed and burn de cover; also he break de pot and de cradle-chair, and after, de window, an' de armoire an' de—vat you call de pendule; —he let fall ink on de carpet, and he spit tobacc' on de wall, and he vomit in de bed.[19]

Through Hearn the seller of cooked crabs explained impatiently "Why Crabs Are Boiled Alive":

And for why you not have of crab? Because one must dem boil 'live? It is all vat is of most beast to tell so. How you make for dem kill so you not dem boil? You not can cut dem de head off, for dat dey have not of head. You not can break to dem de back, for dat dey not be only all back. You not can dem bleed until dey die, for dat de not have blood. You not can stick to dem troo de brain, for dey be same like you—dey not have of brain.[20]

In the *Item*'s columns the charcoal vender bawled his wares:

Cha'coal!
Twenty-five! Whew!
O charco-oh-oh-oh-oh-oh-lee!
Oh-lee!
Oh-lee-e!
(You get some coal in your mout', young fellow, if you don't keep it shut.) [21]

Even odder cries drifted out into the early morning air of the city:

One shouts, or seems to shout, "A-a-a-ah! *She* got." Just what *"She* got" we have not yet been able to determine; but we fancy it must be disagreeable, as the crier's rival always shouts—"I-I-I!—I want nothing!" with a tremendous emphasis on the I. There is another fellow who seems to shout something which is not exactly proper for modest ears to hear; but he is really only announcing that he has fine potatoes for sale. Then there is the Clothespole Man, whose musical, quavering cry is heard at the distance of miles on a clear day, "Clo-ho-ho-ho-ho-ho-ho-ho-ho-se-poles!" As a trilling tenor he is simply marvelous. . . . There is also the figseller, who crieth in such a manner that his "Fresh Figs! seems to be "Ice Crags!" And the fansellers, who intend to call, "Cheap fans!" but who really seem to yell "Jap-ans!" and "Chapped hands!" [22]

When Hearn wrote privately of such things in letters to friends, he often sketched grotesque antic little figures on the margins. He was persuaded, perhaps on an impulse of his own, or at the urging of Fairfax or Bigney, to try something of the kind for the newspaper. After May 1880 many of his stories of street life were illustrated by squat and forceful cuts, signaling to the reader the kind of homely and familiar New Orleanian fare the *Item* was now retailing. Here were the clothespole men in picture as well as in words; here were the French Quarter's laundresses with their baskets on their heads; here was a peddler of charcoal driving a half-broken-down wagon. Sometimes woodcut and words illustrated some more private interest of Hearn's own: a diatribe of hatred against quack doctors, a dissertation on cutthroats, a cartoon of tombstones, so prominent a feature of the city's landscape.

The woodcuts helped the circulation of the *Item*. They were even credited later with saving the paper from failure. Hearn did two hundred of them between May 1880 and December 1880. Colonel Fairfax, eighty-two in 1923 when Ethel Hutson sought him out, raked up his memories of Hearn and recalled something of his manner of executing these illustrations—among the earliest cartoons ever published in a newspaper in the American South.

Hearn carved the cuts himself, "on the backs of old wooden types, which had been used for advertisements," remembered Fairfax. "They were just the right height, you see, to fit into the bed—we used the old fashioned flat-bed press, of course—and every day he would whittle out one of those drawings." 23

The odd dark little gesticulations in the middle of so much close print were a relief and an amusement to the casual reader, and they attracted the more inquiring ones to try to find out who this new man at the *Item* was. The paper began to be more widely read for its strange varieties of learn-ing, for its vignettes of local scenes, for its wayward, unpredictable opinion. The *Item* had a voice that was immediately recognizable. Who else but the man in the *Item* would write with such mock seriousness about "Taxing Cats"?

The New York Times advocates humorously a tax upon cats. . . . the subject of taxing cats is worthy of consideration in a city like ours when everything else has already been taxed,—except a certain domestic utensil taxed of old by Roman Emperors, but which it is not proper to name in public prints.

The difficulty of attending the taxation of cats is, [due] of course, mostly to the peculiar habits of those animals. Cats are nomadic, although they have been errone-ously termed domestic animals, while the dog is really a domestic creature. . . . A cat appears to possess a goblin gift of ubiquity. . . . It always comes when it is not wanted; and when wanted no human being can find it.24

Who but the impudent writer for the *Item* would spend print upon telling New Orleanians "How to Eat Fruit"? 25 His cheerful familiarity with them and their ways gradually won the writer an audience with the Creoles. This was a writer who talked to them about their local manias as if he were possessed by a few of them too. He flattered by loving the oddities of a passionately loved city.

"Latterly it has been said that if New Orleans has any special mania which distinguishes it from other cities, it is the mania of 'talking to one's self.' " So provokingly did the anonymous writer in the *Item* write on March 9, 1879. And he went on:

It were useless to deny so widely recognized a fact as the propensity of people in New Orleans to perambulate their native streets conversing only with themselves. . . . Is it that the people are being driven mad by stupid legislation and business losses and outrageous taxes? God only knows! But they do talk either to themselves or to viewless beings or to the sleepy shadows that fling jagged bits of darkness across the streets on sunny days.

And he made himself one with them in this queerness of habit:

Seeing and hearing these things, we somehow ceased to marvel that some people dwelling in the city of New Orleans should speak mysteriously and hold audible converse with their own thoughts; forasmuch as we, also, dreaming among the shadows, spoke aloud to our own hearts, until awakened by an echo of unanswered words.[26]

The "fantastics" which he began at this time to write, the pieces which did not please Krehbiel, were just another form of speaking to his own heart. In Cincinnati he had been the *Enquirer*'s and the *Commercial*'s sensational reporter, licensed to seek out fights, riots, suicides, murders. In New Orleans Hearn discovered a different character for himself, that of a troubled dreamer who wrote out of daydreams and sometimes nightmares congenial to the city and to himself in his aloneness in the city. New Orleans colored his dreams with particular hues and supplied certain characteristic images, of cracked tombstones, of tropical and venomous plants, but the dreams were his own, the troubled daytime musing of an unfulfilled man.

The ground of his daydreaming can be seen in a letter he wrote to Krehbiel. He described the house in which he was then living as if it were a stage setting and he suggested how dreamlike, even to himself, his living there was. "A hoary dog sleeps like a stone sphinx at a corner of the broad stairway . . . The dog never notices me. I am not of his generation, and I creep quietly by lest I disturb his dreams of the dead South. I go up the huge stairway. At every landing a vista of broad archways reechoes my steps —archways that once led to rooms worthy of a prince. But the rooms are now cold and cheerless and vast with emptiness." Of his own room in this decayed house he wrote: "It is vast enough for a Carnival ball. Five windows and glass doors open flush with the floor and rise to the ceilings. They open on two sides upon the piazza, whence I have a far view of tropical gardens and masses of building, half ruined but still magnificent. The walls are tinted pale orange colour; green curtains drape the doors and windows; and the mantelpiece, surmounted by a long oval mirror of Venetian pattern, is of white marble veined like the bosom of a Naiad. In the centre of the huge apartment rises a bed as massive as a fortress, with tremendous columns of carved mahogany supporting a curtained canopy at the height of sixteen feet. There is no carpet on the floor, no picture on the wall—a sense of something dead and lost fills the place with a gentle melancholy;—the breezes play fantastically with the pallid curtains, and the breath of flowers ascends into the chamber from the verdant gardens below. Oh, the silence of this house, the perfume, and the romance of it." There was a conscious striving toward effect perhaps, a conscious acting out of romantic melancholy. But his loneliness was real. "A beautiful young Frenchwoman appears once a day in my neighborhood to arrange the room; but she comes like a ghost and disappears too soon in the recesses of the awful house. I would like to speak to her . . ."[27]

The city seemed at times unreal, the house unreal. In certain self-indulgent moods he seemed unreal himself, a wanderer out of a tale by Poe, strayed into an ominous place where, try as he would, he could find no real face, hear no vibrant voice, and touch with his hand no warm and human hand. Being so alone in his room, in his walks, and in his work in the stagnant newspaper office, he felt no compunction in continuing in his daily work the idle dreaming of his workless hours.

The "fantastics" ranged from the slight but delicate humor of "The Little Red Kitten," "A Dream of Kites," and "When I was a Flower" to the relatively elaborate and plotted "Aphrodite and the King's Prisoner," "The Fountain of Gold," "El Vomito," "A Legend," and "The One Pill-Box." The slighter ones were usually the better, as if something done only half seriously succeeded in this genre better than something done too earnestly. And when he mixed a certain homeliness of detail with his fantasy he mixed strength with delicacy.

The "red kitten" whose wanderings out into the city and whose death he imagined lived first in observation:

The kitten would have looked like a small red lion, but that its ears were positively enormous,—making the head like one of those little demons sculptured in mediaeval stonework which have wings instead of ears. It ate beefsteak and cockroaches, caterpillars and fish, chicken and butterflies, hash and tumble-bugs, beetles and pigs-feet, crabs and spiders, moths and poached eggs, oysters and earthworms, ham and mice, rats and rice pudding,—until its belly became a realization of Noah's Ark.[28]

He wrote about kites, not kites attached to children, but kites already flown and lost:

We observed last evening the infinitely extending lines of the vast web which the Electric Spider has spun about the world, and the innumerable wrecks of kites fluttering thereupon, like the bodies of gaudy flies . . .

All these represented the destruction of childish ambitions—each the wreck of some boyish pleasure . . .

We dreamed of the kites which children of a larger growth fly in the face of heaven —toys of love and faith—toys of ambition and of folly—toys of grotesque resolve and flattering ideals.[29]

Such "fantastics" were slight but wise, with the reach of an ingenuous amateur philosophizing. More often the "fantastics" were vague, soft, self-indulgent, a morbid dreaming. Scenes of graveyards recurred again and again, such scenery owing its inspiration almost equally to the reality of New Orleans cemeteries and to the pages of Edgar Allan Poe. Life pursued love into burying ground and found it a ghost or a festering body, which was still conscious, but conscious only of deprivation. "And that vague phantom life, which sometimes lives and thinks in the tomb where the body moulders, lingered and thought within the narrow marble bed . . ." [30] What was not death was love, but love burning itself out in lust. A traveler in a strange land found love. It teased him in a picture on the wall of an ugly hotel room. He kissed the picture. A frequenter of cafés found the heat of love, but it was only lust upon the lips of an ugly, unloving woman. A prince in a strange kind of fairy tale was the prisoner of a cruel king who locked him up in a beautiful garden and deprived him of human companionship. He loved, but loved only a smooth-limbed marble statue.

Done with care, the sentences polished, the words delicately chosen, these morbid little pieces, symptoms of a state of mind rather than full creations, made an unforgettable impression upon many new readers of the *Item*. Half understanding what he did, half proud, half ashamed of this work, Hearn wrote in defense of his "fantastics" to the one friend who had the least aptitude for sympathizing with them. To Krehbiel Hearn wrote:

> As to the Fantastics, you greatly overestimate me if you think me capable of doing something much more "worthy of my talents," as you express it. I am conscious they are only trivial; but I am condemned to move around in a sphere of triviality until the end.
>
> . . . But I fancy the idea of the Fantastics is artistic. They are my impressions of the strange life of New Orleans. They are dreams of a tropical city. There is one twin-idea running through them all—Love and Death. And these figures embody the story of life here, as it impresses me. . . . There are tropical lilies which are venomous, but they are more beautiful than the frail and icy-white lilies of the North.[31]

The dreaming "fantastics," the racy sketches of everyday city life, the odd and individual editorials, the book notices, the bits of translation gradually won the *Item* a respect it had not had before. Hearn's interest in their city drew to him one by one a few of the scholars, writers, booksellers, the bookish lawyer or medical man from among the proud and withdrawn people of the older New Orleans world. Not that any general breach was made in the wall of Creole society for the sake of the outsider. But individuals from within the wall reached out a hand to this writer who told them that their ways were not only unique and valuable, but delightful. Hearn was conscious of the charm of the sequestration practiced in the French Quarter. He wrote, in "A Creole Courtyard," on November 11, 1879:

> Without, cotton-floats might rumble and street-cars vulgarily jingle their bells; but these were mere echoes of the harsh outer world which disturbed not the delicious quiet within . . . A guitar lay upon the rustic bench near the fountain, where it had evidently been forgotten, and a silk fan beside it; a European periodical, with graceful etchings hung upon the back of a rocking-chair at the door, through

which one caught glimpses of a snowy table bearing bottles of good Bordeaux, and inhaled the odor of rich West India tobacco. And yet some people wonder that some other people never care to cross Canal Street.[32]

Not yet within the sanctuary, only glimpsing it beyond an open door, Hearn began to love New Orleans. He had come to a halt in the one city in the United States of that time where he might thrive—as a writer and as a person. The region, the city, his position on the *Item* began to give him a chance to discover himself. Cincinnati had let him write, but only out of carelessness. There were plenty of hands to tend the noisy and important machinery of real life: therefore a few might write; Lafcadio Hearn might write, but only if he teased the jaded, uncritical palates of men of the new industry in their hasty reading of the morning paper. Place made a difference. The South meant a relaxation of pressure first, and then a gentle, unemphatic encouragement. In the South of the 1880's, particularly in the odd, untypical corner of the South in which he found himself, there was no stigma attached to the writer's profession. The writer as a professional was an honored man. The community, somewhat timid in bookish matters, rather easily shocked, never following the writer into any lonely or rigorous altitude, yet shyly approved the profession of letters. Like the minister, the lawyer, the medical man, the writer was a figure of importance. There were no industrialists or businessmen to compete with the older professional types for place of honor in the public mind.

The older South was dying. Its means of surviving and prospering were already dead, but the shadowy ideas of a once vigorous and ruthless community, which had always chosen to amuse itself with gentle pleasures, still ruled the social imagination. The city of New Orleans had been the cultural center of a great region of farmers, landowners who might be rude in act but who lived by a code of polite accomplishment. Conversation was important; the written word was important, although less so than the spoken word. The purveyor of a gentleman's reading matter was an asset to society, not a drag or an irrelevance.

What Hearn at last bruised himself against was the limitation of this polite acceptance. The standard for the written word was that of a well bred, neighborly amateurishness. The goad for professional excellence had to prick him from within. But at first what was refreshingly different and important in New Orleans was the fact that society did not urge him to live by some more respectable way of life than writing. Society even rather admired, praised, and made much of one who was clever with words, and appreciative of the local scene.

Therefore at first the South blessed the talent that was in Hearn. It set no stumbling blocks in his way. By being its own unselfconscious self, a rich display of a life uniquely different from the American average, it furnished him not only with a climate for writing but also with a fertile kind of material. Hearn could ruminate and read and write in peace, and arouse a modest, honest, and uncritical liking among a people who gave him, in addition to praise, a roof over his head, food to eat, paper to cover with his meticulous script.

But even in sluggish New Orleans the *Item* was a backwater. And Hearn was becoming ambitious. Toward the end of 1881 there occurred a change which allowed him to exercise those ambitions. At that time there came a climax to the rumors concerning the birth of a new paper in the city. At last it was announced that the *Times* and the *Democrat* were to merge. Hearn of the *Item* was asked to be the literary editor of the new paper. He resigned from the *Item* to accept the position.

"The magic of words . . ."[1]

A phrase used by Hearn in
a lecture to his students at
Tokyo University

9 ❧ *Stepson to New Orleans*

In the early 1880's Joel Chandler Harris, just in the beginning of his
fame, paid a visit from Atlanta to New Orleans, a city where he had
worked for a short time just after the Civil War as secretary to the publisher of a magazine. He found no object in a changing New Orleans
worthier of his attention than Lafcadio Hearn. He wrote a column about
the other writer for his own paper, the Atlanta *Constitution:*

> There is in New Orleans a man of letters who has already made his mark—
> Mr. Lafcadio Hearn, who has managed to translate the body and soul of some
> of Théophile Gautier's writing into English. Indeed, I am inclined to think
> that Mr. Hearn has imparted to his translations a sensitiveness, a delicacy, a
> spiritual essence not to be found in the originals. A ten minutes' talk with
> Mr. Hearn is among my most vivid impressions of a brief stay in New Orleans.
> He struck me as a man capable of putting versatility to new uses. He is a
> specialist in almost every branch of information. I hope to hear that he is writ-
> ing a book which shall be a translation of the mysteries of his own mind and
> imagination.[2]

Such was Hearn's standing among his fellow writers of the new South
a short time after he had begun working for the *Times-Democrat.* It
is doubtful that in their brief meeting Harris and Hearn learned how
much they had in common. Hearn had used Negro material in Cincinnati; Harris had begun to make Uncle Remus flourish. It is improbable that they talked of such things. Hearn's reputation in the
1880's in New Orleans was beginning to be associated with the work of

translation and with the spinning of tenuous essays on abstruse subjects. But the man made a strong impression, beyond that of his writing. Harris went home to share with his family an impression of the appearance of the writer. "I remember," his daughter wrote, "that father once spoke of the unpleasant and sinister effect upon the beholder of that gifted writer's myopic eye." [3]

In such reports as that of Harris in the Atlanta paper, and in gossip and conjecture, was set reverberating the small beginning of Hearn's fame. It was a double reputation, that of a writer who had a magical way with words, and that of a person who was as disturbing as he was remarkable. Stories about the *Times-Democrat*'s odd and indispensable man spread quickly among the writers and editors of the little parochial, ingrown South. At the same time a cloud of reputation was blown northward upon the breath of each returning literary man who had gone downriver to New Orleans to see the carnival, or in 1884 and 1885, to visit the International Exposition. Such men as Charles Dudley Warner, Richard Watson Gilder, Joaquin Miller, Samuel Clemens, and others met Hearn or heard of him and carried back to New York or Boston or Hartford a rumor, an anecdote, and some slight assessment of his work. Hearn, becoming well known locally, began to be a name even among those northern editors who were at this time too cautious to print anything he sent them.

In New Orleans the quiet, abstracted writer became the subject of talk, as well as of local pride. The indiscriminate lively reader gossiped about Hearn's dress, manners, appearance. It became soon a New Orleans resource to speak of him to outsiders as "one of our Southern writers." But Hearn was at the most a stepson to New Orleans, a favored stepson, about whose head an uneasy expectation hovered. He could never be one of them. Yet New Orleans was genial and tolerant. It licensed Hearn to be himself. The forbearance was rewarded: New Orleans had the benefit of a virtuoso performance. And Hearn had the chance to live, to grow, to do ill and to do well as a writer. With the egotism of the shy he carved a conspicuous place for himself in New Orleans in the decade of the 1880's.

Although Hearn watched eagerly for any sign of interest in his words, he hated any interest in his person. If he caught a gleam of such an interest, he misinterpreted it just because he was inordinately suspicious and expectant of slights and cheats. Yet his existence as a *Times-Democrat* editor was the first ordered and kindly era in his life since his school days in England. Encouragement and praise warmed the air around him, and an attentive audience awaited each daily column with suspenseful interest. It was this small circle which spun his lasting American legend. These readers who were acquaintances put into circulation stories about a sedentary man of exquisite sensual imagination, about a writer of delicate and artificial prose, about a sensibility which looked at raw life through the medium of other men's thoughts and words.

There was much truth in this image of Hearn—for the particular period in which it was concocted. This was the most leisurely and literary, the most bookish, period in Hearn's life. Yet this New Orleans audience, who fixed the image of Lafcadio Hearn for the future, knew nothing of his life before or after, and could not guess how rawly he had lived in Cincinnati, or how completely he would give up a stable, ordered existence to start over again—in Martinique and then again in Japan. New Orleans was only a pause, but a necessary pause between adventures.

Yet the emphasis which the New Orleans legend put upon Hearn as a magician of words was not entirely false. He lived, particularly in this decade of his life, in a daylong, nightlong dream of words. The color, sound, feel, and infinitely shifting meaning of words delighted him.

What provoked the spectators of his life was just the reserve, the holding back of himself, which he could no more help than his breathing by the time he had lived through the years that brought him to New Orleans. He wrote later in Japan, thinking back to New Orleans for his analogy: "The world is a carnival-ball; and you must wear a mask thereat,—and never, *never* doff it except to the woman or the man you must love always." [4] Luckily in New Orleans there were a few to whom he could doff his mask: an Irish boardinghouse keeper who became a kind of mother, the editor of the *Times-Democrat* who attracted both an intimate kind of anger and an intimate kind of admiration from Hearn, a young girl who attracted and frightened him but awakened some intimacy of emotion, and a doctor who became the one close friend of this time. These relationships made bearable the lonely way he went in the midst of a rapt attention of which he was for the most part unaware.

Even in the closed world of New Orleans "society" Grace King enjoyed a sensation in discovering that a friend of hers knew Lafcadio Hearn, "even intimately," [5] as she recorded it years later with proper emphasis. To her kind of well mannered reader Hearn's highly colored and occasionally audacious work seemed the pathway of a bright-tailed cockatoo decorating the seemly, proper city with a strident noise and brightness.

Gently and teasingly Henry James once used the phrase "the strange irregular rhythm of life," [6] to indicate how life might surpass fiction. Just so strange and irregular was the leap into light by which Hearn moved in December 1881 when he became translator and literary editor of the New

Orleans *Times-Democrat*. His transition into consequence seemed very sudden, but it had been preparing. From May 1880 until December 1881, he had been contributing translations to the pages of the New Orleans *Democrat*. Each Sunday there were scenes of splendid frozen horror from Flaubert's *Salammbô,* or colorful, amoral descriptions from Loti's Tahitian or African adventures, or a careful lifting of stories from the controversial Emile Zola. These paint-bright paragraphs from the French had caught the interest of those who intended, "God save the mark," as Hearn said, to create "a literary" paper.[7] Hearn's translations under the heading "The Foreign Press" were transferred without a break from the *Democrat* to the enlarged *Times-Democrat*.

The year before Hearn went to work for the *Times-Democrat* he wrote a series of essays for the *Item* in which, as if talking to himself, he attempted to define his ambition in writing. He saw, just beyond his grasp, a form:

There is nothing really so difficult to produce . . . as brief stories whose effect depends wholly upon uniqueness of conception—sketches which although suggested by fact are moulded and colored by imagination alone.[8]

He saw partially what materials he would use:

The collections of traditions, superstitions, legends, fairy tales, goblin stories, impossible anecdotes, supernatural romances to which so much attention has been given in this century, have a prodigious influence upon the use of language and the formation of style.[9]

But matter and manner did not come to life without passion having been breathed into them:

Passion is the mighty electricity which vibrates through all human life and causes all grand vibrations in its flood; it is again the power which creates the music of the instruments, which guides the chisel and the brush, which directs the witchery of the pen.[10]

He stated that to him contemporary American fiction seemed for the most part flavorless:

For strong and characteristic color and sentiment, we must study not this hothouse growth of fashionable intellectuality, which resembles a flower that may be found in the private conservatories, of all climates and countries; but rather the wild plants, the natural blossoms of human life. . . . What is wanted now is something distinct and unique and truthful, which cannot be found in the factitious life of drawing-rooms, but in the workshops and factories, among the toilers on river and rail, in villages fringing the sea line or hidden among the wrinkles of the hills, in mining districts and frontier towns, in the suburbs of vast industrial centers, in old-fashioned communities about which quaint traditions linger . . .[11]

What Hearn would do with these ideas could not be foreseen by him or others. The founders of the *Times-Democrat* were not interested in his ambitions but in his accomplishments. They expected editorial comment, local sketches, and translations. Since the new paper was to be rather showily a literary one, they thought they might use this odd one.

The *Times-Democrat* came into being in the midst of a lively interest. It was a genuine excitement involving the whole of the small, intensely literate public of the city who watched from day to day the drama of the founding of a paper, the gathering together of a talented staff, the issuing of the first numbers. The names of the staff were familiar to the daily readers of the older newspapers. The founding of the paper was a sort of local dramatic performance.

The new journal was the creation of Major E. A. Burke who had been a part owner of the *Democrat*. He believed that his paper, founded in 1875, merged with the older *Times,* founded in 1863, might become "the most powerful paper in the South." Page Baker, who would be the most powerful protective and fostering influence for Hearn's talent during the six years from 1881 to 1887, was named editor in chief. He was a former officer of the Confederacy, a forceful, gifted man. His brother Marion ran the Sunday edition in which the major part of Hearn's writings would appear. A third brother, Henry, was business and advertising manager. George Dupré became managing editor; his brother-in-law, John Augustin, became city editor and reviewer of drama and music. Both men had been shareholders of the *Democrat.* In addition to Lafcadio Hearn, other principal staff members were Charles Whitney, a New Englander, and Honoré Burthe, who enjoyed special local prestige as a descendant of a marshal of Napoleon. Mrs. Marion Baker, Julia Wetherall, wrote occasionally for the paper. An inexperienced young girl, Elizabeth Bisland, contributed verse and wrote about women's activities.[12]

All of them, except Whitney and Hearn, belonged to the local community. They and their like had been sayers and makers of opinion before the war. They were now once more in power after the end of official Reconstruction. The election of President Hayes had brought about a truce in northern management of southern affairs. These New Orleanians were a clever and conscientious people, accustomed to ruling, to inventing, to providing for themselves at the same time they provided for their region. Nothing could ever be again the same for them or their land; any vital prosperity would destroy them in remaking the South; in the meantime, in quiet stubbornness, they set up a pale simulacrum of the past, and prospered.

The Bakers and their associates, without even thinking about it, intended to use the *Times-Democrat* to promote just that amount of superficial change necessary for New Orleans to gain a share of northern prosperity. Alongside Hearn's exotic meditations were black headlines exhorting the community of New Orleans to do those things necessary for success in the new American framework. There were almost daily references to the commerce of the port, to drainage schemes, to plans for street paving. "St. Charles Avenue must be paved," adjoined in bold letters one of Hearn's more remote essays.

Thus the beginning of Hearn's fame as an independent writer, and the time of his happiest functioning as a journalist, belonged to a particular moment in the South, a moment epitomized by Henry Grady in Atlanta and Page Baker in New Orleans. This was a turning point, when in the long southern winter after the war, a small stir of shaky prosperity—in the cities —began to change the atmosphere. It was just the combination of tentative progress and a lagging, backward look which provided the proper place for Hearn in the decade of his thirties. The belief in prosperity made the founding of the *Times-Democrat* possible. The same hope created an atmosphere in which New Orleans staged an improbable but successful International Exposition in 1884 and 1885. The paper gave Hearn his daily living. The Exposition provided him with a subject for a national audience. But the backwardness of the South in the 1880's was as great an advantage to Hearn as the region's superficial flush of prosperity. New techniques might be welcomed; new attitudes were blandly refused. In this naïve, nonindustrial society, where every endeavor was carried on through personal relations and personal arrangements, such a writer as Lafcadio Hearn, concerned with intensely personal and human values, could be let to have his own way. And a newspaper such as the *Times-Democrat* could thrive.

Hearn came to this moment in his life, this six-year pause, ready within the depths of himself to forget the past. Behind his back a door closed. In Cincinnati in 1880 Mattie Foley remarried, this time in all legality, a Negro citizen of the city, John Kleintank. Although Hearn never knew of the event, it was important for him, for Mattie never again reached out a hand after the living Hearn. He was never reminded of her again except in his imagination. He came to his new position, after years of gradually lightening darkness, without a tie of loyalty except to his work. The readers of the *Times-Democrat* found operating before them a poised, varied, and experienced, as well as stimulating, mind. To his editors there must have been something even a little frightening in the deftness with which he moved from one task to another.

Baker learned quickly to let Hearn work without a checkrein. He saw that

Hearn needed not stimulation but appreciation. He undertook willingly to be an appreciator of Lafcadio Hearn. Hearn interested the editor personally as well as professionally, and he took him home to share meals and talk with him in the company of his family. In the office Baker was prepared to sit idle at regular intervals to listen to Hearn read his essays and translations before they appeared in the paper. After office hours he walked out with Hearn to find a place to sit and talk and drink long, contemplative drinks together. He cleared out from around Hearn's footsteps all petty annoyances as well as small duties of the regular newspaper job. He wished to let that sensitive, imperious temperament operate in peace. He was tolerant of the small tyrannies Hearn exacted. He relayed word to his outraged printers that in Hearn's case they were to print his copy exactly as received, down to the last semicolon. What was more important, he encouraged Hearn to hunt a publisher for his books. In one case he wrote a decisive letter of introduction.

Many scenes of his life Hearn almost succeeded in forgetting. The office of the *Times-Democrat* was not one of them. He could look back to that place and that time without any wounding. "Of course it was *really* long ago," Hearn wrote in 1896 to Baker from Kobe, "that we used to sit together —sometimes in your office, sometimes upon a doorstep, sometimes at a little marble-topped table somewhere over a glass of something—and talk such talk as I never talked since." And continuing to look back, he conjured up the scene of work: "I wonder, wonder, wonder whether I shall see you again —and walk up and down on that cocoanut matting—and make noises through the speaking tube to the composing room." [13] Safely beyond the mischances of daily work which had brought on upsets, recriminations, silences, even unlucky letters, Hearn in Japan blandly forgave Baker for the trouble he had given the editor and remembered the best of their relationship. Baker, corresponding somewhat gingerly with his former employee, continued wryly to appreciate. He engineered the syndication in America of some of Hearn's Japanese pieces; he offered Hearn again a job in New Orleans if he would come back; he exchanged pictures of his children for pictures of Hearn's. The tough, elastic relationship which stretched across the later length of Hearn's life was a complex one built in the 1880's upon a strong mutual need.

Page Baker was the kind of man Lafcadio Hearn could never be. Hearn admired him intensely for this, and also occasionally despised him for it. Baker was completely the product of his place and time. He was a natural leader, functioning forcibly and decisively but almost unconsciously within the framework of the half-ruined South. He was able, strong-willed, and in addition, handsome, strong, tall. His kindness to Hearn had naturally a limit: that point beyond which the interests of his paper and society would not be served by Hearn's freedom. Here he was as immovable as Hearn, who had his own implacable loyalties. The two men inevitably clashed in their fruitful partnership. In 1888, not long after leaving Baker's employ, Hearn wrote: "He was always willing to believe any [chamberpot] who told him that what I wrote was scandalous or untrue or offensive to Jesus C. and Co." [14] Hearn should not have said *always:* Baker's latitude was wide, but his proper boundaries were those of a small, somewhat provincial, if brilliant and cultivated, southern city of America in the 1880's.

But in his first year of work for Baker, when the *Times-Democrat* seemed to offer him so much more than any other paper had, Hearn was sanguine and expansive. Serious clashes with his editor were far off. He did not see the fences set up to keep him grazing peacefully within certain bounds. Very quickly Page Baker was pleased too. The work Hearn did was not only good but brilliant. It increased circulation. It attracted the kind of reader he wanted for his "literary" paper. The editor enjoyed, without foreseeing a limitation of this enjoyment, the spectacle of Hearn doing fiercely and exactly just as he pleased.

Each Sunday literary section of the *Times-Democrat* carried Hearn's translations under the heading "The Foreign Press." Here according to his taste were stories, excerpts from novels, biographical and critical articles, anything at all which he wished to put into English from his daily culling of the French and Spanish papers that cluttered his desk. (He had taken Spanish lessons for a time and tried his hand at putting Spanish gypsy ballads into English, as well as occasional articles in the Spanish press of the Caribbean.) Often Hearn's translations appeared in the *Times-Democrat* only a few days after the original appearance of the piece. New Orleans shared, only days late, Paris' sensation over Pierre Loti's unauthorized report of the French Navy's bad behavior in Tonkin in the 1880's. On weekdays Hearn offered occasionally another column of translation headed "Foreign Miscellany." On both Sundays and weekdays he wrote editorials prolifically. Hearn made this part of his work a catchall for his new interests. In his first two years he wrote almost as often for the daily papers as for the Sunday literary section. Later the editors learned to value him more highly, and reserved his energies for Sunday work only.

Much that interested Hearn and New Orleans in the 1880's is inert matter now. But his translations are as vivid now as then. Consulting only his own imperious taste, Hearn in 1882 gave his readers Daudet's "The Curé of Cucugnan," and "The Man with the Golden Brain." He began his long enchantment with Loti and translated "The Legend of the Moons," a Tahitian folk tale out of *Le Mariage de Loti*. He gave his readers Coppée's "The Blessed Bread," and a tight pure plain translation of Zola's "The Fight at the Mill," in two parts. During the same year he offered New Orleans a small choice of the prose poems of Charles Baudelaire, who was not at that time a certified classic.

By selection Hearn turned translation into a personal art, saying things about himself through the words of others. He shared also with the writers he translated an ardent loyalty to the romantic cause. "Every man is subject to an irresistible passion which might be called the thirst for the Infinite," he wrote in an introduction to two stories by Musset. "There are some who seek intoxication in wine, like Noah; others who seek it in women, like Solomon. Do not regard this as an appetite purely human or carnal. It is only the beginning—whether drunkenness of wine or drunkenness of love —it is only the starting of a loftier inspiration. . . . The drunkenness of Wine and the Drunkenness of Woman make us for an instant even as Gods." [15]

Hearn wrote what was probably the first article in English on Pierre Loti on September 23, 1883, and called his essay "A New Romantic." He raised up to a place in the pantheon of romantic heroes the neglected Gérard de Nerval, and on February 24, 1884, in an essay, "A Mad Romantic," wrote: "Like a shadow he walked the icy streets of wintry Paris, dreaming of the Impossible that he sought in vain . . ." [16]

In the latitude allowed him by the editors of the *Times-Democrat,* Hearn wrote not only about the infinite and the impossible of romanticism, but of the equally beguiling possibilities and impossibilities of scientific knowledge. He read Sir John Lubbock's study of ants, and swung off into a ready speculation: "Perhaps when the race of man has perished in some vast cataclysm, such as destroyed the monsters of geologic eras, some ants may found a new and peculiar civilization of their own." [17] Upon the excuse of a news item from the wires, he wrote a memorable phrase concerning "The Fate of the Comet"—". . . the prodigious enchantment of the sun draws them [the comets] nearer to the furnace each time they return." His conclusion was a verbal ecstasy: "But before the sun gives up his flame-ghost to God, strange things will be seen." [18] In the same vein he wrote in "An Atmosphere About the Moon": "Some day the Atlantic and Pacific oceans shall cease their most ancient thunder-hymns, the stainless heaven will no longer be frescoed with clouds, the rivers will die in their couches of stone. Then we shall become as the moon." [19]

He had written earlier in the *Item* about electricity as a new divinity,

"Whiter than moonlight is she; her locks are ceiling lightnings; her eyes sun-bright like the eyes of the vision of the Apocalypse," [20] and he had fallen into the habit of going out alone in the evening along the streets where they were stringing those new powers, electric wires, and of standing below them fascinated to listen to the new kind of music the wind made in them.

Into books of archaeology, anthropology, folklore, Hearn sank himself even as he metaphorically recommended ("When we descend in the diving bell of our imagination"), and came up with bits and pieces, luminous and odd, flashing with suggestion.

On Sunday, October 8, 1882, Hearn significantly reviewed Herbert Spencer's *Principles of Sociology* and called attention to the author's "synthetic philosophy." This was a modest announcement of a theme of importance. But it would take the urging of a friend, and a rereading, to awaken his permanent interest in Spencer. Another handle with which to grasp life was offered him when he first read Edwin Arnold's *The Light of Asia*. This was a decorative retelling of the life of Buddha, pallid if sincere, yet it had a great effect upon Hearn. He had reviewed the book for the *Item* on October 24, 1879, but had continued to read it all through the 1880's. As in his reading of modern science, so in his reading of Eastern thought, stimulated first by Edwin Arnold and Percival Lowell, his imagination was stirred. Hearn lived in and for this faculty at this time, but he was keenly aware that the imagination was troubled, isolated, unhappy in the modern world, anxious for some buttressing explanation that would let it tend to its own affairs and yet give it the comfort of some sort of explicable world above, below, behind. From the time he read Spencer, from the time he read Edwin Arnold, he had two explanations to juggle in his imagination. He tossed these two balls higher and higher till their movement and color at last came together in his mind as one merging, blending meaning.

Originally the Eastern interest was the livelier one. By 1882 he was glad of any occasion which let him write about the East, glad that the subject of that year's Momus parade in the Mardi Gras was the *Ramayana:* he wrote fluently, and much more than was necessary. In June of the same year he wrote in "Hiouen-Thsang": "Who shall say that there is no goodness without the circle of Christianity!" [21] He became so regular in presenting Buddhist lore in his columns that by 1884 he frightened some of the clergy-men of the city. Certain ministers preached sermons against the *Times-Democrat,* and Page Baker had an anxious moment or two. Hearn refused to be intimidated, and jeered at his detractors in an editorial entitled "The Buddhistic Bugaboo!"

Last Sunday was not the first occasion upon which a local theosophist [theologist?] uttered awful warnings from the pulpit against the spread of Buddhism! We were not aware that Buddhism had made any progress upon this side of the Atlantic; but various honorable clergymen have positively averred that such is the case, and one ecclesiast even hinted to his congregation that Buddhism "had its newspaper in New Orleans!" [22]

Although Hearn wrote a good deal, in a rather superficial manner, about the religions of the Far East during this period, he had no sense of a destiny turning him particularly toward India or China or Japan. He was at least as interested in Arabic and Jewish folklore, and in Finnish mythology. He gladly made matter of these hesitancies and happy awakenings. Readers of the folded sheets of the *Times-Democrat* could not predict from one day to the next where the errant writer of the paper would direct their attention.

In order to explore new territories of the word, in order to meditate in peace upon the material which exploded in little squibs upon the literary pages of the newspaper, Hearn needed a steady life, some degree of comfort, and the warmth of a fostering, friendly household. This he found just when he yearned for it at the boardinghouse of Mrs. Margaret Courtney. He had lived since coming to New Orleans in a succession of brutally ugly rooms. He had eaten haphazardly in one public eating house after another, choosing for economy the poorest and most sordid. He had tried to cook for himself, and failed. All this had become a sequence almost unbearable. But at last he found himself able to afford a little decency.

His relish for the Vieux Carré had not deceived him in the matter of how well the inhabitants had consistently cheated him. The economic pressures of the Quarter made his succession of landladies fasten upon him as an available victim. However well he liked the place, he could endure it no longer. He presented his dilemma to Krehbiel in 1881. As a local-color writer there was still an advantage to him in living in the Quarter: "I am living in a ruined Creole house; damp brick walls green with age, zig-zag cracks running down the façade, a great yard with torchon plants and cacti in it; a quixotic horse, four cats, two rabbits, three dogs, five geese, and a seraglio of hens,—all living together in harmony . . ." All this was very well for his writing, but he went on: "But I am getting very weary of the Creole quarter; the people are too infernally wicked to live with, and I think I shall pull up stakes and fly to the garden district, where the orange trees are, but where Latin tongues are not spoken." [23]

Casting about to find a new place to eat, Hearn discovered one day Mrs. Courtney's dining room. Hearn liked the place and came back again. The

house at 68 Gasquet Street (later Cleveland Street) became at last the substitute to him for the domestic life he ached for and believed he would never
achieve. Margaret Courtney cared for him as competently and cheerfully as
she cared for her family and for the other boarders, many of whom were
young medical students. She served a plate of nourishing food. She knew
no airs. She talked sensibly and listened with unaffected interest to the
young reporter of the new paper. She grew fond of Mr. Hearn, and soon
proud of him. Hearn became as famous in the small world of Gasquet Street
as he was in the larger one. And the world of Gasquet Street knew him much
better. Mrs. Courtney's dinner table was the center of a warm and happy
society disregarded by all who mattered in New Orleans. It was only the
anomaly of Hearn's being there that brought Page Baker there, on a horse
as handsome as he was, or George Cable, or Rudolph Matas, or such visiting
celebrities as Charles Dudley Warner, Richard Watson Gilder, and Joel
Chandler Harris.

The good of being at Mrs. Courtney's (he did not live there, but came
daily for three meals) soon showed in Hearn. First there was a physical
change in him: he gained weight and strength and took on a stocky, athletic
look. He swam when he could in Lake Pontchartrain and regained an almost
forgotten skill in deep water. He returned to the boardinghouse from such
easy excursions famished, and then ate greatly and uncritically of the common hearty fare. Upon workdays he began with breakfast at the Courtney's,
returned at noon for the generous southern dinner, and returned a third
time at night for supper.

It was not just the generosity and regularity of the food; it was Mrs.
Courtney herself who was good for Hearn. Margaret Courtney, who
was at this time a woman past middle age, a person of great strength,
capability, and energy, seemed from the first to have an intuitive understanding of the little newspaperman who came to her house one day to
eat, and came back again and again. She thought of him always as Irish.
His faint brogue pleased her. She was American born, but of Irish descent;
her husband was Irish born. She knew in her plain way how to talk to
Hearn, and he to her. He reverted with the Courtneys to some faintly remembered mannerisms of the country places outside Dublin where he had
spent many summers as a child, sent off to be out of the way in the company
of a maid.

Hearn came to accommodate all the other conditions of his life to the
beneficent regularity of his three daily meals at Mrs. Courtney's. He moved
from one nearby address to another—three moves in all—to be convenient
to her. He was first with a Creole family at 39 Constance Street, then with

Mrs. Canterbury at 278 Canal Street, and at last found anchorage in two rooms at Kate Higgins', on the corner of Robertson and Gasquet, just around a corner from Mrs. Courtney's. If Hearn fell ill the two women arranged between themselves to transport his meals from Mrs. Courtney's to Mrs. Higgins'. His cleaning woman was an elderly Creole Negro, Louise Roche. The three women between them, Margaret Courtney, Kate Higgins, and Louise Roche, cared for Hearn's modest material needs. They could not cure his infallible and inevitable loneliness, but they gave him the comfort and the peace and the secure routine necessary for the remarkable amount of writing he accomplished during the rest of his time in New Orleans.

One can judge from the friendly, direct, and entertaining letters he later wrote to Mrs. Courtney that he respected her judgment and admired as well as liked her. He gave her a copy of his third book—*Some Chinese Ghosts*—with the following dedication written on the flyleaf:

> To my kindest and truest friend
> Mrs. M. Courtney
> —by whose generous care
> and unselfish providing
> I recovered that health
> of mind and body
> without which no
> literary work can
> be accomplished,
> Lafcadio Hearn.[24]

Long before he wrote these words on March 14, 1887, the paying guest had become the friend of the family. He gave the Courtney address, 68 Gasquet Street, as his address and received all his mail there. With her quick sympathy Margaret Courtney saw that Hearn had the privacy he needed. There was an unused shed at the back of the lot. To this separate place, and later to another, slightly more dignified room at the front of the house overlooking the street, she carried his meals or sent them by one of the busy boardinghouse servants. Often, in her own coming and going, she stopped to talk with him. Her little girl, Ella, became Mr. Hearn's friend too.

Ella, who was twelve or thereabouts when Hearn first began to eat at the Courtney's, told him stories. He listened quietly. Imperceptibly, with no one else to overhear but Ella's mother, he began to tell stories to the child. Some of them he wrote out, or rather printed, and had bound in the printshop of the newspaper, and gave them to Ella. She kept them, and had them still, forty years later when she was sought out for questioning about the man who had been her mother's indulged and favored boarder.

Another member of the household who became a friend, on a sub-conversational level, was Denny Corcoran, Mrs. Courtney's nephew. He was remembered as a large, simple, good-natured roughneck who carried two guns, was supposed once to have run away from the city under suspicion of a killing, and who, if he worked at all, worked in some dubious capacity at the polls where he was employed to keep voters in line. He was naïve and proud and something of a terror, but at the same time a good soul, as transparent as a child, perhaps simpler than Ella. The chameleon-like Lafcadio could communicate as easily with Denny as with Ella, and enjoyed an occasional walk with the great hulking Denny into the dark slum streets of the city.

The two rooms he went back to from eating at Mrs. Courtney's or walking with Denny were plain and clean. In one was a bed hung with a mosquito net. In the other were a table and a chair, his trunk, and his books. He began to satisfy the luxury of buying books as soon as he was able, at $30 per week, to do so. Some of his bookstores were Fournier's Book Shop on Royal near Toulouse, Julien's on Royal, Muhl's Book Shop on Exchange Alley, Armand Hawkins' Book Shop on Canal. He ordered rare books directly from the great book dealers of Paris. He began to pride himself on the quality of his collection.

Hearn hated his own ignorance as he began to recognize the gaps in his knowledge. He admitted humbly (only to very good friends) his lack of any systematic education, yet what he had had, up to his sixteenth year, was good of its kind, the classical training given in English preparatory schools. So, in New Orleans, in his thirties, he read a great deal and collected stacks of expensive books. They were an odd lot: Creole dictionaries, scientific books for the layman, particularly in the fields of biology, physiology, anthropology, many volumes of folklore, and a tolerably complete collection of the French novelists and storytellers of the nineteenth century.

When he did not require certain books on his desk for research or reading, he put them away carefully into his trunk in a corner of his room. This room to which his friends came to collect him for a joint errand or to sit with him and talk or smoke was excessively bare. The absence of clutter was due not only to Hearn's not caring about things, but to his need for space about him, even in a small room. His friends never ceased to be amazed at Hearn's ascetic self-sufficiency. They told queer tales to each other of his writing habits, how he stood up to a high table, or how he wrote upon the smooth top of an old leather valise set up on the top of an ordinary table.

It was in these rooms that he plotted more ambitious work than he could achieve in the daily manufacture of words for the *Times-Democrat*. Some of

this daily work was vivid, some of it better than he knew, and much of it
—as he well knew—worthless. He had not been able to get his stories from
Gautier published in the regular manner. No publisher would take them.
With grim determination, he saved out of his salary the necessary amount of
$150 to hand over to a publisher, R. Worthington of New York, who agreed,
upon receipt of the author's money, to publish the book.

So, in April, 1882, when he had been at work for the *Times-Democrat* for
five months, Lafcadio Hearn held in his hand his own first copy of his first
book, the title of which was *One of Cleopatra's Nights and Other Fantastic
Romances,* by Théophile Gautier, translated by Lafcadio Hearn. The fresh
sensuality of the stories, the delicacy of the translator's rendering of them
into English, and the ingenuous appeal of the translator's note affixed to
them and signed L.H., New Orleans, 1882, attracted a scattering of tenacious
readers. In his note, Hearn appealed for discrimination:

Naturally, a writer of this kind pays small regard to the demands of prudery. His
work being that of the artist, he claims the privilege of the sculptor and the painter
in delineations of the beautiful. A perfect human body is to him the most beautiful
of objects. He does not seek to veil its loveliness with cumbrous drapery; he delights
to behold it and depict it in its "divine nudity" . . .
It is the artist, therefore, who must judge of Gautier's creations. To the lovers of
the loveliness of the antique world, the lovers of physical beauty and artistic truth,
of the charm of youthful dreams and young passion in its blossoming, of poetic
ambitions and the sweet pantheism that finds all Nature vitalized by the Spirit of
the Beautiful—to such the first English version of these graceful fantasies is offered
in the hope that it may not be found wholly unworthy of the original.[25]

Hearn was sparely reviewed, but he enjoyed the small stir of attention
even when certain of the reviews and a number of letters showed a strong
mood of disapproval, even shock. There was stimulation in the consciousness even of opposition.

With a bound of ambition, he determined that his next book would go
a step beyond his first. This time he would translate the spirit instead of
the word. Out of the folk tales in his collection he would choose and shape
a number of stories, legends, anecdotes from various traditions of the world,
and make a harmonious book of the sequence. His renderings would be free;
there would be more of Lafcadio Hearn in this volume than in his translation of Gautier. When they were finished, his "stray leaves" would be a
various lot taken from the folk literature of the Egyptian, Eskimo, Poly-
nesian, Hindu, Finnish, Arabic, and Jewish traditions. His attitude toward
the stories would make a unity of them.

He called the book *Stray Leaves from Strange Literature,* and in it he gathered the velvety petaled flowers and ignored the coarse and hearty roots of the old tales. In his preoccupation with surface, he softened his subject matter and indulged himself alternately in an easy eroticism and a soft luxury of horror. In smooth words he created landscapes for beneficent dreams:

. . . leaving the forest, they came to a great stretch of gardens lying without a white city—gardens rainbow-colored with flowers of marvelous perfume, and made cool by fountains flowing from the lips of gods in stone and from the trunks of rock.[26]

And he peopled his dream landscapes with dream-fulfilling women:

. . . he beheld a damsel descending toward him unrobed above the hips, after the fashion of her people. Sweet as the moon was her face; her hair was like a beautiful dark cloud; her eyes were liquid and large as a wild deer's . . .[27]

Beheadings, suicides, murders, strange and unimaginable cruelties floated upon the colored surface of these stories, and did not matter. His best stories were exceptions to this general rule. In them (escaping from his own dreaming) the grotesque, the horrible, the grimly humorous imposed their own style. "The Lion," a tale out of the Hindu tradition, was such an exception. It told a macabre story, and then stopped. "The Legend of the Monster Misfortune"—a Chinese story—was another exception, as was "A Tradition of Titus," a terrible story out of the Talmud. The horror of these more effective tales disturbed the graceful smoothness of the whole. And an exception, vigorous, spare, lean, of another nature was his literal translation of passages from the Finnish *Kalevala,* from a French version he had read.

The "leaves" appeared one by one in the pages of the *Times-Democrat.* It was not until the spring of 1884 that he found a legitimate publisher for the patiently made and polished collection. No money was advanced this time by the writer. J. R. Osgood of Boston brought out this second book as a regular commercial venture; Lafcadio Hearn had reached a new stage in his career as a professional writer.

The book received in the Boston publisher's office from an unknown writer in New Orleans might not have gained a hearing at all if it had not been for a letter of recommendation from the writer's own editor. So the book was dedicated:

> To my friend
> Page M. Baker
> Editor of the
> New Orleans *Times-Democrat*

While preparing one book Hearn schemed for others. He wrote to Krehbiel: "Couldn't get a publisher for the Fantastics and I am, after all, glad of it; for I feel somewhat ashamed of them now. . . . Another failure was the translation of Flaubert's 'Temptation of Saint Anthony,' which no good publisher seems inclined to undertake. . . . At present I am also busy with a dictionary of Creole proverbs (this is a secret) . . ." 28

Hearn thus had small disappointments and large hopes to busy him. His life was cushioned for a time from the gross shocks it had known so regularly: hunger, lack of shelter, rejection, fear. But he had not been able to forget such things. And he did not want altogether to forget. He wrote "A Word for Tramps" on December 26, 1884, as an admonition to his good-hearted neighbors to notice things they usually ignored, and to himself not to forget.

He began:

. . . Let us venture to insinuate, in the mildest and most modest manner attainable, just a word or two—not a defense, but a mere plea in abatement, as it were, in behalf of the tramp.

He went on to describe the recent death of a man:

A few weeks ago, the body of a man was found in the woods near one of the towns on our Gulf coast, in the hollow of a huge magnolia tree, into which he had crept for shelter from the cold rain that was falling, hanging his tattered coat as a screen at the entrance. There he perished, alone and untended, with no kind hand to pass him food or drink, to wipe the death-damp from his brow, or to perform any of the last offices of humanity, and no sympathetic voice to whisper words of cheer and consolation in the final struggle. . . . He perished unknown, like a wild beast in his lair, and left no sign or token. What bitterness of heart he may have felt as he lay dying within a few hundred yards of the light and warmth and food and shelter of cheerful homes, can only be matter for conjecture.

He appealed, without much hope of touching her, to the well fed, unthinking woman of gentle habits and sheltered surroundings:

Ah! Flora, if you could but feel for an hour the fierce fires of adversity, the "fever at the core" that so often drives men to madness or despair, and in so many cases was the mainspring that set the tramp in motion, you might still condemn him, but it would be with a gentler and kinder consideration for his infirmities.29

Hearn had no doubt about his own kinship with the tramp; he might have been the man who died in the tree. It was only good luck that he ate well and slept under a sound roof. It was, it seemed to him, too, a piece of good luck that he was beginning to enjoy a small fame in New Orleans. But then, in addition to the usual human hungers, he had a few that could not be fed. Nothing could fill the emptiness of essential loneliness in him.

What he hungered for most was the commonest possession of his friends, a family:

You will laugh at me, [he wrote later to his half sister, Mrs. Atkinson] and perhaps think it very strange that when only thirty-five I began to feel a kind of envy of friends with children. I knew their troubles, anxieties, struggles; but I saw their sons grow up, beautiful and gifted men, and I used to whisper to myself,—"But I never shall have a child." Then it used to seem to me that no man died so utterly as the man without children . . .[30]

He had not been a son; he had not been a father. He had no relations with women except those paid for, and a few uncertain friendships. When he came face to face with his needs and his lacks, something like panic afflicted him. But he knew no way out of his prison. When he reached the time of his life when he might have stepped out of the tight box of his own nature, he was afraid to try. He justified his apartness, his solitariness, his icy loneliness by romanticizing these qualities. And for self-protection, when he dreamed about the woman he desired, he imagined her as an ideal woman, a perfect woman, a woman he could never know—safely unattainable.

In a slight essay, "Spring Phantoms," written for the *Item* on April 21, 1881, he had articulated this idea:

So that when the fancy of a home and children—smiling faces, comfort, and a woman's friendship, the idea of something real to love and be loved by—comes to the haunted man in hours of disgust with the world and weariness of its hollow mockeries,—the Woman that he shall never know stands before him as a ghost with sweet sad eyes of warning,—and he dare not! [31]

The mind had settled the matter, that he was to be one of the deprived. But the body, half wild, rebelled, and sent him out into the streets to hunt a brutal substitute for dreams.

Hearn was morbidly awkward with women he thought his equals. He separated such a woman as far as possible from his common need and made of her a kind of mother, sister, or even intimate younger brother. Thus he metamorphosed his relations with one woman after another in New Orleans so as to sustain a relationship of friendship. With Mrs. Marion Baker, his editor's wife, with Leona Queyrouze, he accomplished this transformation. But with Elizabeth Bisland he could never find the proper key into which to transpose his feelings.

It needed only the sight and nearness of this radiant, self-confident girl (she was sixteen or seventeen when she came first into the *Times-Democrat* offices with some verses to offer to the literary editor) to cause Hearn to retreat into impersonality. He admired her verses almost humbly, was quite dazed by the sight of her, and could hardly speak to her at all. She frightened him to death, this beautiful, assured girl from a decaying plantation who had come into the city to make her own way. Direct in manner, imperious in will,

Elizabeth Bisland succeeded not unexpectedly, for she had Hearn's help in this early acceptance of her work, as well as her own energy and ability. She began writing woman's page copy, and was soon a regular member of the staff.

Hearn kept his mask on, but watched her progress with an interest which was in part dismay. He wrote once to a friend: "The lady-writer you inquire about is probably Miss Bessie Bisland, who writes the 'Bric-a-Brac' for *T-D*, reports Women's meetings, etc., and occasionally writes some superb poetry (I am not joking) over the signature of B. L. R. Dane. She is really a genius poetically, needs only discipline and practice . . . Tall, fair-skinned, large black eyes, and dark hair. Some call her beautiful; others, pretty; I don't think her either one or the other; but she is decidedly attractive physically and intellectually. Otherwise she is selfish, unfeeling, hard, cunning, vindictive; a woman that will make inferno in any husband's life, unless he have a character of tremendous force. You may see her some day; she thinks of settling in New York. A girl that reminds me of a hawk,—although her nose is not aquiline—a graceful creature of prey." [32]

Miss Bisland was ready to admire Hearn, and to learn from him. A little piece he had written for the *Item* on October 21, 1880, "A Dead Love," had been a part of her reason for coming to the *Times-Democrat*. Her liking for it stirred Hearn to revise it in a more ambitious form for the *Times-Democrat*, on April 6, 1884, calling it, in the later version, "L'Amour Après la Mort." (It was better in the earlier form.) Her frank admiration upset him into being stiffer and blanker with her than ever. He stood aside and watched while Miss Bisland easily secured a conspicuous place in the happy make-believe of New Orleans society. This achievement added the last bit of impossibility to the relationship.

Only the accident of her falling ill early in her New Orleans career cracked the wall a little between them. She had a fever and was thought to be dying. Hearn hovered about the premises of the hotel where she lived and helped see that she had food to eat and nursing care. Later, when time had changed their relationship, giving it familiarity and warmth, but never quite removing the element of distrust from it, Hearn then recalled this early moment. Writing to her from Tokyo in 1900, describing a room in his house in which he had hung the likenesses of his friends, he spoke of hers: "On the opposite wall is the shadow of a beautiful and wonderful person, whom I knew long ago in the strange city of New Orleans. (She was sixteen years old, or so, when I first met her; and I remember that not long afterwards she was dangerously ill, and several people were afraid she would die in that quaint little hotel where she was stopping.)" [33]

But in that early time in New Orleans, when they first knew each other, Hearn—except when she was in need—kept his visor up. The sequel of their closer friendship in later years was unexpected and almost improbable.

In writing about Lafcadio Hearn—and she was his first biographer— Elizabeth Bisland succeeded almost in keeping herself out of her portrait of Hearn except as a neutral friend and encourager. But it is necessary now to fill in the obscured angles of Hearn's life and to show her as an actor in that life. New Orleans was only the prelude to their friendship. But his imperturbability at this time was a sham. Every person he met, every place he gazed at with his intense, nearsighted look, changed him. He was not the self-sufficient person his less intimate acquaintances saw: soberly reading, writing, smoking endless pipes, gazing out of his window upon the quarrels or joys of his neighborhood. They did not see what he kept well hidden from them: the quick stir of frenzy, the outbreak of pain or disorder in the mind.

It was easier to be intimate with a person he had never met face to face than with many of his associates in the newspaper office. He had such a friendship with the writer W. D. O'Connor. It came about through O'Connor's noticing some of his work in the *Times-Democrat*. He wrote a letter to the editor praising an anonymous piece on Doré. Baker turned the letter over to Hearn, who answered it gratefully. It turned out that O'Connor was another writer condemned to daily uncongenial labor. He worked a daily stint for the United States Government in Washington, D.C., and had only a small margin of time for his own work. He had written an abolitionist novel, *Harrington,* in his earlier years. He was the herald and advocate of Walt Whitman. He had helped Whitman in 1862 when the poet badly needed help, and had written in 1866 *The Good Gray Poet.* Each man, lonely in his private work, Hearn and O'Connor, discovered a friend in the other.

They felt out the Irishness in each other, argued a bit, and exchanged books, opinions, and encouragements. Hearn felt free to say to O'Connor any incautious thing that came into his head (with Krehbiel he had to preserve a certain tone, with Watkin he could not have an intellectual argument). So, at various times, he wrote to O'Connor:

There is no possibility of praising Whitman unreservedly in the ordinary newspaper, whose proprietors always tell you to remember that their paper "goes into respectable families," or accuse you of loving obscene literature if you attempt controversy.[34]

By purchasing queer books and following odd subjects I have been able to give myself the air of knowing more than I do; but none of my work would bear the scrutiny of a specialist . . .[35]

I do not find it possible to persuade myself that the "mad excess of love" should not be indulged in by mankind. It is *immemorial* as you say;—Love was the creator of all the great thoughts and great deeds of men in all ages. . . . Again, after all, what else do we live for—ephemerae that we are? . . . Would not Love make a very good religion? 36

I am glad to hear you dislike Matthew Arnold. He seems to me one of the colossal humbugs of the century: a fifth-rate poet and unutterably dreary essayist;—a sort of philosophical hermaprodite . . . Don't you think Edwin Arnold far the nobler man and writer? 37

You will be shocked, I fear, to know that I am terribly ignorant of classic English literature—of the sixteenth, seventeenth, and eighteenth centuries. Not having studied it much when at college, I now find life too short to study it—except for style. When I want to clear mine—as coffee is cleared by the white of an egg—I pour a little quaint English into my brain-cup, and the Oriental extravagances are gradually precipitated. But I think a man must devote himself to one thing in order to succeed: so I have pledged me to the worship of the Odd, the Queer, the Strange, the Exotic, the Monstrous. It quite suits my temperament.38

The ease of their correspondence, the ease of their friendship, was a rest for the spirit. The two men never met, but Hearn kept a picture of O'Connor and honored him to the end of his life as the typical man of letters of the United States, overworked, unencouraged, killed off at last by an indifferent public. O'Connor died in 1889.

Hearn expressed to O'Connor the ambitions he had in writing his books. He did not tell him much about his newspaper work. He underrated this daily labor. He did not see the good of this quick-witted, earth-rooted work he did for wages, nor did he think so very remarkable the unceasing, questing hourly life of the senses by which his writer's appetite was fed. He thought everyone lived so.

But he noticed things a man of more complicated human relations might not have seen. The ants upon the baked mud of the yard outside the shed room seemed to have as good a claim on life as he. The terrapin under the step, the stray cat he set up as yard cat, the mouse he trained to eat scraps carefully saved from each meal—these creatures beneath the ordinary notice of the occupied man, Hearn noticed.39 They amused and interested him in a way perhaps impossible to one more entangled with people.

An impulse that had lain asleep under the dirt of Cincinnati and the fierce struggle of his early New Orleans days awoke once more: he began to exercise his childhood's love of the wild and the natural. He fed this interest in trips into the less settled parts of Louisiana. Page Baker sent him out of the city several times to the very depths of the state in search of stories.

At about this time the editors of *Harper's Weekly* became interested in his work (his first article for this magazine was published in 1883). For one assignment sponsored jointly by the *Times-Democrat* and *Harper's Weekly,* Hearn and the Harper artist chartered a lugger to explore the southern shore of shallow Lake Borgne in order to locate an isolated settlement of Tagala fishermen. *Harper's Weekly* on March 3, 1883, carried the sketch "Saint Malo." Hearn described a place sufficiently lonely to satisfy even his imagination:

> Out of the shuddering reeds and banneretted grass on either side rise the fantastic houses of the Malay fishermen, poised upon slender supports above the marsh, like cranes or bitterns watching for scaly prey. . . .
> Below the houses are patches of grass and pools of water and stretches of gray mud, pitted with the hoof-prints of hogs. Sometimes these hoof-prints are crossed with the tracks of the alligator, and a pig is missing. Chickens there are too—sorry-looking creatures; many have but one leg, others have but one foot: the crabs have bitten them off. . . .
> Although the region is included within the parish of St. Bernard, no Louisiana official has ever visited it; never has the tax-gatherer attempted to wend thither his unwelcome way. In the busy season a hundred fierce men are gathered together in this waste and watery place, and there must be a law unto themselves.[40]

Later in March 1883 Hearn went out into the Teche country and wrote about its bayous and bearded trees. Each time he went away from the city he was fetched back upon a short tether. He made himself impatient thinking of other places to visit.

In the meantime he tried to get his friends in Cincinnati to come south to visit him. Farny would find much to sketch, if he came; Krehbiel would find wonders in folk music, if he came. But Krehbiel, and then Tunison, both left Cincinnati without visiting Hearn in New Orleans. Krehbiel went to New York (as Tunison did too) to work for the *Tribune.* He soon became music critic of that paper, with no time to come south. The friend of the Cincinnati days Hearn most wanted to see was Henry Watkin. He urged the older man again and again to come down to New Orleans. He had a place now to put him up, and his friends of the city would be Watkin's friends too. "You must ask for Courtney's Grocery, corner Villere (pronounced *villery*) and Gasquet Sts. The folks are already anxious to see you: I have been telling them so much about you from time to time." [41]

But Henry Watkin did not come, and Hearn did not himself go north to visit him, as he half promised to do from time to time. The weather was never right; he was too busy; he had, besides, a deep-seated dread of seeing Cincinnati again.

The only one of his old friends of Cincinnati who came south to see him was Charley Johnson, cheerful, expansive, affluent Charley Johnson, who had been a reporter for a German-language newspaper when Hearn worked for the *Enquirer* and the *Commercial.* "Charley Johnson's coming down to spend a week with me," Hearn wrote gleefully to Krehbiel in February 1884. "I shall soon be enjoying his Rabelaisian mirth, and his Gargantuesque laughter." [42] He came, and Hearn wrote: "He is the same old Charley. We had lots of fun and talk about old times. He was quite delighted with my library. . . . Johnson seems to have become a rich man. The fact embarrassed me a little bit. Somehow or other, wealth makes a sort of Chinese wall between friends." [43]

A visit from Johnson was something, letters from Watkin and Krehbiel were important, but they were not daily companionship. The place in Hearn's life of Watkin to confide in and Krehbiel to argue with and defer to was not filled in New Orleans until Hearn met Rudolph Matas. Matas became more of a friend than Krehbiel had been, and as much of a support as Watkin. It was the younger man, the Creole Matas, who sought Hearn out. Decades later, the old doctor, full of fame and years, dedicating a room in the library of Tulane University to the memory of his friend long dead and longer gone from New Orleans, recalled how they had met.

He had first seen Hearn's writing in the *Times-Democrat,* admired it, and schemed to meet the author. Matas was then, in 1883, twenty-two or twenty-three years old, a young and promising medical man of an inquisitive open nature. He had not yet become the great Dr. Matas, the inventor of surgical techniques, the teacher, the international figure. He supplemented his beginning doctor's fees with a job as editor of the New Orleans *Medical and Surgical Journal.* He had literary as well as scientific sensibilities. He was not content to admire the anonymous articles and stories in the *Times-Democrat,* he wanted to meet the writer of them. They had made him appreciate his own city in a fresh way. Having come back to New Orleans from studying in faraway places—France, Spain, Mexico—he had been struck by a new sense of New Orleans' uniqueness. He, the son of another Dr. Matas of New Orleans, a Creole of the original Spanish stock of the city, determined to meet this man who wrote with authority, with humor, with wit about his own place. "Who writes those wonderful things—translations, weird sketches and remarkable editorials on your paper," [44] he remembered that he asked Charles Whitney of the *Times-Democrat.* Whitney told him: Lafcadio Hearn. Matas contrived that Whitney, who was a patient of his partner, Dr. Lucien F. Salomon, bring Hearn along with him on a visit to Salomon's office.

Thus, Hearn was introduced to Rudolph Matas, and Matas to the writer whose "things" had so caught his imagination. Matas did not recall how they progressed into friendship, but remembered only the sudden fact. Hearn's own recollection supplies a second link in the welding of their comradeship. In a scrap of an unpublished letter to Dr. Gould, Hearn, looking back to the 1880's, spoke of Matas as "a very dear friend, almost a brother," and remembered that "I first felt really curious about him after having visited him to obtain some material for a fantastical anatomical dream-sketch, and asked him where I could find good information regarding the lives and legends of the great Arabian physicians." [45] He found that Dr. Matas could tell him all he wanted to know, and other common interests and enthusiasms sprang up immediately between them. They fell into the habit of seeing each other almost every day; interest changed to affection, each one feeling a proprietary concern in the affairs of the other.

Matas served Hearn as a physician as well as a friend. He treated Hearn's one good eye when, early in their friendship, he was almost totally blinded, and confined, frightened and despairing, to his room. Curing a local inflammation, leading Hearn out of a literal darkness on this occasion, Matas, Hearn warmly believed, led him toward light when they talked and joked together.

Matas was just the man for Hearn: young, ardent, elegant of mind as well as person. He was a Latin who spoke both French and Spanish as well as English. What was particularly important to Hearn at this moment was that Matas was a man of science with a fearless, asking mind. He could attempt to answer Hearn's unending questions about physiology, biology, sociology, and even enter into discussions with him as to the literary connections of those subjects. Matas admired Hearn, enjoyed him, and had no desire to reform him. His recollection of Hearn was unembarrassed by the contradictions in him. Matas wrote in retrospect: "Both in taste and temperament he was morbid . . . he had an obsession of persecution . . . [but] he was as gentle and tenderhearted as a woman." [46] Matas considered that some of those who wrote later about Hearn exaggerated the fearfulness of Hearn's appearance and the luridness of his behavior. He recalled that one quickly forgot the disfigurement of the eyes in daily association. What he recalled of Hearn's New Orleans' regimen was its sober, almost ascetic rule of daylong and nightlong work, either for the newspaper or himself.

In the days of their intimacy in New Orleans, Matas was a very young uncle to a somewhat older nephew. Together the two young men shared a wider swath of knowledge than either could have enjoyed alone. Their minds played upon each other eagerly. With Matas, Hearn let fall all self-protective barriers. He let the other man see him in spiritual nakedness.

He showed him the emptinesses, the wants, the aches he carried about with him. Matas, less wasteful of emotion than Hearn, gave him good advice which Hearn sometimes heeded. There was a sturdiness of mental and emotional fiber in their connection.

Matas was the best of fellows for the strolls that Hearn had come to love in New Orleans. These were streets Matas had known since childhood. The two men walked out together into the city's murmurous, busy night after they had finished the day's work. They sat long hours over quiet drinks in the excellent small eating houses which Matas as a native took pride in showing off to Hearn. As a seal upon their friendship, Matas introduced him into the sacred seclusion of a Creole house and made him a friend of his wife.

Mrs. Matas knew Creole talk, Creole proverbs, recipes, anecdotes, attitudes, and poured out this knowledge to her husband's friend. Hearn, collecting what Mrs. Matas could give him, and what Mrs. Marion Baker could, filled notebooks with material on Creole cookery, Creole proverbs, Creole folklore. He thought that the coming Exposition, from which the city hoped to gain much prosperity, might be the propitious moment for him to have cheaply published some little booklets on these subjects.

In 1882 he had written with unconscious humor to Henry Watkin: ". . . Neither you nor I can now correct ourselves of habits. We are both old." [47] (Hearn was thirty-two.) Now, Matas helped him to be young again. Behind were the years of terrible, youthful seriousness. In the company of Rudolpho, as he called his new friend, Leocadio, as he signed himself to him, learned to relax and to be carefree. It was Leocadio oftener than Rudolpho, thirty-three rather than twenty-two, who capered in the dark streets of the city in the excitement of their intellectual combustions. It was this rebirth of juvenility that was the sign of Lafcadio Hearn's spiritual prosperity in New Orleans in the middle of the 1880's. He had been serious, far too serious. Now he could begin to let go, and benefit from letting go. His writing began to show a change. He began to go beyond the effort of translation and adaptation, and to stray into a tremulous but original and fresh effort of creation.

"There is something un-
utterable in this bright
Gulf air . . ." [1]

Chita

10 ✹ *The Beach at Grand Isle*

In August 1884 Hearn was tired of work and weary of the city. His editor ordered him out of the office on the first vacation he had had from a newspaper job. Baker suggested a destination, a place on the coast of Louisiana.

Upon an early morning of humid city heat, Hearn went on board a small white boat tied to a city dock, and felt at once the expectation which travel quickened in him. Once under way the little ship turned southward and by some devious water passage left the city far behind, threading a course through bayous, lagoons, lakes, and bays. By sunset it seemed to be nearing some ultimate end of earth. There was more and more water, a larger and wider sky. Skeins of pelicans in raveling patterns turned and wheeled at a great height. There were no more people in the world, only an exhilaration of space. The white boat, dwarfed by the scene, left the last of the mainland behind, crossed the widest bay it had yet traversed, and came to anchor against the lee side of Grand Isle. Even at first glance the island could be seen for the precarious bit of earth it was, a sandbar accidentally grassed and populated, sheltering a calm north shore. The sea could be smelled and felt but not yet seen just beyond the narrow width of the island.

On shore an unexpected apparition awaited the passengers. Drawn up before them was a streetcar of an obsolete New Orleans type, mule drawn, and labeled irrelevantly Tchoupitoulas Street. Krantz, the enterprising German who had invented Grand Isle as a resort for summer-drugged New Orleanians, had picked up very cheaply several outmoded cars from the street railway system and shipped them to an odd fate at this last stopping place. Here upon primitive Grand Isle his ladies and gentlemen from the city did not need to walk the negligible distance from north shore to hotel, or beyond to the beach on the south shore.

Small, light, topheavy with sway, sophisticated with bright paint, the trolley carried its load of chattering passengers slowly southward along straight narrow rails. It moved across marsh populated by long-legged wading birds upon mudflats, then across a waste of abandoned sugar-cane fields grazed upon by the island's half-wild cattle, and stopped under the dense shade of wind-twisted oaks where was the collection of buildings known as Krantz's Hotel. Through the tangle of undergrowth there was a glimpse of surf to the south.

Hearn dumped his bag in the little whitewashed cabin to which he had been assigned, turned his back upon the question of what kind of place he was in, and set out alone and on foot toward the sight of the sea. He walked first under the shade of low trees, then out into the sunlight flooding untended fields, next upon a ridge beside froggy ditches, and found himself very quickly upon a wide flat brown beach exposed to a smashing surf and a fierce, exhilarating wind.

Ahead was a great space of water, no land beyond but Yucatán. Behind was the island, a slight bit of ground which attained no greater height than six feet and seemed threatened by the restless sea. Overhead, a giant sky floated tall clouds. At his feet the sea ravened, wetting his shoes soiled by city dirt. The wind tore at his clothes. Brown sand, blue sky, white clouds, and the infinitely shifting shades of the sea, the noises of the waves, the shore birds, the wind: the dazzlement of sight and sound stunned and absorbed him, a solitary figure, into a moment of ecstasy.

Coming down from this height of emotion, Hearn returned to the hotel and was soon busy exercising his mind upon the place, its people, and the odd contrast these guests made to the life of the islanders, moving about within sight, collecting cattle, hauling in nets full of fish, earning their living as if Krantz and his people were not there at all.

Establishing himself for his stay, setting out his paper and books upon the washstand which seemed suitable for a writing table, thrusting his head out his window, trying the lockless door, Hearn found that his one-room whitewashed cabin was only one of many, set up in straight, neat rows like a small village. When dinnertime came, a loud cheerful gong was struck to call the guests, like children in school, to come to eat. They gathered together in a dining hall which was a separate building, a single room with a lofty ceiling. The kitchen, where the odorous seafood was prepared and gathered up on generous platters to be carried to the waiting guests, was in a nearby building.

The cabins had been slave cabins. This place had been a slave village, inhabited by the Negroes who had worked in the fields and in the sugar house of the plantation which had once occupied this ground. The dining hall had been the sugar house. The kitchen had been the stables. The New Orleanians of the 1880's holidayed, for Krantz's profit, upon the site of the once-prosperous plantation of the time before the Civil War where the firm of Colmenaro and Ribas had planted, cut, and refined the sugar cane. Beyond the grove of trees stretched the barren weedy fields where the cane once grew in orderly dense furrows. The ridges of the furrows still showed. Now, only the cattle of the island strayed up and down the furrows, grazing upon weeds and native grasses.

Hearn accepted Grand Isle as if he were the first person ever to see it. He began at once to come to terms with the place in words. He began scribbling rough notes for his own use and writing letters home to Page Baker, Margaret Courtney, and Rudolph Matas. The hotel so oddly located, the guests, the natives, the waste wilderness dwarfing all human activity: these aspects of Grand Isle Hearn attempted to see straightly and to set down accurately. Released from tasks set by others, Hearn set himself a larger task, to understand all about Grand Isle.

He walked the little paths of the island, from cabin to dining hall, from cabin to beach, from Krantz's establishment to fishing anchorage, from fishing boats to the innocent and inefficient little post office in the cabin of a careless Creole where he posted his letters. In his wanderings from one end of the island to the other (seven miles from east to west, not more than a mile or a mile and a half from north to south), Hearn saw that he had come by chance upon a unique small world. Grand Isle had remained through all the generations of its habitation sufficiently isolated from the larger life of Louisiana and America to develop an odd but complete life of its own.

What captured Hearn's interest was a piece of land fronting the open sea upon its south side in an irregular, wounded sea front seven miles long where the sand was strewn regularly with shells, boards, trunks of trees, wrecks of ships, and occasionally bodies. "These are the skirts of the continent, trending in multitudinous tatters southward to the sea," [2] Hearn wrote of the entire Gulf Coast area. Grand Isle was one of the ultimate tatters, a place geographically apart, far off, disconnected. The life of the island was eccentric to the industrializing, centralizing, "normal" life of the continent.

The islanders, a few hundred in all, lived a harsh, independent life. As their fathers and grandfathers had done, so would they do. And there was a streak of color in their past. The grandfathers, never spoken of in this character, had been the pirates of Barataria, the great bay beyond their own bay, Carminada. The pass between Grand Isle and Grand Terre was the narrow passage by which the pirates escaped their enemies and preserved their loot for the markets of New Orleans. Upon the faces of the grandsons was the look of those who knew they were their own sufficient law. Grand Isle was a blessing for Hearn, a "romantic" place almost suburban to a prosaic modern city (for so New Orleans had become to Hearn). Here was the "Orient"—hitherto found only in books—near at hand.

He listened to the expressive slow guttural French of the islanders and tried to talk to them in their modification of Creole. They soon forgot to distrust this small dark man, or even to think of him as one of Krantz's people. They invited him into their cottages. They mended their nets while he sat by them. Hearn spent long hours on the rickety porch of the post office, watching the island life go on before him as if he had become invisible. He made a particular friend of an eccentric Basque scholar-fisherman who could talk to him of Spain and North Africa, and he trembled shyly in the presence of the scholar's pretty young daughter who served the two men food and drink while they talked.

And all the time he lived as if in another skin as one of Krantz's guests, an odd one, not much of a talker. He missed little in the dining room, on the beach, along the tramway. The resort was an anomaly, set down by accident on Grand Isle, a place haunted by the sea death. But it had its innocence too. Hearn did not miss this quality when he wrote to Page Baker:

I suppose you have not been at Grand Isle—or at least not been here for so long that you have forgotten what it looks like. It makes a curious impression on me: the old plantation cabins, standing in rows like village-streets, and neatly remodelled for more cultivated inhabitants, have a delightfully rural aspect under their shadowing trees; and there is a veritable country calm by day and night. . . . The hotel proper, where the tables are laid—formerly, I fancy a sugar-house or something of that sort—reminds one of nothing so much as one of those big English or Western barn-buildings prepared for a holiday festival or a wedding-party feast. The only distinctively American feature is the inevitable Southern gallery with white wooden pillars. An absolutely ancient purity of morals appears to prevail here;—no one thinks of bolts or locks or keys, everything is left open and nothing is ever touched.

Nobody has been robbed on the island. There is no iniquity. . . . There are no temptations—except the perpetual and delicious temptation of the sea.[3]

That there had been no bad storm for a number of years was an irrelevancy upon which Krantz and his hotel guests prospered. The very beauty of the island—its trees, undergrowth, the grasses of its fields—was vulnerable. It was only the lull between storms that furnished the scenery for vacationers: orange trees for scent, oak trees for shade, oleanders for color. All this decoration seemed permanent to the visitors. They made themselves a routine and set up conventions. Hearn, who talked to the islanders, was like someone let in on a secret: the secret of the destroying wind which might visit the island any summer.

Hearn too set up a schedule and found a sameness in the days as they passed: ". . . the land is the same day after day;—surf, crabs, fish, cats fishing in the canals, Creole boys swimming and selling birds, dinner-bells, cigars on the platform, ladies at piano, and the cattle on a thousand hills— each hill about 8 inches high." [4] To Margaret Courtney he wrote as if to an anxious relative, and emphasized the comfort he enjoyed on the island: "My room is small and cosy; and everybody leaves doors and windows open all day long. . . . There are birds and trees and insects innumerable; and 'mud-daubers' build their nests in every corner;—there are two under the top of my washstand. The board—(I know you want to hear about the board) —is very good. One does not need any wine here; the sea air is wine enough. I have a famous appetite and am getting well tanned." [5] But he admitted in another letter: "I miss your nice beefsteaks, nice legs of mutton, nice cooking. Very little meat here,—and no eggs. Nothing but oysters, croakers, red fish, sheephead, crabs. I am going to turn into a fish and get scales!" [6]

He entertained Mrs. Courtney, Ella, and the others of the family with homely description: "Last night we had rain; and you ought to have heard the frogs. It sounded like a hundred thousand tin horns blowing a big frog's Christmas Eve. Near the house were little fellows who kept saying: 'Polly, Polly, Polly!' but the big fellows in the marsh kept blowing their tin horns. Other frogs said or seemed to say: 'Tea-table, tea-table, tea-table' all the time." [7]

After a night of frog music the fishermen of Grand Isle grappled with taking a living from the sea, and the guests of Krantz's Hotel trooped down to the beach to play. The gayest group disported itself around the pretty figure of Miss Bessie Bisland. The young Woman's Page editor of the paper had come down to the island at the same time that Lafcadio Hearn made his visit. Hearn almost succeeded in behaving, at least in public, as if she were not there. But he sketched her privately upon his letter paper, with her long black hair floating on the waves.

He found it impossible in a crowd to improve his acquaintance with her. And he tried to disapprove of social ease. He wrote in a letter to Mrs. Courtney: "I find no pleasure in talking nonsense to young girls; and if I had to keep company with the people who frequent the dancing-saloon, I should not be able to stand it very long." [8]

Many of his fellow guests at Krantz's Hotel annoyed him. His nerves were exacerbated whenever uninvited humanity pressed close about him. A group of luckless Jews were the targets of his wrath in letters home. Hearn always argued eloquently in public print against anti-Semitism: he had in one case demolished an elaborate French defense of the doctrine. But in this case he was contradictorily and personally ugly. He wrote to Ella Courtney: "Mr. Baker came down last night (Tuesday) and forty Jews went away,—so I am now able to take your mama's kind advice, and try to think there are no Jews in the world." [9]

Marion Baker, with whom he shared some of his island excursions and swims, soon annoyed him too. To Mrs. Courtney he wrote about the man who was his immediate superior on the newspaper: "Mr. Baker simply made me very unhappy here. He seems to be my bad luck. I have got a superstition about him, and in spite of all I can do, I can't help showing my dislike. He is going to-morrow (Monday) and I think I will stay a little longer, just to be rid of him for a while." [10]

Hearn was hard to please, fickle in his regard, constant only in his love for aspects, words, meanings—as he had said of himself in using the phrases of Baudelaire: "I love the clouds—the passing clouds—the clouds of heaven . . ." [11] But in his self-enforced apartness Hearn was very lonely. It was hard to be a spectator only to the warmth that surrounded such a person as Elizabeth Bisland, to whom he would have liked to talk carelessly and brilliantly.

In his loneliness he wandered along the beach. The spectacle of nature disturbed him. He had been reading earnestly whatever he could find on the theory of evolution that seemed to explain himself to himself, as well as all of life. At Grand Isle he beheld gigantic manifestations of the struggle for existence. He watched, appalled and fascinated, the destruction of whole shoals of fishes upon remote areas of the sea border:

Sometimes when winds are variable and breakers run at long angles to the foam-line, strange sights are to be seen. Unknown perils of the abyss, mysterious panics, drive whole nations of fish to flee from the profundities, and infinite multitudes rush to the shallows,—even to the shore itself—followed by enemies in legion. Then begins the gigantic massacre of an entire population,—the destruction of an innumerable race. Pursuers and pursued spring high into the daylight;—millions of iridescent creatures, mad with fear, leap far out upon the sand,—while behind them the armies of porpoises and of sharks slaughter savagely and silently. And above where the sea is most thickly seamed with those sharp fins that sailors fear,—above the churning and the foaming and the prodigious quivering of terror, triumphantly ride the murderous bands of air,—squadrons of shrieking gulls, and wheeling eagles, and fish-hawks, and frigate-birds, hideous of foot and huge of wing. . . .

Soon along the beach is spread so mighty a feast that the birds sicken themselves with luxuries;—they feed upon the eyes only, and only devour one eye of most victims, not seeking even to overturn the flat body in order to tear out the other.

Did Hearn notice his own detail—that *one* eye only of each victim was torn out? At least he read the scene as symbolic.

Enormous slaughter!—appalling cruelty! destruction symbolizing grimly the great contests of human life in which the fiercest and strongest and swiftest survive to exemplify Nature's mystic and merciless law,—symbolizing, too, the stranding of myriad ambitions in the terrific race for wealth, the stranding of countless lives upon the sands of Illusion,—symbolizing, likewise, the loss of unnumbered precious things desperately won only to be wrested brutally from the winner by superior strength and cunning and ferocity in that eternal Battle of Success which is also a tearing-out of hearts . . .[12]

But Hearn did not only meditate upon the sea; he merged himself with it. He made an ecstasy of the simple act of swimming. "I had not been in sea-water for fifteen years, and you can scarcely imagine how I rejoice in it—in fact I don't get out of it at all." [13] So he wrote to the initiator of the trip, Page Baker. Every forgotten joy of childhood and adolescence in the sea mixed with this present joy. He had not been away at all; he had not forgotten. The great space of years dropped away, and he was on the sands at Tramore once more.

He forgot, in writing to Page Baker, to be moderate:

I'd like to melt into the water, and move with it lazily,—tumbling sleepily on the lukewarm sand under big lazy moons;—or become a half-conscious fish to be assimilated by the irresistible stomach of a man-of-war bird. To become a part of the infinite laziness of a man-of-war bird would delight me. Still better to become a cloud floating in the Eternal Blue Ghost and only draw my breath at long, long intervals, so enormously lazy have I been.[14]

He forgot to sleep long. He awoke at four each morning and went down to the beach alone, to swim out, far out, into the colorless liquid, facing the east, letting the dawn come to him in its slow steadiness. Then only he faced reluctantly back toward land and rejoined people, affairs, and complications.

He swam regularly three times a day and had the unusual experience of finding himself possessed of a physical accomplishment which was publicly acclaimed. He was the best swimmer in Grand Isle, better than any guest, better even than the fishermen who from long knowledge of the sea feared and even hated it more than they loved it. Hearn, with his strong shoulders and back, went far out beyond what was safe for most, and swam with what was more than a knack, more than experience, more than practice; he swam as if swimming were more natural to him than walking.

The days at Grand Isle ended. Hearn had to give up the swimming, the free wandering along the beach edge, the talks with the Basque fisherman, the tentative flirtation with the fisherman's daughter, the routine of the vacationer at Krantz's Hotel. "I suppose I must come back on Monday," he wrote just before he left. " 'My poverty but not my will' etc." [15]

Hearn went on board the white steamer once more and left the surf, the brown sand, and the tangled lanes of the island behind. He faced again the sobering routine of newspaper work.

11 ⊱⊰ *Intensifications*

Hearn returned to the city with his eyes dazzled by the sea. "I am weary of New Orleans," [2] he had written even earlier to Krehbiel. With his quick irritability he was even more weary of the city during these later years. Yet he did much good work. He helped make the *Times-Democrat* a distinguished newspaper. He accomplished two more books. He began to be a writer for the national magazines.

As early as this time he saw that he would one day leave New Orleans. But he shuddered at the thought of going to New York, where all his friends seemed destined to go. Krehbiel had gone, Tunison had gone, Miss Bisland was going. And Cable had suddenly gone too, driven out of New Orleans, north beyond New York to New England, fleeing from his own people who thought he had betrayed them.

Hearn too would go north one day. But he held off the time. "New York has become something appalling to my imagination," he wrote to Krehbiel, "perhaps because I have been drawing my ideas of it from caricature . . ." And, his fancy fired, he went on half humorously about the New York of his imagination. It was

. . . something cyclopean without solemnity, something pandemoniac without grotesqueness—preadamite bridges—superimpositions of iron roads higher than the aqueducts of the Romans—gloom, vapour, roarings and lightnings. When I think of it, I feel more content with my sunlit marshes—and the frogs —and the gnats—and the invisible plagues lurking in visible vapours—and the ancientness—and the vast langour of the land. [3]

In adopted southern style Hearn exaggerated both his own and the land's languor. For himself, he talked of lazy or fantastic alternatives to the driven career of newspaperman: he would buy a bookstore, he would rusticate without income in some crumbling coastal city of South America, he would become a doctor and try his skill in the "Country of Cowboys," or go to Japan—"A doctor might do well in Japan." [4] But he continued to write his daily editorials, book reviews, translations. And as for New Orleans, the city stirred out of its postwar lethargy: on December 16, 1884, the long-anticipated World Industrial Exposition opened its gates.

For months Hearn had been involved in his newspaper's scheme to make the Exposition a great success. But when the gates opened, he forgot the maneuvering which had brought the thing into being. He was a child again and opened his eyes and mouth and stared about him with wonder. He went again and again. One night the entire exhibit of the federal buildings was lighted by electricity. Cities then were not routinely lighted by electric power. "Never," wrote Hearn, "did the might of machinery seem to me so awful as when I first watched that enormous incandescence; and after having left the buildings and their myriad lights far behind, I found myself still dreaming of that future cycle of centuries wherein the world's labors shall be performed by automatons, and the great duels of nations shall be fought with lightning." [5]

The crowd, in which Lafcadio Hearn stood, holding its collective breath over the power of this new white light, came from every part of America. For the first time since General Butler's Civil War occupation of the city, New Orleans had become the center of the national attention. The city's streets were crowded, its hotels filled, and many of its private houses opened to visitors of all sorts: casual sightseers, wealthy travelers, newspapermen, independent writers. And although the Exposition was devoted to the New South, even the most casual visitor caught hold of some notion of the older South. It was easy to do so while strolling under the live oaks of the former sugar plantation on whose broad grounds the Exposition had been planted, or in viewing, from the levee nearby, the broad brown Mississippi. Although many of the visiting newspapermen wrote about the new situation of the Negro, or the economic progress of the South, many others wrote about the French Quarter and the stubborn, unchanging manners of the Creoles. Sightseers and scribblers alike sent back word to the North how interesting a place the old city was, how different from their own America, how entertaining its picturesque dirt.

It was just at this moment, when the responsible Southern leaders were trying to make the South a little more like the North, that the lagging, behind-the-times South became a romantic place for the imagination of the North. It was a lucky moment for Lafcadio Hearn, for it opened to him a new career. After the Exposition he was included among the practiced younger writers of the South who could be relied on for essays, stories, novels, all wrapped in the guaranteed glamour of the newly discovered region.

Hearn found himself engaged in writing Creole pieces again, this time for national publication. On January 10 and 17, 1885, the *Harper's Weekly* carried Hearn's "The Creole Patois." In the same magazine on November 7, 1885, with sober words and careful addition of fact to fact, Hearn recreated the life of one of New Orleans' singular persons, Jean Montanet, in "The Last of the Voodoos." Montanet had been a great man among his own people but in his old age "nothing remained to him but his African shells, his elephant's tusk, and the sewing-machine table that had served him to tell fortunes and to burn wax candles on." [6] Remembering other odd corners and strange practices of the city, Hearn was to give his new readers the following year a rich gumbo of information, in "New Orleans Superstition."

On January 3, 1886, the New York *Tribune* (where Hearn had friends) published his piece "The Creole Doctor." Among curious remedies which the poorer people practiced among themselves he listed two he had tried himself: one a cure for fever, the other a cure for inflamed eyes. From his hints one can conjure up a picture of Louise Roche looking after him in his rooms and urging him on to recovery from various illnesses as much by her good nature as by her remedies.

Of more importance to Hearn than this easy revival of his Creole writing was the debut of another kind of writing. *Harper's Bazar* published one of his "Chinese ghosts"—"The Legend of Tchi-Niu"—in October 1885. He was spending his private time on a selection of Chinese tales of which this was only one. When each of them was set, in frail fine colors and harmonious sound, he published it in the *Times-Democrat*. Only "Tchi-Niu" found a national audience at this time.

There was not much of common life about them. They represented rather the most extreme pitch of verbal perfection he was able to reach. They were as polished as beautiful smooth stones. Occasionally there was a faint specter of pathos in them. The first story, "The Soul of the Great Bell," and the last, "The Tale of the Porcelain-God," were a double parable about art and the artist. For the perfect bell or the perfect vase, a life must be sacrificed: ". . . My life for the life of my work!" [7] cried Pu, the first maker of porcelain, and entered the fire.

The texture of these stories was a precious, attenuated tuning of word to meaning. In "The Soul of the Great Bell" he wrote:

And after each huge shock, how wondrous the multiple echo and the great golden moan and, at last, the sudden sibilant sobbing in the ears when the immense tone faints away in broken whispers of silver—as though a woman should whisper, 'Hiai!' [8]

Working upon these "Chinese" stories, six in all, night after night, during all the weeks and months of the holding of the Exposition, when his day hours were filled with another journeyman kind of work, Hearn knew what it was to mix a little of his own life with his work. He estimated the book, *Some Chinese Ghosts,* justly later: "Early work of a man who tried to understand the Far East from books—and couldn't; but then, the real purpose of the stories was only artistic. Should I ever reprint the thing, I would change nothing . . ." [9]

In the meantime, he rushed into hasty and makeshift publication three books he thought the Exposition would help to sell. His trunk at Mrs. Higgins' held whole stocks of unusual material about Creole New Orleans. If some of this old matter could be put together quickly and sold under the noses of the free-handed strollers of the fairgrounds, there might be some money in it. Will H. Coleman had been a friend in New Orleans in earlier days with whom he had enjoyed talking about books. Then he had sold machinery to make a living; now he sold books in a bookshop in the Astor House in New York. Coleman was persuaded to back the three books.

Hearn had only a small share in the one that was best suited for sale at the fair, the *Historical Sketch Book and Guide to New Orleans and Environs.* It was introduced by the publisher as being "edited and compiled by several leading writers of the New Orleans Press." To pad it out to a certain length it included a number of essays as well as factual information on the geography, history, street system, clubs, churches and charities of New Orleans. It printed and identified a few sketches by Lafcadio Hearn, including his "Scenes of Cable's Romances."

The second book of the small set, *La Cuisine Creole,* issued without any name of author or editor, was Hearn's work entirely, a collection of recipes gathered from the wives of his friends.

The third book, a book he signed, *Gombo Zhèbes: A Little Dictionary of Creole Proverbs,* was a compilation he had completed two years before, and which he had put away in his trunk after receiving a rejection. *Gombo Zhèbes* (which is to say Creole herbs or Creole witticisms) belongs to a rare category, the witty personal dictionary.

Among the phrases he pulled out of the living talk of this sublanguage to French are these:

Bon bagout çappe lavie. (Bon bagou sauve la vie.) "Good gab saves one's life."

Bon blanc mouri; mauvais rêté. (Le bon blanc meurt; le mauvais [méchant] reste.) "The good white man dies; the bad remains."

Divant camrades capabe largué quilotte. (Devant des camarades on peut lâcher sa culotte.) "Before friends one can even take off one's breeches."

Li laçasse zozos pariaca. (Il chasse aux oiseaux à paliaca.) "He's hunting paliaca-birds." *Paliaca* is the Mauritian term for the brightly-colored kerchief worn by all young negresses in lieu of hats or bonnets, like the old time Louisiana *tiyon*. "He is hunting for paliaca-birds" therefore means, "He is running after the colored girls." [10]

None of the three books did very well. They came out late. When they appeared, in April 1885, interest in the Exposition was waning. The books were orphans—spurned, neglected, lost. Only the cookbook had a steady sale.

Hearn limited most of his writing about the Exposition to a particular interest he had discovered not long after the opening. This interest was the Japanese Exhibit. He had come upon this small space of quiet and exquisite taste in the middle of the Exposition's large bustle, and had returned again and again to it. He was so rapt away by his interest, and looked so long, that he attracted the special attention of the Japanese commissioner, Ichizo Hattoro, charged by his government with the management of the exhibit. When Hearn, who introduced himself as the representative of both the *Times-Democrat* and the *Harper's Weekly,* began asking questions, Hattoro took particular pains to help him.

Hearn had read books about the East, but this was different: this was touching with his own hands, seeing with his own eyes. Here, in a wash of ink and color upon silk, was the landscape of the East itself: "A flight of gulls sweeping through the gold light of a summer morning; a long line of cranes sailing against a vermilion sky; a swallow twirling its kite shape against the disk of the sun; the heavy eccentric, velvety flight of bats under the moon . . ." [11] So he described what he saw to his readers.

He held in his hand ingenious imitations of insects made out of cotton and paint: ". . . cotton crickets with the lustre of lacquer, and cotton grasshoppers of many colors; the korogi, whose singing is like to the 'sound of a weaver weaving rapidly' . . ." [12] and other small artifacts of curious realism. On this tray were beetles, on another silks. Next, catching his eye, was a display of prints and printmaking. Here were school books, there exhibits of machinery. Hearn could not leave off looking, for even familiar objects had a strangeness here. It was a small sample of an exotic industry, ability, modernity, all familiar qualities, yet expressed in terms of an unknown, a remarkable sense of beauty. On January 31, 1885, *Harper's Weekly* published his article "The New Orleans Exposition: The Japanese Exhibit." For his own paper, on February 24th, he wrote "Oriental Literature at the Exposition." On March 7th *Harper's Weekly* published "The East at New Orleans." For *Harper's Bazar* of March 1885 he contributed "Some Oriental Curiosities."

Later Hearn's friends argued among themselves why Hearn chose to go to Japan in 1890. One or another claimed the honor of implanting the suggestion in him. Some of these pricks of urging may have helped him in the direction of Japan when he was uncertain where to go from New York, but the desirability of doing so was already buried in him in 1885.

He had the relief of a vacation trip after this activity. Charley Johnson came down again in mid-April from Cincinnati, and Hearn went with him by train, "across the Floridian barrens to the sea—a long night and a longer day of steam travel over light powdery soil, the tint of hour-glass sand." [13] The two friends, garrulous about old times, were full of gossip concerning Krehbiel, Tunison, Farny, and the others whom Hearn had not seen since 1877. At the little town of Jacksonville, they admired white buildings and green river. They went out to the beach and swam, to Hearn's delight, in the open surf of the Atlantic. Then they stepped aboard a river steamer and traveled up the St. Johns to the Oklawaha, up the Oklawaha to the Silver River, and so at last to Silver Springs. Hearn's slight sketch of this expedition showed the happiness he felt at getting away:

> Our boat, turning sharply, steams out of the green water into—what can I call it? —a flood of fluid crystal—a river of molten diamonds—a current of liquid light. . . . It might be fifty feet in depth at times; yet every pebble, every vein of the water-glass blades, every atom of sparkling sand, is clearly visible as though viewed through sun-filled air; and but for the iridescent myriads of darting fish, the scintillations of jewel-color, we might well fancy our vessel floating low in air, like a balloon whose buoyancy is feeble.[14]

Lafcadio was rash in the company of Charley. He swam while very hot in the waters of a spring, a plunge into an atmosphere "as cold as death," [15] and came home from his several days in Florida ill with a fever. He felt the effects of his illness into midsummer. He recovered slowly not only from his vacation but also from the harsh bout of work he had endured before the trip.

But when he went back to work, he seemed as if by a jump to have arrived at the gate of new ideas. He had made discoveries in his private reading; he shared these new things with his daily readers. For one thing, he had come upon the contemporary Russian novelists. Whether there was an audience in 1885 for these writers in New Orleans, he did not know, but insisted upon writing about Turgenev, Tolstoy, and "Dostoevski, the Siberian exile," all of whom he had read in French. About *Crime and Punishment* he wrote a Sunday essay informing New Orleans that it was, "perhaps, the most frightful and powerful romance conceived by any modern writer." [16] For another thing, at this time Hearn came into the fullness of his admiration of Herbert Spencer. He had read Spencer's *Principles of Sociology* in 1882, but it was only in July 1885, after a young friend persuaded him to try a second time, that he was confirmed in a permanent idolatry.

The friend was Lieutenant Oscar Terry Crosby of the United States Navy, a nephew of Mrs. A. C. Durno, a hospitable, friendly, social woman, who had persuaded the literary editor of the *Times-Democrat* to come to her house occasionally for good talk and good food. In this kind household Hearn momentarily forgot his wariness. He was ambushed into talking of the books he liked, or of things he had seen. His musical voice dominated the room where the others sat silent to listen. The nephew spoke one day to Hearn of the great enthusiasm he felt for the English philosopher who seemed to be successfully applying the law of evolution to all of human life. Hearn went home to look up Spencer again and was caught by a powerful new interest. He sought out young Crosby for confirmation, agreement, argument. The lieutenant became one of Hearn's perambulating companions.

Out of his own temperament Hearn lent a romance to this new study. Spencer proposed to explain and systematize all of life within the terms of the new theory recently expounded by Charles Darwin, Thomas Huxley, and others. For Hearn there was no deadening and dulling of sentient life in this comprehensive explaining, but a new kind of wonder. He became the most immaterial of materialists.

With the innocence of a bright child, he studied his new master and spread the Spencerian gospel among his friends, some of whom laughed at his naïve ardor. He wrote to H. E. Krehbiel: "Talking of change in opinions, I am really astonished at myself. You know what my fantastic metaphysics were. A friend disciplined me to read Herbert Spencer. I suddenly discovered what a waste of time all my Oriental metaphysics had been. I also discovered, for the first time, how to apply the little general knowledge I possessed. I also learned what an absurd thing positive skepticism is. I also found unspeakable comfort in the sudden and, for me, eternal reopening of the Great Doubt, which renders pessimism ridiculous, and teaches a new reverence for all forms of faith. In short, from the day when I finished the 'First Principles'

—a totally new intellectual life opened for me; and I hope during the next two years to devour the rest of this oceanic philosophy." [17]

To understand the extravagant hope Hearn brought to this new system one must remember that he had had no systematic training in thought, and that Spencer promised beguilingly to make all parts of modern knowledge one sound and solid whole. Hearn had put aside the faith of his childhood (which had been taught him in an atmosphere of hysteria) as irrelevant to the experience of life he had known. Of God, he kept only the god of nature. Spencer let him respect faith even in the act of not believing. Hearn had admired "science" ever since he had picked up the concept in his scattered reading in Cincinnati. Spencer promised to pull into "science" all the various modern studies of man: psychology, sociology, ethics. Hearn had been solitary all his life in the midst of the activity of the world. Spencer held out the hope of significance for the acts of mankind, if not for the individual. Although Hearn did not quite make Spencer's teaching into a faith (he held to another more private one—"I think art gives a new faith . . .") [18] he did set up his own version of Spencer's philosophy as a permanent backdrop to his own life of struggle and crisis. He flavored his writing, from this time on, with evolutionary instances.

And having learned a theory of the mechanics of society from Spencer (and having reinforced himself by further reading in Darwin, Huxley, John Fiske, and others), Hearn no longer so bitterly resented being a victim. His particular misfortunes were a part of a universal process tending obscurely but necessarily toward some distant good end. Having precariously gone through a harrowing amount of "struggle," he prided himself on his sharpness at having "survived." Hearn did not adore what evolution seemed to be accomplishing in the modern world. He fled it when he could. Yet he enjoyed thinking he understood it.

The man who seemed to many of his contemporaries to concern himself only with the personal, the peculiar, and the particularly wayward was in reality always measuring these crotchets against a "scientific" standard. This was a fruitful contradiction in him. It kept him from being altogether precious, although it did not save him from swallowing certain popular errors along with the popular truths of the scientific advance. His belief in "science" had in it a certain saving commonness. It united him with the main current of nineteenth century life.

Spencer was a sort of teacher and preacher in the background of his life. The writers with whom he occupied himself lovingly in translation were his comrades in the ordinary hazards of life, yet they were also exemplars. To him, Gautier, Flaubert, Baudelaire, and the others of the successive train of romantics, realists, naturalists of the time were models in the purity of the word, and in the purity of their devotion to the word. He never particularly admired Zola's theory of naturalism, but he felt a sense of kinship to the man Zola who had been hungry, poor, friendless in his apprentice days, and who had been unmoved from his principles.

Continuing to translate these giants of the nineteenth century, Hearn came to enjoy more intimately two younger writers of exactly his own age: Pierre Loti and Guy de Maupassant. With them he felt a sort of brother closeness. For a decade he vibrated energetically between an imitation of Loti's lush decorativeness and Maupassant's spareness.

Hearn translated Loti again and again. "No writer ever had such an effect on me." [19] Loti was a meteor of the decade of the 1880's, a brightly gifted and facile writer, the kind of man Hearn as a dreamer would like to have been. Loti worshiped the beautiful flesh of mankind upon many different continents. Loti was luminously aware of the beauty of the nonhuman too. Loti celebrated the radiance of the senses in clear bright, colorful phrases, a language which seemed the achievement of Hearn's ideal of a poetic prose. And besides, Loti was fortunate; he wandered the earth, as a French naval officer, on a regular salary, searching for and finding romantic places.

Hearn thought the way the Yankee starved the senses was a scandal, and for him the American southerner had turned out to be disappointingly a kind of esthetic Yankee. Loti made sensation everything. For Hearn, marooned in the arid plain of the American late nineteenth century neglect of the senses, such an emphasis was refreshing. Hearn gave New Orleans the best of Loti's sun-filled romances. He eschewed the foggy ones. His favorites were *Le Roman d'un Spahi,* with its setting of sunbaked French West African desert, and *Le Mariage de Loti,* with its Tahitian jungle background. Hearn enhanced Loti by cutting, concentrating, excising. He translated the memorable phrase "The infinite platitude of the desert," [20] or the vivid bit of exotic description: "Absolutely black butterflies, flying crookedly in somersaults . . ." [21] He could only hint guardedly (because of local prudishness) at the themes of the novels, but served up generous portions of Loti's landscape painting, and essayed now and then a tidbit of his figure painting.

From *Le Roman d'un Spahi,* appeared a sudden and improbable city:

On one side, shutting in the picture, is an arm of the river, with Saint Louis beyond; its straight lines and Babylonian terraces; its bluish whiteness of whitewashing, sprinkled with the red of brickwork, and here and there the yellow plume of a palmtree mounting into the blue sky.[22]

From *Fleurs d'Ennui,* came this apparition of a human figure:

As she passes to and fro through the chamber, she moves with that slight swaying of the hips which is the supreme grace of woman, and which, among us, high heels and narrow shoes have changed into another and artificial something. The women of antiquity must have walked with just such a swaying motion,—which is possible only with bare feet.[23]

Any lengthy translation (Hearn gave only a page or two or three at a time) would have spoiled the effect. For Loti was almost all surface, a brilliant, sensuous equipment brooding upon heat, light, and sex in a contrived image of foreign communities. Hearn, who admired Loti, was not like his idol in any fundamental. Japan was to be the test of the difference between them. Hearn went there in 1890 carrying with him the load of an admiration he felt for Loti's book about Japan, *Madame Chrysanthème.* Yet he found a completely different Japan from the one Loti found.

It was in Japan that Hearn arrived at a just estimate of the Loti whom he had adored. In 1893 he wrote: "To me Loti seems for a space to have looked into Nature's whole splendid burning fulgurant soul . . . He was young. Then the colour and the light faded, and only the worn-out blasé nerves remained; and the poet became,—a little morbid modern affected Frenchman." [24]

His translation of Loti was confined to selected pages; his translation of Maupassant, the only other French writer who occupied him as fully during this time, was more satisfactorily a thing of wholes. He was prevented by the conditions of his employment from handling all the kinds of stories Maupassant wrote. But out of his own reading he chose a remarkable number in a wide range from this contemporary who had a particular significance for him. (Hearn translated between forty and fifty stories; they were the first English versions of these stories; they are perhaps the best in existence, although not readily available today.) Hearn waited for no lapse of time to confirm him nor for other critics to buttress him. He seized upon this recent work of a remarkable contemporary and read, translated, and printed, month after month, the result of his own judgment.

Hearn never corresponded with Maupassant, as he did with Loti. But there was a close, subterranean connection between the two men, although neither one was ever perhaps aware of the fact. Hearn had experienced an unhappy year of early adolescence in precisely the same school background which had helped form the rebellions of Maupassant. They had both—just missing each other—attended the same school, the Institution Ecclésiastique in Yvetot, near Rouen. Apparently Hearn never knew this.

The effort to encompass Maupassant's simplicities (of wording, of meaning) helped Lafcadio Hearn to do his best work in translation. And the effort pushed him to do better work of his own, in a reversion to his own younger simplicities, now understood and projected by a maturer mind. Late in life, Hearn would write more in the manner of Maupassant than of Loti. It was not only the beautifully cool and accurate manner of Maupassant that compelled the respect of his translator, but the matter. Maupassant recalled to Hearn his own short racy reports of Cincinnati low life. Preoccupation with the subtleties of literary ways and means in these sedentary years in New Orleans had taken him a long way from his own quick sympathy for undisguised human nature. Maupassant brought him back to the zest of a plain look at life.

On February 14, 1886, in an essay in praise of Maupassant, he wrote: "Zola would have written a five-hundred page novel upon such a theme as 'Solitude'; Maupassant writes ten and produces an equally durable effect upon the reader's mind. That is the difference!" [25] In trying for English equivalents of the other writer's French sentences, Hearn achieved clean, plain, honest prose. But he achieved also, at times, the extra bite of an imaginative transmutation. The child Simon, in "Simon's Papa," a boy or-phaned and abused, "felt a great crumbling down in his heart." [26] The translation in the 1955 American edition of Maupassant's *Complete Short Stories* reads flatly, "He then felt a great sinking in his heart." Hearn was nearer literally and emotionally to the original: "Alors il sentit dans son coeur un grand écroulement."

In translating from Maupassant, Hearn had to be careful. He had to watch for the limits of patience of his ultimate censor, Page Baker. Only so much Maupassant would go down in New Orleans. At some point or other Baker would draw the line, and Hearn would have to stop, fuming with frustration.

New Orleans began to seem a narrow corner of the universe, changing un-pleasantly, trying to be like Cincinnati. New Orleans was never quite suc-cessful in this effort, but Hearn did not stay to see that something of the Latin, something of the Creole persisted there. It was the normality of progressive industrial America that seemed, in the 1880's, to be threatening his idyl of a Creole city. "Here," he wrote, in New Orleans, in America,

. . . the problem of existence forever stares one in the face with eyes of iron. In-dependence is so hard to obtain,—the churches, the societies, the organizations, the cliques, the humbugs are all working against the man who tries to preserve in-dependence of thought and action.[27]

To get away from the "eyes of iron" of modern existence in the city, he spent longer and longer vacations at Grand Isle. Page Baker tolerated these absences; Hearn's copy could be written anywhere. Even after his prolonged absence from the office in the spring of 1885 (if one can trust an undated letter to Krehbiel), Hearn managed a few days on the beach at Grand Isle. "For bathing—sea-bathing—I prefer our own Creole islands in the Gulf to any place in Florida." [28]

At first the prodigality of nature and human nature on the island dazzled him. He could not decide what to write about. He tried short stories. He tried a melodramatic novel. These things would not do, and he gave them up with relief. With the artist's uneasy faith, he simply waited for sensation to crystallize into idea.

It was only the next year, in the spring of 1886, that Hearn realized that he already had his idea, that he had held it in his hand ever since one evening in 1883, but had not till now recognized it as something he could use. On that night, three years before, Hearn had shared a dinner and an evening of conversation which George Washington Cable had arranged in honor of the illustrator Joseph Pennell. Cable fell to talking of the hurricanes which regularly ravaged the Louisiana coast. He told them of the disaster of 1856 and the horror which seized New Orleans when news came that Ile Dernière, the favorite vacation place of the day, had been swept clean by a storm. Out of a group of summer visitors assembled late and recklessly to dance in the hall of a wooden hotel near the beach, ignoring the accelerating storm, hoping it would pass them by, only one human soul survived. The storm had smashed the hotel and washed the dancers out to sea. The survivor was a child, a little girl. She was found by a fisherman and brought home to his wife. These two lonely, childless people kept her as their own. It was only years later that a Creole hunter recognized the girl from some trinket she was wearing. She was brought back to her proper place in New Orleans society, but she did not love the civilization that had reclaimed her. She rebelled, returned to the coast, married a fisherman and, as far as Hearn knew, lived there still.

In 1883, when Hearn first heard the story, he had not seen the Louisiana coast. He saw in 1886, now that he knew Grand Isle, that he could envision the sea, the coast, the hotel, the visitors, the fisherman and his wife. Grand Isle, in the 1880's, occupied precisely the situation in relationship to New Orleans that Ile Dernière had had in the 1850's—before it was smashed by a hurricane, and left a poor bare sandbar.

Hearn resolved to write his own version of the story of the hurricane and the lost child. Now that he had the thin line of a plot, he could use everything he had observed and experienced on Grand Isle. He announced his project in a letter to Elizabeth Bisland in April 1887. Since she had gone (to New York) he could communicate with her: "I am trying to find the

Orient at home—to apply the same methods of poetical-prose treatment to modern local and living themes. . . . The subject of the whole is one which you love as I—Louisiana Gulf-life." [29]

This book, the most important he had yet tried to write, exercised him to his depths. It was not just an experiment in technique, to make a highly wrought language parallel emotion and mood; it was an attempt to re-create a scene he knew in his blood and bones. There would be more passion in *Chita,* as he came to call the book, than there had been in his *Chinese Ghosts.* This was a new kind of translation, from life, and not from books. And the theme implicit in the story, the appeal of the wild, the natural, the free, was a mood as native to him as the beat of his heart. It was as a spontaneous romantic that he wrote this classic romantic tale.

By the time Hearn announced his ambition to Elizabeth Bisland, he was in the act of accomplishing it. He had visited Grand Isle two or possibly three times after his first visit in 1884. He began writing *Chita* while on Grand Isle in 1886. He finished the book on another visit there in the early months of 1887. In between these visits, in the offices of the newspaper, in his quiet room, whenever he could find time to work upon his island story, he forgot New Orleans, forgot the *Times-Democrat,* forgot Lafcadio Hearn. He stood again on the beach at Grand Isle. Placing himself there in his imagination, he saw in his mind's eye everything that the child Chita had seen, experienced everything that she had experienced. And by intensifying all the stories of storms told him by many Grand Islanders, he whipped up a fearful hurricane of the imagination, fit to wash Last Island away.

He was most sure of his theme when he stood upon the actual sand of the coast, or swam in the lettuce-green water of the Gulf. In July 1886 he wrote a letter to Rudolph Matas (who was away from New Orleans on a visit to Spain) full of the joy of indubitable inspiration:

My first swim made every muscle as sore as if I had been beaten with a stick; but at the end of the first week I hope to be as brown as a seal and as hard as a piece of wood. I am going to remain a month. Meanwhile I have separated myself from my beloved books, being determined to devote myself wholly to literary work, not to literary *pleasure.* . . . At half-past four I rise to bathe and to view the birth of the morning—the advent of the light—the blossoming of the vast and Mystical Rose of Sunrise. Sea-birds follow me out, and fly low over me, with their sinister little sharp cries; and I feel at intervals weird little touches, as of phantom hands,—the bodies of tiny fish touching my own.

So I wait for the poet's pentecost,—the inspiration of nature, the descent of the Tongues of Fire. And I think they will come, when the wild skies brighten, and the sun of the Mexican Gulf reappears for his worshippers,—with hymns of wind and sea, and the prayers of birds.[30]

He grasped the essence of his story in such rare moments of ecstasy, but in the commonplace intervals between these moments he was as business-like and careful as he could be. For the human part of the story, he seized upon the image of his splendid friend, Dr. Matas, to stand for the father of the lost child. He wrote to Matas in March 1887 asking for specific and immediate help in a small problem of colloquial talk:

I would like a few words of greeting, in Spanish, in Catalan, or both—such as a child might be taught to say to a father, coming home, every evening.
What is a good phrase for "poor little girl" and "poor little child"—phrases of compassion—short and quick—uttered in a moment of awful excitement?
Half my sketch is done; the other half, alas!—is still a chaos of notes, perfected pages, outlines, idea in embryo,—all tangled up; a half-suggested thing, like a *subject* partially dissected.[31]

For his own unrealistic telling of the story Hearn could dispense with the literal ending. His child of the coast was never snatched away from her foster-parents. Her life was not tragic. It was the father, searching for the lost daughter, who was tragic. His finding and losing her almost simultaneously as death struck him down was the only real reminder of common human fate in the story. The rest was lyrical—a song of solitude and the sea, and man's relationship not to man but to nature.

The book, as it grew into shape in his imagination, became a thing of moods and images. It fell into three parts, three moods of a tone poem. Part I, "The Legend of L'Île Dernière," held the mood of the destroying sea. Its climax was the image of the fragile wooden hall and its dancers smashed by the wind and waves of the storm. Part II, "Out of the Sea's Strength," held the mood of the calm sea. Its image was that of a child playing by the shore. Part III, "The Shadow of the Tide," held the mood of human loss. Its image was a dying man stretching out his hand toward love.

Chita was weak in plot, weak even in ordinary humanity. It was as if a story had been told by a gull or a great wave. The attempt to make a plot, to round the corners of human suspense (not the storm's suspense, which was superb), was awkwardly carpentered. Yet *Chita* was the rise to a youthful climax. It was a spontaneous, fervent emotional prayer to the wildness of sea, sky, sand, and marsh of the first land the writer had loved since he was a boy in Ireland.

In finishing *Chita* Hearn experienced a rare, extravagant moment of hope. Publishers seemed to want his manuscripts. He was apparently no longer bound to the regularity of a job such as he held in New Orleans. There were probabilities in the air. In February 1887 he wrote in this mood of expectation to his friend W. D. O'Connor. He told him that he had become a contributor to *Harper's Magazine* and that he was "going to have the honour of a short sketch of myself in it—of course, in connection with the New Southern Literary Movement. And I will also soon have the pleasure of sending you a new production, just got, or getting out by a Boston house—my 'Chinese Ghosts'; brief studies in poetical prose, if you like." [32]

The Boston house was Roberts Brothers. Ticknor had rejected the book, but acceptance by a smaller firm soothed Hearn. Probably he was pleased, too, by the attention the book received in *The Nation* for May 26, 1887. The unsigned reviewer seemed to think that "the author, possibly, has been in the Middle Kingdom," and he added: "His style is exquisitely polished, his vocabulary is the cream of language, and his six stories are told with literary art." But a certain "lascivious coloring," as the reviewer rather heavily put it, displeased him, and he ended with a nice compromise of disapproval and encouragement: "Altogether the impression made upon a Western reader of Mr. Hearn's semi-Chinese production is not pleasant," but there is in it "a promise of better things to come." [33]

With his *Ghosts* published and reviewed, his *Chita* completed, Hearn was expansive. For him expansiveness meant irresistibly the desire to travel. And so he ended his cheerful letter to O'Connor: "How delightful it would be if you could take a trip with me in March, to the Floridian springs, to windy Key West, or to the palmier Antilles, where we might watch together the rose-blossoming of extraordinary sunrises, the conflagration of apocalyptic sunsets. Is it impossible? My dreams now are full of fantastic light—a Biblical light: and the World-Ghost, all blue, promises inspiration. Could we not celebrate the Blue Ghost's pentecost together? Affectionately . . ." [34]

Hearn was nudged on toward a break with the *Times-Democrat* by a development in the management of the paper. About this time the Louisiana Lottery Company—a thriving and many-sided organization—gained financial control of the paper; no member of the staff was let go, but there was a general uneasiness among staff members about matters of tenure and policy. Hearn applied himself to the study of the schedules of steamship lines in the Caribbean. He believed that with a regular if intermittent income he could now travel and write independently.

In March he wrote to O'Connor persuasively (he was attempting to encourage and persuade Lafcadio Hearn): "In Trinidad I can see South American flora in all their splendour; in Jamaica and, especially, in Martinique, I can get good chances to study those Creole types which are so closely allied to our own. I want to finish a tiny volume of notes of travel—Impressionist-work—always keeping to my dream of a *poetical prose*." [35]

A new friendship, perhaps the last he made in New Orleans, inclined him particularly toward Martinique. One day in 1887, looking about in a book-shop, he made the acquaintance of a young Creole, Miss Leona Queyrouze. She knew of Lafcadio Hearn, and admired him and prevailed upon him to call upon her. At the end of his first visit to the shuttered, well bred Creole house, when Hearn had taken tea and admired her books, he said to her abruptly, "I would like to look upon you as a younger brother; would you mind?" [36] On this basis he fixed the relationship, and came again.

Leona Queyrouze made a small book out of her recollection of his visits. After he left New Orleans, Hearn wrote to Matas: "Sorry you did not meet Miss Q. Would so much have liked your idea of her. I am not *sceptical* now; but do not know what to do. I fear to write to her. All fire and nerves and scintillation; a tropical being in mind and physique, and I could never be to her what I should like to be." [37]

Each time he came to call, the door was opened to him by Marie, Miss Queyrouze's maid, a light-skinned colored girl from Martinique. Hearn was very curious of her speech and asked her many questions about her native land. Miss Queyrouze remembered that Marie called him, in her childlike Creole fashion, "Missié Lacadee." She recalled too that Hearn talked French to Marie and said to her: ". . . Tell me something new about your beautiful country . . . You know I am going there sometime, before long." [38]

In May two events were decisive in causing Hearn to act. *Chita* was accepted for publication in *Harper's Magazine* and presumably for book publication later. And the article by Charles W. Coleman, Jr., "The Recent Movement in Southern Literature," appeared in the May issue of the magazine. It annoyed Hearn slightly for its tone of personality and gossip, but the pages devoted to him, side by side with those about Cable and Harris and others, seemed the assurance of his acceptance as a writer in the competitive American scene.

Hearn resigned from the *Times-Democrat* as of the end of May 1887. He left his books in boxes at Mrs. Courtney's with instructions to Rudolph Matas to take charge of them and send them to him when he wrote. He had then only to say goodbye to Mrs. Courtney, Matas, Page Baker, Leona Queyrouze, and a few others, and go.

By going, he stepped out of security as he had done ten years earlier. It had been a beneficent decade, a long slow time of sauntering under the sun and shade of the wide Louisiana sky. He had changed during that time as the city changed. He was a surer man than he was when he first set foot upon the levee. As he had once turned his back on Cincinnati, he now turned away from New Orleans. He had little time for nostalgia. He looked past gratitude and regret toward the expectation of new things: the iron streets of New York, the sea, and archipelagoes of islands full of promise.

12 ❧ Underneath Pelée

Upon a day in July 1887 Lafcadio Hearn stood at the rail of the steamer *Barracouta* more than a week out from New York as the ship made its way deliberately into the bay of St. Pierre, Martinique, advancing through a fleet of island vessels, brushing dangerously the impudent packing-case canoes of the boys who dived for coins the passengers flung over the rail.

On the trip southward the small man, blind in one eye, peering at sights through a collapsible pocket telescope, had seemed an odd and separate figure to the planters going home to the various islands, and to the gold hunters on the way to British Guiana. If Hearn was conscious of the curious glances cast his way by these men of affairs at the intensity of his absorption in things that could bring him no gain, he ignored the fact in looking greedily at every succeeding island the *Barracouta* passed in review: St. Croix, St. Kitts, Montserrat, Dominica, and finally the violet bulk of Martinique. The far-off view of the island resolved itself into a shallow half-moon bay, a city, and a mountain, as the ship moved nearer and nearer to the land. The prosperous port of St. Pierre, facing the Caribbean near the northern end of the island, seemed overhung by the steep green slant of Mont Pelée, a splendid single peak toward which all the other tormented uprearings of the island led as to a climax. The city, built upon stone terraces, was a streak of yellow-bricked façades and red-tiled roofs compressed between the sea and the humped green hills which were the lower parts of the volcano.

In this landfall Hearn's sense of discovery was as startled and delighted as any gold hunter's in stubbing his toe upon a field of nuggets. He knew that he had found one of his particular places. During the *Barracouta's* short stay in St. Pierre Bay (the city was only a port of call on the cruise southward to Guiana), Hearn confirmed his first happy intuition by a hasty exploration of the city and its surrounding hills. St. Pierre seemed a bright pocket of out-of-date customs and beliefs. The dress, speech, manners, animation, and grace of its "fruit-colored" population were infinitely attractive to the susceptible voyager. Walking the stone pavements upon which the bare feet of the city's people made a whispering sound, Hearn knew that he could make matter out of this place.

The journey which had brought him to this unpremeditated goal had begun the previous spring on the day he left New Orleans. On that hopeful morning of early June he closed his desk at the *Times-Democrat,* and left Page Baker's domain permanently behind him—setting out for the dangers and delights of New York City. On the way, he stopped in Cincinnati, going out of his most direct route in order to see Henry Watkin once more.

Without warning he appeared in the familiar print shop, and saw, over the shoulder of the older man, who, crying, embraced him, both the long-remembered Sphinx and the grandfather clock. Watkin's shop was all he cared to see of the city; he was afraid of Cincinnati. He remained with Watkin all one afternoon. When he went out through the door late in the afternoon to catch his train to New York, he thought that it would be easy to come back again; but he never did, and he never saw Watkin again.

The train east carried Hearn very quickly to the dreadful city of his imagination. He did not have to enter the city alone. Henry Krehbiel and his wife were at the railroad terminus in New Jersey to guide him through the confusion of arrival. They offered him the shelter of their apartment on West Fifty-seventh Street. Thus, under their protection, Hearn let himself relax, and enjoyed the size, power, and splendor of New York, the quality of "wealth-force and mind-power" [2] as he termed it at once in a letter to Henry Watkin.

Krehbiel, who had been benignly sure of himself when he was only a police reporter with large ambitions in Cincinnati, had expanded ten years later in New York into a figure of solid authority. He edited the music column of the New York *Tribune* fluently and weightily. Hearn saw in his old friend the pride of place a journalist might occupy in the city. Krehbiel's contented tenure of such a position, and the happy settledness of his domestic life, gave Hearn a twinge of wistful envy.

Krehbiel discovered during the days that Hearn was with him that he did not now altogether approve of his friend. He feared something apparently unstable in him. Hearn seemed to be as juvenile, ingenuous, and reckless at thirty-seven as he had been at twenty-seven. Yet he had obvious gifts; he might do something remarkable. Krehbiel guided Hearn about the city, and helped him do the small but necessary things to make him known in New York's journalistic and publishing world. He introduced him to some of his fellow employees on the *Tribune*. He pushed Hearn into going personally to call upon Henry M. Alden, the editor of *Harper's Magazine*. Alden, who had recently accepted *Chita*, was keenly interested in meeting the writer from New Orleans with whom he had only corresponded. He found Hearn more extraordinary than he had expected. Alden was at this time the most eminent of all American magazine editors. Hearn was aware of the importance of this friendship. He wrote succinctly to Matas: "Mr. Alden pets me, almost like Page did." [3]

The strangeness of New York fostered another sudden intimacy. Hearn came to know Elizabeth Bisland better in New York than he ever had in the long years of their acquaintance in New Orleans. Recently Miss Bisland had written him to congratulate him upon the publication of his book *Some Chinese Ghosts*. He had answered gratefully, and they had achieved an ease in corresponding that they had never had face to face. In New York, Hearn ventured to call upon her. His first effort failed, but he made an entertaining story of his failure in a note he sent her:

DEAR MISS BISLAND,—A small creature rang the bell at 136 Madison Avenue. A large and determined concierge responded, and the following converse ensued:
  S.C.—"Miss Bisland—?"
  C.—"No, sir!"
  S.C.—"Miss E-liz-a-beth Bisland—?"
  C.—"No, sir!"
  S.C.—"Isn't this 136 Madison Avenue?"
  C.—"Yes.—Used to live here.—Moved."
  S.C.—"Do you not know where—?"
  C.—"No, sir." . . .
Then I wandered away down a double row of magnificent things that seemed less buildings than petrifactions—astonishments of loftiness and silent power—and wondered how Miss Elizabeth Bisland must have felt when she first trod these enormous pavements and beheld these colossal dreams of stone trying to touch the moon. And reaching my friend Krehbiel's house I made this brief record of my vain effort to meet the grey eyes of E. B.

                                        LAFCADIO HEARN [4]

The second time he went out into the city to find her, he succeeded. He spent an evening bewildered by enjoyment. She talked to him of his own writing, and of how they both loved Grand Isle. "I met Miss Bisland again," he wrote to Matas. "She has expanded mentally and physically into one of the most superb women you could wish to converse with. I am inclined to suspect her alleged cruelty and hardness of character are to be accounted for by the impatience of a very keen strong mind with trivialities and egotisms." [5]

During these hurried days in New York, Hearn found old relations changing and new ones coming into existence. He continued to admire Henry Krehbiel but no longer deferred to him. He began over again with Elizabeth Bisland. In Henry Alden he discovered a new friend and adviser. Although he was harassed by the problem of getting off for the West Indies, he found time for some pleasant irrelevancies. He went for a walking trip up the Hudson with Krehbiel. He went alone to Coney Island to find by swimming in it that the Atlantic Ocean was cold. But at the end of these weeks in New York he had not secured any practical help for his expedition. Alden did not offer him any advance for work that might be done, or even any assurance of publication. He simply held out to Hearn the offer of a lively interest in anything the writer might send him from the Caribbean. Therefore, with no more money in hand than he had had when he set off from New Orleans (but not much less, since he had scrimped on living expenses by staying with the Krehbiels), Hearn got himself ready to go.

The Krehbiels accompanied Hearn to the dock on the day he left New York. Hearn was conscious of a perceptible cooling between himself and them. He no longer asked or took Krehbiel's advice. He had also overstayed his welcome. Mrs. Krehbiel had been friendly at first, but her hospitality had tightened into something merely formal. The Krehbiels in seeing Hearn go, and Hearn in bidding them farewell, experienced on both sides something of relief. Hearn had accepted too much from them to be quite happy in their company. Having launched himself outside the regularity of salaried journalism, and yet being determined to go on writing, Hearn inevitably asked too much of friends, and so ruined friendships.

But in turning away from the Krehbiels waving goodbye to him from the pier, Hearn dropped his responsibilities and became for a time simply an organism for registering pure sensation. As the *Barracouta*, a "long, narrow, graceful steel steamer, with two masts, and an orange-yellow chimney," [6] moved steadily south from New York toward the West Indies, Hearn measured each day the increase of blue in the water. "I ask the ship's doctor whether it is really true that the West Indian waters are any bluer than these. He looks a moment at the sea, and replies, *"Oh, yes!"* Upon the third day one who knows, a native of the French island of Guadeloupe, "observes that the sea is 'beginning to become blue.' " [7] Upon the sixth and seventh days the sea began to be peopled by ghosts of islands, peaks seen far off. And, "The first tropical visitor . . . boarded our ship: a wonderful fly, shaped like a common fly, but at least five times larger. His body is a beautiful shining black; his wings seem ribbed and jointed with silver, his head is jewel-green, with exquisitely cut emeralds for eyes." [8]

The first city of the Indies he saw, Frederiksted in St. Croix, was not a disappointment: "The water of the harbor is transparent and pale green. One can see many fish, and some small sharks. White butterflies are fluttering about us in the blue air. Naked black boys are bathing on the beach . . ." [9] The trip's climax occurred farther south in the Windward Islands. It was in St. Pierre, "As under a perpendicular sun, I wandered down the narrow, curious, yellow painted streets of Martinique," [10] that Hearn realized his surrender to the tropics. It was too much, he wrote Rudolph Matas humorously, to be staidly respectable, or even prudent, in such a place.

Before he set out on his adventures his young medical friend had lectured him for his own good with mock solemnity, but also with some seriousness, about desirable prudences. Hearn reported first from New York how well he had so far obeyed: "I have observed one of your prophylactic injunctions so far; I have been strictly chaste. I think also that I shall be at all events very temperate all the time . . ." [11] But easygoing Martinique had undone him. "My great and good resolves came to a furious termination at the delicious, dreamy little town of St. Pierre, Martinique. . . . It's all very well to speak of the sy—coccus and the other; but I'd like to see *you* live from one of these purple ports to another, in a condition of compulsory laziness, and in view of all the tantalizing things, and continue to neglect the Apples of Paradise." [12]

Reacting through the entire range of his being, from physical to imaginative to cerebral, Hearn found delight. He wrote more circumspectly his joy to Elizabeth Bisland: "Imagine old New Orleans, the dear quaint part of it, young and idealized . . . made all tropical, with narrower and brighter streets, all climbing up the side of a volcanic peak to a tropical forest, or descending in terraces of steps to the sea;—fancy our Creole courts filled with giant mangoes and columnar palms (a hundred feet in height sometimes); and everything painted in bright colours, and everybody in a costume of more than Oriental picturesqueness;—and astonishments of half-breed beauty;—and a grand tepid wind enveloping the city in one perpetual perfumed caress . . ." Such a place was St. Pierre. "I love it as if it were a human being." [13]

His time in the port was short. The *Barracouta* fired its signal gun and rolled a battery of echoes against the side of Mont Pelée. Hearn went on board reluctantly to finish his tour of the islands and his visit to Guiana. Although he visited Barbados, and the coast of Demarara, and touched at Trinidad and St. Lucia on the way back, he remained loyal to Martinique. He abandoned the *Barracouta* when it stopped once more under the shadow of Pelée on its way north to New York. It would return on another round of the islands in the fall. He could return to the city then, and carry with him a stack of sketches to sell to Henry Alden. And if he sold them, he might return to Martinique before the winter winds chilled his susceptible bones, and stay indefinitely. Hearn acted on this plan by turning his back upon the ship before it had sailed out of sight. He picked up his light bag and made his way into the city to find an inexpensive room in which to spend the rest of the summer.

Hearn returned to New York in September on the stub end of his ticket and his resources. No friend met him at the dock; there was no buffer between him and the city. The blasting, impersonal breath of New York shriveled him. He did not venture far into it, but stumbled blindly into the door of the first waterfront hotel he came upon, the United States Hotel, at the corners of Water and Fulton streets.

Krehbiel was out of town. Miss Bisland was out of town. Krehbiel did not make any effort to see Hearn when he returned to the city. Hearn wrote to Miss Bisland when she came back, but declined to see her. He sought out only Alden with a desperate single purpose, and pushed before him the long, segmented sketch he had made of his past summer's experience, an essay he called "A Midsummer Trip to the Tropics."

Alden liked the essay and bought it immediately, paying Hearn a prompt and needed $700, and promising its early appearance in serial form in *Harper's Magazine*. (The *Magazine* still held Hearn's *Chita*, as yet unpublished.) Hearn had a few things to do to get ready to go back to Martinique. He had to buy another steamship ticket. He had to buy clothes. He had to get in a good supply of the yellow paper he always used. He felt that he would need a camera to illustrate the sketches he was going to write.

Seeing Hearn rattling about so blindly on the dangerous streets, Alden took pity on him and invited him to his house at Metuchen, New Jersey. It was a fresh, virginal, New England sort of house upholding all the elder virtues of the region from which the family had been transplanted. Alden himself was an epitomized New Englander. He was the eighth in the line of direct descent from John Alden. He was born in Mount Tabor, Vermont, labored as a bobbin boy in a mill in Hoosick Falls, New York, and worked his way through Williams College. He taught school and contributed a few articles to periodicals before he was hired by the Harper publishing firm in 1863. He became editor of *Harper's Magazine* in 1869. In 1887, when Hearn first knew him and was impressed by him, Alden was a figure of great authority in the publishing world, a man of fine presence with his good clean-cut features and beautifully groomed silvered hair and beard. He was a benevolent, conscientious purveyor of good things, and also a shrewd manager. He had pushed his magazine's circulation beyond its near competitor, the older *Atlantic Monthly.*

Hearn enjoyed the untempestuous atmosphere of this house in the country, and the society of Alden's family. He always got on best with the young, those who had not yet been completely formed by the world into which they were growing up. He charmed and was charmed by Alden's young daughter, Annie Alden. It was to her he wrote, in a moment of dissatisfaction with Martinique, how well he had liked Metuchen: "You don't know what pleasure your letter gave me. It made me see Metuchen again,—the parlor, the garden, the road bordered with golden-rod,—the fields . . . How I wish for just twenty minutes of that light bright northern sky." [14]

This visit established Henry Alden as a new and necessary mentor in Hearn's life. Alden took the place that Krehbiel, and then Page Baker, had once occupied. Krehbiel had lost his place through the attrition of years of separation and the gradual loss of common enthusiasms. He had not regained it when Hearn came again into association with him in New York. Page Baker, whom Hearn had much admired in his first years with the *Times-Democrat* had lost his place through Hearn's impatience of the paper's cautious policy of censorship of what he wrote and translated. He had also lost almost all Hearn's regard, for a time, when in New York Miss Bisland told Hearn how once years before Page Baker had shown her one of Hearn's incautious letters from Grand Isle, one in which he had been harshly critical of her. Hearn then wrote a rash letter to Baker, the "most insulting," [15] said the editor of the *Times-Democrat,* that he had ever received. It took years of silence, and then a characteristic, fresh approach from Hearn—as if he did not remember the incident—to bring the two men back into a wary kind of friendship. Thereafter they corresponded irregularly between Japan and Louisiana for the remaining years of Hearn's life. (In 1907, three years after Hearn's death, Baker wrote: "He was a rare genius and in some respects, a most extraordinary human being, but taken altogether he was quite impossible.") [16]

Recklessly making and unmaking heroes, Hearn had always a need for them. In 1887 Alden filled this necessary place. Alden, with his fine manners, settled opinions, success in a world which frightened yet allured the writer, seemed the most to be admired of friends, and the most kindly of advisers.

After the conclusion of his visit with the Aldens, Hearn returned to the United States Hotel to make his small preparations for going. "I am going back to the Tropics," he wrote confidently to Rudolph Matas, "probably for many years. My venture has been more successful than I had hoped: and I find myself able to abandon journalism, with all its pettiness, cowardices, selfishnesses, forever." [17] He did not tell his friend that he had spent $400 of his slender $700 for a camera he did not know how to use. Saying goodbye to Miss Bisland whom he had not had the courage to see again he wrote: "Goodbye, with best regards and something a little more, too." [18]

On October 2nd Hearn took ship for the West Indies. He had again booked passage on the familiar *Barracouta*. Nothing interrupted the prolonging of expectation but an unlucky stumble; he wrote jauntily of the accident to Annie Alden: "P.S. I forgot to tell you that I fell down a hatchway of the *Barracouta* without any other result than surprise." [19] With no more bad luck he came again to the now familiar indentation of Caribbean blue which was the bay of St. Pierre, Martinique.

Here, in the late autumn of the tropics, which was not a blazing and a fading away but a quickening into new life under the drying trade wind, Hearn tried to become an inhabitant, a citizen, an unnoticed comer and goer on the streets. But at first it was difficult. In this small, isolated tropical city a stranger was immediately remarked and frankly stared at. Hearn's remarkable energy in walking the narrow sidewalks in the blazing sun, his pertinacity in lugging with him a heavy, awkward camera, his persistence in cajoling canoe boys and washerwomen into letting him take their pictures made him a momentary celebrity. But the boys who lazed away hours between ships' docking soon grew used to him and his attempts to speak Creole to them. And the idlers on the bridges over the Rivière Roxelane soon became accustomed to seeing him among them as they enjoyed the pretty spectacle of the younger washerwomen up to their knees in cold water, beating the white wash upon the boulders of the stream, and crying reproaches upward to them for their bold eyes. Hearn soon went about his own urgent business almost unnoticed, getting to know the topography and human geography of every steep street of the city, stopping to dream upon the blue line of sea and sky enlarging to tremendous dimensions as he climbed sweating up the cobblestones to his room. He was busy, but puzzled, almost dazed, by the richness of his material. He did not yet know what to do with it, or what his role here was to be.

It was a surfeit of beauty. It had knocked all the poetry out of him, as he said. Description, however sensitive and finely drawn, was not enough. He was already dissatisfied with what he had done in "A Midsummer Trip." That had been pure impressionism, good enough in its way, but now that he was in the tropics and of the tropics, and felt the vital thrust of its life, the mere painting of pretty pictures seemed a stupid kind of activity. He wanted to learn, to feel, and with the old reflex of the newspaperman, to report. And yet he did not want to chatter with the confident mindlessness of the daily feature-story writer. He made jokes of the predicaments in which he got in trying to talk to people or to take pictures of them, but he did not pretend to believe that this chatter, which made entertaining letters, was the thing he wanted to do in his yet unwritten essays about the real and unselfconscious life of Martinique.

Miss Alden of Metuchen was the recipient of such a bonus of little considered and amusing fare when he wrote to her of the disastrous day when he first tried to photograph the little canoe boys:

There were 17 *canotiers* that day; and I could not tell which was which,—for when I went to pay off, every little brown, black, and yellow boy in the neighborhood took all his clothes off, and joined in,—so that it seemed as if I had a hundred boys to pay off.

Then I got the 17 in a line, surrounded by a shrieking mob. I paid at one end, and as fast as I did so, the recipients ran to the other end of the line,—so as to make the paying seem eternal and incomprehensible. I ran away!

And the horrid little naked boys ran after me. I took refuge in the fourth story of the tallest building in St. Pierre,—the house of the photographer De Pay; and a mob collected before the door.

There was a general attack up the stairway:

. . . And police had to be sent for so that I could leave the building. Then everybody began to cry; and I felt quite sorry—but what else could I do? In the afternoon, all financial troubles were adjusted; and order prevailed.

My next story will be about two of these horrid little boys.[20]

His letter had the elements of an amusing article, of the kind Alden might have used. But this was not what Hearn wanted to do with the "petits canotiers." That distillation had to wait a slow growth in his imagination. He did not want to show off these people as odd or different. He wanted to be able to write about the islanders as if he had lived their lives himself.

While waiting for his impressions to settle into proper shapes and sequences, Hearn became uneasy about his income. Alden had paid for *Chita* —at least for its use as a magazine story—the previous spring, and had given him quick money for "A Midsummer Trip," but neither piece had been used in the magazine as yet, and Alden seemed to be in no hurry for new material. If Hearn had known in October 1887, when he returned to Martinique, that it would be October 1888 before any new material from him appeared in Alden's magazine, he might have despaired. (*Chita* appeared in April 1888, and "A Midsummer Trip" in three installments in July, August, and September of the same year.) After having had his hopes buoyed up by flattering attentions in New York, Hearn had thought that his literary way would be smoothed by one acceptance after another. Now, with expenses for his camera eating away his short supply of dollars, he saw the end of his resources approaching. And he did not even have the comfort of knowing what he wanted to write.

He enjoyed a modest room, No. 6 Rue du Bois-Morin, on a narrow street overlooking the harbor and the green peaks curving down to the water. He could look over his shoulder each morning to see if Pelée were clear or not, or down the steep slant to the docks to see what ships were in. Each morning he ate a piece of fruit and drank black coffee, took up a towel, and made his way down the stone terraces to the beach for a brief swim. As he wrote to Miss Annie, this was a daily ritual of many of the business and professional men of the city: "After half an hour, or an hour's swim, we go home, or to offices; and the day's work begins." [21]

Each morning in November he hurried back to his room to spend longer and longer days at work upon a story his ambition had at last decided upon. It was to be of the same length as *Chita* and was to be called "Lys." It was to tell the effect of a journey to the cold North upon an ingenuous Creole girl, a nature made by the tropical suns and rains. And, running ahead of himself, he had an enthusiastic plan for a pendant to "Lys," a story to describe the "total fascination and enervation of a Northern nature by the tropics. I am going to keep it for the last," he told Alden, "because I don't think you could put it in the Magazine. It will be called "Nini." [22] Hearn knew that he was not yet ready to write with authority about the island, and could only search in himself for a subject.

In a mood of morbid uncertainty he suddenly had his books, which were stored in New Orleans, sent to Henry Alden's house in Metuchen. It was perhaps a gesture to compensate his editor for the work he was not sending him. These books were the only things of value he owned. Hearn called upon Dr. Matas to send them, and Alden to care for them, as if he were conferring a favor. He hoped, he wrote to Alden, that the books would be an amusement for him and his family, and he pictured them upon the shelves in Alden's house in a room he remembered from his visit there in September. He sent Matas some money to pay for the freight, but apparently it was not enough, and both Matas and Alden had to spend some of their own to oblige Hearn in his generosity. One can discern, through Hearn's replies to letters from Alden, that Alden found the care of the books onerous, but that he shouldered the burden conscientiously. He took out an insurance policy for $2,000, and he catalogued them, something that Hearn had never done.

His editor let Hearn know something of the responsibility the books were to him, and Hearn, intensely touchy, was stung. He felt a reproach for this care he had put on the other man, and possibly too a reproach concerning money he may have borrowed and not repaid. He sent Alden what was in effect a will, leaving his books to his editor in case he himself should die. Whether Alden's letters justified this move cannot be known. Only Hearn's precipitous answer is in existence: "I also send a little document you spoke of,—an olograph [*sic*] that is enough to settle your claim to the books, in extreme circumstances." [23]

But at last, triumphantly, on December 8, 1887, Hearn wrote: "I send you 'Lys'; it gave me a good deal of work, and still I can't tell what it is." [24] He asked, almost apologetically but urgently, that if Alden liked it, he send payment for it immediately in French francs. Hearn's letter tried to mask his anxiety to sell the story and receive prompt payment. He wrote from a new address, Morne Rouge, a small mountain town two thousand feet higher into the interior of the island.

On the coast hot and humid weather continued into the normally dry season, and an epidemic threatened. Smallpox had walked off a boat and scattered some cases around the harbor. At Morne Rouge, Hearn enjoyed a freedom from contagion and heat, but shivered susceptibly in air that seemed like October in New York. He noted interestedly the stunted palms of this higher altitude, and watched the top of Pelée cover and uncover, and waited for Alden's answer.

When the rains abated, he walked the looping, twisting roads across the mountaintops nearby, and met the carrier girls coming and going with their heavy loads. He stopped to talk to the good-hearted woman who rented him his room, or to her daughter, and was soon caught in the interest of digging out of their shyness the many *zombi* stories they knew, and the Creole songs they sang. He began almost absentmindedly taking notes. If he hesitated over a word or a phrase he had help near at hand:

I call upon Adou to explain. [So Hearn wrote later.] Adou is the daughter of the kind old capresse from whom I rent my room in this little mountain cottage. The mother is almost precisely the color of cinnamon; the daughter's complexion is brighter—the ripe tint of an orange. Adou tells me Creole stories and tim-tim. Adou knows all about ghosts, and believes in them. So does Adou's extraordinarily tall brother, Yébé—my guide among the mountains.[25]

Adou and Yébé's cottage had a *chapelle* over the door, a shrine inhabited by a doll-like virgin. Everywhere along the mountain paths and roads were shrines, large and small; and the speech, manners, and devotions of these country people showed Hearn that these shrines were living centers of worship. In Martinique, for the first time since his adolescent rebellion, he saw the faith of his childhood as a possible, poetic system of belief. His mind did not relent, but his imagination was aroused.

Some time later Hearn had a letter from Henry Alden. His editor had not liked "Lys" at all, and did not hold back from telling Hearn why. The vehemence of Alden's opinion stunned the lonely, isolated writer. Here was a blow both to his pride and to his pocket. Alden reproached Hearn for what he conceived was a lack of moral fiber in the story. Hearn had exhibited at some length the disintegration of purpose in northern natures cast upon tropical shores. Hearn in his shock agreed abjectly with everything Alden said. Whether the story was as reprehensible as Alden thought, or as poorly written as Hearn came to think, no later reader could judge; Hearn destroyed "Lys" in the first form in which he wrote it. He later included a very slight sketch under the same name in his *Two Years in the French West Indies.*

Hearn's reply to Alden did not hide his deep dejection:

Your letter was not at all harsh;—too kind, perhaps; and, as in most such cases, *opened my eyes.* I saw at once the faults, and judged them probably as severely— no, more severely than you.

"Chita" was a long slow piece of work, I had no right to attempt such a thing as "Lys," under present circumstances: perhaps I was mentally sick when I wrote it. I must confine myself to brief sketches until I can feel secure to attempt a good solid careful piece of long duration.

I am not sure of myself now at all,—may be mentally out of gear without knowing it.[26]

Hearn did not at first admit to himself the resentment he felt at Alden's confident judgment upon him as a moral being and a writer. At the moment he yielded completely to the other's sentence. "I thank you more for having made me see my faults and be ashamed of them, than I can say." ". . . Whatever one could feel toward a father I feel toward you." And: "How ungrateful I seem to myself to have been, and how good and kind and patient you are!" In sending Alden a new piece of work he said: "Perhaps when you read it you will be able to write 'my dear boy'—as you did before I sent you that horrible 'Lys!' " [27] But the suppressed emotion persisted, and would flame out with inordinate heat later.

From the suspense and disappointment of his mountain sojourn Hearn returned to St. Pierre near the end of January 1888. He was in the nadir of uncertainty concerning his writing. "There is something wrong about it,— something that bewilders me. I have either lost some faculty, or am acquiring some new one," [28] he wrote to Alden. He was lucky to find a room in which to wrestle with his uncertainties, for it was Carnival time.

One returning from the country to the city in the Carnival season is lucky to find any comfortable rooms for rent. [So Hearn wrote later in "La Verette," a recollection of this time.] I have been happy to secure one even in a rather retired street—so steep that it is really dangerous to sneeze while descending it, lest one lose one's balance and tumble right across the town. It is not a fashionable street, the Rue du Morne Mirail; but, after all, there is no particularly fashionable street in this extraordinary city, and the poorer the neighborhood, the better one's chances to see something of its human nature.[29]

In his poor room overlooking the poorer street, where all of human nature was exposed to view, Hearn sat and tried to write, and watched the life moving along the pavement under his window. He had come back not only to Carnival, but to plague and to quarantine; no ships could land at Martinique, or leave. The smallpox which had only threatened the city in the fall now raged unobstructedly through the communities of the poorer folk who, out of superstitious horror, had refused to let themselves be vaccinated.

The streets are so narrow in this old-fashioned quarter that even a whisper is audible across them; and after dark I hear a great many things—sometimes sounds of pain, sobbing, despairing cries as Death makes his nightly round—sometimes, again, angry words, and laughter, and even song—always one melancholy chant: the voice has that peculiar metallic timbre that reveals the young negress:

> Pauv' ti Lélé,
> Pauv' ti Lélé!
> Li gagnin doulè, doulè, doulè—
> Li gagnin doulè
> Tout-pàtout!

I want to know who little Lélé was, and why she had pains "all over. . . ." [30]

Wanting to know about Lélé and about many others, Hearn could almost forget himself and his meager situation, and begin to lose his identity in the life that flowed along the rough and broken pavement of the Rue du Morne Mirail. The woman who carried a heavy burden in a large straw basket on her head, the brawny worker in torn shirt and ragged trousers who strutted by whistling, freehanded and proud, the bright scattering of scrubbed children running home from the free schools, the graceful girls, the old women whom life had worn—all this was not a parade, but a company among whom he lived. Hearn complained bitterly to Alden during this period of not having enough money to get out of the city or even out of his room, but confinement to the street and to the room bred a deep familiarity in him to the scene, a familiarity which was without contempt. He could not help but be compassionate of the people of the Rue du Morne Mirail; they had so much spirit, humor, and sweetness, qualities flowering on the edge of hunger, disease, and death.

The center of intelligence of the neighborhood was the shop of Manm-Robert, next door to the house in which Hearn lived. Manm-Robert was a sharp, kind woman who sold cigars to the *békés* (the rich whites), nursed all the people up and down the street when they were ill, and found time to invite Hearn to seat himself in her rocking chair for a leisurely bout of conversation. He was soon gently leading her out into the telling of zombi tales, into describing her remedies for those who had been so unfortunate as to let themselves be *quimboisé* (bewitched), or into explaining the usages of Creole words.

Playing in the street just below the balcony where Hearn often sat with a book or a manuscript were three pretty children, Mimi, Maurice, and Gabrielle. Their mother was Yzore, the graceful slender *calendeuse,* who dressed always in white *douillette* and violet foulard. She calendered, or painted yellow, the madras squares ready to be made into turbans. And not being able to support herself and her three children upon this skilled patient work, she sewed *moresques* and *chinoises,* the sleeping garments for the siesta. Hearn often heard her hand-cranked sewing machine across the narrow street. At night he heard the children seated on the step beside their mother asking her endless questions. One time they asked about the stars:

"Ça qui ka clairé conm ça, manman?" (What is it that shines like that?)
And Yzore answers:
"Ça, mafi, c'est ti limiè Bon-Dié." (Those are the little lights of the Good-God.)
"It is so pretty—eh, mamma? I want to count them."
"You cannot count them, child."
"One—two—three—four—five—six—seven." Gabrielle can only count up to seven."
"Moin peide!—I am lost, mamma!" [31]

Yzore and her children were friends of Manm-Robert's too. They depended upon her. It was in Manm-Robert's shop one day that Hearn heard Yzore complain of bad times. The quarantine had hurt the island in many ways. There was little money coming into her hands, or into the more provident Manm-Robert's either.

Upon the last day of Carnival Hearn watched the children, who knew nothing of hard times, grow more and more excited. " 'Vini ouè!—vini ouè!' cry the children to one another—'come and see!' " [32] Hearn ran, as the children ran, to the end of their street to see the masquers pass. And as the hours of this great day passed (Ash Wednesday in Martinique), the crowd accelerated into one surging parade of dancing, singing bodies, faces, flung arms and legs. Late at night the Devil came by:

> He is clad in red, wears a hideous blood-colored mask, and a cap of which the four sides are formed by four looking-glasses;—the whole head-dress being surmounted by a red lantern. He has a white wig made of horse-hair, to make him look weird and old—since the Devil is older than the world! Down the street he comes, leaping nearly his own height—chanting words without human signification—and followed by some three hundred boys who form the chorus to his chant . . .

> "Bimbolo!"
> "Zimabolo!"
> "Bimbolo!"
> "Zimabolo!"
> "Et zimabolo!"
> "Et bolo-po!" [33]

After the Carnival was over, the children still played at being masquers, and started at the sound of any drum to run and see the dancers. But the street grew deadly sober; many died and were taken away in the night. Hearn watched while one face after another in which he had learned to look for a friendly greeting, disappeared. The worst death was Yzore's, for to Hearn, who hardly spoke to her, she had become a figure in his busy imagination. He had found out her story: she had had a white lover who died young; he had left her and the three children a small income; it had been taken from her by the dead man's other family, his white family. Yzore "was brave;—she abandoned the costume of the upper class forever, put on the douillette and the foulard—the attire that is a confession of race—and went to work." [34] And now the work did not matter. "Very early yesterday morning Yzore was carried away under a covering of quick-lime: the children do not know; Manm-Robert took heed they should not see." [35] The little furniture Yzore had accumulated was sold. When the auction drum sounded, Mimi thought it was the Carnival again: where are the masquers, she cried. Manm-Robert

> . . . utters all the dark thought of her heart for them:
> "Toua ti blancs sans lesou!—quitté moin châché papa-ou qui adans cimétiè pou vini pouend ou tou!" (Ye three little penniless white ones!—let me go call your father, who is in the cemetery, to come and take you also away!) [36]

Looking at such sights, hearing such words, Hearn was as close to human bedrock as he had been on the mud of the river landing in Cincinnati. He was back to the motives proper to such places, and he bent all his skills to the service of just such simple insights.

Before he could explore his new knowledge, he was struck down himself, not by the smallpox, but by typhoid fever which had begun attacking the Europeans, immune to the first disease.[37] Walking out under the sun one day, he found the brightness insupportable. He fell down, and had to be carried home, when it was found out by the excited crowd who gathered round him, where *Missié* lived. For almost six weeks Hearn lay helpless in his room while the fever rose and broke four times. He had no means to pay for nursing. He had not even means to pay for his room, but all his neighbors, these people of mixed blood with whom he had become friends, looked after him. Manm-Robert even went out before dawn to pick certain herbs upon the mountainsides which she thought were necessary for him. These neighbors of the Rue du Morne Mirail tended him as kindly and attentively as if he had been one of them.

When the worst of his sickness was over, with the help of a few of his more well-to-do white friends (Hearn had met some of the professional men of the city—a notary, a photographer, a planter or two) he was carried up to Morne Rouge to recuperate. He wrote a proud letter on April 19, 1888, to Alden, telling him that he had been "seriously ill," [38] but predicting his rapid recovery. In April and May he was better, seeming to spring up into a renewal which was both physical and emotional. He came back from his illness to a steely kind of poise and confidence. He knew now what he wanted to do, and he had already unconsciously collected much material he could use. He began sending sketch after sketch to New York. The magazine which had at last begun to publish what he had left behind before he ever set off for Martinique, accepted his new work.

Strong again, and with a little money in his pocket, Hearn in the summer began taking little trips into the island. A visible presentment of the fresh wind that was blowing in his mind seemed to strike him upon the face at

Grande Anse (now Lorrain), on the Atlantic side. The waters blown upon by the trade wind struck this black volcanic shore with a gusto Hearn exulted in. He scandalized his friends who had come with him from St. Pierre by walking out to experience the wind when everyone else stayed indoors. Something in the look of the place—the blue sea, the black volcanic sand— seemed to awaken a memory. Perhaps it was a fugitive recollection of the Greek island of his birth.

Starting back for St. Pierre, he and his friends stopped overnight at a plantation. Here Hearn saw something of polite Creole country life, and was full of pity for the young Creole misses, who were so constrained and dull. Theirs was "a naïveté that borders upon the stupefying. Those who have been brought up in France form a sort of coterie apart. They are deemed a little bit shocking, a little bit dangerous, because they have opinions of their own, and read novels, and subscribe to reviews, and sometimes say sarcastic things . . ." [39] So he wrote to Annie Alden.

At night he saw something of the underside of plantation life. Their host led them out of the constricted politeness of the house to listen to the drums and watch the dancing of the plantation workers. Hearn tried to take down the words of the feverish, pulsating songs, even when all that he understood was a rush of gibberish. He never forgot the windy torchlight, the quick nervous hands beating the drums, the weaving rhythm of intoxicated legs.

On the road once more, they climbed the underpinnings of Pelée the next day. Seeing the mountain thus from the south and the east as well as from the west, looking up at its various sides from its magnificent bastions, Hearn was seized by an impractical ambition: to climb the mountain to its top.

In the company of some of his friends, men who could afford a little jaunt away from the city, Hearn set off by carriage in the darkness before dawn on the morning of September 12, 1888. One of the friends was Léon Sully, the professional photographer, whom Hearn now depended on to take the pictures he still believed necessary for his articles. He had learned a little about the use of the camera, but did not trust himself for this difficult job.

The mountain climbers left their carriage at a friend's house in the foot hills, and changed there into rougher clothes. Two splendid-bodied cane field workers from the plantation led the way up the steeper slope. The climb was one of the most difficult things Hearn ever stubbornly forced himself to do. (Only his later climb up Fuji, when he was an older man, was harder.) The next day, with full appreciation of the feat, he wrote to Alden: "Yesterday I made the ascent of Pelée to the extreme top,—also had a swim in the crater. Today I feel as if I had been 'broken on the wheel'—cannot move. . . . I think I must have fallen more than two hundred times." [40]

In spite of these exertions Hearn had a rare moment on Pelée. He swam in the slightly warm water of the crater, hopped over crevices whose bottom he could not see, teetered on the edge of precipices, and shouted, laughed, and suddenly grew quiet. In writing about the experience, Hearn imputed to the entire company the emotion that was his particularly:

Now all look serious;—none speak. The first physical joy of finding one's self on this point in violet air, exalted above the hills, soon yields to other emotions inspired by the mighty vision and the colossal peace of the heights. Dominating all, I think, is the consciousness of the awful antiquity of what one is looking upon—such a sensation, perhaps, as of old found utterance in that tremendous question of the Book of Job: "Wast thou brought forth before the hills?" And the blue multitude of the peaks, the perpetual congregation of the mornes, seem to chorus in the vast resplendence—telling of Nature's eternal youth, and the passionless permanence of that about us and beyond us and beneath—until something like the fullness of a great grief begins to weigh at the heart.

For all this astonishment of beauty, all this majesty of light and form and color, will surely endure—marvelous as now—after we shall have lain down to sleep where no dreams come, and may never arise from the dust of our rest to look upon it.[41]

He experienced not only a fresh feeling for the blind beauty of nature, but also an access of understanding for the poignant limitations of man. This oblique reference was his subject in every sketch he was writing. His washerwomen battered to death by boulders in a sudden cloudburst, his little canoe boys swept out to sea in a packing-box boat, his cane workers lured to death by a ghastly superstition, his carrier girls made old before their time, or crippled into crooked shapes by rheumatic pangs—all these people of his stories lost nothing in the perspective of a beautiful, unfeeling nature.

Hearn was in no mood to idealize man or nature in Martinique. He was familiar with the literature that had done so. "Nothing could be more material than this tropic life . . ." he wrote to Alden. "The romance of Bernardin de Saint-Pierre never could have taken place in Martinique; I doubt if it ever did in Mauritius. There are Virginias, but no Pauls." [42]

There was only artificiality in making a romance of life upon the island. His sketches instead were attempts to capture only the unconscious beauty of everyday labor, life, and belief. The infinite pains he took with words became here subservient to his respect for common life. He learned the Creole word for each step of the day's work in the life of the "blanchisseuses":

The young girl first learns simply to soap and wash the linen in the river, which operation is called "rubbing" (*frotté* in creole):—after she can do this pretty well, she is taught the curious art of whipping it (*fessé*). You can hear the sound of the fessé a great way off, echoing and re-echoing among the mornes: it is not a sharp smacking noise, as the name might seem to imply, but a heavy hollow sound exactly like that of an axe splitting dry timber.[43]

Finding the exact word and using it to describe the habitual daily effort of body and mind defined the spiritual stance of the doer of the work.

Hearn used his senses as vigorously in these new sketches as he had the summer before in describing the look of the islands, but he buttressed ears and eyes with knowledge. He found out exactly how his canoe boys made their boats. He learned the routine of the carrier girls' day, and how much weight they carried how far. He worked these facts into the strong structure made by feeling, and there was no loss, but a gain, in power. For the first time he learned to unite the virtue of the reporter to the virtue of the exquisite handler of words.

And with no sense of turning away from life, he read as many of the old explorers' and priests' books about the first days of Martinique as he could find. He had had no books at first, and suffered. Now one of his new friends turned over to him his library where Hearn browsed with sensuous enjoyment. He discovered a strong, cross-grained hero in Père Labat, one of the builders of the Martiniquan colonial society, and retold his life in an essay, "Un Revenant." He found a poignancy in the fact that the good which Labat had done—the factories, the fortifications, the churches built— had crumbled into dust while the cruelty, of which he was capable at times, lived after him: in Hearn's time mothers frightened little children into obedience by the name of Pè Labatt. "Un Revenant" was Hearn's strongest reach into biography.

Meanwhile in St. Pierre he had made a sweet order in his life. He exposed his satisfaction to Dr. Matas: "I keep house! It is the only earthly way of living comfortably here! No one thinks it scandalous,—even if your house-keeper be young and pretty, and have a baby suspiciously like you. . . With me, however, there is no romance in the business as you might have sus-pected. I have just a good, plain, sensible little housekeeper who is really a *bonne,* and that's all!! You see, I could never do literary work and have any nonsense going on in the house." [44]

He lived in utter simplicity, and had time to look and listen and to write. Cyrillia (about whom he wrote a tender essay of appreciation in "Ma Bonne") took care of him. She fed him native messes cooked in earthenware pots, cleaned his rooms, and fussed over his coming and going in the hot sun. At night when he could not read—the light of candles or lamps being too poor for his meager sight—he pulled a rocker out onto his balcony and listened to the life of the neighborhood. Cyrillia, like a faithful dog, sat on the floor of the balcony beside him, and asked him naïve questions. One night she amused herself with the shape of the clouds moving across the moon, finding, as Hearn wrote later

. . . wonderful things in them: sheep, ships with sails, cows, faces, perhaps even *zombis.*

"Travaill Bon-Dié, joli,—anh?" (Is not the work of the Good-God pretty?) . . .

"Would you like to look at the moon with my telescope, Cyrillia?" I asked. "Let me get it for you."

"Oh no, no!" she answered, as if shocked.

"Why?"

"Ah! faut pa gàdé baggaïe Bon-Dié conm ça!" (It is not right to look at the things of the Good-God that way.) [45]

He shocked her by trying to explain to her that there was no such thing as the sky, that it was only air:

"My dear Cyrillia, there is no sky to touch. The sky is only an appearance."

"Anh, anh, anh! No sky!—you say there is no sky? Then, what is that up there?"

"That is air, Cyrillia, beautiful blue air."

"And what are the stars fastened to?"

"To nothing. They are suns, but so much further away than our sun that they look small."

"No, they are not suns! They have not the same form as the sun—You must not say there is no sky: it is wicked! But you are not a Catholic!"

"My dear Cyrillia, I don't see what that has to do with the sky."

"Where does the Good-God stay, if there be no sky? And where is heaven?—and where is hell?"

"Hell in the sky, Cyrillia?"

"The Good-God made heaven in one part of the sky, and hell in another part, for bad people— . . ." [46]

And he left off teasing her, and listened to her version of the cosmos seriously and sympathetically. He had a photograph of her daughter made and hung up in her room to surprise her, and found her in front of it talking to it as she talked to her footless Virgin in a tiny box-top *chapelle.*

In addition to the good terms he and Cyrillia had come to, and the daily ceremony of friendship with the inhabitants up and down the narrow street, Hearn had now a pleasant entanglement with a circle of acquaintances in the city. Léon Sully, the photographer, was a companion as well as an associate charged with picture taking on the climb up Pelée and elsewhere. (Hearn had given up trying to be his own photographer.) Testart, the Creole from New Orleans, climbed the steep road to Morne Rouge, when Hearn was living there, to bring him an important letter from New York, and to stay to talk. Cornilliac, a delightful elderly medical man with literary leanings, gave Hearn the freedom of an old, well stocked library. His closest friend in St. Pierre was Léopold Arnoux, a notary, and an amateur scholar. It was to Arnoux that he dedicated his Martinique book. It was probably of Arnoux, "mon cher ami," that he thought first on that day thirteen years later when in Japan he read in a callous daily paper that the French colonial city of St. Pierre had been completely destroyed by the volcano Pelée.

Occasionally Hearn called upon a young Frenchman from the Vosges, in his house upon a hillside, where he was engaged in recovering slowly and dubiously from a tropical fever, and who was watched over hauntingly by a self-effacing Martinique girl in *douillette* and foulard. When Félicien, as he called this friend in the sketch, and Lafcadio, sitting together on the terrace to watch the sunset flare across the bay and disappear, grew quiet, the girl was alarmed:

> "Pa combiné, chè!—pa combiné conm ça!" (Do not think, dear!—do not think like that!). . . .
> "And you, Missié," she said to me, in a tone of gentle reproach;—"you are his friend! why do you let him think? It is thinking that will prevent him getting well."
> "Combiné" in Creole signifies to think intently, and therefore to be unhappy—because, with this artless race, as with children, to think intensely about anything is possible only under great stress of suffering.[47]

Hearn too began to believe that thinking in this climate was bad for him. Thinking seemed in the eternal heat to curdle his brain. Yet for many months he lived almost entirely in his room, writing and writing, completing sketch after sketch, and then busying himself with a long story about a slave girl who chose to die with the white child entrusted in her care rather than to save herself in a slave rebellion.

He had heard the story, which was based on fact, when he visited the plantation near Grande Anse. *Youma* was to be better in its parts than *Chita*, more solid and more human, but it lacked the charm of that frail story. It had too many digressions, curious and interesting though they were. It came to life too late. Though when it was first published it was more respectfully reviewed than *Chita* had been, *Youma* never held the continuing audience of the other book. *Youma* had the fault of all Hearn's longer, more elaborate efforts without the particular passion which had filled *Chita;* it had no naturalness of plotting or development. His gift was for short efforts where the development was all given. What he learned in his best work to do was to convey a single vision, a climax of cause and effect all in one.

In working and planning, the murk and heat of Martinique began to stifle him. He wrote more slowly, and then less and less, in the spring of

1889 after the long effort of *Youma*. Again his supply of money grew short. Alden had not used as many of his sketches as Hearn thought he should have used. In October 1888 *Harper's Magazine* had printed "La Vérette." It was only in the following July (when Hearn was back in the United States) that it printed "Les Porteuses." In all, only three pieces by Hearn appeared in 1889, and three in 1890. Hearn was restive: he had voluntarily given up showing any of his work to another publisher. He began to blame Alden in his imagination for the bad situation in which he had found himself in Martinique: out of money, ill, shut up by the quarantine from all escape. The worst of the situation to him was that he could not proofread his work before it was printed in the magazine.

Upon this issue Hearn almost broke with his editor. He wrote to Alden:

I feel that I cannot any longer endure the pain of seeing myself in print as some-body else. The whole "style" of the composing room,—the changes,—the changes by omission and punctuation and reparagraphing and condensation,—destitute me of all personality to an extent that discourages me utterly. No kindness and no money can help me to bear the torture of it. . . .

Illustrations that contradict the text; text abbreviated and made colorless to form not a page—but a parallelogram of type; and the writing of a long year to see only this! And I have been working so hard to please you, and to please myself by polishing and coaxing into life another story! Why should I give it to be changed and discolored and have every drop of soul squeezed out of it.[48]

The writer smoothed over this outburst in another letter. But when the quarantine lifted, he could not stay any longer. He was ready now to complete his articles on Martinique and to shape them into a book. He could do this work best near New York so that he could interfere with any heartless mishandling of his words. Hearn borrowed enough money from Léopold Arnoux to pay his various debts in Martinique, and to buy his passage back to New York.

He boarded his ship on a day early in May 1889 and looked back to the city and its attendant mountain with a fear that he would never see the place again: "It seemed," he wrote Matas, "like tearing my heart out to leave Martinique." But in the same letter he said quietly, "I have got over a sort of crisis, however, which isolated me more than I would have liked to be isolated from the world at large: the distrust of myself." [49]

13 ❧ *Cyclopean Streets*

New York seemed more impossible than ever when Hearn returned to
the city on May 8, 1889. He stopped only long enough to collect a bundle
of proof from the publishing office, and to try to see Joseph Tunison.
He had probably renewed his friendship with this companion of the
Cincinnati streets during an earlier stay in New York. But during this
stopover he failed to waylay him. He missed Tunison at his apartment,
and left the following outraged note:

DEAR JOE,—By the time this reaches you I shall have disappeared.
    The moment I get into all this beastly machinery called "New York," I get
caught in some belt and whirled around madly in all directions until I have
no sense left. This city drives me crazy, or, if you prefer, crazier; and I have
no peace of mind or rest of body till I get out of it. Nobody can find anybody,
nothing seems to be anywhere, everything seems to be mathematics and geom-
etry and enigmatics and riddles and confusion worse confounded: architecture and mechanics run mad. One has to live by intuition and move by steam.
I think an earthquake might produce some improvement. The so-called im-
provements in civilization have apparently resulted in making it impossible
to see, hear, or find anything out. You are improving yourselves out of the
natural world. I want to get back among the monkeys and the parrots, under
a violet sky among green peaks and an eternally lilac and lukewarm sea—where
clothing is superfluous and reading too much of an exertion—where everybody sleeps fourteen hours out of the twenty-four. This is frightful, night-
marish, devilish! Civilization is a hideous thing. Blessed is savagery! Surely a
palm two hundred feet high is a finer thing in the natural order than seventy

times seven New Yorks. I came in by one door as you went out at the other. Now there are cubic miles of cut granite and iron fury between us. I shall at once find a hackman to take me away. I am sorry not to see you—but since you live in hell what can I do? I will try to find you again this summer.

Best affection
L.H.[2]

This was his valedictory of the season to New York. The frustration he experienced made him willing to try a venture in Philadelphia. There was a young medical man living there who had recently put out his shingle as ophthalmologist, and who had been corresponding with Hearn warmly and persistently since just before the writer left New Orleans. At that time a medical student, George Milbry Gould had written Hearn his admiration for *Some Chinese Ghosts.* Hearn had enjoyed Gould's letters during the months he lived in Martinique. Gould seemed to reverence writing and writers, praised Hearn's books, and asked Hearn's advice about his own technical and semitechnical writing. He was interested in such things as the theory of color, and sent Hearn pamphlets he had written on such partly philosophical and partly medical subjects. He was apparently that rewarding combination of scientist and literary man with whom Hearn always got on best. He imagined him to be something like his *hermano* of New Orleans, Rudolph Matas. The lonely writer, isolated on his French tropical island, did not note, or think important, certain differences of opinion that showed up at once between the two correspondents.

Writing letters to a new friend was easier than talking to him face to face. Hearn told Gould things he had never told others. He spoke of his appearance. "I am five feet three inches high, and weigh about one hundred and thirty-seven pounds . . ." [3] He spoke frankly to this medical man, who was studying the diseases of the eye, about his own disabled sight. He even gave Gould a brief history of his birth and parentage, so far as he knew it. He sent Gould a photograph of himself in exchange for one of Gould. He was charmed to find his unknown correspondent surprisingly young; he had thought him, from his tone, a good deal older than he was.

Assuming the man in Philadelphia to be a person of the same impulsiveness and ardor as himself, he said things that he intended to be taken with the proper salt of understanding: "I have a badly-balanced nervous make-up," [4] he flung out once, with no explanation. He could not know that the reader of his letters had a literal mind, as different as possible from his own, and that his exaggerations, fancies, sparkles of wit, were taken as solemn fact. Gould, a categorizer of human types, began at once to classify Lafcadio Hearn.

Hearn wrote freely to this unknown correspondent about many of his favorite, long-pursued private notions:

Are you perfectly, positively sure there is really a sharp distinction between moral and physical sensibilities? I doubt it. I suspect what we term the finer moral susceptibilities signify merely a more complex and perfect evolution of purely physical sensitiveness.[5]

Of course, I am not a believer in free will. I do not believe in the individual soul —though in the manifestations of a universal human, or divine, soul, I am inclined to believe, or to have that doubt which almost admits of belief. . . . Perhaps I may say that I would call moral feelings, as distinguished from those termed physical, the sensitiveness of perception of suffering in others—of the consequences of acts. But can those be thoroughly developed before those which conduce to self-preservation? I imagine the reverse to be the case. By the super-refinement of the earlier sensations comes the capacity for the "higher sentiments." It is true that moral standards are very old, but those existing are also very defective.[6]

Ingenuously he put himself in Gould's power:

Is it always a safe and encouraging thing to trace one's ancestral history, supposing one to be philosophical? In your case it is. A fine physical and mental man can feel sure from the mere fact of his comparative superiority that he has something to thank his ancestors for. But suppose the man be small, puny, sickly, scrofulous, —the question of ancestry becomes unpleasant.

As for me, I know I have a good deal in me *not* to thank my ancestors for.[7]

Toward the end of his stay in St. Pierre, Hearn wrote Gould: "If you could find me in Philadelphia a very quiet room where I could write without noise for a few months, I would try my luck there. New York is stupefying: I know too many people there; and I want to be very quiet—only to see a friend or two now and then, when I am in good trim for a chat." [8] Without having had time to receive an answer, Hearn left New York and went straight to Philadelphia and to the street and the number he knew from Dr. Gould's letters. He paused at the door, No. 119 South 17th Street, and found the brass plate with the name—George M. Gould, M.D.—on it, and was somewhat reassured. He pushed open the door, found the doctor within, and was greeted by him with an apparently unmeddlesome curiosity and admiration. Gould at once offered Hearn a room in his house (he lived in the house which held his offices), and did not put a date upon his hospitality.

Hearn had little if any money to pay for a room elsewhere. With characteristic rashness, he accepted this gift of time from a man he did not know. To get his work done, he would have sacrificed himself as well as others, and in this instance Gould begged for the privilege of taking care of him—or so Hearn recalled. The boon of being let off for the interim from scrambling about, trying to find a cheap place to live, moving because he had no money, losing or rescuing his bags, dodging creditors—this was too tempting to turn down.

He was at once filled with an uncritical worship of his benefactor, and settled down to work in his own room in the Gould house. He had everything he needed: a desk spread with proofs to correct, plenty of yellow paper on which to compose new pieces, and as a bonus, three meals a day, a good bed to sleep in, and conversation with a new friend.

Gould, as an eye specialist, insisted on examining Hearn's eyes as almost his first act of hospitality. He found Hearn's nearsightedness deplorable and extreme, but could not prevail upon his guest to accept eyeglasses. Hearn was stubborn in his belief that glasses strained his one good eye. He had settled upon a personal solution: the pocket magnifying glass and the folding telescope. He would not change his habits.

Hearn was not easy about accepting so much help from Gould. He wrote Elizabeth Bisland that he did not know when he would be in New York again, that he was simply "drifting." [9] Without telling her that he was at the moment without funds, he said: "I am peculiarly situated, tied up by a business-muddle—tangled in necessities." [10] He also wrote to Alden asking him to find him some part-time work in New York, but Alden found nothing, and Hearn stayed on in Philadelphia into the summer.

In an attempt to repay Gould in the only way he could, Hearn pushed the name and abilities of the young doctor, who aspired to be a writer as well as an eye specialist. He sent pamphlets and articles written by Gould to Alden, and predicted to his editor that the doctor's projected "philosophy of spectacles" would be a great work. He said later that he helped the doctor with a medical dictionary which Gould was at that time editing, that he introduced Gould to the editors of various magazines, and that he even wrote a piece for him which Gould signed and sold under his own name. Gould later denied the more material help. A balancing of Hearn's and Gould's opposing statements and motives is the only arbitrator between them.

Outside his own sphere of competency, Hearn was in awe of the doctor only two years older than himself, but a man of few fears and compunctions. He seemed assured in all those things about which Hearn was unsure. Gould did not hesitate to tell Hearn how ignorant he was, and Hearn humbly agreed. Gould was benign; he would teach Hearn how to get along in the world, how to order his thinking, his morals, and his manners. Hearn was moved to a strange hero worship. Gould was not only his friend, he was his master, his brother. In one letter written after this first quick growth of friendship, Hearn ebulliently called the doctor "Cher frère et père et ami." [11] In another note he called him his "dear teacher and brother." [12] At the height of his fervor of admiration he wrote to Alden: "How wonderfully a strong well trained mind can expand a feebler and undisciplined one, when the teacher has pleasure and time to teach!" [13] Not only was Hearn's head turned by this solicitous attention, but in gratitude he became almost a child. He called Gould "Dear Gooley," and signed himself, whenever he had occasion to write to his new mentor, "Hearney boy."

It is through Hearn's letters of this time—letters to Gould when the doctor was away from Philadelphia, letters to Alden and Tunison and Miss Bisland in New York—that one can partially reconstruct the bemused Lafcadio of the period, happy in his own undisturbed work upstairs, coming downstairs only to admire and to abdicate responsibilities. Gould knew everything that he did not; from him he would learn how to live in the bewildering world of modern power and complexity.

Yet he took his daily meals somewhat dauntedly under the eyes of both Dr. and Mrs. Gould. He wrote teasingly to the doctor, before the spell had been broken, how the presence of the two of them "bewildered" him at meals, "when I was asked two questions at the same time,—one by you in a voice of command,—the other in a small dove-voice, like the 'still small voice' of the prophet, by Mrs. Gooley." [14] Gould did not undergo such teasing with any grace; he was literal-minded. Hearn had to be careful of his wayward tendency toward irony. He had to restrain himself to please this serious and proper man. He did not know if he pleased Mrs. Gould, who remained tight-lipped in front of her husband's guest. Hearn tried awkwardly to help her when Gould was out of town; he ran to answer the doorbell for her, he fed the cat.

So much worship from a gifted man turned Gould's head too. His response was selfish, although there was an appearance of generosity upon the surface of the facts. In helping Hearn, he pursued two private interests. Gould had just failed going into the ministry before going into medicine. He was a natural admonisher. He was confident that he could remodel Hearn's character into one suitable for a man of genius. He saw also in Hearn a prime example of an idea he was riding, an idea that was becoming an obsession with him: that ". . . intellect is largely, almost entirely, the product of vision." [15] So he attempted to manipulate Hearn, and coldly studied him, as if Hearn were an object and not a person. As the summer went on, and Hearn came out of the dream in which he had lived while happily completing his West Indies book, he began to be conscious of something chilling in Gould's attention. He became uneasy and wanted to get

away. Hearn had seemed at first delightfully pliant to Gould. In his anxious-
ness to please his teacher-friend, Hearn had unconsciously bent greatly.
But he had not changed at all. And when, in the end, he began to resent
Gould, and moved on to another scene, he was the same Lafcadio Hearn
who had first come into Gould's sight, full of preposterous notions and
deplorable practices.

After Hearn was dead, Gould wrote two books in which he put down the
disappointment and the malice which had been aroused in him by his experience with Hearn. There were valuable individual insights in these
books, but they were spoiled by Gould's obsessive special pleading. In his
chapter on Hearn in *Biographic Clinics,* 1906, he demonstrated to his own
satisfaction that everything about Hearn, good or bad, was determined by
myopia. In his curious *Concerning Lafcadio Hearn,* 1908, he made several
contradictory claims: that Hearn was a monster, that he was a genius, that
he was a peculiar kind of limited genius because he was nearsighted.

This growth of Gould's ideas centering upon his guest of the hot summer
months of 1889 did not reach perfection of form till many years later. Yet
Hearn, feeling something strange in Gould's regard, began to shy away
before the summer was over. There was no full break between them, but
when Hearn was able to get away to New York in October he went with a
sharp sense of relief.

He had finished his work on the Martinique book; he had finished the
proofreading of articles already set up and ready for the magazine. He had
lived in the Gould house for five months. He had the prospect of payment
for a number of articles and sketches. He wanted to be in New York for the
printing of the West Indies book. He borrowed $40 in cash and left with all
good wishes. After he had been in New York for a few days, he wrote Gould
of other immediate needs, and the doctor sent him $20 more. Hearn sent
Gould his note for $60, and his warm thanks.

He arrived in New York at the end of October 1889 to find himself becoming famous. *Chita* was being read. *Youma* was about to come out in serial
publication in *Harper's Magazine.* He was going to write something for
Miss Bisland for the *Cosmopolitan.* He had under his arm a story, "Karma,"
which *Lippincott's Magazine* accepted almost at once. And the book he had
just finished assembling, *Two Years in the French West Indies,* was the
largest book he had yet done. Nothing he would ever do again would be as
various and as comprehensive.

Hearn's first days in the city were occupied with scrambling about trying
to find a place to live. He went almost automatically to the one hotel he
knew, the dreary United States Hotel, near the Battery. Then hopefully he

moved into entirely different surroundings upon the invitation of Mrs. Daniel M. Rollins, a writer, whom he had met through Elizabeth Bisland.

He had liked Mrs. Rollins very much, finding her a comfortable, motherly woman. As Alice Wellington Rollins she wrote fiction, light verse, and travel essays. She had pleased Hearn before he met her by writing a favorable review of his book *Some Chinese Ghosts* in *The Critic* in March 1887. They had exchanged letters before they met.

Mrs. Rollins and her family lived in a spacious apartment in the Novarro Buildings at 170 West Fifty-ninth Street, an apartment adjoining the rooms of Kate Douglas Wiggin and her husband, as well as near those of the bachelor scientist and businessman Ellwood Hendrick and his sister, Anne Hendrick. Mrs. Rollins hospitably invited Hearn to come up to Fifty-ninth Street and enjoy the company of this little colony. Hearn, who was sick of his hotel, hesitated for a little but agreed. He arrived precipitately but found that Mrs. Rollins' son had had to give up his room for him. "I could not stay at the Rollins'," [16] he wrote Gould, and he went back to the United States Hotel.

During this time of moving about from one address to another in the city, he applied hopefully to Henry Alden for an advance, apparently on the Martinique book. But he was turned down again. The growing resentment Hearn felt showed in the report of the conversation he made to Gould (to whom he still reported his activities as if to a teacher):

He had nothing definite to say about anything, and avoided all direct questions except one,—to which he said:— "Oh us! the Harpers will not make any arrangement with anybody on time like that."
"Nothing to expect?—no show?" I asked.
"No: but it is much the best for you, I assure you," he said, fleeing away to catch the ferry boat.[17]

Hearn more and more disliked the working out of his informal agreement with his publishers, although he continued to submit everything he wrote to them first. He hated piecemeal publication in the magazine before book publication even though he was paid more through this arrangement. He scorned the typographical style of the magazine. He disliked the liberties the magazine editors took with his essays—omitting, condensing, changing his preciously contrived paragraphs, his sentences, even his punctuation. He wanted to give up magazine work altogether, to receive a lump payment for each assemblage of essays that could be made into a book. Yet in the case of *Two Years in the West Indies,* he conformed to his publishers' practices. He gave Alden essays out of proper order and let them appear one by one in the magazine. There, changes were made in them, and the touchy writer choked with anger over the illustrations which as he thought misrepresented his words. The regard he had for Alden began to fray. Resentment began to change to distrust; for, with Hearn, any differences between him and a friend grew gigantically into suspicions of deliberate betrayal.

But in his early weeks in New York, he had little time to devote either to fame or to his growing discomfort with his publisher. He continued to hunt for a good cheap room. He had asked Joseph Tunison to see if he could find a place near him, on West Tenth Street, and Tunison told him, after the fiasco of the move to Mrs. Rollins', that there was a handy room near his place. Hearn hastened to look at it, and planned to move in. But he found that it could not be heated in the winter, and cold winds were already blowing steadily down the long avenues. Tunison said gruffly: come in with me. And Hearn did. He remained with Tunison at 149 West Tenth Street for the rest of his time in New York City.

Lafcadio thought that Joe loved him as he loved Joe. But although Tunison ably defended Hearn's memory after Hearn's death in articles in the paper he edited at that time, the Dayton *Journal,* and expressed disgust with Gould for his strange and perverse treatment of Hearn, Tunison yet wrote to Gould—before the appearance of Gould's book about Hearn—on December 21, 1906: "I never pretended to be a friend. I was merely one to whom he resorted when all the rest cast him out. He never found me wanting, but he got few letters from me and none that were flattering." [18] This revelation, which would have been another shattering confirmation to Hearn of the justification of his suspiciousness, apparently never burst upon him. He went through life innocently thinking that Tunison thought of him as he thought of Tunison. Years later in Japan he even begged Tunison to come join him there; he could arrange a teaching job, and Tunison would save expenses by living with him. Tunison did not come.

Early in Hearn's stay in New York, Henry Harper secured the writer's wary consent to attend a dinner the publisher was giving at the Union League Club to honor the painter Edwin Abbey. He wanted to show off Lafcadio Hearn too. Harper deputed Henry Alden to see that Hearn fulfilled his rash promise to come. Harper recalled that Alden told him that he had literally to hold onto Hearn by the slack of his unaccustomed dress suit to get him into the banquet room. Then Hearn made himself small, ate little, and at first talked not at all. William Dean Howells, seated on Harper's left, indicated to his host the small, odd-looking figure beyond Harper, and "asked who he was."

I reminded him [wrote Harper] that I had introduced him on arrival, and added, "Surely you know who Lafcadio Hearn is?"

Howells jumped up, went around to Hearn, and remarked that the name Hearn, by which I had introduced him meant nothing to him; but that there was only one Lafcadio Hearn, and he was so pleased to meet him that he wanted to shake his hand again.[19]

Hearn was not immune to warming praise. He knew Howells by repute, and the figures of Howells' circle. He particularly admired, and had admired since the 1870's, Howells' friend Henry James. As the party grew smaller toward the end of the evening, Hearn forgot himself and talked and was listened to. ". . . He and Alden were the last guests to leave the club after dinner," [20] wrote Henry Harper.

The dinner at the Union League Club marked the official recognition of the writer by the powers of the New York literary world. *Chita* and his current series of essays from the West Indies were making an impression. Howells underlined his approving handshake with a handsome review of *Youma* in "The Editor's Study" in *Harper's Magazine* the following September. Unsigned as usual, it was distinctively Howells in its praise as well as its reservations. He found the writer a throwback "to earlier ways of looking at human nature." He did not use, but implied, the word "romantic." And romanticism was for the moment out of date among the cautious realists and naturalists of the New York literary scene of the early 1890's:

We do not refuse the pleasure offered us by Mr. Lafcadio Hearn because we find our pleasure chiefly in Tolstoï and James and Galdós and Valdés, and Thomas Hardy and Balzac at his best. In Mr. Hearn the public has learned to know an artist of those who think with color; and perhaps one doubts whether it might not be better for him to paint his sketches rather than to write them. As a painter he is of the most modern school: an impressionist who puts on pure color, and loves to render light in its fiercest and brightest and gayest tints; it is as a fictionist [however] that he seems a reversion.

Howells found the story of the West Indian slave girl "a poem," but at the same time thought that there was a certain amount of "overdoing" in it. Yet he discerned that nothing could be done with Hearn but accept him:

That [the "overdoing" it] is really a matter for him to settle himself with his readers at large; criticism cannot do more than note his characteristics; it cannot teach him anything, or mend him, or mar him. What it can be certain of and grateful for is the fact that in the great array of mediocrity and passivity, here is a positive talent that vividly distinguishes itself from all others, and joys in its life and strength. The love of doing the things that it does is evident in all his work; and it is this that in *Youma* charms and recompenses and promises. It is the sign manual of the poet; the impress of authority and might.[21]

Thus Hearn impinged upon the American critical consciousness in the early 1890's as a self-possessed, completely individual voice, something of a puzzle, but markedly complete. Howells' generosity conferred an official recognition, but it also crystallized the general appreciation of Hearn in a half-truth. For at this moment Hearn was leaving behind much, learning much. After several tries he had found he was not a storyteller except when the story was given, and given in a legendary form. He was also at this time dissatisfied with his ten years' allegiance to the caressing beauty of surfaces. He was attempting to translate his perceptions more rudely. He was for the rest of his life to struggle against his own sensuous susceptibilities, and to try to see beyond appearances to the skeleton of motive. And it was not much noticed either that Hearn was a social critic. This faculty would grow in him, and not diminish.

Hearn had soaked himself for two decades in the juices of the French writers of the nineteenth century. He had learned much from realism and naturalism but had continued to exercise the romantic outlook with a good conscience. Romantic method he might find inadequate; romantic temperament was something he could not slough—it was native to him.

If a realist was a person who described only what he knew, then Hearn was a realist. But then he went a long way to find his facts. Howells, who was a classic realist, happily limited himself to those facts that came within his sight every day. He never went out of his way to find subjects, scenes, or characters. By this standard Hearn could not be considered a realist.

If the naturalist's practice (if not theory) was to picture the usually dark or hidden side of life, then Hearn was a naturalist. But Hearn, who had lived much of his life among the low and the poor, did not find averages, integers, or good statistics among them. He could find only color, humor, pathos. He could not qualify as a naturalist.

Hearn was as committed a determinist as Zola. Half his nervousness in the face of the America of the last decades of the nineteenth century was due to his belief in the large, impersonal forces which were building and destroying for the future. But he felt that he had not the time to wait for the good which would come of this progress. He preferred to consider the ephemeral graces which survived by accident. He was happy in giving to whatever he sketched of this haphazard survival some charm of design. His design was always the individual, lopsided design of romantic beauty. He had not the patience or the weightiness for the slow building up of effect from detail.

Hearn was beginning to find himself. He was also humanly pleased with others for finding him too. "I am much stronger in New York than you imagine," he wrote Gould, beginning to pull away from his advising, "and my future in it is plain and perfect sailing. . . . I am only embarrassed at the moment. I am quite a lion here." [22] Like a son escaping from a too anxious father, he assured Gould he could now make his own way. This was his first step toward independence.

His second was accomplished in a burst of anger. He found out that Gould had made private use of some of the manuscripts and notebooks he had left behind in his house in Philadelphia. Gould had used them as the basis for a series of lectures he was making before local clubs and civic organizations. Hearn was easily brought to hold a low opinion of himself, but he was always high and mighty about his work. He was also touchy to the point of mania about anyone stealing or spoiling a literary right.

He sent Gould a telegram and amplified his outrage in a letter. "If there is anything in an idea, to make it public before printing it, ends the writer's property in it, and in all likelihood, must result in preventing his ever again being able to lay claim to it. I do not see how you could have done it. I could not have done it, even privately, with your idea of what a Tree means. Are *you* a humbug, too!!" [23]

His final progress into independence came as he realized that he had not been so welcome in Dr. Gould's house as he had thought. Hearn had believed that the Goulds loved him. Finding that the quality of the feelings Dr. and Mrs. Gould had entertained toward him had been mixed freed him from domination. The instrument of enlightenment was a letter from Mrs. Gould, who wrote sharply demanding a proper and formal thank you for all that she and her husband had done for him in Philadelphia. Hearn tried to reply correctly:

My dear Mrs. Gould, I am very sorry you should have experienced any annoyance on my account. I wore my welcome out at your home, and made a good many clumsy mistakes, no doubt; but I should deem myself very low and very contemptible indeed if I should feel anything but gratefulness and affection to those who endured me so long. I fear I proved a disturbing element, instead of a pleasure, in your home-life at times,—and whatever feelings you might have against me in consequence, I should consider perfectly natural under the circumstances, and like you nonetheless. I was somewhat selfish in staying so long: but I was anxious especially about my book, and if I had not had the rare good luck to be helped in that way, the book never could have been prepared as it has been. . . . If I have been a great affliction to you, you will find some small pleasure in the result of the work, perhaps,—the pleasure of knowing that you made the book possible.

He finished with an awkward apology, after imputing to her the opinion that he was "horrid":

I know I'm very horrid; but I really can't help it,—and at all events I'll never be horrid to you any more, except on paper. . . . Now please don't feel worried about anything in regard to—

Your horrid, horrid little friend
LAFCADIO HEARN [24]

He lost his temper when he received almost immediately an additional letter, this one from Dr. Gould, adding his request to Mrs. Gould's, that he write a proper thank you for the hospitality he had received:

MY DEAR GOULD:

Your letter asking me to write Mrs. Gould, was received only after answering hers. *Her* letter, however, was illuminated by yours; and as I know myself no match for a woman in diplomacy, I simply ask you to read it, and understand it. It strikes me that Mrs. Gould is very desirous to terminate our relations even in the matter of correspondence, and that we can accommodate her in this without any ill feeling.

Yours, etc.
L. HEARN [25]

In spite of this curt letter, the dying relationship was partially patched up between Hearn and the doctor, and they continued to write to each other, but less ardently than before. Hearn could not break off till he had paid back his debt—which seemed to be growing, encompassing not only the cash he had borrowed, but the board of the previous summer. Hearn became obsessed with the idea of paying Gould back. But he had no money to do so. So, on the edge of a tremendous row, the connection wore thin.

Yet, walking the "cyclopean streets" of New York, Hearn could almost forget Gould and the resentment he felt for the favors the man had done him. He salved his heart with a new idolatry.

In Philadelphia he had written letters to Elizabeth Bisland that were more intimate than he had dared to be in her presence. He told her once about wandering in Fairmount Park where

Thousands and thousands of carriages file by, each with a pair of lovers in it. Everybody in the park seems to be making love to somebody. Love is so much the atmosphere of the place—a part of the light and calm and perfume—that you feel as if drenched with it, permeated with it, mesmerized. And if you are all alone, you will look about you once in a while, wondering that somebody else is not beside you—. But I forgot that I am not writing to a stupid man, like myself.[26]

"Karma," which was published in May 1890 in *Lippincott's Magazine*, was the story which Gould afterward claimed he had bullied Hearn into writing. (He prided himself on having had Hearn write something sensible and modern and American.) "Karma" was a failure as a short story, but it has an autobiographical interest, for it was filled with Hearn's personal feelings of the time. It was written as if it were a letter to Miss Bisland, and he sent it to her to read in manuscript.

It is the story of a young man who, in proposing marriage to an impossibly exalted and virtuous young woman, finds that she makes a condition: he must be completely honest with her, and write for her an account of his life, sparing no shameful episodes. So, in an agony of candidness he writes out for her the story of a shameful episode in his past (it is never clearly specified), is judged, forgiven, and then accepted by her.

Miss Bisland did not like "Karma." The humble attitude of the man toward the woman in the story could not have pleased her—she, who prided herself on working upon a common level of effort with every man she encountered in her career. And she carefully ignored the personal signalings from Hearn to her in the story. Whether Hearn privately told her of his own troubling past, his marriage which was not a marriage with Mattie Foley in Cincinnati, is not known, but it is probable. Elizabeth Bisland later knew of this episode. After Hearn's death she very carefully concealed it, and then, when she was forced to do so by Gould's ugly and partial allusions, she defended Hearn's reputation by relating the story of the relationship with economy and honesty.

In 1889 the friendship quickened when Hearn left Philadelphia and moved to New York. At the end of his first day in the city Hearn wrote to Gould: "I have seen Miss Bisland, and her wonderful sister, and her superb brother . . .":

> Miss Bisland is prettier and more astonishing than before. She has a cozy home in which I smoked a cigar and took supper. She works for four papers at the same time, —a very brave girl: works often eighteen and twenty hours at a stretch, and still keeps fresh and rosy and gracious as a jessamine. And I really can't remember much of the last part of our chat, because it was 1 o'clock; and I got at once sleepy and filled with dreams on my feet, so that I don't know how many foolish things I said or did.[27]

He went back again and again to watch the expressions upon her pretty, mobile, self-confident face:

> When I see Miss Bisland [he wrote to Gould in November] I feel out of the world for a while, and get bewildered . . . Next day the enchantment evaporates, and I think "What an ass I have been,—I won't go there any more." Then a letter comes, and I argue with myself; "Why not?—the sensation of getting bewitched is so delicious: yield to it,—make a story out of it." [28]

Analyzing Miss Bisland and his reactions to her, he wrote some time later, again to Gould:

She is a sort of goddess here—keeps a Southern salon: it is hard to get to talk to her. She is a witch—turning heads everywhere: but some of her best admirers are afraid of her. One told me he felt as if he were playing with a beautiful dangerous leopard, which he loved for not biting him. As for me she is like hasheesh: I can't remember anything she says or anything I myself say after leaving the house: my head is all in a whirl, and I walk against people in the street, and get run over, and lose my way—my sense of orientation being grievously disturbed. But I am not in love at all,—no such foolishness as that: I am only experiencing the sensation produced upon—alas!—*hundreds* of finer men then I. A woman-admirer (she has the astounding art of making women love her, in the blindest, most unselfish way!) told me that she was Undine,—she had no soul yet; but the spiritual awakening would make her all transfigured some day. I suppose this is true. She is energetic as a man, and thoroughly business when business is concerned,—has some thousands of dollars in the bank, and is quite proud of having made it all with her own little head.[29]

(Hearn's admiration for Miss Bisland made Gould jealous; his pupil was asking another kind of person the questions he used to ask him, was deferring to another the way he used to defer to him.)

Hearn felt for Miss Bisland a mixture of alarm and delight. What she felt for him remains an enigma, except that it contained admiration, and a desire to help him. It was a strange, but apparently mutually satisfactory, relationship in which the two of them performed a little ballet of meeting, dining, writing, advising, giving and receiving gifts. They were witty, deferential, sympathetic toward each other, and never really close at all. It was a romance without consequences, as if the fact had been silently decided between them.

As far as the rest of the world was concerned, Elizabeth Bisland constituted herself a guardian spirit to Lafacadio Hearn. She was proud of this difficult, gifted friend whom she had known since she was sixteen years old, and who had been kind to her then. She wanted to help him now, and she knew that she could. She had lost her terrors of the city and its people. She put Hearn in the way of meeting as many of her literary friends as he would consent to meet.

Elizabeth Bisland and her friends lived on the edge of the great world of letters, not in its center. They were busy, competent professionals, working for magazines or newspapers, writing an occasional book. Hearn was a find for them. He belonged by rights to the other, more important world of letters, but he did not claim the privileges of that world. They knew that he was going to be famous. They enjoyed in his company the relish of connoisseurs sharing a flavor that the rest of the world was going to know soon enough. From among these friends of Elizabeth Bisland, he extracted one real friend of his own.

This friend was Ellwood Hendrick. In the fall of 1889 Hendrick was twenty-eight years old, a buoyant, independent bachelor who enjoyed books and writing, but was too facile, or too lazy, to do much writing himself. He was a chemist by profession, and fell naturally into the scientific attitudes and expressions Hearn adored. He was, however, making his living at this time as an insurance agent.

The occasion of Hearn's meeting Hendrick was a dinner given by Alice Wellington Rollins. Hearn had consented in an incautious moment to come, but had stipulated that it be an easy, informal occasion. Mrs. Rollins had agreed but could not forbear asking a few good friends to share her new interest. She began to realize that her party might not be a success when her guest of honor was very late appearing.

Ellwood Hendrick, who lived in the same apartment house as Alice Rollins, and was an old friend, had been invited to dinner. Hendrick never forgot the evening, and many years later wrote an account of it.

As he often did in New York, Hearn lost his way coming to the party. When, at eight o'clock, he arrived at the imposing entrance to the Novarro Buildings, the doorman thought that he was some sort of help, not "carriage-company" at all. He was sent upstairs in the service elevator, and stumbled blindly from the kitchen into an interested circle of strangers, all staring at him. "He wore," wrote Hendrick, "what we called 'spring-bottom' trousers which even then were out of date, a pea jacket, immaculate linen, and he carried a big, fawn-colored sombrero."

He was greatly embarrassed. We tried to make things pleasant for him, but the seven or eight of us were too many for him. He hadn't a word to say. He merely nibbled sparingly. Then the visitors began to arrive, and that nearly undid him. He sat off in a corner, rose as if in pain when introduced to anybody, and for the rest of the time he hugged his knees.

With compassionate eyes Hendrick watched the suffering going on in front of him, and at last took Mrs. Rollins aside to suggest that he take Hearn away. She approved. He came up to Hearn and said that he had an engagement later in the evening, that his way was Hearn's, and perhaps the two of them could go along together. "It seemed as though I were saving his life."

At first in silence they walked down Sixth Avenue. Hendrick gave up the pretense of another engagement as Hearn thawed out. They turned into a beer cellar and "talked till two in the morning." Hendrick, trying to remember the quality of Hearn's talk, wrote:

He did not hold the floor. His usual posture was with one hand over his blind eye, because someone had once told him it was ugly and offended people. There was a touch of Irish accent in his speech, and he was so modest that his frequent revelations were often put as though they were incidental suggestions. We discussed the ways of simple people, of children, of dogs, of children with dogs, of what dogs knew and their point of view. We ventured over into philosophy and into abstractions and back again to human reactions, the sequelae of emotions—everything.[30]

Hendrick saw the talker home but came back to his place to rouse him up at ten or eleven the same morning for more talk. For the rest of the winter and spring the two men met nearly every day. They thrashed out all possible agreements and disagreements and settled happily upon a majority of the former. Hendrick was twenty-eight years old to Hearn's thirty-nine when they first met. He had not been hurt by experience as Hearn had been, or spoiled by good luck. He had quick and intuitive sympathies and understandings. He had the gay, asking kind of mind to which Hearn responded most easily. There was an easy give and take between them. It was a natural, fortunate kind of friendship, and it endured till the end of Hearn's life and, for Hendrick, beyond that event. The letters Hearn wrote the younger man from Japan were the frankest he wrote in that fourteen-year period.

Hendrick was a chemical engineer and by education and temperament a pure scientist, but money kept tempting him into the applied side of science and into business. When Hearn met him, Hendrick was the special agent of the Commercial Union Assurance Company of London. Earlier he had managed the Albany Aniline and Chemical Works of Albany, New York. He married in 1897 and went into business with two brothers-in-law. The firm they organized, Pomeroy Brothers, was a member of the New York Stock Exchange. Hendrick was active in this family firm, but continued to serve from time to time as a consulting engineer, and at last settled into the scientific life. He became a lecturer in chemistry at Columbia University and the Curator of the Chandler Chemical Museum. He wrote a number of chemical textbooks and books popularizing the study of chemistry. He contributed to the *Dictionary of American Biography*. In 1919 his occasional light effervescences upon general subjects were collected in a volume he called *Percolator Papers*.

Hendrick was a cheerful skeptic and once wrote an essay saying that St. Paul had ruined Christianity. He wrote another essay against war and offered a plan for international duels to be fought to the death by representatives of the disagreeing nations. He wrote "A Plea for Materialism," and asserted in "C_2H_5OH" that alcohol, while not good for individuals, was often very good for societies, endowing those that drank reasonably with a sweetness and moderation which was wholly lacking in abstaining societies.

In the winter of 1890 Hendrick was Hearn's best bulwark against New York. The two men saw each other often and talked "as usual into the night with great earnestness and ardor concerning all the things there are," [31] or so Hendrick remembered. Hendrick came down to West Tenth Street after his workday was done and called for Hearn. They would go out together into the dark streets of winter to walk for blocks and blocks, or turn into some homely eating place for beer and sausages. They made a curious contrast in appearance. Hearn was small, dark, and habitually contained in gesture. Hendrick was a large man of fashionable appearance, careless and sweeping in gesture. But each found an agreement in the mind and the temperament of the other.

Hearn told Hendrick many fugitive things about himself. He told him of the occasion in Memphis when he tried to kill the man he saw abuse a kitten. " 'It has been,' he continued with a whimsical sigh, 'one of the great regrets of my life that I did not kill him.' " This vivid memory, this sharp regret, was preluded by a statement on ethics. Hendrick remembered that their conversation went as follows:

"There is nothing," I exclaimed, "eternally right or eternally wrong!"
"Oh yes, there is!" said he, and this with finality, although his statements were usually offered in the form of suggestions. "One thing is always wrong—always: to cause suffering in others for the purpose of gratifying one's own pleasure; that is everlastingly wrong." [32]

After Hearn's death, after many acts defensive of Hearn's reputation, Ellwood Hendrick's conclusion was: "Lafcadio Hearn was a mystery to his friends as he is to us today." [33]

Hearn could accept one friend more. It was more difficult to accept a brother. A letter came to him one day in New York signed James Hearn. The writer said he was a farmer in Ohio, and he said that he was his brother. James Hearn had seen a picture of the writer Lafcadio Hearn in a Cleveland newspaper and ventured to write. Lafcadio to James was truculent and suspicious. He addressed his correspondent as "Dear Sir" and asked impolite questions:

What is your full name?
What was your mother's name prior to her marriage?
Of what place was she a native?
Where is she? [34]

James (who was in fact Daniel James Hearn, the only other living child of Charles and Rosa Hearn) knew less than Lafcadio the answers to these questions, and he did not even remember the appearance of their mother, but he convinced Lafcadio that he was his brother. Lafcadio apologized and asked him if he had not been with their Uncle Richard Hearn as a child. "Where is he? Please tell me something about him." And: "You ought to have on the calf of each leg, three lines [marks made at the time of baptism] made by our mother. Perhaps you have them without knowing it." [35] James replied and sent Lafcadio the portrait photograph of their father, completing his revelation. Lafcadio began his third letter, "My Dear Brother," and full of emotion, interest, and curiosity, poured out to James everything he himself knew of their parents.

James had not, as Lafcadio thought, been given into the care of Richard Hearn, but sent away to a school in England, to a Dr. Stewart in Alton, Hampshire. He had stayed there till he was sixteen and then, in 1871, he had come to the United States. He had lost all his belongings in the Chicago Fire in October of that year, a year when Lafcadio, not far away in Cincinnati, was enduring a bad time too. James was practical and resourceful, if not much luckier than Lafcadio. He had engaged in a variety of small enterprises, succeeding, failing, trying again. He had been in the tea business, and in tobacco growing. He had been a miller and got miller's asthma. He had owned a farm and lost it, and rented land since. He had a wife and children. He sent Lafcadio a picture of the baby, Gracie.

Really, I think that is my baby! [wrote Lafcadio hungrily to the brother he now believed in.] It has my eyes anyhow—mother's eyes almost. . . . I think you must have stolen some of my soul, to make Gracie with. She certainly looks more like me than you. I am going to ask which is her father, when I get up there to see you.[36]

He lectured his brother sharply on the proper care of children's eyes. He told James a little about himself. "To give you the details of my life would be tedious and uninteresting on paper. It has been a very varied, blundering, foolish existence—sometimes rather shocking then creditable. . . . I have no wife or children; had various temporary relationships with women, in which I was the dupe until I succeeded in obtaining the wisdom of experience." He expanded into a small pride in his work: "I won my way into something higher and better by patient hard work. I was for seventeen years a journalist; I am now a littérateur by occupation . . ." Always he came back warmly and insistently to their mother's sufferings: "What if there is a 'skeleton in our closet'? Did not he make it? I think only of her. I have thought only of her, and of you, all my life—rarely of him. It is the mother that makes us . . . And I would rather have her portrait than a fortune." [37]

James had written a little stiffly, as if afraid that Lafcadio might not think much of a farmer brother. Lafcadio answered: "You know nothing of me, of

course, but when you do, you will laugh at your own suggestion, that I
might wish my brother to be an aristocrat. I only trust he is not more indifferent to external appearances and to social formalities than I am; for
I have the reputation of being an outrageous person . . ." [38]

Lafcadio repeatedly sent his love to Ohio, but he did not go there. He had
not the money or the time. And he feared to open up this relationship with
his past. He feared memory. And he still distrusted this brother, particularly
his lukewarm attitude to their mother. Lafcadio continued to put him off
while he involved himself in a complicated scheme for escape from New York
to a place farther than Ohio. They exchanged a few more letters after
Lafcadio went to Japan. After his brother's death, James Hearn said to an
interviewer:

> I think I've done as well as my brother. It's very different, of course. He was a
> genius in one way, but he didn't have any business head. But he did have a gift
> of language, and he suffered for it. I'd like to have met him. I offered to pay his
> expenses to Ohio, but he went off to Japan in a great hurry. Queer, tenderhearted
> sort of fellow he was, I believe.[39]

Hearn's departure was almost a necessity. He loathed New York, and he
did not find work there with which to supplement his income from books.
He might have been persuaded to go to the West Indies again, or to South
America. He had even suggested to Alden once that he might go to Greece
and make stories from the folk customs of the people of the Greek islands.
The decision to go to the East came as an accident. He was in the process
of realizing he could not stay in New York and remain his own man. He
would be forced into admitting that the easy part-time job he had talked
about was an illusion. He would have to take on a full-time newspaper job.
The only answer was flight, flight which could be translated into words
which editors would buy. Flight for Hearn was an exercise of integrity, a
legitimate movement of his spirit.

A casual suggestion by William Patten, an art editor at Harper's, early
in his stay in New York, had ignited his imagination. They had been talk-
ing of Eastern books, and Patten said to Hearn: Why do you not go to
Japan? Hearn had just finished reading Percival Lowell's *Soul of the Far
East,* and he had earlier read and cherished Edwin Arnold's *The Light of
Asia.* Gould too had suggested Japan, but Hearn had been too unsettled in
Philadelphia to decide anything. His earlier longing to go somewhere east-
ward revived.

In addition, his one chance at a part-time job in New York had failed
demonstrably. The *New York Times* had offered him work in reviewing

French books and commenting on French intellectual trends. But nothing was on hand to review when the offer was made, and little turned up.

From the moment Patten spoke to him of going, his mind was made up. On November 28, 1889, he wrote an outline of a possible book he might write on Japan. It was detailed, comprehensive, and remarkably prophetic of what he actually did do in *Glimpses of Unfamiliar Japan*. In this plan, drawn up to persuade Harper & Brothers that his going was a sensible course, he stated too just what his idea of a travel book was:

> In attempting a book upon a country so well trodden as Japan, I could not hope—nor would I consider it prudent attempting,—to discover totally new things, but only to consider things in a totally new way. . . . The studied aim would be to create, in the minds of the readers, a vivid impression of *living* in Japan,—not simply as an observer but as one taking part in the daily existence of the common people, and *thinking with their thoughts*.[40]

Hearn submitted his proposal to Harper's. Patten added his active support. He persuaded one of the firm's illustrators, C. D. Weldon, to say that he would go with Hearn. Patten next secured free transportation for the writer and artist. He went to Montreal and talked to the president of the Canadian Pacific Railway, Sir William Van Horne, and fired him with zeal for the project. Van Horne promised free transportation from Montreal to the West Coast of Canada and on to Japan by steamer. In return Hearn was to write an article about the beauties of the route. Van Horne had a genuine interest in the East, and was so persuaded of the good of the trip that he guaranteed to the adventurers an additional cash gift of $250 when they came up to Canada to begin their journey.

Only Hearn's editor hung back from joining in the enthusiasm. He was used to the scrapes into which Hearn got himself, and saw difficulties ahead. But Alden entered into talks with Hearn about the trip, and even cautiously reduced to paper the terms upon which he would consider giving the trip his blessing. He outlined what he wanted from Hearn on the trip, what he would be paid, and at what rates, if the articles Hearn wrote should prove acceptable. But no contract was drawn up. No advance was given. It was to be Hearn's adventure; the risk was not to be shared by his publisher.

Hearn fumed and threatened. On February 3, 1890, he wrote about his money problem to Alden. "I have no assurance of any means beyond $250 to be paid at Montreal. Even supposing myself able to earn something before the date of starting, such a sum would, according to present indications, barely enable me to procure a few absolute necessities for the journey, and pay a few small debts."[41] He was worried about the money he owed to Arnoux in Martinique and to Dr. Gould in Philadelphia.

Alden saw to it that Hearn got a series of small jobs to do for the publishing house. He was handed Anatole France's *Le Crime de Sylvestre Bonnard* to translate. This he did in two weeks—with the help of a girl, "a typewriter" as she was called then, whom Alden sent down to West Tenth Street. He was given $115 for this quick job. He was given two magazine supplements to get together for future issues of *Harper's Magazine*. Hearn did these at top speed. He paid his Martinique debt. He got together some clothes. He bought a few books and a supply of yellow paper. He was terribly busy, but he had time to quarrel with Henry Krehbiel.

Hearn's leap into rage was partly the result of nerves stretched too far upon possibilities. But his willingness to be angry with Krehbiel had an old and long-developing cause; he saw that the intimacy he had thought would last forever had not outlived circumstances. It made him unhappy and rudely angry with Krehbiel. Krehbiel had shown him little regard for many months. When they were together the two men found little to talk about. Hearn refused to let the friendship die a decent quiet death. (Krehbiel, when Hearn was dead, slurred over the fight, and presented himself to the world as having been always his friend and benefactor. And he did so with only a slight juggling of the truth. What was good about their association had warmed them both in the cold days in Cincinnati. The essential fertilizing influence of one upon the other endured.)

The breakup came with comic speed. Hearn had seen very little of Krehbiel since before his first trip to Martinique. Now at the time of his getting ready to go to Japan, he went to Krehbiel's apartment for a pair of shoes he had left there and never claimed. Through some accident of not being able to identify himself to the maid, or to impress her, Hearn was turned away at the door without his shoes. He thought he had been treated as a thief or a vagrant, and wrote Krehbiel this opinion in intemperate language. He intimated that if Krehbiel wanted to see him before he went away, he should have to come to him. Krehbiel replied: "Dear Hearn— You can go to Japan or you can go to hell." [42]

By the time Hearn was ready to set off, Elizabeth Bisland had already left town, on a trip around the world. He had spent a last evening with her of which he spoke ten years later: ". . . Such an evening . . . in a flat off Fifth Avenue, New York, where a certain divine person and I sat by a fire of driftwood, and talked and dreamed about things." [43] He had groped to tell her, before she went away, how much his meetings with her had meant: "Such visits . . . that helped me to forget the great iron-whirling world and everything but yourself. You made a little space of magnetic sunshine for me . . ." [44]

After she had gone, across the space between them, he wrote: ". . . After looking at your portrait, I must tell you how sweet and infinitely good you— can be, and, how much I like you, and how I like you—or at least *some* of those many who are one in you. I might say love you—as we love those who are dead (the dead who still shape lives) . . ." [45]

Never having conquered the distance between them when they were to- gether, he was happier in their relationship when she was gone. He put her image away in his imagination where nothing could mar it.

In leaving New York, Hearn was going through a familiar process, break- ing some relationships, loosening others, tearing himself away from people as well as the scenes of one life, preparing himself for another. "All those irrational partings,—self-wreckings,—sudden isolations,—abrupt severances of attachment," [46] these were the phrases Hearn used in an essay, "A Ghost," which he had written for *Harper's Magazine* the previous winter, and in which, defining a particular type of human being, "the civilized nomad," [47] he tried for his own satisfaction to understand his way of breaking out of the chrysalis of one environment before going on to a new one. Writing in this vein, Hearn softened and romanticized a streak of cruelty and self-punish- ment in himself.

He left New York in the company of his new associate C. D. Weldon on March 6 or 8, 1890. He had spent the previous day with Ellwood Hendrick toward whom he had felt in these last few months only a growth of com- fortable affection. Weldon and Hearn first traveled north from New York to Montreal. There they collected their tickets and the promised $250. Aboard the Canadian Pacific Railway train they crossed the continent, much of it under a late spring snow, and Hearn looked wonderingly at the plains and the mountains. At Vancouver, British Columbia, they boarded the *Aby- sinnia*. The ship began its crossing of the Pacific on March 17th.

At dawn on April 4th Hearn saw the cone of Fuji lifted above the dark shore of Japan.

". . . Impressions so multitudinous and so sharply novel come to me every day that the mind refuses to digest them. Everything seems enchanted now." [1]

Hearn to B. H. Chamberlain from Yokohama, April 1890

14 ❧ *Yokohama: Anteroom to Japan*

The sight that Hearn had at dawn of Fuji lifted above Yokohama was a punctuation of hope for the newcomer. He left his trunk and suitcase in a hotel, asked the word for "temple," hired a kuruma (jinrikisha), and spent the day being pulled from one sacred place to another, calling out *tera* (temple) indefatigably, and prolonging his exploration into the early hours of darkness.

He wrote in "My First Day in the Orient":

There is some charm unutterable in the morning air, cool with the coolness of Japanese spring and wind-waves from the snowy cone of Fuji; a charm perhaps due rather to softest lucidity than to any positive tone,—an atmospheric limpidity extraordinary, with only a suggestion of blue in it, through which the most distant objects appear focused with amazing sharpness. . . . The street-vistas, as seen above the dancing white mushroom-shaped hat of my sandaled runner, have an allurement of which I fancy that I could never weary.

Elfish everything seems; for everything as well as everybody is small, and queer, and mysterious: the little houses under their blue roofs, the little shop-fronts hung with blue, and the smiling little people in their blue costumes. . . .

And perhaps the supremely pleasurable impression of this morning is that produced by the singular gentleness of popular scrutiny. Everybody looks at you curiously; but there is never anything disagreeable, much less hostile in the gaze: most commonly it is accompanied by a smile or half smile. And the ultimate consequence of all these kindly curious looks and smiles is that the stranger finds himself thinking of fairyland. Hackneyed to the degree of provocation this statement no doubt is . . .[2]

His practiced reporter's eye noted too the mixture of Western objects with Eastern ones—"the line of tiny white telegraph poles . . . a shop of American sewing-machines next to the shop of a maker of Buddhist images; the establishment of a photographer beside the establishment of a manufacturer of straw sandals." He knew that he would have to examine more carefully these incongruities, but, "On the first day, at least, the old alone is new for the stranger, and suffices to absorb his attention." [3]

During long hours Hearn climbed steps, stood before gates, passed into shadowy, incensed interiors, and not knowing what was old or new, significant or mean, paid his respects to one altar after another. Being small and dark he did not look very foreign himself, as Hearn noted appreciatively; he might have been a citizen from one of the corners of the Empire. Children stumbled against his legs in courtyards—for he stood stock-still to stare—and smiled at him. Students heard his halting inquiries and stopped to practice their English in answering him. Grave priests served him tea. Treasures of one sect after another were pulled out of polished chests, dusted off, and shown this grave and reverent stranger. Across the gulf of difference there was communication.

If the priests took him for some queer kind of pilgrim, what did Hearn take himself for? He could not have said. His rushing out to embrace Japan upon his first day there had something disproportionate in it. It was a reaction not strictly accounted for by an assignment from a magazine or by his own poignant desire to make a living out of his traveling. Yet he knew that what he was so eagerly doing, going from one shrine to another, was more important to him than any reason he could give, more important than copy for a magazine, more important even than the book he would carefully make of these tingling sensations. He had had a talent for letting a new place knock him off balance. It was happening again, and he welcomed the discomfort and rapture of the familiar experience. He knew, without words to explain, that this overturning of himself was good.

A student in a Buddhist temple asked him why he offered alms to Buddha:

"Are you a Christian?"
And I answer truthfully:—
"No."
"Are you a Buddhist?"
"Not exactly."
"Why do you make offerings if you do not believe in Buddha?"
"I revere the beauty of his teaching, and the faith of those who follow it." [4]

In another sacred place of impressive approaches (a Shinto shrine) he came to an altar expecting some benignant or frightening image, and was confronted with his own face in a mirror. Hearn stared at himself, the seeker, looking back out of the frame of this new land; he was startled into wondering if the discovery of self was to be the end of all his searching.

At last Hearn signaled his kurumaya to return to the hotel. He watched the straw hat bobbing up and down upon the head of the man who was pulling him, and he noticed the design of flying sparrows on the blue towel with which he wiped his sweating face. He thought of "chills, congestions, and pleurisy." [5] In his hotel, too tired to rest, he listened to the song-cry of the blind woman outside: "She will come and rub your weary body 'above and below,' and make the weariness or the pain go away." [6] Beauty was here, but beauty as he had always found it, mixed with the pain of effort and endurance.

The next day and the next Hearn continued to explore Yokohama, its streets and neighboring hills and beaches, and forgot or ignored the formal reason for his trip. He and Weldon had agreed to carry on their researches separately. Hearn had not liked the partner assigned to him and was glad to be rid of his company. However, he had a companion for his discoveries. In one of the Buddhist temples of his first day he had fallen into talk with a young student. Akira Manabe offered to be his guide.

One day they went by train through narrow valleys to the once great city of Kamakura, and to the island of Enoshima. In a belfry of one of the temples of Kamakura, Hearn swung a great beam to sound a bell six hundred and fifty years old: ". . . A sound deep as thunder, rich as the bass of a mighty organ,—a sound enormous, extraordinary, yet beautiful,—rolls over the hills and away. Then swiftly follows another and lesser and sweeter billowing of tone; then another; then an eddying of waves of echoes. Only once was it struck, the astounding bell; yet it continues to sob and moan for at least ten minutes!" [7] It was as if something in his own book, *Some Chinese Ghosts,* had quivered to life.

In Kamakura he saw too a picture of the King of Death, Emma-O, with "eyes of nightmare." [8] He saw too the Daibutsu, with eyes of peace, "the half-closed eyes that seem to watch you through their eyelids of bronze as gently as those of a child . . ." [9] Here were astonishing contrasts, astonishing ranges of thought and feeling.

Akira Manabe was the first of the many Japanese Hearn persuaded to tell him stories. The first sketches of Japan he would write would be punctuated by the talk of Akira, his smiles, his small jokes, his astonishments at the questions Hearn asked:

"Akira, do the Japanese always keep their vows to the gods?"
Akira smiles a sweet smile, and answers:—

"There was a man who promised to build a torii [a sacred gate] of good metal if his prayers were granted. And he obtained all that he desired. And then he built a torii with three exceedingly small needles." 10

Accompanied by Akira, or alone, Hearn continued to look and to make notes on everything. In these first days in Japan he lived an unsparing cycle of inquiry, affirmation, and discovery. He commented wryly on the fullness of his reaction four years later: "Today I spent an hour in reading over part of the notes taken on my first arrival, and during the first six months of 1890. Result, I asked myself: 'How came you to go mad?—absolutely mad?' It was the same kind of madness as the first love of a boy." 11

On April 25th he reported on himself to the friend who had never laughed at him, never criticized—Henry Watkin in Cincinnati:

Here I am in the land of dreams,—surrounded by strange Gods. I seem to have known and loved them before somewhere: I burn incense before them. I pass much of my time in temples, trying to see into the heart of this mysterious people. In order to do so I have to blend with them and become a part of them. It is not easy. But I hope to learn the language; and if I do not, in spite of myself, settle here, you will see me again. If you do not, I shall be under big trees in some old Buddhist cemetery, with six laths above me, inscribed with prayers in an unknown tongue, and a queerly carved monument typifying those five elements into which we are supposed to melt away.12

Hearn was in love with a new place. He knew how much he had to learn, and knew too he could not accomplish this education in the time his journalistic assignment would allow. He had half decided to overstay his assignment, and yet he did not know how it might be arranged. But he found a good base for his explorations in a cheap and decent hotel on the waterfront. Carey's, at Number 93 Yamashita-cho, a hotel frequented by sailors. The American, Carey, who ran it, "was kind, a good man to the bones of him." 13 Hearn was afraid of circumspection and respectability, but he did not mind such a place as Carey's where he could slip in and out and not be noticed. Writing in 1894 Hearn looked back nostalgically at this first place of refuge he had found in Japan. It was an island of safety in a swirl of activity, "an atmosphere of sailors and sealers and mates and masters of small craft . . . a salty medium of water-dogs." 14 In 1894 Hearn would have liked occasionally even to escape from his family and go back to such a disregarded freedom. He wrote then to Chamberlain: "I feel a great temptation this summer to take a run by myself to Hakodate, and plunge into the little hotel kept by Carey the mulatto there. (You may remember I lived at his house in Yokohama . . .). It would be healthy for me, refreshing: I like rough men who don't get too drunk, and I get along with them first-rate." 15

During the irregular hours he spent in Carey's hotel, resting from his expeditions, Hearn wrote the article he owed for his free passage to Japan. In November 1890 *Harper's Magazine* at last published his "A Winter Journey to Japan." Van Horne, the president of the Canadian Pacific, never asked for anything else. He saw the article in the magazine, liked it, and attempted to thank Hearn:

> If you know where to reach Lafcadio Hearn I will be glad if you will tell him that I think his article in the November *Harper's* "A Winter Journey to Japan" is one of the most charming things I have ever read. It appeals the more strongly to me perhaps because I have lived so much in the scenery which he describes. I wondered how he would treat the subject which has become somewhat hackneyed. I am surprised and more than pleased—delighted.[16]

Whether Hearn ever heard this expression of thanks is not known. Many years later Van Horne again offered the writer free passage, this time back to America, at a time when Hearn was considering a visit, and again needed help. But the trip was never accomplished.

If Hearn had been willing to write a number of quick facile sketches about Japan in the manner of the one that had pleased Van Horne, he would have accomplished all that his publisher wanted of him. But he wanted more of himself. Because he found that he could not fulfill his own ambitions under the publisher's conditions, he became angry with his editor. The only solution for Hearn was to smash things.

Something in one of Alden's letters to Hearn angered him. He joined other angers to this initial one. He had found out after coming to Japan, that, justly or unjustly, he did not like C. D. Weldon. He was further angered when he contemplated the fact that Weldon was to be paid more per page than he was. He thought he had had an agreement about the turning over of the advance from the Canadian Pacific to himself; Weldon had not done so. Brooding, Hearn fed every nagging discontent he had had to his general wrath. The Harper firm had not supported him as they might have in his various writing adventures. They had never given him an advance. They were noncommittal, overcautious, disingenuous. They had a vile and ugly method of editing his copy, of rearranging his sentences and paragraphs; their typography was ugly; they were businessmen—the last word was an epithet. Filling the background of this present unhappiness with his publishers was his older, unresolved trouble with Dr. Gould. All these things united in one misery which he resolved by a desperate explosion.

He first hurled at Alden a hasty request that the editor hand over Hearn's books to Dr. George Gould. He wrote to Alden:

I have received a letter from you. I have also sent you a positive request to turn over my books to Dr. Gould. I am under larger obligations to him than to you, or to anyone else in the East: he wants to be paid for his kindness and his expenses, and I have nothing else to pay him with—thanks to your generous scheme to render it impossible for me, under any circumstances, to earn more than $500 a year. Whether you are offended or not has ceased to be of the least concern to me:— you abandoned me in the middle of the epidemic after getting me to make a will in your favor; you broke the promises which you voluntarily made; you lied to me in every possible manner for the purpose of duping me into the power of your brutal firm, which deals in books precisely as they might deal in pork or hay. I could have forgiven all that;—but your desire to utilize me simply to illustrate the idiocies of a sign-painter, rather overreaches the plan.

What do I care about your vulgar Magazine, anyhow?—What inducement have I ever had to alter my work to be spoiled in it? . . . Your miserable $20 per 1000 words—who cares for it at *your* conditions.[17]

There was a P.S. almost rubbed out: "Ask Harry Harper whether he thinks the theft of that $37 which he stole from me still bothers his idiotic mind." [18]

Hearn's suggestion that his publishers had cheated him out of the small, definite sum of $37 was something he firmly believed. There was in the last hurried weeks in New York a slurring over or a misunderstanding of a verbal agreement as to the payment to be made to Hearn for the supplements he compiled for *Harper's Magazine*. For the rest of his life Hearn cherished the belief that the sum agreed upon was $137. He had received only $100.

In writing this letter Hearn had enlarged a few specific complaints into a general denunciation—poured out rapidly, disjointedly, incoherently. It was the kind of letter that his wife would learn to hide in a drawer and show him a week later, to receive his thanks for intercepting it. Alone, angry, undeterred, Hearn in 1890 wrote several more times to Alden, making himself angrier and more abusive in the intoxication of his own words. "Please to understand that your resentment has for me less than the value of a bottled fart, and your bank-account less consequence than a wooden shithouse struck by lightning." [19]

Alden was shocked, and failed to appreciate the style, a swinging Irish profanity in which words had gained complete control of the writer. He replied to these impossible letters with icy good manners. He denied his or his firm's responsibility for Hearn's various misfortunes. He pointed out that the agreement that they had made prior to Hearn's departure from New York was unofficial and nonbinding. Alden also forgave Hearn, or told him he forgave him. The editor's reasonableness infuriated Hearn further. Friendship was like love to Hearn. There was no rationality to it.

In his ordinary dealings with people Hearn was moderate, even timid, in claiming his rights. But when his work was involved he could be caught up in intemperate excesses of mood. He then tried to hurt and punish those who seemed to him to have betrayed him. In this particular storm of anger which marred his first weeks in Japan, Hearn even sent back to Alden the copies of his book contracts. Alden refused to stop sending Hearn's royalties to Japan, as Hearn demanded, but consented to break off relations with him.

"Hearn has utterly cast me off," [20] Alden wrote to Dr. Gould, gladly giving up to him the books which had been a care and an unwelcome burden.

In the fury which possessed him, Hearn finished with Dr. Gould too. He sat down in his room at Carey's Hotel and wrote out an extravagant and unasked personal note. At the same time he authorized Gould to demand his books from Alden:

Apr. 30, 1890

I owe Dr. George M. Gould, of Philadelphia, the sum of $500,—for board and lodging during the summer of 1889.

And in lieu of ready money, I give to him, unconditionally, my library, now in the possession of Henry M. Alden (Editor of Harper's Magazine), at Mr. Alden's private residence, Metuchin, [*Sic.*] New Jersey.[21]

Hearn, before leaving New York, had put before Gould the temptation of doing just this thing: he had given him at that time a letter to Alden asking Alden to hand over the books to Gould. Gould did not use this first authorization, but Hearn thought he had, when, after writing intemperately to Alden, he found that the transaction had taken place almost immediately. Hearn was then triumphant at this disclosure of greed and underhandedness in his former friend. He did not ever see his own deviousness in the matter or the way in which, by setting traps for his former friends, he made them behave more badly than they would have done.

Alden, upon being berated by Hearn, had with utmost speed sent the books to Gould. Gould had accepted them. Gould's sin was now in Hearn's mind the one he had thought the doctor would be guilty of; he had got hold of the books; he did not give them up. Hearn had used the word "unconditionally" in his personal note to Gould, in speaking of giving up his books to him, but he had not really meant the word even in using it. He had been experimenting dangerously upon Gould's human nature. Hearn did not in his heart feel that he owed the doctor anything. He thought his books valuable, and with some justice. When Gould accepted both the books and the note, and did not rebate any of the money, or sell the books and share the profit with Hearn, or even send back to the writer his IOU's, Hearn completed his disillusionment. After a few requests to Gould for specific books out of the collection which he still referred to pointedly as "my" books, he had nothing more to do with Gould. He spoke of him after this time as one who had gulled him. He distrusted and disliked him with all the force of a revulsion from the extravagant deference he had used toward him in the first months of their friendship.

Hearn was now alone in a strange land. He had deprived himself of any security he might have had, and he had made himself ill with anger. Yet, when he wrote to Joseph Tunison on June 10th, a faint cheerfulness and anticipation infused his bitterness:

> It was a bad business for me, this trip to Japan. First, the artist, who is an ignorant brute and unbearably disagreeable, went back on his word to make the first payment from the C.P.R.R. over to me. Secondly, I found rates of living higher in Yokohama than New York. Thirdly, the conditions of the Harpers rendered living by literary work wholly out of the possible. Fourthly, I could not get out of Japan. Fifthly, I could not get employed.
>
> So I have been having a much worse time than in the West Indies. I have broken altogether with the Harpers: to continue would have been an encouragement of the policy of starvation. I am going to settle in an out-of-the-way part of Japan as a school teacher. The position will be open to me in September. Meanwhile I am teaching a little—just enough to keep me from sinking. To do literary work in Japan requires much time. I suppose I must stay at least five years to write a book. The language is extraordinarily difficult. The climate is very cool in winter and very hot in summer. The country is, however, full of the strangest charm. . . .
>
> Well, I will write you better things as soon as I get settled. I am so upset now that I am a poor correspondent. I am afraid I must resign myself to melt into this Orient and be buried in it—out of the hearing of European tongues or the sight of European faces, in a little village where no stranger ever goes.[22]

The general smashup of his affairs was in some way necessary to Hearn. As soon as he had completed his job of breaking up things, he began energetically to rebuild his life. He saw no more of Weldon who had been the outward sign of his bondage to the hated agreement. (Weldon was perhaps not so insensitive as Hearn thought. He made a drawing of Hearn which showed an appreciation of the writer's loneliness in setting out on this journey, a small figure seen from behind, lifting a shabby suitcase.)

Even while receiving blows and giving them, Hearn looked about to find a way to live. He had brought two letters of introduction with him. One, given him by Elizabeth Bisland, was to Mitchell McDonald, an American naval man whom she had met during her journey around the world. McDonald was Paymaster of the United States Navy in Yokohama. He was also a principal owner and promoter of the Grand Hotel of Yokohama. In him Hearn met the kind of honest, downright man of affairs he admired at once. He was so unlike Hearn that nothing ever spoiled their friendship.

He began helping Hearn almost at once. Hearn, in the middle of his quarrel with his publisher, rashly sent back an unopened royalty check which he needed badly. He happened to tell McDonald what he had done. The captain went at once to the postal authorities of Yokohama, got the check back, and persuaded Hearn to accept the money. He also lent or gave money to Hearn during the crisis. For the rest of his life Hearn depended on Captain McDonald for good judgment in all practical matters.

William H. Patten had given Hearn a letter to Professor Basil Hall Chamberlain of Tokyo Imperial University. Hearn sent off this letter the day he arrived in Yokohama. Chamberlain was interested at once. He had already read *Some Chinese Ghosts.* Letters began going back and forth between Yokohama and Tokyo. They were full of eager askings and answerings, and as much concerned with linguistics, folklore, and other widely ranging intellectual matters as Hearn's momentary needs. Shortly Hearn went up to Tokyo, met the professor, and confirmed the liking he had had for the letter writer. In this spare, decisive figure, a man of his own age but of an infinitely more settled position in life, Hearn found at once someone to look up to, to admire, and to depend on.

Chamberlain, an Englishman, had lived in Japan since 1873. He was one of the most distinguished scholars in the country, being a master of both spoken and written Japanese, and an authority upon the origins of the language. No Japanese could detect any foreignness or stiffness in his conversation. He spoke Japanese like a cultivated native gentleman. He had translated the oldest Japanese document, *Kojiki,* into fluent and entertaining English. He had written a book about the primitive indigenous people of the islands, the Ainu. He had written a book about Japanese classical poetry. He had also edited an excellent and amusing book about Japanese customs, *Things Japanese,* a dictionary of facts and customs. With his friend W. B. Mason he was engaged in revising Murray's *Guide to Japan.*

In his first letter Hearn had mentioned tentatively the name of the only Japanese he had known in America, the friendly manager of the Japanese exhibit at the New Orleans Exposition of 1885. "I believe Mr. Ichizo Hattori belongs to the University," [23] he wrote to Chamberlain, thinking that this name, thrown out at a hazard, might turn out to be useful. It was; Hattori was in 1890 a Vice Minister of Education.

When Hearn first wrote to Chamberlain and gave him the fortunate name of Hattori, he thought that any help he might get would be something to add to his regular income from *Harper's Magazine.* But in a few weeks he had broken with his publisher, and needed help urgently. Chamberlain and

Hattori went about their helpfulness at the ritualistic pace possible in Japan, and before they could act, Hearn was out of money, or badly frightened of being so. He had to find something to do at once.

One day he walked into the offce of the headmaster of an English-language school, the Victoria Public School, and persuaded him to hire him as a tutor. The headmaster was evidently impressed by Hearn's list of published books, but he gave the writer only a meager kind of job; Hearn was to tutor one bright boy for several hours each week. That pupil's subsequent recollection, published in 1936, nails into place a lost moment in Hearn's career.

Edward Clarke, a boy of mixed Western and Japanese parentage, a partly crippled fifteen-year-old student, was called one morning into the office of the head, to be introduced to a small foreigner whom the head called "a literary gentleman," [24] who was to tutor him in his English lessons.

Sitting in a chair in the office was "a short, broad-shouldered man, somewhat swarthy of hue, with a fine head, the dark hair on it beginning to grizzle, and already slightly silvered at the temples, clean-shaven except for a moustache, and what struck me most at the time, very clean looking." [25] The boy shuddered for a moment at the strange aspect of the man's blind eye, but checked himself. He remembered his own twisted foot, and how he had suffered from being stared at. Lessons were arranged at once. The new tutor was to help young Clarke for a period of a half-hour every weekday morning, and one hour every Saturday morning.

The experience Clarke had as Hearn's first student in Japan was very short, but it had a quality he never forgot. Hearn showed nothing of his trouble to the boy, but awakened his curiosity and a fine excitation toward learning. Edward Clarke was flattered by this teacher who behaved as if teaching him were the only thing he had to do in the world. Hearn asked the boy if he wished to write, and told him sharply never to go into writing unless he had either genius or an income. He set Clarke to writing essays which he corrected with stimulating asperity.

Clarke wrote:

> . . . I do remember a trick of his, . . . he would burst out in praise, as I fancied, but even as I was mentally patting myself on the back, he would come down with a crusher, and lay me out flat! This sort of thing: "Aha, this is *very* good, ve-ry good, my boy! You have surpassed yourself! The words are well-chosen, the manner quite elegant, the grammar superb, but (a slight pause, then) *it is not English!*" [26]

Clarke also remembered the suddenness of the end of this experience. After a few weeks he was told that "Mr. Hearn had gone away." [27] The pupil only half understood the drama of his teacher's appearance and disappearance. The headmaster had been charmed with the tutor, and asked him to stay at his house, but, his wife being continually shocked by the man's damaged face, he had had to ask him to leave. Hearn fled back to Carey's Hotel.

This kind of melodrama was the usual accent of Hearn's shifting from one environment to another. But, agonies and embarrassments aside, Hearn was more sure than ever that he might make something of Japan: "If I have the chance, I think I shall be able to make myself valuable," [28] he wrote to Chamberlain. He was thinking of his writing, but it seemed that he might be able to teach, and to do well in that career. On an early visit to Tokyo, he had fallen in one day with a foreigner who disclosed to him that he was a teacher in the public-school system of Japan. Hearn learned from him of the extraordinary willingness of the government to hire foreigners, and the advantages that a foreigner, especially one who could teach English, might have in the system.

He wrote about this conversation to Chamberlain: "An English teacher whom I met here, has given me some information about Japanese schools; and from what I could learn through him, I think I should be very glad to serve as English teacher in a public school for several years, if desirable. I should not be at all particular as to what part of Japan I might be sent, nor for how long a period my services might be required." [29]

The necessities of the Japanese government chimed with his own. The government, in its formidable attempt to mold the country into effective competition with the West, had made the English language a required subject on all levels of learning. There was always a need in some corner or other of the vast centralized system of public education for another English teacher.

Chamberlain looked about for such an opportunity for Hearn, and by midsummer—perhaps with the help of Hattori—he found one. There was a vacancy for a teacher of English in Matsue, a city in Shimane Prefecture, far to the south and west of Tokyo across Honshu on the Japan Sea. The governor of Shimane Prefecture, Governor Koteda, was in Tokyo and willing to interview this candidate for a position in his district, and to decide at once whether to hire him. Koteda was an able, upright man of the old tradition, a governor with a strong paternalistic interest in everything which went on in his province.

Koteda and Hearn met and respected each other. Koteda offered Hearn the position; Hearn accepted. A contract was drawn up in July or August. Under its terms Hearn was to teach English in two schools in Matsue, the Middle School and the Normal School, during the next school year, starting in September. He was to receive in yen the equivalent in American money of a monthly salary of $100, but in unsophisticated Shimane Province it would be worth much more.

He wrote to Elizabeth Bisland several letters trying to tell her what he had found in Japan:

DEAR ELIZABETH,— . . . I feel indescribably toward Japan. Of course Nature here is not the Nature of the tropics, which is so splendid and savage and omnipotently beautiful that I feel at this very moment of writing the same pain in my heart I felt when leaving Martinique. This is a domesticated Nature, which loves man, and makes itself beautiful for him in a quiet grey-and-blue way like the Japanese women, and the trees seem to know what people say about them—seem to have little human souls. What I love in Japan is the Japanese—the poor simple humanity of the country. It is divine. There is nothing in this world approaching the naïve natural charm of them. No book ever written has reflected it. And I love their gods, their customs, their dress, their bird-like quavering songs, their houses, their superstitions, their faults. And I believe that their art is as far in advance of our art as old Greek art was superior to that of the earliest European art-gropings . . .

. . . Now, as for myself—I am going to become a country school-master in Japan —probably for several long years. The language is unspeakably difficult to learn; —I believe it can only be learned by ear. Teaching will help me to learn it; and before learning it, to write anything enduring upon Japan would be absurdly impossible. Literary work will not support one here [in the port city of Yokohama], where living costs quite as much as in New York. What I wish to do, I want to do for its own sake; and so intend to settle, if possible, in this country, among a people who seem to me the most lovable in the world.[30]

Koteda found out that the future teacher of English in Matsue could not make his way there without help; he advanced Hearn 80 yen.[31] Nothing remained for Hearn but to turn his back upon the misty wrinkled coast, the port city with its Western sewing machines side by side with Buddhist religious wares, and the decayed and gentle villages nearby which contained the relics of medieval greatness.

With Akira Manabe, who was willing to go with him as interpreter, Hearn set out for Matsue in the Izumo district of Shimane, on the other side of Honshu.

The train moved out of the city and away from the crowded streets. It came to a rocky coast where mountains massed across the way they were to go, and there were many tunnels. Glimpses of the sea appeared on the left between black plunges into the hills. Then there were little valleys among the mountains, and rice fields gave way to tea terraces where long green rows of even rounded shrubs made hillsides look like gardens. The hills swept back, and rivers cut across the plain on which the train now steadily went forward. A long pure shape of mountain slope moved out from behind the hills: Fuji, half seen, then wholly free of obstructions. Hours of travel, and the cities of central Honshu began to pass the window, with farms and fields right up to the edges of the populous areas, canals and rivers cutting through the crowded centers, streets with houses close together, each house decorated with the upward curve of the roof line whether the roof was of thatch or tile. Nagoya was behind them. After dulling hours of travel came Osaka and the port of Kobe. Now on the left were the sails and islands of the Inland Sea, and hills again pressing close and hoary with trees on the right. Then the track emerged upon a vast plain, just out of sight of the sea. There was again the freshness of farmland, active with small stooping, lifting, carrying figures. The massed ranges of central Honshu had withdrawn to a blue line far off. But standing up like individuals in this great plain were single mountains, and groups of mountains, whitened on their tops by masses of bare rock. At last the train reached Okayama and stopped under an echoing shed where the partly covered space rang with the cry of vendors selling lunches and tea.

Hearn and his companion had reached the end of rail travel on their journey. They must turn away now from the coast and go through the mountains. With Akira's help, Hearn hired two kuruma which seemed very light for the rough journey ahead of them. "Over the mountains to Izumo, the land of the Kamiyo, the land of the Ancient Gods," they would go, "a journey of four days by kuruma, with strong runners, from the Pacific to the Sea of Japan . . ."

Through valleys most of this long route lies, valleys always open to higher valleys, while the road ascends, valleys between mountains with rice-fields ascending their slopes by successions of diked terraces which look like enormous green flights of steps. Above them are shadowing sombre forest of cedar and pine; and above these wooded summits loom indigo shapes of farther hills overtopped by peaked silhouettes of vapory gray.[32]

Hearn had been only an unusually perceptive tourist in Yokohama and Kamakura. Making this journey across Japan he began to take part in the life of Japan. Near the end, when Hearn and Akira spent a night in a village near the Japan Sea, he saw Japanese life as more than something exotic.

They were dancing the Bon-Odori that night, the dance of the festival of the dead. Hearn spent few of the hours of darkness sleeping, but slipped out of the inn to watch and to become a part of a monotonous, fascinating pulsation of dim color and repetitious sound. "All together glide the right foot forward one pace, without lifting the sandal from the ground, and extend both hands to the right, with a strange floating motion and a smiling, mysterious obeisance. Then the right foot is drawn back, with a repetition of the waving of hands and the mysterious bow." [33]

He lay down to rest at dawn, his mind vibrating to the music and the motion. In this journey he had begun to see the common humanity of the Japanese. Wayfarers and innkeepers did not seem to think of him as a foreigner at all. In the music of the Bon-Odori it was not the strangeness of the music that had held him, but an emotion caught in its unfamiliar intervals, "something not of only one place or time, but vibrant to all common joy or pain of being, under the universal sun." [34]

He was finding here in Japan not the strange, but a repetition of something familiar, a something common that he had found in other places, in the streets of Cincinnati, of New Orleans, of St. Pierre.

Next morning Hearn and his friend took ship, a small vessel which carried them westward from Yonago along the coast in the open Japan Sea, then into an islanded lagoon, then up a river clear and fresh between mountains and marshy fields, and at last into the center of a city. Anchorage was just short of, and in the shadow of, a long, slightly arching white bridge just where the river flowed toward them out of a lake. The sky above was blue and high and far-reaching. Behind them, the way they had come, was the cold gray peak of Daisen. Nearer to them mountains scalloped the horizon on every side of the city and were blue or greenish-blue. The life of the place rippled the river's and the lake's banks with activity. Matsue was bright, contained, yet lively. Nothing of Europe or America had had anything to do with shaping it.

15 ❧ Land of the Gods

In medieval fashion Hearn was bowed into the Tomitaya Inn on August 30, 1890, and there slept his first night in the city of Matsue, the governmental center of Shimane Prefecture, the older Izumo, in tradition the land of the gods. He awoke to find that his balconied room, hanging over the north bank of the swiftly flowing current of the Ohashi River, was a good place to muse upon the early-morning stirrings of the community. The water of the river flowed across his outward gaze from right to left, having narrowed into swiftness and strength in issuing out of the lake. Before him was his anchorage of the day before where lay the small steamers which served the various ports of the nearby coast of the Japan Sea. At other wharfs the shadowed figures of fishermen loosed their slender tapering boats to catch the current and move quickly downstream to the fishing grounds in the lagoon beyond the small mountain range which seemed to shut the river from freedom. Early stirrers in the life of the city had begun to move across the bridge which spanned the river just beyond its exit from the lake. These dawn figures were lighted by the rising sun which shone, from behind the volcanic cone of Daisen, past them, past the bridge, to give color to the lake and to its ring of mountains receding to the west. Although Matsue was an inland city, several miles up the Ohashi River from the Nakaumi Lagoon, an inlet on the Japan Sea, yet it was a city set in the midst of flashing waters. Its habitations, one-story and of unpainted wood, bordered the lower

end of Lake Shinji and the lake's outlet into the Ohashi River. Its neighborhoods were laced with canals and moats only a generation ago defensive of
Matsue's massive castle. This stronghold of the Matsudaira family stood now
empty and unused upon its hill in the center of the city, surrounded by
magnificent pines and great walls, open to the games of children and the
strolls of the solitary-minded. The castle was a fitting symbol of the essential
nature of the place, a nature denied not by habit or mood but by edict.
Matsue was still medieval, although its medieval function was gone. Japan
had moved by law out of its indurated Middle Ages into the modern world,
but Matsue, far from trade routes, with no occasion for industry, had not
changed very much in the twenty-two years since Japan had declared itself
part of the community of nations. Matsue was a city still recognizably divided
into samurai, merchant, and priestly quarters. Everywhere there were signs
of the live functioning of Shinto, the older of the two religions of Japan.
These things Hearn began to notice in the two days he had of freedom to
walk and look before he took up his position of teacher in the city.

Upon the morning of September 2nd, Hearn reported first to Governor
Koteda at the prefectural office, a painted frame building, large and ram-
bling, and then, nearby, to the Middle School, a building of similar Western
style, almost like a New England American building, to meet his classes and
begin a new career. Hearn was curious about his pupils, and they about him.
They were boys of twelve to sixteen years of age, accustomed to obeying and
revering their teachers, but under a quiet decorum they hid a stir of interest
in the new foreign teacher. When the dean of the school, who was also a
teacher of English, Sentaro Nishida, brought the new master into the room
the boys looked at the stranger with childish, candid eyes wide with expectation. Here was a small man, dark as many Japanese, blind in one eye,
quiet of movement, speaking his language to them hesitantly, slowly, in a
low musical voice. Nishida had prepared them for this day's lesson before
he introduced them to the new teacher. He remained in the room for a time,
helping Herun-san, as the new master was named to them, to call the roll
and to establish a routine.

This day and the next and the next, awkwardness and confusion gradually
dispersed. Nishida was always there to help. Herun-san began to enter into
communication with his students. The new teacher puzzled the boys at first,
but they soon felt the stimulating pressure of good teaching. He was always
painstakingly clear and insistent in his methods. He spoke to them in short,
simple sentences. He wrote principal words upon the board in a beautiful
script. The half-blind teacher, whose understanding seemed to run just ahead
of their striving, began to interest his students as a person too.

He caught their imaginations. He was polite and dignified and satisfactorily remote. He told good stories when they were tired and bored with
drill. He came to them from far-off places and had the air of having seen
much and experienced much. This was a vague excitement to boys who had
never been far from the small city of Matsue. As Herun-san came to know
these pliable boys better, he challenged them softly and insistently. He asked
them to write short essays in English. He required them not only to exercise
new words and phrases, but to be honest in their statements, and to try to
think. He upset them in a healthy disturbance of complacency so that for
the first time in their lives they thought about their own feelings, their own
daily living habits, the ideas among which they lived.

Teaching every school day his youthful students of the Jinjo Chugakko,
or Ordinary Middle School, and four times a week the slightly older pupil-
teachers of the Shihan-Gakko, or Normal School, Hearn learned the routine
of a new profession. He pleased the administration of public education in
Matsue who were also somewhat dazzled at having a writer on the teaching
staff. Still, he was lonely. (Akira Manabe, his companion of the road, stayed
only a short time in Matsue.) Hearn worked his curiosity hard to fill in what
might have been empty hours for a foreigner in a strange city. He learned all
the odd corners of Matsue, the cemeteries, the street shrines, the public buildings, the castle grounds near enough to the school for a daily stroll, and all
the places of interest within the distance of a walk or a short kuruma ride
from the central point of the white bridge across the Ohashi River.

Upon September 14th he made his first considerable journey. He went to
Taisha. This was the ancient shrine of Izumo, the oldest sacred place of
Shinto in Japan, in the village of Kitzuki, twenty and more miles west of
Matsue. The teacher of English found that he must consume much time in
the going. He had first to cross Lake Shinji by boat, and then, by kuruma,
travel miles across a plain crossed by streams and a river and bordered on
each side by mountains. He arrived in Kitzuki after dark.

He liked what he first saw: the shopping street hung with lanterns, the
long avenue beyond the village leading gently uphill to the shrine enclosure,
an approach under pines, and over a number of bridged streams, and the
enclosure itself, an area of generous spaces among ancient buildings, dusky
and indistinct against the mountains, the shaggy Yakumo-yama.

At the Inabaya Inn he was pleased by a solicitous reception. This seemed
to be the kind of inn, clean, well staffed, elegant, which one could surprisingly
find even in the smallest places in Japan. The proprietor accepted Hearn
without fuss as just another pilgrim. The teacher from Matsue was well fed
and sheltered, and awoke at dawn, to the thudding of the nearby pounding

of rice, to push aside the heavy wooden shutters and look out at this new world.

He explored by daylight the village and the shrine. He familiarized himself with the generous graveled spaces of the sacred enclosure where occasionally, among the massed and reverent pilgrims, would move the slight and graceful shapes of the "daughters of the gods," the young dancing priestesses, and where might be heard the music of the gods, the flutes and drums of the priests. He learned to make the circle of these grounds counterclockwise, as the course enjoined by belief. He watched behind blowing curtains the white-robed priests performing movements like a slow solemn dance, and he stared upward at the mysterious crossed beams of the oldest and most sacred building, the style of which had been set before the memory of man. He enjoyed perhaps most of all the sacredness of the very trees and rocks and soil, for before the buildings had been built (and they were often rebuilt for ritual reasons and because of fires) this ground itself had been sacred. He learned that Taisha, at least this space sheltered by pines and cedars, had been sacred to pilgrims for three thousand years.

On Sunday night Hearn went back to Matsue, his head filled with the greatness of this small place, pleased by the friendly reception he had had there.

They knew him in Kitzuki after this first visit, and welcomed him back when he returned. And he went again and again, rising early on Saturday morning, a day of freedom from teaching, and coming home late on Sunday night. He enjoyed Kitzuki intensely. There was the shrine for wonder; there were many small shops for curiosity; there was the inn for comfort. There was also a pretty little beach a short walk away, down a hill, through a narrow street—a walk ending in an open space facing a curved bay with a decorative rock just offshore. There was a branch of the Inabaya Inn facing the beach. Here was everything Hearn admired in Japan: an ancientness encumbered with customs, a little town unmodernized, an inn of good Japanese style, a place to swim.

Although thousands of Japanese from all the islands of the Empire came to visit the great shrine of Izumo, particularly during the seasons of pilgrimage, this one pilgrim could not escape becoming well known there. The small dark foreign teacher from Matsue became a personage in the village and an honored and habitual guest at the inn. He was known too at the cake shop across the narrow street from the inn entrance. Here he customarily purchased a special kind of cake, white on the outside, chewy and dark brown on the inside, which he took home to Matsue to offer to his students as a special treat when they came to call and to drink green tea with him.

The maids who brought his meals and fetched his shoes came to adore him. He was kind, he was aware of them, and he tried to talk a baby kind of Japanese with each one of them. They attempted to protect this odd one, who was so full of enthusiasm and sudden starts of liking and disliking. One young maid, O-tani Yasuda, never forgot how he awoke full of energy in the mornings, and insisted on opening for her the wooden, sliding shutters, barriers to the sun and air. She did not mind either his juvenile enthusiasm for the long approach to the shrine, which he liked even better than the shrine enclosure itself, an enthusiasm which caused him to keep up late this same seventeen-year-old maid to carry a lantern for him on his accustomed strolls at night under the old pines. Down at the beach inn the young maid, Miss Tani, as he called her, learned to laugh at him, and to let him see she laughed, for he did not mind, when he came in from swimming all day, and complained loudly of a blistered back. She, and the others at the inn, learned at last not to be afraid when he swam far out, almost beyond their sight. They had been sure at first he would not get back. But he did, and he explained to them complacently, "My body never sinks." [2] O-tani never ceased to admire, when she was no longer afraid, the way he could lie upon his back upon the water, and lift his arms above his head, and folding them, rest his head upon them with the utmost ease.

One day there was a festival in the street of the inn, a festival of the particular shrine of the street. Herun-san took O-tani Yasuda with him when he went shopping that day. She never forgot the day, for he bought for her a hairpin, a costly tortoiseshell hairpin. It cost two yen; one could live for a month on that. It had a design of waves and a seabird. But she was too shy to eat with him, when he asked her to, or to have her picture made with him. He said things to her innocent listening that he seldom said to anyone else. He told her that he had no parents, and that he missed very much the love of mother and father.

Sixty-nine years later, O-tani remembered these things.

Seeing the great Taisha shrine at Kitzuki was Hearn's definitive experience of the "way of the gods" which had survived in its authentic humbler forms in this part of Japan. Elsewhere it was masked by the forms of Buddhism, or manipulated in a nineteenth century effort to make it serve the state. In Kitzuki, and in the little shrines of Matsue, he saw how important was this force in the life of the people, and how unthought of, and natural. He wrote in his first book about Japan, a book formed by his experiences in Matsue:

Buddhism has a voluminous theology, a profound philosophy, a literature vast as the sea. Shinto has no philosophy, no code of ethics, no metaphysics; and yet, by its very immateriality, it can resist the invasion of Occidental religious thought as no other Orient faith can. Shinto extends a welcome to Western science, but remains the irresistible opponent of Western religion; and the foreign zealots who would strive against it are astounded to find the power that foils their uttermost efforts indefinable as magnetism and invulnerable as air.[3]

Kitzuki gave Hearn his first understanding of the Japanese ability to take in the new and yet not give up the old, the trait of maintaining a distinct being while greedily absorbing whatever it could use of other cultures. Kitzuki was the beginning of his groping for the secrets of the national character. The childishness of the religious myth, the dignity of the ritual, the loyalty of performance tying all Japanese together in the state of devotion—all these things generated power. Hearn was interested and inclined, without a shred of fellow faith, to be sympathetic.

If Kitzuki hinted to him of the mystery of Japanese life, Matsue came to mean the decency of daily common existence. In this small compact city, isolated from the rest of Japan, Hearn was gaining confidence in his performance of the role of teacher and was even finding opening before him the delight of participation in the general life of the place.

For almost at once the foreigner, who was gentle and good to the boys of the Middle School and stimulating to the older students of the Normal School, had become a prominent citizen in the ingrown, self-appreciative community. And here, for once, Hearn did not resent attention. Here attention was so gentle and undemanding (at least so it seemed to him at first), that he hardly felt any pressure from it.

He wrote to Chamberlain:

To escape out of Western civilization into Japanese life is like escaping from a pressure of ten atmospheres into a perfectly normal medium. I must also confess that the very absence of the Individuality essentially characteristic of the Occident is one of the charms of Japanese social life for me: here the individual does not strive to expand his own individuality at the expense of every one else.[4]

The governor invited him to call, and showed him his art treasures. Miss Koteda, the governor's daughter, sent the new teacher the gift of a caged songbird, an uguisu. It had a remarkable voice, and seemed in one of its phrases to be repeating again and again a particular Buddhist prayer. Hearn, with his new interest in the way Buddhism had penetrated into everyday life, was charmed by this bird which uttered an approved religious sentiment.

The soft and fervent interest of Matsue flustered and pleased him. He did a thing he had never done before; he made a public talk. Astounded at himself, but proud too, Hearn wrote to Chamberlain in October:

I had to make a speech before the educational association of Izumo the other day, and in citing the labours of Darwin, Lubbock, Huxley, and others, I quoted also Tylor's delightful little book on Anthropology. My speech was on the Value of the Imagination as a Factor in Education. The Governor ordered it to be translated and printed;—so I am being for the moment perhaps much more highly considered than I ought to be.[5]

It was extraordinarily lucky for Hearn that the Western ideas current in Japan were identical with those which had shaped his own amateur knowledge of science and philosophy. There was in these colleagues of his the same tremulous admiration for the social applications of evolution which he had learned from his private reading in New Orleans, New York, and Martinique. Spencer was a god here too.

The new teacher, with his respect for Japanese customs, and his up-to-date interest in the ideas of the West which the Japanese felt they must make their own, became a sort of pet of Matsue. The newspapers of the town considered his every move. His fame abroad was probably exaggerated in Matsue, but could not fail to please. A man of letters was a great person in this unindustrialized society.

At the end of October the new teacher consolidated his position in the community by moving out of the Tomitaya Inn into a rented house of his own. He did not accomplish this move without a quarrel, but progress in Hearn's life was always accompanied by quarrels. In this case he was mortally offended by the conduct of the innkeeper, not to him, his guest, but to the man's own child. The proprietor of the inn had a little girl with a disfiguring disease of the eyes. Hearn, who was particularly sensitive to any trouble of the eyes, remonstrated with the man, and found that the landlord had no intention of spending his money to save the child's sight. Hearn burst out in hot anger, and refused to stay under the roof of such a father. Later he gave the man money for the necessary treatment, and saw that the child's eyes were saved; so Mrs. Hearn remembered.

Away from this moral ugliness, Hearn expanded into a life-observing and life-sharing routine in his new little house, a house he called his "bird-cage house," [6] because of its smallness and fragility. It had a beautiful situation from which to observe the life of the city. The house fronted upon the lake just above the bridge, on the same northern side of the water as his inn. Even before he rose from the padded coverlets which were spread in the center of his small matted room, he could hear the morning noises of the city, the swift hollow patter of geta (wooden clogs) upon the bridge nearby, and the sharp clapping of hands in the Shinto salutation to the sun at its rising. When he raised himself from his prone position, and pushed aside the shoji already warmed by light from the east, he could see river, bridge, and early-morning risers. It was of this scene that he wrote in his essay "The Chief City of the Province of the Gods."

His colleague, the dean of the Middle School, Sentaro Nishida, came often to this house to talk with Hearn. It was remarkable and fortunate how quickly the two men became friends without waiting for time to seal the bond, or for supposed national differences to fade. Perhaps Nishida's youth and unusual intelligence had something to do with his disregarding the usual barriers. Hearn was as usual impetuous in friendship; this time he was justified. Nishida, twenty-nine to Hearn's forty, became another of the younger friends so necessary to him, another Krehbiel, another Matas, whom Hearn treated as a contemporary uncle to whom to take his troubles and with whom he could relax, be foolish, and with whom, in this case, he could innocently drink a little too much sake, and laugh, and quote poetry, and be ambitious.

It was to this house that his students first came to sit and ask shy questions of their teacher—they were almost inarticulate in admiring and asking. "Sometimes they scarcely speak at all, but appear to sink into a sort of happy reverie. What they come really for is the quiet pleasure of sympathy. Not an intellectual sympathy, but the sympathy of pure good-will: the simple pleasure of being quite comfortable with a friend." [7] So Hearn wrote later.

In the classroom formal acceptance upon the part of the boys had long ago quickened into something else. They had had, before Hearn, another Western teacher. He was a missionary, of a thick-skinned, obtuse kind, who had tried to proselytize them and had derogated their Japanese customs and beliefs. The new master was very different. He honored their ways, perhaps more than those ways were honored by the Japanese masters. Even in Matsue the school was the agency of change of the Meiji government. Hearn was firm in telling his students to be Japanese. He was also a little upsetting in making them look at themselves and think about themselves as no one else ever had. He was always open to their ambitions, their troubles, their joys. They found him, in spite of his foreignness, as true a figure of the teacher as they had all their lives been taught to admire. Yet he was a teacher imbued with qualities they could like as well as respect. He had warmth of opinion and an unpretentious candor. He was exciting as well as kind.

In his turn Hearn was finding satisfactions in the job of teacher. He had never taught, and he found that at least in Matsue he liked to teach. He enjoyed the drama of the teacher-student relationship. Although he was impatient of the regular teaching hours and the time away from his writing, although he hated the monotony of drillwork, yet he knew that he could learn more about Japan from his students than from any other associates. They were naïve, soft-natured, half formed, and utterly honest.

The schools in Matsue were instructive in their very existence. Matsue, although upon a remote coast and unserved by a railroad, yet came under the central government's anxious scrutiny in every phase of education. The Middle School with its three hundred boys was only one of a number of institutions grouped together upon extensive and pleasant grounds. These buildings served all the educational needs of the community except the higher levels of college and university training. There was a Normal School where 150 boys and girls studied and in their final year practiced teaching. For this purpose a kindergarten and an elementary school were attached to the Normal School. Girls attended the elementary school with the boys, but at the age when the boys entered the Middle School the girls, if they went on with their education, were trained in special schools. Hearn, by the terms of his contract, was required to teach in the Normal School as well as in the Middle School, but found that he did not spend much time there and had little contact with the students; they were not allowed to visit their teachers. Most of his teaching time, and all his private friendships, were with the boys of the Middle School. Yet Hearn was keenly interested in the other schools, and visited them, making notes for future articles. He was charmed by the kindergarten which allowed the children to learn while playing with colored papers in light, attractive rooms; he thought of Spencer's theories of learning in which the needs of the body and the needs of the emotions took precedence over the needs of the pure intellect. He noted with approval the skillful teaching of science in the elementary grades. Yet what would happen to traditional Japan when these children grew up? Hearn was in a genuine quandary. Two of his dearest enthusiasms seemed irreconcilable.

So, coming to this remote part of Japan where the old ways were still powerful, Hearn found that he had not escaped the central problem of Japan: the merging into effective functioning in the modern world of the ways of tradition and the ways of science. Hearn's own position was in that area of conflict.

Nishida made Hearn's practical functioning as a teacher easy. He also brought Hearn into the quiet communings of the faculty in their room apart where, between periods, and before school opened, each day these grave gentlemen sat about a hibachi and smoked long Japanese pipes with minute, decorative bowls. Hearn, always a devoted smoker, enjoyed this most ceremonial form of tobacco appreciation. He secured a Japanese pipe of his own, tapped his pipe as gravely and satisfiedly upon the porcelain edge of the hibachi as the others, and enjoyed the stillness of such moments between the demanding hours when he stood up to face his students.

Outside school, Nishida invited Hearn to his house. Nishida was a kind, generous man who seemed not to be conscious of the barriers supposed to be separating the Eastern man from the Western man. He and Hearn built a true friendship very quickly, making little of the improbabilities of such a bond being formed as it was. His wife was the first Japanese woman Hearn knew, his family and house, the first Japanese household into which Hearn was accepted. Nishida, who was a man of frail health himself, began worrying about Hearn's own solitary and possibly unhealthy regime alone in his small house on the lake.

Even in temporary quarters, without having yet settled to any solidity of existence, Hearn was glad that he had come to this place to which he had been assigned by chance, and not to one of a hundred other cities. He appreciated at once that he could not have come to a place where there was more of the old Japan visible, still a part of everyone's unconscious living and breathing.

Matsue and its community of forty thousand souls had been yoked by the prefectural government to the new modernizing energy of the central government. The old feudal system was legally dead; the samurai class had been impoverished for a generation. Yet the remoteness of Matsue allowed much of the tone of the pre-Meiji Era to survive.

Governor Koteda, whose seat of office was not the castle, but the Western-style prefectural office down in the town, was pleased to keep the older ways green by rituals, ceremonies, and public festivals. These celebrations were empty of power, but faithfully held together the forms. It was only twenty-two years since the rule of the shogun and his daimio had been upset, his two-sword men stripped of their position and bit by bit of their income, and both daimio and samurai absorbed into a more modern allegiance to the nation in the person of the Emperor in Tokyo. But here old ways, at least in manners, persisted. Soon there was no one in Matsue more solicitous of preserving the old ways than the new foreign teacher of English of the Middle School and the Normal School.

Foreigners seldom came to Matsue, which made it easier for the town to accept this particular one who was so eager to learn, and not just to teach. (Yet the city was anxious for him to teach that one essential that Japan must learn in order to compete on equal terms with the Western world, that one indispensable tool, the English language.) Matsue was so disarming that Hearn forgot his usual suspicions and became almost social. In his room at the inn, in his little birdcage house on Lake Shinji, he received fellow teachers and students, and from these quarters went out to parties, club meetings, to dinners, to talks, to civic occasions.

He lived less and less like a foreigner. He taught in Western clothes, as did most of the Japanese teachers; but when he went home he learned, as they did, to put off trousers and stiff-collared shirts, binding coat, and hard shoes, and put on instead the loose-fitting kimono and sandals. With his usual single-track devotion to adapting himself to a new place, he gave up Western food (there was not much to be had in Matsue) and lived on the lighter, daintier, but perhaps not so filling, Japanese food. As winter came on, Hearn warmed himself only in the Japanese style—in his paper-thin house—by the not very adequate glow of the porcelain charcoal-burning hibachi, and its winter adaptation, the *kotatsu,* an ingenious but simple device for conserving the warmth of the hot charcoal by covering both the hibachi and the legs of those huddled around it with a quilt or comforter.

But these pots of heat were set in the middle of breezy rooms whose outer parts were as cold as outdoors. This was the snow country of Japan. Early in the winter the wind blew from the mainland of Asia across the Japan Sea and began to pile drifts against the fragile houses. Hearn watched the snow descend in its erratic but inexorable fall with something like a despairing consent. There had to be a flaw in Izumo; this was it. The province of the gods was cold in winter. Hearn would have to suffer for his enchantment. He shivered and shook at home, in school, and hurrying alongside the snow-banks between his two destinations. He had no knack for making himself comfortable.

Within a few weeks he suffered something more than discomfort. He had to leave off his teaching and go to bed, solitary and frightened in his chilly house. He was ill with some respiratory infection for several weeks. He wrote in January 1891 to Professor Chamberlain:

I myself am very sick. I boasted too soon about my immunity from cold. I have been severely touched where I thought myself strongest—in my lungs—and have passed some weeks in bed. My first serious discouragement came with this check to my enthusiasm; I fear a few more winters of this kind will put me underground. But this has been a very exceptional winter, they say. The first snow-storm piled five feet of snow about my house, which faces the lake, looking to Kitzuki. All the mountains are white, and the country is smothered with snow, and the wind is very severe. I never saw a heavier snowfall in the United States or Canada. The thermometer does not go so low as you might suppose, not more than about twelve above zero; but the houses are cold as cattle barns, and the hibachi and the kotatsu are mere shadows of heat—ghosts, illusions. But I have the blues now; perhaps tomorrow everything will be cheerful again. The authorities are astonishingly kind to me. If they were not, I do not know what I should do.[8]

Recovering from his illness in a comfortless house, it seemed the most natural thing in the world to consent to Professor Nishida's kind arrangement for him to marry and be taken care of. The proposal was a sober and conventional Japanese one, managed in traditional, respectable fashion by an estimable go-between, Professor Nishida himself. It was a considered bond, contracted for the benefit of both parties to the contract. Nishida had seen the helplessness in Hearn's management of his daily practical affairs. He was also a friend of the young woman's family, an impoverished samurai family, and saw the benefit that would come to her and her people through this relatively prosperous if unconventional marriage.

Setsu—meaning "true," a name sometimes rendered familiarly by the diminutive Setsuko—was the twenty-two-year-old daughter of the Koizumi family of Matsue. Koizumi was an honorable name. The family had belonged to the retainer class, samurai, sword-men of the daimio: but Koizumi was a name of honor only, now; its function was gone. Setsu's grandfather had been a tutor in the family of the lord of the castle in his days of power. He and his descendants, like small but proper aristocrats after the French Revolution, like minor plantation people after the American Civil War, had survived the social revolution of 1868 with their principles and their manners intact, but with no homely skill or knack for making a living in a changed world. Their income, a measured supply of rice given annually by their feudal lord, was cut off. They had no training in commerce, nor did they wish to compete with the other classes learning eagerly to make their way in the new world of the Meiji Era. In marrying the foreigner, Setsu was helping her family to whom she owed her first duty always. Herun-san seemed cheerfully willing, as a proper Japanese son-in-law, to take on the obligation of caring for them all. And marrying an outsider was no concern of hers, if her elders agreed to it; it was only one step further along the road of obedience and deference on which she had been set from childhood.

The marriage was accomplished in its proper forms, probably in the month of January 1891. Lafcadio married Setsu in the Japanese ceremonies only (for if he had married this Japanese woman in a foreign ceremony she might lose her citizenship and her native property rights): the intimate family ritual of the exchange of rice wine in the presence of witnesses, and then the proper registration of the fact with the town authorities.

Hearn may not have followed all the involutions of the thinking of the Koizumi family in being brought to this unusual marriage for their daughter.

But he was lonely; he was unable to look after himself; he was willing to agree with Nishida to this proper solution for his solitariness, perhaps at first without looking very far into his future or Setsu's.

In spite of the ceremony of marriage being clothed in all proper Japanese forms, in spite of Hearn's own desire to be properly Japanese, the two of them had to create an accommodation of their own within the forms. Nothing in the background of either of them could prepare them for the problems, the complications, the ramifications of this marriage. The remarkable thing was that the two disparate human beings did achieve a relationship of solidity and permanence.

But all the circumstances were strange for the new wife. "When I went to him, I found only one table and a chair, a few books, one suit of clothes, and one set of Japanese *kimono*." [9] Mrs. Hearn wrote thus in her *Reminiscences,* a book of naïve truthfulness, valuable for the qualities that were in her from the beginning: sound sense, delicacy of apprehension, a firm will. In January 1891, in spite of being frightened by the oddity of her husband, she began to try to bring order into his life.

It would have been easy for no one. It was particularly hard for a Japanese whose manners were fixed by custom for each possible situation. Although Hearn loved Japanese things extravagantly, an extravagance Setsu noticed at once, he did not conform his manners very greatly to Japanese usage. He had no patience with people or customs displeasing to his sense of fairness. There was never any disguise in his anger. Over his previous abrupt leave-taking from the inn, Setsu at once suffered too.

She wrote:

A man moved into our neighborhood and called on him. This man had been in the same hotel on Zaimokucho, and was a friend of the hotel-keeper. He came to borrow a corkscrew. After greeting him, Hearn asked, "Is it you who stayed at that hotel in Zaimokucho, and were a friend of the hotel-keeper's?" The man answered, "Yes, I am his friend." Hearn replied, "I dislike you because you are that strange and unsympathetic fellow's friend. Sayonara. Good-bye!"—and left him and went inside the house. This man naturally did not understand what the trouble was, so I tried to explain, but I was very much embarrassed.[10]

When they left the house by the lake and went to live in another house, the easily aroused pity of both of them added to their nondescript collection of movables one small cat. She wrote, recalling these days when they came closer step by step toward an understanding of each other:

We moved with a maid and a pussy-cat. One evening in the early spring of that year while the air was yet chill and penetrating, I was standing on the veranda admiring the sunset on the lake, when I saw, directly below the veranda along the shore, four or five naughty children ducking pussy up and down in the water and cruelly teasing her. I begged the pussy of the children, brought her back to the house, and told the story to Hearn. "Oh, poor puss!" he exclaimed. "What cruel children they were!" And he held the shivering pussy right in his bosom to warm her. That time I felt a great admiration for him.[11]

From the beginning Hearn's carelessness about money alarmed her. As a proper Japanese wife she began to manage and to conserve their income. Hearn was grateful and pleased. A similar recklessness about his own health, the way he wasted himself in his writing, alarmed her even more. She found him white-faced, unconscious of his surroundings, in a trance of concentratedness at his desk late one night, and was frightened. She even went to Nishida-san to ask, innocently and hesitantly, if Hearn were not a little mad. He reassured her that Hearn was behaving only as other devoted writers did. She gradually accustomed herself to his habits, shyly responding with a bloom of happiness to his un-Japanese openness of pride in her as his wife, his extravagance in clothing her in expensive materials. The young wife, not beautiful, but with a distinction of refinement, expanded into confidence in her honored position as the wife of the foreign teacher and author.

As for his own attitude toward this marriage he had contracted, Hearn was quixotic and extreme. He considered himself bound. He paid no attention to the common practice of the single foreign male in Japan; his idol, Loti, for one, had married and got unmarried in Japan as easily as he had rented a house and given it up. The general Western attitude toward Oriental legalities (this was the decade that produced *Madame Butterfly*) affected Hearn not at all. Through enduring many kinds of social persecution, he had achieved a perfect freedom from the tyranny of social convention. In this freedom he bound himself harder than ever to his own private standard.

During his first year of marriage he wrote to Ellwood Hendrick with whom he was always frank: "My household relations have been extremely happy. The only trouble is that they begin to take the shape of something unbreakable, and to bind me very fast here at the very time I was beginning to feel like going away." [12]

Two years later he wrote to Hendrick what a transformation marriage had made in his life, how it had exorcised the "hunger for the eternal feminine." "Marriage seems to me the certain destruction of all that emotion and suffering,—so that one afterwards looks back at the old times with wonder. One cannot dream or desire anything more, after love is transmuted into the friendship of marriage. It is like a haven from which you can see the dangerous sea currents, running like violet bands beyond you out of sight." [13]

During 1891 he wrote to Professor Chamberlain an opinion which had not been formed by analysis and abstraction: "But how sweet the Japanese woman is!—all the possibilities of the race for goodness seem to be concentrated in her. It shakes one's faith in some Occidental doctrines. If this be the result of suppression and oppression—then these are not altogether bad. On the other hand, how diamond-hard the character of the American woman becomes under the idolatry of which she is the subject." [14]

Of all errant bachelors Hearn was most needful of, and when loaded with the burden most grateful for, the weight of a family. He had never belonged to a family in any way that could count, and he was delighted with the acquisition of Setsu's father and mother, grandfather and grandmother, family servants, and all the ramifications of duties, obligations, and benefits which having a family in Japan entailed. He never quailed visibly at the prospect of supporting them. He spent hours with the grandfather, who was his own favorite. The old man was not only an interesting person in himself but also a relic of the old Japan Hearn had fallen in love with.

The strange match functioned better than Hearn's friends might have expected, better than Setsu's family had hoped. With the well learned abnegation of the Japanese woman Setsu simply accepted Hearn. "He never had the least patience with anything he disliked. I was still young then, and not used to the world, so this peculiarity of Hearn's caused me embarrassment many times. This was Hearn's innate temperament, and I thought it good." [15] Helping her too in these earliest years was the fact of Hearn's teaching and writing; these activities were admired in Japan; Setsu was proud of her odd, combative, generous husband.

Each one changed the other as they progressed into intimacy. Hearn was never quite the proper Japanese husband. He was too demanding of Setsu, in company, conversation, and ideas, and he made more of his wife than was decorous. They created their own language, "the Hearnian dialect," a baby Japanese matched with a baby English, in order to talk at all. Speaking their private language gropingly, they sometimes laughed. This was not proper either. Laughter with a geisha was customary, but giggling with one's wife was unseemly.

Hearn had lived in a stoic bareness in the inn and the small house by the river. Such soldierly living was no longer suitable. He was able to adopt larger and more ample ways because, as a teacher, he was able to save money. A sign of affluence was his move in June 1891 from the house on Lake Shinji to a house near the castle enclosure, a house called Kitabori, Northern Moat. Going to live in these new circumstances, where there was space for the whole family he had undertaken to support, was a move not only into comfort but into delight.

16 ❧ *Kitabori*

Hearn lived only five months, from June to November 1891, in the rented samurai house called Kitabori, between the castle hill and a neighboring wood filled with doves, but it seemed a long pause of contentment. It was a time in his life that seemed later an epoch; Kitabori signified to him all that was beautiful in Japan, and much that was significant. Even today the idea of Hearn in Japan calls up the image of Hearn in Kitabori. Yet he lived and worked, and changed his ideas for twelve years more, after he moved out of this house.

What seemed wonderful at first was the difference in himself. He was hardly the same man who had been so angry in Yokohama, so harassed and houseless in New York. Here he was sheltered and clothed in substantial dignity and moved about his modest affairs in an aura of importance. The house itself, the center of his new life of marriage, teaching, and writing, was the symbol to him (as he showed in writing of it in several essays) of everything good he had found in Matsue. Under the new regime of his wife's practical management, Hearn lived and breathed with quiet satisfaction. Setsu had grown quickly accustomed to Hearn's difficult ways and had begun smoothing away from around her husband's feet all the petty daily complications, the many critical annoyances which in other places had distracted him and kept him from his work. Now he learned to resign the care of such things to Setsu and to use his own time for writing. Japan seemed to promise him many books. That he became, in his own house, a beneficent tyrant, Hearn innocently never knew.

Hearn's peacefulness in Kitabori was made possible by the comparative affluence his salary and his occasional royalties from America brought him. (There was a small flurry of these royalties during his first year in Japan from work he had done before he left New York, but this American income soon stopped, and Hearn lived for several years almost entirely on his teaching salary.) His modest prosperity enabled him to live in Matsue like a well-to-do man. His house, in a row of similar walled and gardened houses facing the castle moat (once the houses of the chief retainers of the Daimio, houses near the castle for a quick call to service in the days when *samurai* was a function instead of a word denoting, as it did in 1891, a fading, impoverished, dispossessed class) was spacious and well designed. It had a kind of beauty new to Hearn, but regulated by a thousand years of Japanese experiment in making utility elegant: clean straw-matted floors, a shining framework of bare wood, sliding walls which opened room to room for spaciousness, or opened the inner house to a view not of a street but of varying views of the private garden spaces within the walls.

Hearn's salary allowed the retaining of a gardener who kept the shrubs and trees, the raked graveled areas, a little pool, an area for chrysanthemums, all in order. The gardener was not just another servant, but another individual, to be talked to and listened to, from whom to learn things. Hearn picked up quickly the names of the plants, the trees, the birds, butterflies, cicadas, even the snakes, the frogs, and the dragonflies of the little pool. He asked not as a naturalist, although in these observations he satisfied an often thwarted willingness to be entertained by the antics and instincts of all small, nonhuman beings. He asked primarily to find out how such a person as the gardener looked at these things: how such a one named these creatures, thought of them, felt about them. It was a literary, artistic, and associative concern that Hearn had for this carefully cultivated and exquisite Japanese nature. Without moving from his place—a cushion before a low table where he ate or wrote or contemplatively smoked—he could sit still and be part of a composition. His house, his garden, his place in the life of the city formed a pattern of human gentleness and relished naturalness, each held close to the other without enmity.

Despite the occasional alarms he caused his wife, his daily existence seemed to him to move now at a gentle productive pace unrelated to the frustrations and lunges of despair in which he had lived for so many years. He seemed hardly the same person as the Lafcadio Hearn of a year ago. Yet it was the same perceiving eye which watched the dragonfly hovering over the surface of his miniature lake, or followed the beautiful curving path of the snake who lived on the edges of the pool and had got used to accepting from the bemused writer the crumbs of a half-finished meal. " 'I am giving you this food so that you will not eat the frogs,' he told the snake." [2] So Hearn spoke one day to the snake, as Mrs. Hearn remembered, and he reassured her about snakes in general: " 'When I was in the West Indies, studying, the snakes would often crawl up my left arm, over my shoulders, and down my right arm. But I paid no attention to them and kept on studying. Snakes are not harmful; they are not bad.' " [3]

Setsu wrote, many years later, of the man who had impenitently angered innkeepers and patiently kept a pet snake: "It may seem funny for me to mention the fact that Hearn was an extremely honest man. He did not have the least evil in his mind. He had more delicate and kindly sentiments than a girl. During his childhood he had always been teased by malicious people until he cried. The keenness of his sensibility was astonishing." [4]

Many times in his house where understanding warmed the edges of his solitude, Hearn looked up to see one or two of his students standing wordlessly in the doorway, asking for his attention. Hearn would push aside his papers from the low table in the center of the room or on the polished boards of the veranda, and invite them to share a silent enjoyment of the humming air of summer, or a showing to one another of family treasures the boys had brought with them, a scroll, a book, a carving. Hearn might show them, in return for what the boys had brought him to see, the beginning of his collection of pipes, beautifully carved, carefully put together.

The loading of the pipe, the ceremonious smoking, the cleaning, and the careful putting away of this instrument of the esthetic enjoyment of tobacco were activities in tune with other Japanese joys, of tea drinking, of calligraphy, of poetry-card games. Hearn was disciplining himself in the pulses of his being to move as the people in these islands moved, to speak as they did, to enjoy as they did. He had an ulterior motive for this elaborate camouflage, but also found genuine pleasure in conforming a body and a mind racked by Western competitions to a slower time, a curiously different way of looking at life. Hearn never forgot he was going to turn his experiences into publishable articles and books. Yet he adored these things in themselves. This regulation of the body and the mind was a satisfying discipline. It was an adjustment he had never been compelled to make elsewhere. He responded with a passionate attuning of his whole being.

Several of the students who were unconsciously teaching the teacher became almost worshipfully attached to him. They were puzzled by him, a Westerner more Japanese than their fathers, yet with a delightful aura of foreignness about him. He had come to them from the West, a place as strange to them as the East had been to Hearn. These boys were also ambitious. Hearn might help them. These particular students, the ones named by Hearn in his essays, Ishihara, Otani-Masanobu, Adzukizawa, Shida, and others, in their growing up at Matsue, found Hearn the most interesting man in their city. He became the center of a steadfast hero worship.

The writer observed these students keenly, and described them in his essay "From the Diary of a Teacher":

Masanobu visits me seldom and always comes alone. A slender, handsome lad, with rather feminine features, reserved and perfectly self-possessed in manner, refined. He is somewhat serious, does not often smile; and I never heard him laugh. He has risen to the head of his class, and appears to remain there without any extraordinary effort. Much of his leisure time he devotes to botany—collecting and classifying plants. He is a musician, like all the male members of his family. He plays a variety of instruments never seen or heard in the West, including flutes of marble, flutes of ivory, flutes of bamboo of wonderful shapes and tones . . . He first explained to me the uses in temple music of the taiko and shoko, which are drums . . . On great Buddhist festivals, Masanobu and his father and his brothers are the musicians in the temple services . . . When Masanobu comes to the house, it is usually in order to invite me to attend some Buddhist or Shinto festival (*matsuri*) which he knows will interest me.[5]

He wrote of Adzukizawa:

Adzukizawa bears so little resemblance to Masanobu that one might suppose the two belonged to totally different races. Adzukizawa is large, raw-boned, heavy-looking, with a face singularly like that of a North American Indian. His people are not rich; he can afford few pleasures which cost money, except one,—buying books. Even to be able to do this he works in his leisure hours to earn money. He is a perfect bookworm, a natural-born researcher, a collector of curious documents, a haunter of all the queer second-hand stores in Teramachi and other streets where old manuscripts or prints are on sale as waste paper. He is an omnivorous reader, and a perpetual borrower of volumes, which he always returns in perfect condition after having copied what he deemed of most value to him. But his special delight is philosophy and the history of philosophers in all countries. He has read various epitomes of the history of philosophy in the Occident, and everything of philosophy which has been translated into Japanese,—including Spencer's "First Principles." I have been able to introduce him to Lewes and John Fiske,—both of which he appreciates,—although the strain of studying philosophy in English is no small one. Happily he is so strong that no amount of study is likely to injure his health, and his nerves are tough as wire. He is quite an ascetic withal. As it is the Japanese custom to set cakes and tea before visitors, I always have both in readiness, and an especially fine quality of kwashi, made at Kitzuki, of which the students are very fond. Adzukizawa alone refuses to taste cakes or confectionery of any kind, saying: "As I am the youngest brother, I must begin to earn my own living soon. I shall have to endure much hardship. And if I allow myself to like dainties now, I shall only suffer more later on." 6

Among these formidable young admirers the teacher was able, in the frame of mannerliness that was his own as well as Japanese, to be angry with them when he was disappointed, and to upbraid them when they did anything unworthy. He became good company for impressionable and ide-alistic boys who wanted to go beyond their limited schooling in Matsue and see something of the great world—of Japan, or even beyond, those places from which Herun-san had come to them.

In Matsue, Hearn was as much a member of a community as it was possible for him to be. He admired the governor. He adored his friend Nishida. He encouraged his students. In a small way he was a patron of local artists. He went to banquets, he made speeches, he tolerated public attention. Yet he was not predictable, and he never modified his curiosities, however embar-rassing they might be to those who had made themselves his sponsors.

Hearn did not let kindness intimidate him. In April 1891 he stirred Ni-shida into doing what he had never done before. He pushed Nishida into going with him to visit the nearby village of the outcasts, *yama-no-mono.* This was a place Hearn had discovered on his walks around the lower shores of the lake. He wanted to see for himself these people who were excluded from the carefully regulated functioning of Japanese society. They did jobs no one else would handle (in this case the handling of rags, waste paper, and junk), and lived apart, completely cut off from the other Japanese.

Hearn sent a letter about this experience to an English-language paper, the *Japan Mail,* and saw it published on June 13, 1891. Three years later he used some of the same material for a talk before the Asiatic Society of Japan (in Kobe, October 17, 1894). It appeared again in his third book on Japan, *Kokoro,* in 1896. He could not forget it.

In writing about the experience, he described the appearance of the place, the attitude of Matsue's citizens to this village, the songs and dances peculiar to these separate people. He was also interested in his friend's manners, and the villagers' manners, upon meeting:

The settlement is at the southern end of Matsue, in a tiny valley, or rather hollow among the hills which form a half-circle behind the city. Few Japanese of the better classes have ever visited such a village; and even the poorest of the common people shun the place as they would shun a center of contagion; for the idea of defilement, both moral and physical, is still attached to the very name of its inhabitants. Thus, although the settlement is within half an hour's walk from the heart of the city, probably not half a dozen of the thirty-six thousand residents of Matsue have visited it. . . .

Centuries of isolation and prejudice have fixed and moulded the manners of the class in recognizable ways; and even its language has become a special and curious dialect.

I was anxious to see something of a class so singularly situated and specialized; and I had the good fortune to meet a Japanese gentleman who, although belonging to the highest class of Matsue, was kind enough to agree to accompany me to their village, where he had never been himself. On the way thither he told me many curious things about the *yama-no-mono*. In feudal times these people had been kindly treated by the *samurai;* and they were often allowed or invited to enter the courts of the *samurai* dwellings to sing and dance, for which performances they were paid. . . .

I was extremely surprised at the aspect of the place; for I had expected to see a great deal of ugliness and filth. On the contrary, I saw a multitude of neat dwellings, with pretty gardens about them, and pictures on the walls of the rooms. . . .

A crowd soon gathered to look at the strangers who had come to their village,— a rare event for them. . . . There were no exchanges of civilities, as upon meeting *heimin;* a Japanese of the better class would as soon think of taking off his hat to a *yama-no-mono* as a West-Indian planter would think of bowing to a negro.[7]

The visit was finished by the willing performance of the kind of danced and sung ballad for which these people were known. (Hearn so prevailed upon the fastidious Nishida that later he had several of the ballads copied down and sent them on to his friend after he had left Matsue.)

It was Hearn the unshockable, the investigator of the waterfront of Cincinnati, of the alleys of New Orleans, the back roads of Martinique, a man who could never learn a proper prejudice, who talked to these outcasts, who watched their dances, and took down notes on their songs. It was not respectable Japan which pulled on him, but the whole range of Japanese life. There was something here that he had never seen before, a whole nation functioning in a culture of tradition, not a culture of legal contract and of reason as in the West. Before, he had found his material only on the fringes of society; here he found it everywhere, from top to bottom.

Hearn's was still the reporter's eye. The level range of his gaze, the keenness of his observation were qualities he had cultivated in working long hours for daily newspapers. The latent sympathy he had for outcasts was his own quality, as was his skill, grown to a complex tool through years of practice.

He learned even when he did not know he was doing so, small facts, large ones, attitudes, atmospheres, beliefs. Every transaction in a shop taught him something: of shopkeeper's manners and beliefs (there was nearly always a Daruma upon the god-shelf); of the Japanese way of handling money (it was always slipped between paper, since it was an offense to pass unwrapped money from one hand to another); of management, a family affair.

Every meditative stroll added knowledge to the thing seen, the thing felt. The Gesshoji cemetery, which was the burial place of one of the Matsudairas, had a giant stone turtle, its formidable head upreared in apparent regard of the pool some distance away on a lower terrace. It was said to walk there lumberingly at night to drink. There was another lonely cemetery on the northwest outskirts of the city which Hearn liked; a poet was buried in these grounds. Visited almost regularly on his way home from school was the shrine of the fox god, of Inari. He would take the route that led under the great trees of the castle grounds, and around the corner of the castle's crumbling outer walls, to the shadowed enclosure where fox images seemed to have multiplied almost as if by nature. They lined walks, they stood at corners of courts, they were ranged in rows, they stood half buried in the loamy vegetation:

The rustic foxes of Izumo have no grace: they are uncouth; but they betray in countless queer ways the personal fancies of their makers. They are of many moods, —whimsical, apathetic, inquisitive, saturnine, jocose, ironical; they watch and snooze and squint and wink and sneer; they wait with lurking smiles; they listen with cocked ears most stealthily, keeping their mouths open or closed. . . . Time has bestowed upon them divers speckled coats of beautiful soft colors while they have been sitting on their pedestals, listening to the ebbing and flowing of the centuries and snickering weirdly at mankind. Their backs are clad with finest green velvet of old mosses; their limbs are spotted and their tails are tipped with the dead gold or the dead silver of delicate fungi. And the places they most haunt are the loveliest,—high shadowy groves where the uguisu sings in green twilight, above some voiceless shrine with its lamps and its lions of stone so mossed as to seem things born of the soil—like mushrooms.[8]

Hearn might linger till almost dark at the fox god's shrine, bemused by time, and turn to go, and in going, hear the syncopated music of the priests' drum and flute played at sunset for the gods. Even the most regular routine seemed in Matsue to be accompanied by ritual and an outworn beauty. All these things might disappear, and he hastened to collect for memory what samples he could find.

He gathered stories from every street, every bridge crossing, every shrine. The warming weather of spring allowed him to range more widely. In March his contract had been renewed. He did not have to worry about the coming year. He could use the summer months to travel east and west.

Usually he took his young wife with him. She was still in a quandary between astonishment and admiration at the behavior of her husband, but she was a great help to him as an interpreter and handler of funds. She had learned to laugh as well as to praise, finding that he did not mind sympathetic laughter.

On July 20th they hired a boat at a village north of Matsue and were rowed along the "iron coast," as Hearn had learned with proprietary pride to speak of this forbidding Izumo edge of the sea—precipices, broken only by small inlets hiding fishing villages—to Kukedo, the "cave of the children's ghosts." The good swimmer could not resist the smooth, deep sea, and before they left the shelter of the harbor slipped out of his clothes and into the water. He amused his wife and amazed the hired rowers by showing them the various strokes and styles of swimming he knew. The swell of the sea made him leave off and climb aboard. The magnitude of the cliffs along which they now rowed made them all silent:

A tremendous line of dark iron-colored cliffs, towering sheer from the sea without a beach, and with never a speck of green below their summits; and here and there along this terrible front, monstrous beetlings, breaches, fissures, earthquake rendings, and topplings-down. . . . And though the wind to-day seems trying to hold its breath, white breakers are reaching far up the cliffs, and dashing their foam into the faces of the splintered crags.[9]

Hearn wanted very much to swim again in the first great cavern into which they floated, but the rowers screamed their fright at him. They were afraid of sea spirits; they made him afraid of sharks. Rather sulkily, as his wife remembered, he stayed in the boat for the exploration of the cave. They moved out of it by another entrance and passed along cliffs to enter a second cave, dedicated to Jizo and to the dead children who took refuge around the skirts of this compassionate Buddhist incarnation. In this second cave the boat grounded on a gravelly shore, and the passengers got off upon the slippery stones to pass among the little cairns which the dead children were said to pile up each night. Hearn knocked over a few in scraping past them and piled up others in the required penance. He was delighted with these beliefs, and hunted and found the other expected signs of the children, small footprints on the wet sand.

Later, Hearn wrote an essay about the expedition. He was learning what to leave in, what to take out. For singleness of effect in the written account, he left out his wife's presence. The essay had a more solitary, musing quality than the mood of the actual visit, which was a playful occasion. By the time of writing his thinking had changed the quality of his memory.

When Hearn returned to a fishing village on the neighboring coast, they found a little hotel, where a crowd soon gathered to stare at the foreigner. Hearn was beginning, with the help of his wife, to understand spoken Japanese. He listened to the harangue of the innkeeper to the curious crowd. His recollection of what the man said in vehement Japanese he put into English thus:

"You-as-for! outrageousness doing,—*what* marvelous is?
"*Theatre* is not!
"*Juggler* is not!
"*Wrestler* is not!
"*What* amusing is?
"Honorable-*Guest* this is!"

But the crowd, not to be stopped, pleaded with the innkeeper:

"Oba-San!
"O-Kayo-San!
"Shoji-to-open-condescend!—want to see!
"*Though-we-look-at, Thing-that-by-looking-at-worn-out-is-not!*" [10]

Hearn laughed, and forgot to resent this staring which was so innocent. While he and Setsu ate, and the crowd gazed through holes poked by curious fingers in the opaque paper screens, Hearn amused himself by making little holes himself and pushing toward those outside little pieces of pears and radishes which, after a moment of surprised hesitation, they ate.

A few days later in this pleasant summer of sightseeing Hearn went again to Kitzuki where he was now a familiar customer of the Inabaya Inn. But this was to be an exceptional visit. He had a letter of introduction from Nishida-san to the hereditary high priest of the Taisha Shrine. The Guji received the foreign teacher of Matsue in full ceremony among his priests of this oldest and most sacred spot of Japan. He invited Hearn, the first foreigner so privileged, into the inner chambers where even few Japanese had gone, and showed him the treasures of the shrine, the most precious of which was the simple wood fire drill with which the sacred fire was kindled. (Hearn in time secured for B. H. Chamberlain a replica of this drill, and through Chamberlain it was sent to the British Museum in London.)

Hearn never scrupled from behaving with an expected courtesy. As the Japanese were accustomed to doing, he had prostrated himself before the high priest, "a majestic bearded figure, strangely coifed and robed all in white, seated upon the matted floor in hierophantic attitude." [11] With his knack for taking on the coloration of his surroundings—an insect's or a butterfly's or a chameleon's skill—Hearn penetrated these most reserved defenses. Then, with his unsurrendered intellect keenly awake, he criticized, appreciated, enjoyed. He was the first Westerner so to be received at Taisha, and he was neither humble nor proud, but curious and charmed. Senke Takanori, the Guji of Taisha, was impressed by the directness and unself-consciousness of his visitor. He told him the history of the shrine while showing him its precious relics. He had arranged for his visitor a display of the music and the dancing of the shrine. Then, retiring to his house, and reappearing dressed as a private gentleman, he entertained Hearn there with a more informal courtesy.

This reception in the most sacred place of Izumo raised Hearn to an unheard-of eminence in the community in which he lived. Nothing else he ever accomplished could equal this event in the opinion of Matsue. The practice of Shinto in Matsue, and the experience of being received at Shinto's fountainhead, Taisha, impressed Hearn. Shinto was not peripheral; it was essential to the understanding of the Japanese.

He wrote in a letter to Basil Hall Chamberlain: "If it were possible for me to adopt a faith, I should adopt it," speaking thus of Buddhism,

. . . but Shinto seems to me like an occult force—vast, extraordinary—which has not been seriously taken into account as a force.[12]

While Hearn was responsive to every shade of meaning in the forms with which he was received at Taisha, in the forms of his private life he was still careless. His wife had received word from him to join him in Kitzuki (during this visit, or another) and came from Matsue. "I went to the hotel, and found him absent; he was bathing in the sea. His money was in a stocking and scattered around . . ." [13] Hearn was in deadly earnest about earning money and saving it now that he was married, but had no idea how to guard it in daily life.

During the same carefree summer Hearn and his wife made a trip to the east of Matsue, along the shore of the lagoon on which a ship had carried him from Yonago when he first came to Shimane. He wanted to go back to Shimoichi, the little village where the summer before he had first seen the bon-odori. He had the bitter disappointment of finding that the police had forbidden the dance.

His wife wrote:

Hearn was much disappointed and felt very annoyed about it. "The police are worthless! The old customs of Japan, very interesting customs, are discarded. It is the Christians who are to blame; they cast aside all the Japanese ways, and try to imitate Western things," Hearn said disgustedly.[14]

They made up for their loss in Shimoichi by finding the bon-odori in other villages along the coast. The foreign teacher and his Japanese wife were welcome in most of these small places, but in some they were looked on with suspicion. At Otsuka the villagers stopped their dancing, and, frightened at the sight of the foreigner, picked up little bits of sand and mud and threw pellets at him. But even this dislike was not vicious, only a frightened ignorance Hearn found easy to understand.

He was sure he was the gainer in this not always easy association with naïve villagers. He wrote to Ellwood Hendrick that he had been "travelling alone with my little wife, who translates my 'Hearnian dialect' into Japanese," and he said confidently, with no false modesty, "I am the only man who ever attempted to learn the people seriously; and I think I shall succeed." [15]

This trip to find the bon-odori was undertaken in August between the 12th and the 25th, and it had a good conclusion, a stay in Mionoseki, a small half-circle of a fishing village near the tip of Cape Miho. This was a place where the fishing, the shrine of the god Koto-shiro-mushi-no-Kami, and a beguiling and famous group of pines upon a ridge were the only interests. It became a favorite place with Hearn. It was a lost little village which he was sure would not change. Even its particular absurdity, the fact that one could get no eggs there because the god of Mionoseki hated eggs, had an endearing quality.

Mionoseki had only one street, which ringed the little harbor at the foot of its steep bluffs. The inn where they stayed was near the southern end of this semicircle. It had balconies hanging just above the deep water and overlooking all the activities of the place. One could sit upon the balcony and watch the fishing boats sail in and out past the stone breakwater which protected the village from bad weather. Hearn found he could dive into the water from the balcony of his room. Before returning to Matsue in the little steamer which docked at the small pier in the harbor, he promised himself to return. The trip of two hours, in which conversation was muted by the throb of small busy engines, was a voyage of many varying views of near rocky shores, blue mountains in the middle distance, and the white-topped cone of the Fuji of Izumo, the cold high peak of Daisen. From the open Japan Sea the ship made its way steadily and methodically past the more erratic patterns of sailing boats into the Nakaumi Lagoon, past the small city of Sakai, past the flowery islands of Daikonshima, and into the mouth of the Ohashigawa, and so upriver to the familiar dock in the center of Matsue.

Hearn wrote enthusiastically of such trips to Ellwood Hendrick and Elizabeth Bisland in America and to Basil Hall Chamberlain in Tokyo (probably also to Captain Mitchell McDonald, but his letters to him have not survived). His relations with Professor Chamberlain had changed slowly and subtly. It was now Hearn, the seasoned dweller among the remote Japanese of the Japan Sea coast, who lectured the city dweller on habits, beliefs, manners. Chamberlain and his friend W. B. Mason (whom Hearn had not yet met) were engaged in editing a new edition of Murray's *Guide to Japan*. To Hearn they entrusted the revision of the section on Shimane Prefecture.

This was another excuse for traveling about in the countryside, if one were needed.

In Matsue and in the neighborhood his gentle persuasiveness had allowed Hearn, in these months as the teacher of the Ordinary Middle School, to pass where others did not go. He had made friends with a curious assortment of teachers, priests, innkeepers (he was the enemy of one), fishermen, wood-carvers, shopkeepers, a governor, and others. He had the advantage, for an intended chronicler of Japanese life, of living a Japanese life. He could speak with some authority of Japanese women, of household shrines, of various household customs. He lived among them. Yet, in spite of his admiration of Japanese things, in spite of the long-stemmed pipe he smoked, the kimono he wore, the sympathy which inclined him to these things, he could never become at all Japanese himself. Knowledge of Japan subtilized his knowledge of America and of Europe, but he was irreparably a Westerner. Such an uncomfortable position gave clarity to further study of Japan.

He continued to study Japanese human nature daily among his students. The manners, reactions, and adolescent thoughts of the boys added to the total of his knowledge of Japan and gave that knowledge a specific rather than a general cast. Purposely he set daily essay subjects for catching the shy emotions and opinions ordinarily hidden from a commonplace teacher.

Hearn's decision to leave this place where he was well suited as citizen, teacher, and writer was due to two prosaic reasons. He suffered very much in Matsue from the cold in the winter. He could make more money in a larger city. His wife too wanted to move on. She had none of Hearn's romantic attachment for this old, traditional Japan. She had suffered from poverty in her growing up in Matsue. The place was not dear to her.

Hearn wrote to Chamberlain that he wanted to find another school, preferably at a larger salary and in a warmer part of Japan. Chamberlain busied himself diplomatically consulting the proper officials in the bureaus of the Education Department. Hearn began the new school term in Matsue, but awaited word to go. In October he received, through Chamberlain, an offer from the government, of a post in the large government college in the city of Kumamoto in Kyushu, the southernmost island of Japan. Hearn's salary would be twice what he received in the land of the gods. He accepted. There was no need to persuade his wife.

Hearn needed more money. He had not got his notes in order yet for a book. He was not receiving very much in royalties from the United States. His style of life had increased tremendously in taking on a family. Yet, in accepting, Hearn suffered a twinge of remorse, and an imaginative foretaste of the nostalgia he would feel from this time on for Matsue and Izumo.

He set himself to argue the reasons for going. In the comfort of his doubled salary he would be able to put together the book of impressions he owed to his initial experience of Japan. And in Kyushu he would have new experiences, see a different part of Japan, out of which to make a second book. Hearn knew perfectly well that he did not write books to live, but that he lived to write books.

On the day he and his wife left Matsue, November 15th, there was a gathering at the dock early in the morning. There had been other, earlier ceremonial leavetakings, gifts, banquets, formal goodbyes, but this informal waving of caps and cheering as the little lake steamer pulled away from the bridge was the farewell Hearn remembered for the rest of his life. There had been an epidemic of cholera. The schools had been closed. Many of the uniformed students had been marched like soldiers out of town for safety. It was dangerous to be in a crowd. But

. . . an hour after sunrise, some two hundred students, with their teachers, assemble before my gate to escort me to the wharf, near the long white bridge, where the little steamer is waiting. . . .

Other students are already assembled at the wharf. And with them wait a multitude of people known to me: friends or friendly acquaintances, parents and relatives of students, every one to whom I can remember having ever done the slightest favor, and many more from whom I have received favors which I never had the chance to return,—persons who worked for me, merchants from whom I purchased little things, a host of kind faces, smiling salutation. . . . I most miss friend Nishida. He has been very sick for two long months, bleeding at the lungs, but his father brings me the gentlest of farewell letters from him, penned in bed, and some pretty souvenirs. . . .

The little steamer shrieks . . . And as the gray wharves recede, a long *Aaaaaaaaaa* rises from the uniformed ranks, and all the caps wave, flashing their Chinese ideographs of brass. I clamber to the roof of the tiny deck cabin, wave my hat, and shout in English: "Good-bye, good-bye!" And there floats back to me the cry: "Manzai, manzai!" (Ten thousand years to you! ten thousand years!) The packet glides out of the river-mouth, shoots into the blue lake, turns a pine-shadowed point; and the faces, and the voices, and the wharves, and the long white bridge have become memories.[16]

17 ᔕᖾ Buddha on a Hillside

The brave goodbye at the dock in Matsue was only the beginning of a
long farewell. The little steamer crossed Lake Shinji smartly and deposited its passengers upon the opposite shore in front of a number
of kuruma stations, the kurumaya crying out eagerly for patronage.
Here Hearn turned to say goodbye to the head of the Ordinary Middle
School, to the director of the Normal School, and to an admiring student
who had accompanied him this far.

He had then to engage vehicles to carry himself, his wife, a cook, and
a maid farther along the way to Kumamoto. He had brought his own
kurumaya who would pull one of the light-wheeled, fragile vehicles
across the mountains which barred the way to the south. There followed
several days' jolting passage through wooded gorges, alongside green
rivers, step by step up rice terraces, and down again, with stops each night
in inns unused to foreigners. They passed over the backbone of Honshu's
mountains and came down at last to the port of Hiroshima.

In this prosperous city the little group, followed by much masked
curiosity, took ship upon an Inland Sea steamer and for a day and night
sailed along Honshu's coast to the extreme southwestern tip of the
main island at the Straits of Shimonoseki. Across this strait they docked
at Moji. They all, not Hearn alone, felt strange here, and wondered
at the difference in speech and manners in this southernmost island of
the Empire.

They traveled west by train the fifty miles to the double city, Hakata-Fukuoka, a port for ships going to China, Korea, and Siberia. And then they turned south to travel the last seventy-five miles of their long journey into the interior of this island far from Matsue, far from Tokyo, and farther still from Dublin, Cincinnati, or New Orleans.

Below Hakata the train moved through a landscape flamboyantly volcanic. Two ranges stroked backward upon each side of the track. Contained within this generous valley were fields stubbled with the recent cutting of the rice crop and decorated with the bamboo frames upon which the rice still hung drying. A warmth of sun upon the fields and the windows of the train, an easy growth of weeds in ditches, a tangle along the edges of the fields, a slight heedlessness of outline recalled another South to Hearn, and differentiated Kyushu sharply from the severe elegance of Honshu. The mountains to the west removed themselves and showed the sea, and then closed in again. The train pulled up a slight incline to mount a wide plateau and then ran downhill to come into the small north station, the Kita-Kumamoto, and then into the surprisingly large and modern Kumamoto station. The city was much farther than Matsue from the great centers of the Empire, but the fact was not evident. The railroad which was bringing a new teacher of English to Kumamoto had long been an open way for the invasion of the West.

It needed only the sight of the Higher Middle School (also called the Fifth National College of Kumamoto in Kyushu) to create in Hearn a sharp sense of disappointment. This alignment of great stone and red-bricked buildings might have stood in Philadelphia or London. The halls into which he walked for the first time were inhumanly long and cold, and the walls were thick, as if shutting life out. The place was large, but it was not size alone that daunted the new teacher. In introducing himself to the director, in finding out his schedule of English and Latin classes, he was impressed by the school's very complicated and impersonal organization. He saw for the first time how out of the way Matsue had been.

Although Hearn was quick to feel a chill in the air, and soon exaggerated the coldness he thought he had discerned, there was a basis for his intuition. He was very much on trial. A fellow teacher at Kumamoto, writing sympathetically many years later, disclosed that the director had hesitated to accept the new teacher because of his appearance.[2] (Hearn was the only foreign teacher at that time teaching in the public schools of Kumamoto.)

Hearn disliked the city when he first saw it, and he had not had a good first impression of the school, but he wrote cautiously optimistic reports back to Nishida: "The teaching is not so easy as in Matsue . . . But the students are extremely good." [3]

The good things of Kumamoto were curiously mixed with the bad. The director and the staff were polite but impersonal. The new teacher made no friends among the teachers as he had in Matsue. He had no helper with his classes as he had had in Mr. Nishida. The students, older than his Matsue boys, were almost men, excellent workers but seemingly hardheaded and hardhearted. Hearn was left free to teach as he wished, but the twenty-two hours a week first agreed to lengthened soon to twenty-seven, and he had to work hard privately to keep up with his classes in Latin. The students had been poorly prepared in English, and at first many of them did not understand him at all. He had no appropriate books; all those furnished by the school were worse than useless. He had to draw the substance of his lessons out of his own experience and imagination. At least his salary was excellent; he was to be paid the equivalent of two hundred American dollars a month, and he and Setsu were intoxicated with the idea of saving a great deal of money.

But he was not sure at first that he would receive this beneficent salary. Due to a political struggle in the Diet, remote in Tokyo, there was some doubt that he or the other teachers would receive their monthly wages or that the school itself would exist much longer. An economy measure threatened the existence of the Fifth National College at the beginning of his first year there, 1891–1892. There were revivals of this uncertainty in succeeding years, with consequent delays in the payment of the teachers' salaries. Hearn was only one among many affected, but he took this poisoning of his security as a personal affront [4] and wrote distressed letters to Chamberlain in Tokyo, asking him to find out the fate of the school.

The Diet reconsidered, the school survived, the salaries were paid. Hearn's general doubts subsided into prickings of discontent. He settled his family in a house in the city (the school was outside the city proper, to the northeast) rather than accept quarters on the campus where he would be under the direct eye of the authorities. He wrote to Nishida: "I live nearly two miles from the school . . . So that my kurumaya's coming with me was a lucky thing. My house is about as large as that in Kitabori-machi, but not so good, and the garden is horribly ugly." [5]

Of his predecessor Hearn said: "The last teacher was a missionary, and, a *fraud*—as many missionaries are. I was astonished to find none of the boys had been trained by him to compose, or to talk. He had simply *wasted* their time. The conditions of his appointment rendered proselytism impossible; he left in disgust." And he added: "I have to struggle against the unpopularity of my predecessor. That will be all right soon." [6]

Hearn liked Mr. Kano, the director. "He has told me to teach as I please for the present; and having discarded the readers adopted for the three upper classes, I am filling up the time with conversation, and some slight instruction about English literature. The choice of readers was disgraceful." [7]

Over a year later Hearn was still teaching without books, but he thought that this direct engagement with the minds of his pupils was an advantage. He wrote to Nishida on January 15, 1893: "As for my own classes, they still give me no books at all; and I teach entirely by word of mouth and chalk. Still, considering the short time given to each class, I believe this is best. The main thing is to teach them to express themselves in English without books to help them." [8]

Hearn liked to keep his teaching life completely separate from his family life. When he returned to his house at the end of a day, he subsided into comfort and unselfconsciousness. He removed the Western suit of clothes, which, like the other teachers, he wore as a badge or uniform of his profession, put on his *tabi* and kimono, and set to his own work in an atmosphere devoted to his contentment. He was conscientiously a father to the whole family of relatives and servants. When he found that his kurumaya had lied when he left Matsue, and deserted his wife to come with him, he sent him back and hired another man in Kumamoto. He saw to it that the maids had chances, as the members of the family had, to walk out in the evening and amuse themselves by looking at the brightly lighted shops of sweets and toys and flowers. He gathered together all the household, including the servants, after supper, and they played games together and sang. But when he wanted to work—to study or to write—the house kept itself quiet for his sake, strictly enjoined to this quietness by Setsu, and Hearn had space and leisure and comfort surrounding him whose completeness he never questioned or thought much about.

This ease was good for him. "I have become very strong, and weigh about twenty pounds more than I did last summer," [9] he wrote to Nishida before the year 1891 was over. This cushioning of strength made it possible for Hearn to do several things at once: to teach, to write, to observe himself and his family in their new place.

The others were almost as strange in Kyushu as he was. "It was very funny about O-Yone when she first came," he wrote to Nishida, about the maid he and Setsu had brought with them from Izumo. "Nobody could understand her Izumo dialect (she is from Imaichi) . . ." [10] The fact that they felt as alien in Kumamoto as Herun-san made the whole family feel more at one with him. He in his turn was becoming almost unconsciously a provincial from Shimane-ken, slightly out of place and amused here in this ugly, Westernizing city.

He did not neglect to keep up with his friends and students in Matsue. He had heard very soon from three of his pupils, Otani, Adzukizawa, and Tanabe, and from others later, and he answered them with real affection, seeing also how well as a writer he could use these boys who were his friends. In November he wrote to Otani: "You have been kind enough to offer to find out for me something about Shinto. Well, if you have time, I will ask you to find out for me as much as you can about the miya of the household . . ." [11] that is, about the household shrine. He soon got beyond casual questionings of both Otani and Adzukizawa. He offered to help them by payment for work done. They would be aided in going on to higher schools; he would be aided in his writing.

He wrote to Adzukizawa: "I want to know only what is done every day in *Izumo*. It's no use to send me anything out of books . . ." [12] He knew, too, exactly what he wanted in a translation from such a helper: "Now for a word in general about translations for me. If I ask you to translate something, *please never try to translate a Japanese* IDIOM *by an English* IDIOM. That would be no use to me. Simply translate the words *exactly,*—however funny it seems." [13] Through these boys Hearn wanted to get as bone-close to customs and words as he could, to understand through the arrangement of words Japanese thinking and feeling.

He was exceedingly detailed and ruthlessly specific in getting out of Otani and Adzukizawa what he wanted from them, but outside these matters he relaxed into friendliness. He wrote them about his own situation, and did not hesitate to correct their English, give them advice, and help them in a familiar way. He wrote to Adzukizawa, "As to other matters, I advise you to keep and use whatever spare money you may have, for the purchase of books. You may never have again so much time for private study as you have now: take advantage of it as much as you can." And admonishing him, affectionately, "Don't write—'Yours respectively' but, if you wish 'respectfully.' 'Respectively' means 'concerning each one.' But my dear pupil need not write 'respectfully' at all . . ." [14] Adzukizawa wanted to come to Kyushu to live with Hearn, but Hearn did not ask him to come. He was not sure of himself yet.

To Otani he wrote: "As for advice about literature, I can only say that you should try to read modern authors rather than old ones . . . [And]

I should advise you especially to study the literature of your *own* language, and to look to foreign literature only for what may give new strength and grace to your own. . . . I think it is a great mistake to teach English literature in Japan." [15]

Hearn's private work progressed well. In his more public work, he began all over again. Teaching in Kumamoto was very different from teaching in the little world of the Middle School of Matsue. He had to get used to the large grounds, the Western buildings, the brisk, impersonal manners of the staff who were all harried by the atmosphere which drove the students too. By the time the Japanese student reached the level of the Higher School, education was a competition for place in life, not a gentle and personal leading out of a young mind into delight, as it had seemed in Matsue. Hearn was pleased at first only by the large bathhouse, and by the separate building for the teaching of judo; these institutions were in the Japanese style, and the old good manners seemed still in use in them. He admired too the learned teacher of Chinese, a man much like the one who had taught the classical language in Matsue. There was not much of the gentle old tradition in the Fifth Higher School. The atmosphere in Kumamoto was harsh.

It was enough to make a teacher quail to come into a classroom and find at first only stolid, expressionless, apparently indifferent faces confronting him. There was even at the beginning a deliberate lapse of manners. They had had so little good training in English that, not understanding the new teacher, they did not try but, shielded by his short sight, they read, studied other subjects, or amused themselves in the far reaches of the room.[16] Hearn's natural ability, operating without books, and perhaps the better without aids, quickly touched even the deliberately unfriendly ones, and they were soon learning English without knowing it.

Hearn wrote about his methods in the Kyushu classroom later. "Sometimes I would write familiar stories for the class, all in simple sentences, and in words of one syllable. Sometimes I would suggest themes to write upon, of which the nature almost compelled simple treatment." [17] Then, learning to follow his spoken words, learning how well he could tell a story, his students began to ask him for stories. Hearn then, when he and they were tired, stopped the repetitious, patient work at the blackboard and softly, slowly, entrancingly told them tales, from the Arthurian legends, from Hawthorne, from the folk stories he knew.

As he came to know his students, wrestling each September with a fresh, unmannerly, unwilling group and making them responsive, he came to respect the effort they could put into their work. The college comprised five years of classes; the first two were the same as the last two of the Ordinary

Middle School, and three years were added for the strenuous preparations for the great universities. The ruthless weeding out of students at each stage of their education, particularly before matriculation in the universities, had much to do with making this a time of tension. Life in a Japanese college was a competition which trained intellectuals to take part in a game in which there were too many players and too few prizes.

There was another reason for the harshness of the Fifth Higher School. These were "Kyushu men," or at least they tried to be. Kyushu had different manners from Izumo, and prided itself on directness, straightness, stoic bareness of gesture. Hearn felt naked in this blast of will without amenity. He came grudgingly under the tutelage of Nishida's explanations to respect the elder virtues of this stern and militant part of the Empire. He came to admire the Kyushu quality, stoicism in the face of suffering, action in the face of provocation, but he never really liked Kyushu as he had gentle Izumo.

He tried to understand the reasons for the ugliness of Kumamoto. ". . . It is the most uninteresting city I was ever in, in Japan." [18] "There is nothing beautiful here." [19] ". . . A vast, straggling, dull, unsightly town is Kumamoto." [20] The city had been burned to ashes in the time of the civil wars when Japan was trying to change itself from a feudal to a modern state. There was the ruin of a gigantic castle from which there came bugle calls of an encampment of Japan's modern army. There was a famous shrine. But most of the city itself was dull.

Yet the mountains which surrounded the city were interesting, and the countryside beyond them could be imagined as beautiful. The peaks to the west were near and sharp, those to the east farther away and grander, in their center the volcano Mount Aso. The very sources of the Japanese spirit were supposed to live still in the unspoiled villages of Kyushu. But Hearn was as if tied to the ugly city. "I can't travel here, though, as in Izumo. Almost every place worth seeing is too far to go without several days' vacation and a special passport, and the city itself is a disgusting blank." [21] So Hearn wrote on February 12, 1892, to Chamberlain gone far away to England by way of envied scenes in the Phillipines, and other warm, moist lands of southeast Asia.

In living and working in Kumamoto, Hearn had to face the fact that Japan was not after all "redemption from all the sorrows of the nineteenth century," [22] as he had thought. The nineteenth century was here in Japan too, as well as in him, and he could not get away from it. That he could not now go off freely, without responsibilities, to Saigon, or Manila, or Hong Kong, for fresh illusions, was good for his work. He strengthened his powers by enduring revelation, but doing so was a purgatory. He blamed Kumamoto for his spiritual discomfort.

Yet in Kumamoto he thrived on the regularity of his life. He was comfortable in his family relations. He did not by any means live in all things as a Japanese. He had given up at least partially a Japanese diet, and gone back with much satisfaction to beefsteaks and beer, and was pleased that he gained on this fare. He asked his wife's advice too frankly to be really Japanese, but he propitiated her, when he could, by observing some little Japanese rituals of behavior. When they went out, he let her walk properly a few steps behind him. He let her, for the sake of a seemly Japanese household, wait upon him. (It was easier to give in in such matters, he wrote Chamberlain.) She handed him his garments each one in proper order upon his rising in the morning. He let her arrange the eating order at their table in a Japanese hierarchy. And he deferred with real feeling to his wife's grandfather, when the old man arrived from Matsue to take up once more his place of honor in the household.

The grandfather, who in Japanese fashion had relinquished his duties and responsibilities to his children (the term was *inkyo*), and lived only the delightful and serious life of contemplation, was Hearn's favorite among the relatives he had acquired. He too called him "Grandfather," and sought out his company. The old man liked to walk, and persisted in doing so in Kumamoto. He regarded the city, whose people all talked strangely to him, and who had such different ways from Matsue, as a kind of wilderness. He steered himself by the sun or by the shapes of the peaks or by the smoke of Mount Aso to the east. If he got lost, he sat down upon the matted floor of some hospitable shop, calmly smoked his pipe, and waited for his grandson-in-law, or for one of the servants, diligently hunting him, to find and take him safely home. When he arrived at the house, he gravely told them all—thankfully gathered about him—his day's adventures. Hearn cared for him gently, and coaxed stories out of him, of his own life, of the older legends, of the history of Japan of the time of his youth. The old man was a walking museum of old ways, old thoughts, old ideas. He had the beautiful manners and habits of the sheltered, disciplined samurai kind, and was oblivious of the nineteenth century.

Hearn had need of the comfort of his family relations. Nothing else was comfortable during this first winter in Kumamoto, not even the house. Kyushu was occasionally treacherously cold. The large house shook to winds which blew in all directions the ineffectual heat of the charcoal braziers. Hearn endured his second winter in Japan and learned very thoroughly that Japan was not tropical. There were exceptional days of grateful, sluggish warmth. More often he was cold in this house that had no heat except for hands and feet, and thought wistfully of Martinique. He told his wife again and again about this island in a blue sea far away, and promised to take her there one day.

The moral climate at the school was not entirely comfortable for him, although he had broken down the stiff reserve of his students and was happy with them, sequestered in his classroom. Outside, in the corridors or in the teachers' room, he still experienced what seemed to be indifference or enmity. He thought these others seemed unwilling to talk, and only coldly greeted him as they passed in the halls. Hearn did not try to find out if his initial impression was mistaken. The other teachers found him affected. He was more pointedly Japanese than many of his colleagues in daily outward habits. Conspicuously, it seemed, he smoked his Japanese pipe when the others smoked cigars, or drank sake when they drank beer.

He on his side had only contempt for his colleagues: "Now the old men whom I have met were of a larger breed. They thought in a narrow circle,— but fully, and originally, and well, so far as I could divine from interpretation. They gave me ideas. The class I am now in contact with have no ideas. Under such studies as they have made, their brains seem to have shrivelled up like kernels in roasted nuts." [23]

When the weather was good, the foreign teacher removed himself from the company of his students and his fellow teachers and went off alone. His favorite place was a cemetery on the crest of a small hill north of the college grounds. He had seen a path one day and followed it up a weedy hillside to a place where he could sit, his back comfortably braced by a worn stone Buddha, and eat his lunch in peace.

Here he could look out to the fields beyond the school, beyond the city, beyond the nineteenth century. The farmers working below him, often a man and his wife, lifting and lowering, cleaning fields, planting seedlings, were performing the gestures of centuries. Braced by the pedestal of the Buddha whom he had adopted as a friend, Hearn felt here less alone than below among the preoccupied, uninterested teachers and ambitious students. He found the movements of the farmers more significant than the conversation of the professors. He would open his box lunch and use his chopsticks busily upon the cold rice, the red beans, the bits of fried fish and pickles packed for him. Then he would often fill out the hour with reading or strolling about on his hilltop.

If he walked a few steps away from the stone image he had a long view to the east of Mount Aso. The great shallow-coned volcano was in plain sight only twenty miles away, and signaled a perpetual threat in the slow pouring upward of its smoke. It had scattered white ash upon the city in the past and might do so again. On several occasions earthquakes forced the family to spend the night in the garden away from the shaking house. Hearn was thoroughly frightened of these manifestations, and yet earthquakes gave him ideas. They were the fit symbol for the crazy temporariness of all things Japanese. (Houses, cities, habits, ways of thought might disappear with equal readiness. Such changeability merely reinforced the premise of Buddhism: only the eternal remained; all embodied manifestations passed away.)

The defenselessness of his family who shivered through particular earthquakes and who without him would be subject to other shakings became a great reason for strength in Hearn. He wrote to Hendrick in February 1893:

I have at home a little world of about eleven people, to whom I am Love and Light and Food. It is a very gentle world. It is only happy when I am happy. If I even look tired, it is silent, and walks on tiptoe. It is a moral force. I dare not fret about anything when I can help it—for others would fret more. So I try to keep right.[24]

In the center of the family, all holding themselves carefully quiet to let him work, he sat at a table and set down words on yellow paper. In addition to his primary urge to write, he had a second motive; he had to keep this group of people all fed and clothed and sheltered. He could not have stopped now if he had wanted to, and he could not now afford the luxury of pauses.

Nothing of Hearn's (except four articles in two years in the *Atlantic Monthly*) was being published at this time in America. He had only his teaching income during his early months in Kumamoto to support him until he renewed his friendship with Page Baker, his imperious and intelligent editor in the 1880's. Baker, still editor of the New Orleans *Times-Democrat,* was a little wary of renewing acquaintance with Hearn. But in late 1891 or early 1892 Hearn took up their relationship as if nothing had happened, and Baker tacitly agreed to do so too. Hearn was a writer about whom the literate public was curious. He suggested to Hearn that some of his shorter pieces might do well in the *Times-Democrat.* Baker suggested also a syndication of this writing. He was prepared to take on the management of the business. Hearn agreed. The articles began appearing in the *Times-Democrat,* and in other papers in February 1892.

Hearn was a little ashamed of what seemed to him the hasty way these pieces were rushed into print. He wrote on February 12th to Chamberlain on the way to England: "Perhaps you may see on your way some newspapers containing fragments of mine. They are not the best, and please don't judge me by them. But as I was offered the sum of $800.00 for four MSS. (which must be recast later) by a syndicate (English, American, and Australian) I accepted." [25]

The extra money was gratefully received by the writer working long months upon the shaping of his first book about Japan. "Really, it is very queer; but you seem to be the best friend I've got outside of Japan. You really do things for a fellow . . ." [26] So he wrote to Baker.

He was lonely in spite of busy work and soft-mannered relatives surrounding him in a nest of kindly care. He needed at this time talk with friends who had an understood, shared experience and background. He needed such companionship as he had had in Cincinnati and New Orleans. He wrote to Joseph Tunison in July 1892, reaching out a hand to a friend whom he was afraid he would not see again:

Would you like to come to Japan? I wish to put this question a long way ahead of my hope. If you have married, or have taken the editorship of some paper, and have fine prospects before you,—put my question by. If you are quite free, and would like a happy, contemplative, extremely peaceful existence—with ample leisure for study—a life without pressure of any sort, why, think about it a little. . . . Should cost be an obstacle in the way of your coming, I might be able to advance what you want. While in Japan, should you need money or anything else, I would be able to fix everything. So also, for the question of your return, if you get tired. I think, if you wish to take a teacher's position here, you would make your way very successfully. . . .

Did you never get my letter from Matsue? I wrote you twice since I came to Japan—not much to boast of: but you did not write to me at all.[27]

Nothing came of the letter.

While trying hungrily to build a bridge between himself and his friends in the United States, he heard from people in England whom he had never thought to know: these were his half sisters, children of his father and his father's second wife, the pretty golden-haired woman his father had once taken him to visit in Dublin, and been scolded for doing so by his aunt.

There were three sisters surviving this marriage: Elizabeth Sarah Maude born August 18, 1858, when Lafcadio was eight and beginning to grow used to being alone in his aunt's house in Rathmines; Minnie Charlotte born July 27, 1859, when he was nine and forgetting all but the dimmest things about his father and mother; and Posey Gertrude born May 30, 1860, when he was ten years old. He had never seen them or heard from them before. They had read about him or seen his picture in a magazine or newspaper.

These children of Charles Hearn's second marriage had apparently led sheltered lives since their birth in India and the tragedy of their parents' early deaths. Two of them were married. The unmarried sister, the one they called Lillah, eventually came to America to see Daniel James Hearn. All three of the sisters (according to Nina Kennard, who knew them) wrote to Lafcadio, but only Minnie received an answer. She must have written gently and persuasively to allay his suspicions. The picture she sent him (a face pretty and delicate, with large dark eyes and a prominent nose) disarmed him further. Hearn was touched and interested, and wrote to Minnie Atkinson (she was a wife and mother, living in comfortable middle-class circumstances in England). A short, intense correspondence followed.

In June 1892 Hearn begged her to teach her children to love him:

. . . For if they see me without previous discipline, they will be afraid of my ugly face when I come—I send you a photo of one-half of it, the other is not pleasant, I assure you: like the moon, I show only one side of myself.[28]

In September 1893 he was to write (still from Kumamoto):

I am really living in a hideous isolation, far away from books, and book-shops, and Europeans. My happiest sojourns . . . have been in little fishing villages, and little queer unknown towns, where there are no big vulgar hotels, and where one can dress and do exactly as one pleases.[29]

At this same time he wrote:

The more I see your face in photos, the more I feel drawn toward you. . . . But imagining won't do always. I should like to know more of you than a photograph or a rare letter can tell. I don't know, remember, anything *at all* about you. I do not know where you were born, where you were educated,—anything of your life; or what is much more, infinitely more important, I don't know your emotions and thoughts and feelings and experiences of the past. What you are now, I can guess. But what *were* you,—long ago? What memories most haunt you . . .[30]

In this way he began and carried on a correspondence which endured for three or four years but no longer. Hearn suddenly stopped writing. It was as if in these hard-driven years he could not go on communicating with this respectable, sheltered, infinitely distant sister. Writing to her and hearing from her scraped his nerves. It was too great an expense of emotion. He wrote once to Chamberlain how "sky-blue" or rather "indigo" letters "from relatives in England" made him.[31] Also, he could not quite forgive them for their mother.

Hunting elsewhere for a friend, he began an easy correspondence with W. B. Mason, Chamberlain's friend who had earned a living for many years as a civil employee of the Japanese government. Mason lived in Yokohama. Hearn had never met him, but Chamberlain put the two men in touch with each other. Hearn was to send Mason material for the next revision of Murray's *Guide to Japan*. From Kumamoto to Yokohama there began a lively exchange.

"You write the most delightful letters," said Hearn to Mason, "but I haven't the faintest ghost of an idea who you are. I don't know whether I ought even to try to find out. It is charming to know one's friends as amiable ghosts thus." [32]

With Mason, whom he knew to be situated something like himself, married to a Japanese wife, caught by a dull job, prevented from using his gifts as he should, Hearn shared many ambitions and doubts which grew rankly now. Kumamoto did not provide a climate for self-encouragement but for self-examination, prickings, proddings, discomfort. Japan was not, as it had seemed in Matsue, one world, but many. It had the same contradictions as the other worlds he had known.

Here was an ambition: ". . . My whole study must be the heart of the commonest people." [33] (His third Japanese book would be called *Kokoro*—heart things.) Hearn wrote this sentence from Kyoto at the end of July 1892 where, escaping from school and Kyushu, he had taken his wife for the beginning of a long vacation which was not to end until he had visited not only the ancient capital, but Osaka and Nara and Kobe and had gone back to the Japan Sea coast and beyond to the unknown Oki Islands.

It was the people he met along the way on this journeying which held him, not, as it had been in his first days in Japan, the temples and shrines, houses, gateways, avenues. In the train going to Kyoto he was struck with the perfectly unconscious and patterned beauty of the drooping sleeves of the women who held onto the swaying straps above their heads always with the left hand, and let the sweep of the kimono sleeve hide their sleepy faces. It was the innocent family circles, questioning children, answering fathers, at zoos or in temple grounds, talking back and forth, not noticing him, whom through Setsu he overheard and understood; it was these inhabitants to whom he paid closest attention, not their habitat: the curved gate towers, the tall pagodas, the stone paths, which had now become his habitat too.

Hearn gazed dutifully at the magnificences of Kyoto and Nara and the beautiful natural setting of the port of Kobe, but it was the simplicity of the west coast for which he hungered. At Kobe he and his wife boarded a large modern steamship and sailed all the way around Honshu through the Straits of Shimonoseki and along the northwest "iron coast" to the little port of Sakai (beyond Matsue, near it, but apparently far enough away for Hearn not to visit). He had been in Sakai before, and the general aspect of the cliffs and the lagoon of Naka-umi, and the high peak of Daisen were familiar. But he gazed eagerly in the other direction. He had his head set upon voyaging forty miles out into the Japan Sea to the Oki Islands where no foreigner, except seamen from strayed warships, ever went, and where few Japanese from the main island went either.

He had more than his share of hard traveling in going to Oki, and Setsu—

without his particular relish for the advantages of such conditions—had too. Even Hearn got tired of dirt, bad smells, bad roads, and spoke once longingly of the comfort of the house awaiting them in Kumamoto, but in retrospect the good things spread a glamour over the difficulties. He was always cocky about having been to Oki.

He had never set off on a journey with such expectation as he did in the uncomfortable little steamer which carried him out of Sakai Harbor on a long swinging voyage of many hours' duration toward these unknown islands. Hearn, perched upon a deckload of melons, not able to sit, stand, or stroll, smoked his pipe in a kind of rapture.

The Oki Islands were not so primitive as he had been taught, but were sufficiently remote to be entertaining, and they were beautiful—with drowned steep little harbors, fantastic mountain shapes, small villages with no roads in between. The smell of drying cuttlefish in most of the settled places would have daunted most travelers, but Hearn took this as a comforting sign of tradition, and almost relished the smell. He enjoyed the trips by various kinds of boats between islands and between villages. In the settlements he found the same open-minded and open-hearted society he had loved first in Izumo; no locks were upon the doors because there were no thieves.

Hearn spent a month in the islands, traveling about till he was often bone-tired but never bored, looking, making notes, hunting folk material, not finding a great plenty of it, but picking up ideas as if out of the air. He kept a little pencil notebook during this time, a notebook that survived.[34] One day along the way he scribbled down in it something about the importance of the irregularity of art, an idea he had inherited from romanticism, an idea strengthened in Japan, an idea now ready to be worked out.

When he and Setsu were ready to start home, they did a rash thing. Hearn wrote to W. B. Mason on August 31st: "All along the journey I have been tormented by an insane desire to steal other people's servants. The temptation was very strong at Kyoto, where the hotel maidens were veritable *tennin;* but I did not yield to it till I got to Oki. At Oki we found a pretty Shizoku [samurai] boy working in the hotel as a servant of people who had once been retainers of his family. We stole him, and I am now teaching him how to swim. He is so intelligent that I cannot think of having him only as a servant. When we know more of him, we may do something else for him." [35] (They had noticed the sensitive boy. Setsu had spoken to him and found him to be of her own class by his way of talking. They had told him they would take him with them to Kyushu if he would run away and meet them at the port. He had done so.)

At Mionoseki, Hearn and his friend Nishida sat upon a balcony of the inn facing the half-moon harbor, and talked away long easy hours. When Nishida had left, Hearn wrote him: "We felt quite lonesome after you went away, and especially at supper-time—when there were only two mats, instead of three, laid upon the suzumi-dai, overlooking the bay . . ." [36]

It made Hearn lonely merely to think of going back to Kyushu. During this grateful summer absence from the particular problem of Kumamoto, he wrote to Mason about the general problem of Japan. A part of his journey had been made in a giant N.Y.K. (Nippon Yusen Kaisha) steamer. Waiting at Moji, at the Straits of Shimonoseki, he considered the contrast between this modern vessel and the one on which he had recently traveled. This was, he said

. . . A splendid steamer, but patronized extensively by foreigners . . . The voyage was pleasant enough; but I prefer the dangerous little Japanese steamers where you can squat down on deck in a yukata and smoke a little brass pipe, and become agreeably acquainted with everybody. The N.Y.K. is a chapter in the modernization of Japan which I am tired of seeing. Professor Chamberlain spoke to me about the variability of one's feelings toward Japan being like the oscillation of a pendulum: one day swinging toward pessimism and the next to optimism. I have this feeling very often, and I suppose you must have had it many times. But the pessimistic feeling is generally coincident with some experience of New Japan, and the optimistic with something of Old Japan . . .

But with what hideous rapidity Japan is modernizing, after all!—not in costume, or architecture, or habit, but in heart and manner. The emotional nature of the race is changing. Will it ever become beautiful again? Or failing to become attractive, can it ever become sufficiently complex to make a harmony with the emotional character of the West? It is really a very, very hard thing to study, is the Japanese soul. And ever so much of what I wrote in my forthcoming volume of Japanese sketches seems now to me wrong,—now that I have lived so long out of Izumo. I see no literary inspiration ahead. I can imagine no means of consoling myself except by plunging into the study of Buddhism—making a sort of prose-poem that no Japanese will ever look at. But who—not a madman—should try to write a book for Japanese to read, after having acquired some knowledge of things?

Well, they have no reason to love us *en masse,* at least. Here, across the strait, is the city bombarded by us . . . We bombarded unhappiness into the country— beyond any doubt. Force sowed the seed; the future will gather the black crop. In the eternal order of things, I suppose it is inevitable that every race should be made as wretched as possible; and all who cannot accept wretchedness as a necessary part of life must be exterminated. But again, in the eternal order of things, what is the use? What is even the use of the life of a solar system—evolution, dissolution, —re-evolution, re-dissolution, forever more? Really Buddhism alone gives us any consolatory ideas on the subject; but it is now vulgar to mention Buddhism to the Japanese.[37]

After the small adventures they had had in Oki, and the days with Nishida in Mionoseki, Hearn and his wife were ready to start home. They went again to Sakai, near Mionoseki, and missed the ship which was to have taken them the easy way by water around Honshu. They had no choice now but to make the journey overland by kuruma, the third time he had done so, as Hearn noted. The rains had washed out roads, and the going was difficult. For three days they struggled across the mountains to Kurashiki where there was a train.

Mrs. Hearn recalled many years later how one day, their kurumaya, having jogged on into the early dusk without finding a good place to stay, remembered that there was a settlement just beyond where they were, a place of only seven houses, but where one family took in guests.

As I remember, it was about ten o'clock when we reached the inn. It was really a small, shabby farmhouse with a queer atmosphere about it. The *andon* (paper lantern) gave a very poor light, and the proprietors were an old man and his wife. We saw three bravo-like men talking there. We were shown to a room upstairs, and the old woman left us a tiny lamp and never came up again.

It was right after the floods . . . and we heard the torrent rushing down the near-by river-bed. The noise of the water—"*Go—go*"—made a terrific sound.

Now and then the room was lighted by fireflies which flew into and out of the house; there were great numbers of them. While we were looking out of the window, we felt some kind of insect come swarming around us as if something were thrown over us on our hands and faces. They were very nasty insects. Sometimes crickets came and sang close beside us as we knelt on the floor.

We occasionally heard the bravo-like men talking, and the stairs would creak from time to time. We thought that the bravos were climbing up, and we could not help thinking of tales of the olden days which we had read in books of adventure. The old woman brought us our dinners on trays. I asked her what those insects were, and she told us that they were called *Natsu-mushi* (summer insects), and that there was nothing unusual about them. It was indeed an isolated spot, and we felt as if we were living in a dream. Hearn said, "This is an interesting place, and I should like to pass another night here." Those hotels for foreigners with modern facilities in Hakone and elsewhere were not to Hearn's liking, but this kind of inn fascinated him.[38]

After such discomfort and stimulation, Kumamoto caught Hearn up in routine once more in September 1892. Not much was different at the school. There were new boys to tame. There was soon a new director to watch warily and wonder about; Mr. Sakurai replaced the admired Mr. Kano, and Hearn was not sure of this silent young man who made him no confidences and with whom he conversed eerily in French.

In December there was one great addition to his well-being. He found a better house, at 35 Nishihoribata, Tsuboi, and, what was more important, a house with an interesting garden. In the midst of a comforting monotony at home and at school he was able to save money. By February 1893 he reported to Hendrick, "My little wife and I have saved nearly two thousand Japanese dollars between us," and in July he wrote to the same friend: "We have now nearly $3500 between us . . ." [39]

The interest in his writing was now the difficulty of writing simply about simple things. He continued, with the help of his former students, to gather material for essays about customs, manners, folk sayings and songs, childrens' games, popular poetry. He continued to work up more formal essays about the national psychology. But his best new work was of happenings in "common everyday" life. Some of these things he saw, some his friends told him, some were found in the newspapers.

He wrote to Mason for help in November 1892:

It occurred to me, however, to ask you to help me in an easy way—by writing me a few lines about anything touching or noble in common everyday life which you might happen to see without wishing to use. A maidservant, a child at school, an aged man dying among the memories of the past and the disorders of the present, a bit of kindness by the roadside,—any "heart-thing,"—I would like to know. I collect all I can, and write them, and put them in drawers. In time they work themselves out. [40]

He wrote to Nishida for similar help:

You say, if you were to tell me about the noble things the common people do, you would never get done. Indeed, *one* strong fact would give me work for two or three months. [41]

His imagination worked strongly, and he was confident of its function, but it had to be stoked with facts. Daily life even in Kumamoto was not barren of such facts.

One day a murderer was brought back for trial to Kumamoto from Fukuoka where he had been hiding since his crime. In the railroad station, the Kita-Kumamoto station north of the city (where Hearn was a single, silent watcher), the policeman who was guarding the manacled man turned the prisoner to look at the woman he had widowed, the child he had orphaned. The murderer dropped on his knees and begged forgiveness of them. The hard Kyushu crowd watching with intense interest wept. Hearn wrote a short narrative about this scene, a sequence in which no word was wasted and in which emotion compelled without any visible urging. [42]

A few times Hearn broke away from his routine and went out into the countryside. One time he and his kurumaya, an elderly man, paused to rest on a bridge. The old man told Hearn how, twenty-three years before, during the civil war, he had seen Kumamoto burn, and how here on this bridge he had been caught and held by some of the Satsuma rebels disguised as peasants in straw hats and cloaks. These grim men with long swords hidden under their garments had threatened him and made him hold his tongue while they ambushed and cut off the heads of three officers who came ignorantly upon them. They had gone away when that work was done, leaving him shaking upon the bridge. He had gone back to the city and found work with the other army.

"Who were the men that you saw killed on the bridge?"
"I don't know."
"Did you never try to find out?"
"No," said Heishichi, again mopping his forehead: "I said nothing about the matter until many years after the war."
"But why?" I persisted.
Heishichi gave me one astonished look, smiled in a pitying way, and answered,—
"Because it would have been wrong;—it would have been ungrateful."
I felt properly rebuked.
And we resumed our journey.[43]

Such expeditions only punctuated the regularity of his life. In the new house, a house with a room beneficently warmed for Hearn by an American Franklin stove, he finished in January 1893 the writing of the last chapter of his first Japanese book, *Glimpses of Unfamiliar Japan*. Not only his work prospered but his whole being was soothed and softened by the fact that now, in his third winter in Japan, he could be warm. He had had glass shoji installed in the sliding walls of his study, and the ugly, efficient stove was enthroned in a place of honor. "My folks say I have never said a cross word since I had a warm room. Heat thus appears as a moral force. Just think how holy I should be could I live forever under the equator." [44] So he wrote to Chamberlain on February 18, 1893.

He had some trouble in persuading his publisher of this period, Houghton Mifflin Company of Boston, to take the full, expansive manuscript. (It had to be published in two volumes.) He was to spend much of the next summer correcting the big bundles of proof sent from Boston to Kumamoto, and putting his last marks upon material which seemed to belong to the past. Already he was moving toward a new conception of Japan.

But while Hearn looked hungrily ahead into new hopes, doubts, and questions about his function as a writer, his book stated honestly his first fresh impressions of Japan. He later underrated what he had done in the book because when it was finished he had left behind forever the frame of mind which had created it. But in *Glimpses* he conveyed the necessary state of delicious openness in which he had for a time lived. Upon the shallow, delicate canvas of the book he put down what he had seen with the eye of an impressionist painter. There was here only the beginning of a troubling of the surface in such an essay as "From the Diary of an English Teacher."

In Kumamoto, finishing what he had begun in Matsue, he needed all the stability he had to cope with new irritations at the Fifth Higher School. In January 1893 he wrote to Nishida: "The school here is getting rather disagreeable. I think they are trying to get rid of me." [45] He did not fling himself out of the situation as he might have done if he had been single. Animal comfort gave him the strength to endure a spiritual discomfort. He saw now with a freezing skepticism how little he knew Japan, and how much he disliked some of the things he knew.

He wrote to Chamberlain on January 17th:

The illusions are forever over; but the memory of many unpleasant things remains. I know much more about the Japanese than I did a year ago; and still I am far from understanding them well. Even my own little wife is somewhat mysterious still to me, though always in a lovable way.

He meditated upon how little one could know of the thoughts and feelings of people one saw even every day:

My cook wears a smiling, healthy, rather pleasing face. He is a good-looking young man. Whenever I used to think of him I thought of the smile, I saw a mask before me merry as one of those little masks of Oho-kumi-nushi-no-kami they sell at Mionoseki. One day I looked through a little hole in the shoji, and saw him alone. The face was not the same face. It was thin and drawn and showed queer lines worn by old hardship. I thought, "He will look just like that when he is dead." I went in, and the man was all changed,—young and happy again,—nor have I ever seen that look of trouble in his face since. But I know when he is alone he wears it. He never shows his *real* face to me; he wears the mask of happiness as an etiquette. . . .[46]

When spring came again in 1893 Hearn was not so shut up with his human problems. He could go once more on good days up the path behind the college buildings to the cemetery on the hill. He had written to Ellwood Hendrick of this resource:

From between the tombs I can look down on the Dai Go Koto Chugakko, with its huge modern brick buildings and its tumultuous life, as in a bird's-eye view. I am only there never alone. For Buddha sits beside me, and also looks down upon the college through his half-closed eyelids of stone. There is moss on his nose and his hands—moss on his back, of course! And I always say to him: "O Master, what do you think of all this?—is it not vanity? There is no faith there, no creed, no thought of the past life nor of the future life, nor of Nirvana—only chemistry and cube-geometry—and the most damnable 'English language.' " He never answers me; but he looks very sad—smiles like one who has received an injury which he cannot return—and you know that is the most pathetic of all smiles. And the snakes twist before my feet as I descend to the sound of the bell. There is my only companion for you! but I like him better than those who look like him waiting for me in the classroom.[47]

In the warming weather he had also his own garden to stroll in, a strictly ordered piece of nature, fashioned to look like a wilderness, decorated with fifteen boulders transported from the bed of the Shirakawa River. He had learned to enjoy the un-human beauty of these ancient surfaces, handled by water, wind, time, but not by man until set up by him to be admired. He began to understand through looking at stones the Japanese attitude toward nature, a nature not endowed with sexual or supernatural or even any human qualities, but apprehended nakedly, neutrally, purely.

In April, Hearn greeted a long-anticipated guest. The spare, energetic figure of Professor Chamberlain appeared in the doorway, was robbed gently of his shoes, and brought into Hearn's study to sit companionably, to smoke, and to talk. The two men had much to say to each other. Chamberlain had been on a long visit to England, and Hearn, now more immobile than he had ever been, questioned his guest about all the places he had seen. He had also new ideas about Japan to try out upon the rational, witty surface of Chamberlain's mind. It was for the professor mostly a listening to Hearn's talk. Hearn had been so starved for company that, after the professor was gone, he found himself talking, as he reported ruefully in a letter, to the ghost of the professor across the table.

When he had no friend across a low table to whom to direct his notions, he had to write to one. Hearn was becoming very conscious of his extreme solitariness. He did not fit in with the progressive world of the Fifth Higher School of Kumamoto. Yet it would have been foolishness to think he could go home to America (America after all was where he was from, rather than England), and prosper there. He studied the great Western civilization in the perspective of his Japanese world.

Suppose I should seek a place as teacher of English literature. Everybody thinks he can teach English literature, and the public doesn't care particularly; it takes its pabulum largely on trust. On whose trust? Oh! the trust of trustees—and the respectable people. Now I am not respectable. I am under the odium theologicum of every Christian faith. Small and mean as I am, I am spotted. Don't imagine this is vanity! It is just like a prostitute trying to become an honest woman, or a convicted thief endeavoring to get employment. There is nothing great about it. If I had any position worth hunting up, the cry would be raised that an atheist, a debauchee, a disreputable ex-reporter was corrupting the morals of the young under pretence of teaching literature.[48]

Continuing his argument with respectability, in April 1893 Hearn wrote to Hendrick:

I am unable to sympathize fully with the normally moral man. In fact, I don't think he *is* normally moral. . . . Of course, morality, pure and simple, has nothing to do with the matter. It is a question of force, self-balance, self-control, intellectual power of a certain order.[49]

Following Herbert Spencer, Hearn believed that a man had to be a good animal before he could begin to be a good man, that there had to be physical beauty before there could be moral beauty, that the moral qualities were added as extra gifts to the proper functioning of the instincts, that an imposed respectability was a falsehood.

His impatience was temperamental:

How frightful to have to live altogether according to the proprieties! I'd rather die. Everything charming in life, as in Japanese art, is Irregularity and Eccentricity. The Perfectly Regular, the Mathematically Correct, is barbarism and cruelty. Nay, it is a violation of all Natural law; for all tendencies to evolutionary progress come in the shape of invisible tendencies to deviate from the common herd.[50]

Ignoring the world of the herd and the sphere of respectability, it was the duty of the artist, poised, not knowing how or why, upon the balance of his intuitions, to look after his own interests. Hearn's particular interest at this time was the invention of a kind of fiction.

Of such things he wrote to Ellwood Hendrick. Sometimes he comfortably gossiped with him. In 1891 he heard of Elizabeth Bisland's marriage to Charles W. Wetmore, evidently a prosperous marriage, allowing the wonderful Elizabeth to travel and write, and to do very much as she pleased. Now he considered her, at a great distance, probably settled in a world of fashion and money, so far removed from him as never to make a sign to him again. (There was a period of silence, but Elizabeth Wetmore took up the correspondence again, and Hearn responded eagerly.)

Admirable and wonderful she is; but I certainly cannot think of her as of human kin, altogether. That used to be my feeling in the South;—in New York she became wonderfully sweet and bewitched me in a sort of way,—made me think of the charming side, which with her is one of innumerable facets. . . .

But, while eternally grateful to her (for instance in regard to Major McDonald), I would not like to be at her mercy if I were worth a pawn in her chess-play. I think she looks at men like pawns, and has about as much real sense of kinship with them as a supernatural being would have. Then supernatural people are capricious. What would change her,—perhaps!—would be motherhood. But then again, I can only imagine motherhood for her as a sort of condescension to humanity,—just as one of the ancient goddesses might have condescended to become incarnate,—just for an elegant recreation.[51]

Hearn continued to teach her name, as a typical woman's name in English to his students, writing it upon the blackboard and calling upon the rows of uniformed boys to repeat it mesmerically in chorus, E-liz-a-beth Bees-land.

He kept her picture in his study, attaching to it, as it may have seemed to his wife, a sort of religious veneration.

In the summer of 1893 Hearn had little attention left over for anything going on outside his own house. He concentrated with a frightful energy upon this one place. His wife was pregnant. Nothing so important had ever happened to Hearn. He was full of a terrified joy. With characteristic inefficiency in counting, he estimated to his friends that the child would be born in September or even earlier. But he had all the hot summer to wait, and the change to the cool of autumn, before the child, his son, was born in November.

During this time the family was busy and happy and did not much regard him and his intensifications. All the women made baby clothes. Before the birth customary messages of congratulation came from the remotest branches of the family in Shimane Province. Hearn liked his family better than ever in the homeliness of its concern with the coming birth and the openness with which all of them, mother, father, grandparents, servants, took part in the preparations. This did not help him much who had in his own mind taken on the entire pregnancy himself. He had finally to go away for a few days alone to help himself.

He went one week in July to Nagasaki, but the heat was intolerable; he stopped in an ugly Western-style hotel, and he came back for all his exertions with only the ghost of an idea for a story. But "The Dream of a Summer Day," a transformation of all his discomfort, was well worth the trip. He used his own experience of sultry Kyushu summer weather as a piquant frame for the retelling of the old Japanese fairy tale of Urashima:

Fourteen hundred and sixteen years ago, the fisher-boy Urashima Taro left the shore of Suminoye in his boat.
Summer days were then as now . . .[52]

After the school term began again in September, Hearn hurried home each day. During the final weeks of waiting the family followed an old custom and borrowed a baby, to accustom the mother and the family to the handling of a child, and to let them grow used to having one among them. Hearn was awestruck at the baby's Buddhistic calm and doubted that he could have one who would be so supernaturally agreeable. He hardly dared touch him.

As the time of the birth approached, the calm of the others in the household seemed monstrous. He wanted a doctor for his wife. Setsu preferred the customary midwives, and her husband mistrustfully consented. When the two midwives were sent for and arrived to push aside the distraught husband, Hearn disliked the old women on sight. He knelt beside his wife during her labor and prayed in anguish to the child being born, "Come into this world with good eyes!" [53] The midwives, ferocious as old witches as they seemed to him now, got him out of the room. He tried shakily to work in the room adjoining.

When he heard the thin cry of his newborn child, Hearn experienced such sensations as he had never had before. He rushed in and hugged the old women, scandalizing them completely. It had been a normal birth. Hearn called in doctors to assure himself that all was well. That same night he began writing letters to all his friends about this remarkable happening:

Dear Hendrick,—I have been waiting several weeks to tell you of an event which occurred later than I expected. Last night my child was born—a very strong boy, with large black eyes; he looks more like a Japanese, however, than like a foreign boy. He has my nose, but his mother's features in some other respects, curiously blended with mine. There is no fault with him; and the physicians say, from the form of his little bones, that he promises to become very tall. A cross between European and Japanese is nearly always an improvement when both parents are in good condition; and happily the old military caste to which my wife belongs is a strong one. She is quite well.—Still, I had my anxiety, and the new experience brought to me for a moment, with extraordinary force, the knowledge of how sacred and terrible a thing maternity is, and how even religion cannot hedge it about sufficiently with protection. Then I thought with astonishment of the possibility that men could be cruel to women who bore their children; and the world seemed very dark for a moment. When it was over, I confess I felt very humble and grateful to the Unknowable Power which had treated us so kindly—and I said a little prayer of thanks, feeling quite sure it was not foolish to do so. . . .

Dear H., I have not slept last night; I am going to rest a little;—good-bye for a short time, with love to you.[54]

Setsu recovered quickly. The child thrived. The father watched over his son pridefully and nervously. He could not understand or ever get used to the existence of the child. Hearn's life was changed. He had known no goad before like fatherhood. Never for a single instant did the pressure let up, to secure the future of this son he had brought into existence.

His letters continued to tell his friends about the baby whom he first called Leopold Kazuo Hearn but who soon became only Kazuo and then playfully Kajiwa or Kaji. Kaji's hair was chestnut and wavy; he no longer looked Japanese; he was going to be taller than his father, and how was the father to educate him? Should he take him to Europe or to America for his schooling? The future was something to be afraid of now, for in that future something might happen to him, the provider for the child and the child's mother and all the willing helpers of the household who waited on the boy hour after hour.

By the following April, when Kazuo was a sturdy five-months child, able to be strapped comfortably to his mother's or his grandmother's back, he was ready as a proper Japanese child to begin his life's expeditions to various sacred places of the islands. Hearn took Setsu and her mother and the boy on a several days' trip to the Kompira Shrine on the smallest of the main islands of Japan, Shikoku. It was a happy trip. The sights were entertaining. The weather was good. Along the way the family group was accepted as one belonging to the scene. Hearn was pleased at being taken sometimes for an Ainoku (half Japanese). Hearn wrote a long letter about the trip to Chamberlain, calling it "The Adventures of Kaji."

After this respite it was necessary to go back to Kumamoto to finish the school term. Hearn was more unhappy in the school than he had ever been. In his new situation as the father of Kazuo, he was obliged to do his best to support his son, but he no longer felt constrained to be tolerant of wrongs. He was convinced, perhaps wrongly, that he was not wanted at the Fifth Higher School, that there was some sort of conspiracy among the teachers against him, that one among them particularly was in touch with the vague but menacing entity of "the missionaries," who he was sure were his enemies. Probably he made matters worse by calling upon the silent young head-master and talking obliquely to him about his "enemies." Still, he did not resign.

In the summer he had a chance to look for other opportunities. He was apparently worth more as a writer than he had been. His essays and stories were appearing with some regularity in the *Atlantic Monthly*. He had had three sketches in the magazine in 1893. He would have another in July, one in October, one in November in 1894. He would have five in 1895. The piece published in July 1894, "The Red Bridal," with even the critical Chamberlain praising it, seemed a success in his new vein, a writing out of contemporary life: this one from a newspaper report, the story of the double suicide of a young couple not allowed to marry but not prevented from lying down together upon a railroad track.

As the father of Kazuo, Hearn felt obligated to have a more independent and demanding attitude. He must do something for himself. About this time he wrote to Page Baker: "Could you get me anything to do if I started in the spring for America? . . . If you could get me something anywhere south of Mason and Dixon's line, I should try to be practically grateful in some way." And: "Or can you get me anything educational in Spanish America?" [55] Hearn did not pursue these rather large requests but allowed his questions to ravel out into indefiniteness.

On July 10th he left Kumamoto for the central cities of Honshu to explore other, nearer possibilities. He went alone, leaving Setsu and the boy and his family in Kumamoto.

His first stop, on July 15th, was with Mason in Yokohama. He liked the man as well as he had liked the letter writer. "I have been intimately acquainted with Mason for more than a million years, and understand, I think, just why you like each other," Hearn wrote to Chamberlain. "Mason is what Goethe would have called 'a beautiful soul.' " [56] Mason introduced Hearn to his wife and his two boys, eleven and fourteen. It was the same half-European, half-Japanese household as Hearn's. Mason's daily drudgery in the Department of Posts and Telegraphs (where he had been for seventeen years) was something Hearn could understand. Mason had a keen eye for life and a steady interest in literature. The two men found another common interest that sealed their friendship. Mason invited Hearn almost at once to go swimming with him. Hearn continued his report to Chamberlain, who had been responsible for his knowing Mason: "We passed today at Kamakura swimming and indulging in debaucheries of beefsteak, whisky and lemonade, gin and ginger ale and beer. His son was with us—and I like the little man very much; we soon became friends . . ." [57]

Another night Mason invited him to dinner, this time a very proper Japanese meal. Afterward, Mason's wife and sister-in-law played the *koto* for the men. Then the two boys were allowed to run outdoors, full of excitement, and set off a display of fireworks. As Hearn remembered, there was a "great big warm moon. One of those evenings that never die:—But I fear"—again he was writing to Chamberlain—"all these experiences will demoralize me. After rescue, a castaway enjoys too much the food offered; a physician stands by to prevent him eating enough. My ghostly part was really too hungry for such experience, and feels longings not wholesome for it;—sympathy is the supreme delight of life. I ought now to meet some horribly disagreeable foreigners,—so as to have my pleasure checked a little. Besides, I am much too happy to write essays and sketches." [58]

Hearn had a theory that his writing came out of his unhappiness only, that kindness made him dumb. But he had been starved for companionship in both Matsue and Kumamoto. He had written about this loneliness in Matsue in 1891 (before taking on family responsibilities and stifling open wishes to go home):

One's best friends have a certain far-offness about them, even when breaking their necks to please you. There is no such thing as smacking a fellow on the rear, or chucking a fellow under the ribs. Such familiarities are terribly vulgar in Japan. So each one has to tickle his own soul and clap it on the back, and say "Hello!" to it.

And the soul being western, says:—"Do you expect me always to stay in this extraordinary country. I want to go home, or to get back to the West Indies—at least. Hurry up, and save some money." [59]

In Matsue people had been exceptionally kind to him in his loneliness. In Kumamoto he had not even had standoffish kindness. Coming into the circle of earthy goodness and genial understanding that he found at Mason's unhinged his emotions from his critical faculties. Going on to Tokyo on July 17th was a continuing debauch of happiness. He was not only enjoying the kind of talk and ease of association he had missed for years; he was also relieved temporarily of the pressures of which the sight of his family daily reminded him. The trip, which was to have been a solution of his economic problems, first helped them by letting him forget for a little while the intensity of them. He did not lose Mason whom he had just discovered. He went down to Yokohama occasionally to see him, and to meet other people there. Among them was the young scholar and poet Nobushige Amenomori, who was to be important to him later, someone to whom he could apply for knowledge in Buddhist lore.

In Tokyo, Hearn took up residence in Professor Chamberlain's house. Chamberlain was away at the time, escaping Tokyo's summer heat in the mountains of Hakone, but his personality permeated the comfortable, well run house at 19 Akasaka Daimachi. To his absent host Hearn wrote on the day of his arrival:

At your house all was in waiting for me; but the dog first made my acquaintance,—running before to the gate. He is now watching my every movement as I write,—and we are good friends.[60]

He had the care of well trained servants, excellent meals, a bed with a wonderful mosquito net and, what was most intoxicating, a varied library. Hearn spent hours going through these books—about Japan, about language, about folklore, books scientific, and books literary. "Did any philologist ever before, in this mortal world, coolly tell his friend,—'Just take along with you any of my books you wish to read?' " [61] But Hearn was meticulously careful. He put back each book into its proper place after savoring not only its contents—reading bits, skimming much—but also enjoying, as he told the professor, Chamberlain's own notes upon many of the pages. About the books on Japan, he said: "I really had no idea until now how much had been done in certain lines; and feeling that all I could do would be only to add a few bricks to the great Babel, I have become properly humble,—I hope." [62]

He read freely, following his straying interests in many directions. "How touching Tolstoi is! Still, the fault of the beautiful religion of the man is simply that it is unsuited to the real order of things. Resentment, as Spencer has not hesitated to point out, is not only essential to self-preservation, but is often a moral duty." [63] He generalized upon the thinkers of the past hundred years. "The most religious men of the nineteenth century are the infidels—the 'atheists and blasphemers.' " [64] Books could not distract him from other pleasures. Chamberlain's house stood in an area of trees. "The enormous laughter of the crows every morning amuses me very much." [65]

He reported to Chamberlain the enjoyments of his new friendship with Mason:

Mason said a pretty thing the other day in the train. Opposite to us were sitting little mothers with their children. Both mothers and children were good to look at,— and the little white feet in snowy *tabi* seemed scarcely of this world. Mason looked at the dainty picture with a caress in his eyes, and said: "If those people could only feel for us the sympathy we feel toward them!" Indeed the whole question of life in Japan to a sensitive westerner was summed up in that half-utterance. The unspeakable absence of sympathy, as a result, perhaps, of all absence of comprehension, is a veritable torture.[66]

Even in saying such a thing Hearn felt a twinge of guilt and began to think of what he must soon be doing, turning toward his family again. "Now the idea of returning into the life of Japan is a growing terror to be overcome. I have been partly demoralized by my Tokyo days. I need a little medicine of unkindness—want to be sickened for a time of Yokohama, etc." [67]

Hearn had been to see a Japanese publisher of books in English upon the very day of his arrival in Tokyo, and concluded with the firm of Hasegawa a tentative agreement for the publishing of a series of finely bound fairy tales. He had delivered two finished stories to them at the time. He promised others. Such a good beginning of a publishing venture, undertaken on his own initiative, pleased the writer. Perhaps he was at last learning how to deal with publishers. (He was to say once: "Publishers are enemies.") [68] He was accomplishing in Japan what he had vainly planned as far back as those muggy days in Martinique when he had made notes about a Creole Red Riding Hood and a Creole Cinderella.

Hearn started homeward full of confidence at least in his writing but with no particular solution for his life in Kumamoto. On the way he had one more pleasant demoralization. He took a side trip into the Hakone Highlands to stay for a few days with Chamberlain at the Hotel Fujiya in Miyanoshita, enjoying in spite of himself the kind of luxury most Westerners demanded and succeeded in getting in Japan. But for Hearn the now slightly awkward

Western arrangements were of no real importance. What was luxury was to talk with the professor late into the cigar-scented night upon a veranda, looking out at stars which swung in their regular course behind the cone of Fuji.

Hearn returned to Kyushu by boat and train and arrived at his house on July 31st. There were earthquakes in August to upset him. There was the imminent opening of school to give him a slight nausea of anticipation. There was the dullness of Kumamoto to emphasize the excitements he had been through. It was no wonder that when there came to him, as it seemed providentially, the good offer of a full-time job upon an English-language newspaper in the city of Kobe, he quickly accepted.

Yet giving up the security of teaching in the public-school system was painful. He might be giving up a certain good to gain an uncertain ill. He could not know how his adventure would turn out. "We're beginning to pack up," he wrote to Chamberlain on October 2nd. "I'm sick—not attending school, just pleasantly sick. I thank the Gods therefor." [69] He had waited until after the opening of the school year to disrupt himself, his family, and the school. But he had resigned his position and was now going.

There had to be much done in a great hurry. Some of the more extraneous members of the family had had to be sent sadly back to Shimane, there to await a possible word to rejoin the others, if it were convenient, in Kobe. Hearn had had a failure with the boy he and his wife had "stolen" in the Oki Islands. He had been sheltered and clothed, sent to school, treated like a member of the household, but nothing had penetrated an impervious shell of hardness. He had worried them all very much, as Hearn rather neutrally put it. The servants had all cried one day when he ran away. But he had not ever relented into affection. At last Hearn had had to send him back, sore that he had never understood the stubborn, apparently unfeeling boy, nor he them.

Hearn hoped that in Kobe he would be nearer his friends in Yokohama and in Tokyo. But Kobe, close to Osaka and Kyoto, was not really near to these other cities; they were many hours of train travel away. He hoped that his writing would make up for the secure monthly salary he was giving up in Kumamoto. But there was no sureness in the prospect. He did not know if he were betraying Kazuo, himself, and the family in giving up his government job and going away from Kumamoto.

However, it seemed a good time to leave. "I have just sent off my eleventh paper, finishing my second book on Japan . . ." [70] he wrote to Chamberlain on September 22nd.

As for his family, those who were accompanying Herun-san, they were eager to go. Kyushu had never been their home. Setsu was pleased at the thought of moving to one of the great cities of Honshu. "There is a nomad restlessness in this race . . . Even the sweetest Japanese woman has something of this Tartar soul . . . she is ready tomorrow to pull up the pegs and travel a thousand ri." [71]

In the second week of October, having finished his engagement as a teacher at the Fifth Higher School in Kumamoto, Hearn arrived in Kobe to take up once more his old profession of newspaperman on the English-language publication the *Kobe Chronicle*.

18 ❦ A Kobe View

Hearn, his wife, the child Kazuo, Setsu's parents, two female servants, and one extra male relative arrived in Kobe some time during the second week of October 1894 after a journey by train and steamer from Kumamoto. Hearn's Izumo family wondered at the Western strangeness of the busy port city. Half the passers-by seemed to be redheaded seamen or tall blond merchants.

Hearn was soothed by finding his memory true that Kobe was at least beautiful. The steep, wooded Rokko Range closed it in and sheltered it on the north with a line of three-thousand-foot peaks. The city's avenues ran parallel to the range, each one making a step up toward the mountains. Hearn noted with appreciation how from any street one could look down at the water.

Kobe was a complex place. It was one of the two greatest ports of Japan. It had a thriving foreign colony prospering artificially under the special protection of treaty rights forced upon Japan at the time of the opening of the Empire. The houses in the foreign section were of Western style. There were churches, clubs, warehouses, docks, shipping offices, and a confusion of the masts of ships from all over the world. But Hearn, reacting like a Japanese to this display, was comforted by his observation that beyond the foreign quarter there was not much of the West. And indeed at this moment, when Japan had won an aggressive war against China, treaty rights in such ports as Kobe were about to be lost by the bankers, traders, and shippers who had prospered by them.

One of the anomalies of Kobe was the existence of a number of foreign-language newspapers. To one of them, the *Kobe Chronicle,* Hearn owed his chance to live and work in the city. To acquaint himself with what his job was to be, and to meet his new employer, Hearn deposited his numerous family in a hotel and went straight to the *Chronicle* office.

The editor of the *Chronicle* was Robert Young, a vigorous, youthfully energetic Scotsman whom Hearn liked at the first handshake. He knew his business, and his views were, as Hearn said, "liberal," meaning for Hearn scientific, evolutionary, not obscured by too much regard for the influential missionaries of the foreign colony. Young had had previous experience on the English *Saturday Review.* This practical, large-minded man spoke at once to Hearn of giving up to him most of the editorial writing. Hearn was pleased. He saw that he was to be a general assistant and that the job might be interesting.

He was pleased too by the kindness Young and his wife showed Setsu, and the practical way in which they helped the whole Hearn family to begin housekeeping in this strange, bustling town. Hearn wrote to Sentaro Nishida on October 23rd: "He treats me like a brother; his wife pets Mrs. Hearn; and we feel quite happy so far. Of course the work is hard; but it is my old profession. I write all the Editorials . . . I am allowed perfect freedom to write just as I please." [2]

He told Nishida about the house the Youngs had helped him find. "We have a little house now,—foreign upstairs and Japanese downstairs. It is not very nice, but it will be very warm in winter . . ." [3]

Hearn, getting quickly settled to the job, was a wonder to Young in his productiveness and inventiveness. Apparently the two men met each morning. Hearn's subject for the day's editorial was set. Young recalled in 1907 the way Hearn worked:

It was remarkable with what ease he could turn out an article. As soon as the subject was decided upon he would go to his own room, where he had a specially high desk to suit his defective eyesight, and sitting there with his nose not more than an inch from the paper he would write industriously for an hour until the article was finished.[4]

Hearn should have been happy, but he nursed instead a contradictory anger. He felt he had been forced out of teaching, and he blamed his friends Chamberlain and Mason for sins of omission. "I can't guess whom to be vexed with—you or Mason," he wrote to the professor, "but I have been feeling resentful. Both of you knew, or ought to have known, that I was in the Kwakto-Jigoku [hell] for two years, but neither of you would move a pen to help me out of it. Well, I suppose you consulted over me together (unfair!—two against one!) and concluded it was best to let me stick it out. And it was,—since it forced me out of a service which has become unbearable. Still, I feel a little mad at you both. For either of you I should have broken my back to help if necessary, without waiting for finely detailed explanations." [5] It must have seemed a little difficult to be so fiercely attacked for a failure to discover what he had wanted of them. The rest of Hearn's letter was friendly.

The letter explains why this new work, at which Hearn was so grimly dexterous, was such a strain upon him. He went at it, not liking it, but doing it with a dreadful celerity and facility.

The editorials of the *Chronicle* were limited by the outlook of the readers of the paper, mostly English-speaking merchants, military men, consular employees, visitors to Japan. There was no literary comment, not much depth of study of anything, but short familiar comment upon the topics of the day, things Japanese which affected the daily lives of this foreign enclave in Kobe, and American and English topics in which these readers had a passing interest. A few of the editorials were tinctured by Hearn's own interests, but they were not highly charged by his imagination. Hearn was determined to supply what was desired. Some of the titles of his editorials were: "The Kurumaya Question," "Japanese Educational Policy," "Japanese Physique," "The Race-Problem in America," "Earthquakes and National Character," "The Republican Victory in the United States," "The Question of Male and Female Equality," and "A New Chance for Buddhism."

Hearn tried to write these things off the top of his mind, and devoted his evenings to his own work. But his strength drained away, and his eyes suffered. He was more silent than usual, more reserved, and more saving of himself in company.

Mrs. Young, meeting him occasionally when the two families visited each other, found Hearn a curiosity. He came to her house, rang the bell and, without thinking, greeted her in Japanese. He did not think whether she were Japanese or not, and she caught him up on this lapse, somewhat outraged. Hearn was gravely courteous and corrected himself, but did not see the outrage.

Hearn's editor would have introduced him to the English-speaking colony, but Hearn was unresponsive to such opportunities. His avoidance of introductions was very noticeable in Kobe, where all the non-Japanese knew each other and huddled together in their amusements.

Hearn was determined to make a success of his job. He had to save his nights for writing. In this routine he discovered that he missed the ingenuous friendships he had made in teaching, and also the ideas for his writing which teaching had always given him. When he left off scribbling at the paper and went out into the city, it was to take long solitary walks. ". . . He wore the shabbiest of clothes out of doors with the object apparently of escaping observation, and confined his walks to back streets or localities not generally frequented by Europeans or Americans." [6]

Yet when Hearn could be enticed to meet some of the editor's friends for a meal and for talk (which Hearn missed and poured out onesidedly in his letters), he could be charming. Young wrote, "In the company of a few friends, however, he would thaw out, and, having a wonderful memory, was an excellent raconteur, and would illuminate from his wide reading any subject under discussion." [7]

He wrote Ellwood Hendrick in December 1894: "I am writing one article a day for one hundred yen a month. Exchange is so low now that the one hundred represents something less than fifty in American money. And my eyes, or eye, giving out." [8] In January he wrote a letter that seemed the necessary consequence of his December information. "Since I wrote you last, you dear old fellow, I've been through some trouble. Indeed, the very *day* after writing you, I broke down, and had to remain three weeks with compresses over my eyes in a dark room. I am now over it—able to write and read for a short time every day, but have been warned to leave routine newspaper work alone. Which I must do." [9]

Young had lost his editorial writer. Hearn had proved to himself that he could not go on with this work which wasted both his sight and his time. Yet he did not know what to do. He writhed upon his bed in a room as closed in and dark as his prospects. His abused sight recovered more quickly than his emotions. He floundered among his problems: he had failed at teaching, he had failed at a return to newspaper work, he was in danger of blindness, he was immobilized with a family dependent on him. Even if he recovered his sight and his health and his ability, he did not know if he had any material to work with. The crisis in his health coincided with a crisis in his writing. He did not know whether Japan could give him anything more. In March, after several weeks of self-eating idleness, he wrote to Professor Chamberlain: "I feel just now empty and useless and a dead failure." [10]

His coming to Kobe had completed the swift downward slide of his feelings into disillusionment. He saw here as in Kumamoto a gifted, clever people throwing away from themselves as quickly as possible all the qualities he had admired in them and taking on a graceless, shallow Westernization.

Yet he had missed the West in spite of himself. Coming back within the stimulating hum and whir of the West's energy, he had jeered at Japan's smallness:

Coming out of my solitude of nearly five years to stand on the deck of the *Kobe Maru* on the 10th, I felt afraid. I saw myself among giants. Everything seemed huge, full of force, dignity, massive potentialities divined but vaguely. A sudden sense of the meaning of that civilization I had been so long decrying and arguing against, and vainly rebelling against, came upon me crushingly. . . .

How small suddenly my little Japan became!—how lonesome! What a joy to feel the West! What a great thing is the West! What new appreciations of it are born of isolation! [11]

He looked more sharply and less sympathetically at his surroundings than he had since he first arrived in April 1890. "My conclusion is that the charm of Japanese life is largely the charm of childhood, and that the most beautiful of all race childhoods is passing into an adolescence which threatens to prove repulsive." [12] Justifying himself to himself, as well as to Chamberlain, he wrote:

As for my changing my conclusions—well, I have had to change a good many. The tone of "Glimpses" is true in being the feeling of a place and time. Since then I've seen how thoroughly detestable Japanese can be, and that revelation assisted in illuminating things. I am now convinced, for example, that the deficiency of the sexual instinct (using the term philosophically) in the race is a serious defect rather than a merit, and is very probably connected with the absence of the musical sense and the incapacity for abstract reasoning. It does not follow, however, that the same instinct may not have been over-developed in our own case. [13]

Continuing his recriminations, bitterly wounding to himself, he wrote:

You can't imagine my feeling of reaction in the matter of Japanese psychology. It seems as if everything had quite suddenly become clear to me, and utterly void of emotional interest: a race primitive as the Etruscan before Rome was, or more so, adopting the practices of a larger civilization under compulsion . . . There are no depths to stir, no race-profundities to explore: all is like a Japanese river-bed, through which the stones and rocks show up all the year round—and is never filled but in time of cataclysm and destruction. [14]

Very painfully he said in another letter: "I had a sensation the other day, though, which I want to talk to you about. I felt as if I hated Japan unspeakably, and the whole world seemed not worth living in . . ." [15] Yet into this ugly mood in which he lived for some weeks, tied to a house in which he could do no work, fearful of his future, bitter about illusions broken and left lying about him in jagged, ugly pieces, there had come a kind of salvation.

Two women had come to the house to sell ballads:

One took her samisen and sang; and people crowded into the tiny yard to hear. Never did I listen to anything sweeter. All the sorrow and beauty, all the pain and the sweetness of life thrilled and quivered in that voice; and the old first love of Japan and of things Japanese came back, and a great tenderness seemed to fill the place like a haunting. I looked at the people, and I saw they were nearly all weeping, and snuffling; and though I could not understand the words, I could feel the pathos and beauty of things. Then, too, for the first time, I noticed that the singer was blind. Both women were surprisingly ugly, but the voice of the one that sang was indescribably beautiful; and she sang as peasants and birds and semi sing, which is nature and is divine. They were wanderers both. I called them in, and treated them well, and heard their story. It was not romantic at all—smallpox, blindness, a sick husband (paralyzed) and children to care for.16

Perhaps he still had his vocation. He could be interested in human nature in its endearing mixture of goodness and badness and ugliness and beauty. And after all, as he had remarked in the middle of his trouble in Kumamoto, "The Japanese are still the best people in the world to live among . . ." 17 He could write about these people and continue his arguments with himself on paper as to the larger changes going on in Japan, and make some sense out of his difficulties—readable, publishable sense.

Hope, when it came, came with a big gust. To Chamberlain in April 1895, after many months of illness and stagnation, he wrote:

. . . I must do better some day with something or acknowledge myself a dead failure. I really think I have stored away in me somewhere powers larger than those I have yet been able to use. Of course I don't mean that I have any hidden wisdom, or anything of that sort; but I believe I have some power to reach the public emotionally, if conditions allow.

One little story which would never die, might suffice—or a volume of little stories. . . . I might write an essay on some topic of which I am now quite ignorant —by studying the subject for the necessary time. But a story cannot be written by the help of study at all . . . It must be a "sensation" in one's own life—and not peculiar to any place or time.18

Hearn began climbing back to the confidence and the fullness of well-being necessary to his writing. He recovered at a time when walking out in the streets of Kobe he was hissed at and jeered at as a foreigner. National feeling was inflamed against all Westerners because Russia and Germany threatened by diplomacy to take away from Japan the fruits of her war.

Hearn studied this new belligerency with mixed feelings. He enjoyed Japan's showing the West that she was not to be sneered at; he feared what Japan would become in her new hardness. But it was matter for thoughts and words, and more and more busily his head hummed with new ideas.

His fears that he would not be able to support his family proved illusory. His writing was now appearing regularly in the United States, at this time in the *Atlantic Monthly*. His first Japanese book, published late in 1894, had had a good reception in both the United States and in England. He decided to try life in Kobe on the income from his writing alone. The period was a busy and fruitful one.

In close proximity to the representatives of the West who lived in Kobe—merchants, missionaries, consuls, teachers—Hearn did not keep for very long the glow of enthusiasm he had experienced for his own civilization. Kobe presented him with Western sights and sounds he had almost forgotten in the interior. "Carpets—pianos—windows—curtains—brass-bands! how I hate them!! And white shirts!—and yofuku! [Western clothes] Would I had been born savage; the curse of civilized cities is on me . . ." [19]

In wartime, Japan was moving rapidly toward the independence of a modern Western nation or back to the independence it had had under its first Tokugawa rulers. "It's an ugly business, this war. It may leave Japan absolutely independent, as in the days of Iyeyasu. But will that be best for her? I am no longer sure. The people are still good. The upper classes are becoming corrupt." [20]

All these thoughts gathered to conclusions in Kobe. He could loose his discursive intellect upon such matters, and write essays. His emotions went into the stories about the people among whom he moved every day.

He considered more narrowly and critically his own style. In recent years he had accomplished a reversal of aims. "My first work was awfully florid," he wrote Chamberlain in a letter in January 1893. "Self-control was the hardest thing to learn." [21] A month later he was arguing the same subject: "After years of studying poetical prose, I am forced now to study simplicity. After attempting my utmost at ornamentation, I am converted by my own mistakes. The great point is to touch with simple words. And I feel my style is not yet fixed,—too artificial. By another year of study or two, I think I shall be able to do better." [22]

A concern for words carried him to another insight. "By saying half-a-thing one can produce more effect than by saying, or rather trying to say, all." [23] This was in a letter to Ellwood Hendrick, of June 30, 1893. To the same friend he wryly deprecated inspiration: "The best work is done the way ants do things—by tiny tireless and regular additions." [24] Humble about words, his tools, he was not humble about the artist's attitude: "The largest thought accepts all, surrounds all, absorbs all,—like light itself. The ugly and the beautiful, the ignorant and the wise, the virtuous and the vile,—all come within its recognition . . ." [25]

By November 1895, after a year in Kobe, he expressed a newly grown ambition, but said it indirectly, shyly, with superstitious reverence for the quality he had found in himself: "You think me too dissatisfied, don't you?" he wrote to Chamberlain. "It is true I am not satisfied, and already unable to look at my former work. But the moment a man can feel satisfied with himself, progress stops. He can only move along a level afterwards; and I hope the level is still some years off. (I see a possibility to strive for; but I am afraid even to speak of it—so well out of reach it now is.)" [26]

The year that had begun in fear ended in confidence. He had lived and saved out of the income from his writing without working for wages. "I have up to September made about two thousand yen (Japanese money), and prospects of making about four thousand in 1896." [27] Some time during this period he was able to send again for the old grandfather to come to them from Shimane-ken. He was now properly caring for his family. Kobe itself, even in the quality of its irritations, was stimulating. He had here every Japanese quality, the oldest, the newest, and all possible strange mixtures. Kobe sharpened his wits.

Its physical situation was pleasing too. The western suburb of Hyogo held an open parklike space between the mountains and the sea. Here there were amusement grounds and an aquarium. Hearn, his family following along behind, often joined the crowds. He enjoyed these heedless, gawking strollers more than the sights they stared at. These people were his sights. He enjoyed the precipitate, awkward steps of Kazuo who ran in and out among the legs of tolerant adults. He bought toys extravagantly for the child.

Hearn liked Hyogo. He thought of building a house for Setsu on this open side of Kobe. Land was cheaper here, and there were good walks nearby. But he held off; he mistrusted his future. Kobe had given him time to do his own work, yet there were intimations of other opportunities about to come to him.

On December 13, 1895, he received an important letter from Dr. Toyama, president of the College of Literature at the Tokyo Imperial University, the greatest and most influential school in Japan. The letter followed a tactful oral communication through Professor Chamberlain. Thus informally and formally Toyama proposed to Hearn that he consider becoming a teacher at the university. What was offered to him specifically was the Chair of English Language and Literature. Toyama had studied earlier in Michigan; at Tokyo Imperial University he supervised the study of English; he was aware of Hearn's growing literary reputation, and he wanted to strengthen his department by adding him to it. He told Hearn almost shyly that he had read him in the *Atlantic Monthly*.

Hearn quickly raised the point of the possibility of his salary being lowered if he attained Japanese citizenship. Toyama said he was in darkness on this matter and would make inquiries. Usually foreign professors were appointed for two years; the Diet would be asked to appoint Hearn for three years. He added softly: "In our college you shall not be troubled by such underlings as you seem to have been with in Kumamoto." [28]

Toyama continued his persuasion in a second letter written on December 20, 1895. He described the minimal teaching hours, and said: "I have no doubt you will have plenty of time to carry on your literary work, and I hope your work will not suffer in quality by your coming into contact with the University people, as you will have a new field in the investigation of the character of the Japanese people."

"Shall I wish you a Merry Christmas," [29] was Toyama's friendly conclusion. Hearn was pleased but at the same time skeptical and independent.

He foresaw, too, another difficulty. Kazuo's birth in November 1893 had decided him to become a Japanese citizen, and he had instituted the laborious process shortly afterward. He had never before this time worried about any troubles except those in the present. When he looked at the child, he feared the future. The only other alternative, to convert his family's citizenship to his own, was not a real one. His family did not want it, and Hearn listened to them. "My folks won't hear of becoming English citizens, and losing power of acquiring property in the interior," [30] he wrote to Chamberlain. It was true that persons of foreign citizenship could not own property outside certain areas in the open ports. These were rights defined by treaties, which might be abrogated. And worse could happen. In a period of antiforeign feeling, persons of foreign citizenship might be ordered out of Japan or deprived of employment or even suffer violence. Hearn imagined himself dead and his family fending for itself. His picture of his family's future was as small landholders in Izumo. If he died, with his wife's and child's citizenship changed to his own, this safe settling of his family could never take place.

If he lived, and his citizenship and his wife's remained as they were, one British, one Japanese, there were dangers too. As an alien, he might at any time be ordered out of Japan. He could not own land in his own name. If he died—always he returned to that possibility—his wife might be deprived of his property. "Previous to the coming into force of the revised treaties, and while there yet obtained in Japan extra-territorial jurisdiction of the treaty-powers, properties left intestate by the foreigners that had married Japanese wives used to go, not to their families in this country, but to their relations at home." [31]

What of the salary changes which might accompany his imminent acquisition of Japanese citizenship? His sharp query might discourage

Toyama and the university from going much further in the negotiations. He had enjoyed living in Kobe without having to work for a monthly salary. Perhaps he should continue as he was. At least he would require the university to conform to his desires before he would go there.

Hearn had good reason to suspect what action the university authorities might take in dealing with a foreign teacher eccentric enough to become a Japanese citizen. Theoretically they should have congratulated him; practically they might pay him as they paid Japanese professors. He had known teachers to whom this had happened. But if he did nothing, he put his family in danger. He could improve his family's situation only by becoming a Japanese citizen. The reason was too urgent to deny.

Yet in doing so, he struggled in his own mind, not because he particularly disliked becoming a Japanese citizen or because he held onto his British citizenship with any excessive loyalty. He saw clearly that the change of citizenship would be an advantage not so much for him as for his family. As a solitary, rootless writer, willing to find his material where good or bad luck deposited him, he could have managed without any change. Holding the passport of a British citizen, he could have gone anywhere he liked. As a teacher he would be sure of more money. The Japanese colleges and universities paid foreign teachers more than they paid Japanese teachers.

Discussing his situation in a letter to Chamberlain, he admitted that he might in the future like to "travel *a little* for literary material. But I cannot imagine any circumstance, except banishment by the Tenshisama, that should prevent me from making my home in Japan. . . . The Japanese are still the best people in the world to live among;—therefore why wish to live elsewhere? No one will ever, or could ever, love me any more than those about me now love me;—and that is the most precious consideration in life aside from the mere capacity to live." [32]

He knew, however, that he gave up a certain margin around his life in making this choice. Marriage had bound him in one degree; Japanese citizenship limited him even more seriously to one set of circumstances for the rest of his life. He knew also that in spite of the affection of his family he would continue to be lonely in Japan. There was a gulf of difference between himself and his neighbors, even between himself and his family, that would never be overcome. He steeled himself to forget such irrelevancies, and petitioned the imperial government to let him become a citizen.

In the slow process there were many papers to sign, many interviews to which to submit, much silent suspicion to endure. Hearn was interviewed; Setsu was interviewed. They were called for meetings in government offices. On other occasions officials came to the house. The process begun in Kumamoto continued in Kobe. Hearn was in part amused, in part annoyed.

Setsu was asked if he were a good husband, and was questioned closely for proof.

Yet Hearn rested in the conclusion that this was the only proper thing for him to do. It was the only way to safeguard his wife and his son. He had been frightened twice recently, once by the temporary loss of his sight, and in February and March 1896, he was seriously ill again with an infection of the lungs. The doctor found in addition heart trouble and hardening of the arteries. Hearn made little of it and never discussed his health with his family, yet he was haunted by the chance that he might die and leave his family helpless.

He was beginning to realize that he would never again be free. He was now, and he acknowledged it sometimes sorely, only a satellite moving about his family center. He could no longer fling off into a new orbit when he felt a stronger pull. It was only in his thoughts that he ranged. And even there freedom was an illusion. He was bound by his task of converting stray impressions, sensations, ideas into form. The ambition which ruled this process was becoming every year more austere, stern, and peremptory.

In order to become a citizen, he had to belong to a Japanese family. Setsu's family was conscious of the honor they were willing to accord him by adopting him into the family as a son. (Setsu had in childhood been adopted by another family, the Inagaki family, and had to be readopted by her own family, the Koizumi family, for this second adoption to take place; adoption was a common device in Japan for the proper passing along from one generation to another of a name or a function or money, but the process could become infinitely complicated.)

Hearn was therefore to take his wife's name, Koizumi, an old Samurai name in Izumo, for his Japanese family name. He was free to choose a first name for himself. He explained the matter to Ellwood Hendrick in a letter written from Kobe in September 1895 during part of the long wait for government action:

> I am waiting every day for the sanction of the minister to change my name; and I think it will come soon. This will make me Koizumi Yakumo, or—arranging the personal and family names in English order—"Y. Koizumi." "Eight clouds" is the meaning of "Yakumo," and is the first part of the most ancient poem extant in the Japanese language. (You will find the whole story in "Glimpses"—article "Yaegaki.") Well, "Yakumo" is a poetical alternative for Izumo, my beloved province, "the Place of the Issuing of Clouds." You will understand how the name was chosen.[33]

If he were going to become a Japanese citizen, it would be as a provincial from that western and ancient land. The mountains behind Taisha, the first place he had loved in Japan, were the Yakumo-yama, the Yakumo Mountains.

At last in February 1896 the government sent him formal notice that he was a new person with a new status. He signed his Japanese name Y. Koizumi, almost as if he were an impostor.

He entered his new situation as a Japanese citizen at a time when his reputation as a writer was growing. At least as early as June 1895 his second Japanese book, *Out of the East,* was published in the United States by the Houghton Mifflin Company. This book, following so closely upon *Glimpses of Unfamiliar Japan,* strengthened and enlarged his reputation not only in the United States and in England but also in Japan.

With the usual inconsequence of weekly and monthly reviewers, there was a mixture of uncritical praise and biased blame dealt out to the new book. The writer in the London *Athenaeum* of August 24, 1895, dismissed Hearn because he associated himself with the Japanese, and the Japanese were savages lacking in Western morality. Edmund Buckley in the *Dial* of April 16, 1895, was out of sympathy with Hearn's dislike for Western missionaries but praised his essays "Of the Eternal Feminine" and "Jiujutsu." On the other hand the *Atlantic Monthly* of June 1895 found in the two books, reviewed together, "sympathy and exquisiteness of touch." [34]

Hearn gave little regard to the reviews but was glad of attention which helped sell books. The fact of having achieved a second Japanese book gave him a much readier confidence. He thought he had begun to do in *Out of the East* what his dissatisfaction with *Glimpses of Unfamiliar Japan* had compelled him to try. The book was less concerned with the surface of Japanese life than the realities. It included stories and formal essays as well as personal narratives, broken by anecdotes and observations. Reading the book was a varied exercise. It was like walking at different rates of speed through the same landscape. A gradual change in style was beginning to be visible too. Hearn was learning how to shock with simple words. In "Bits of Life and Death" came this calmness after the description of a murder, a hacking with swords of a helpless victim: "Ichiro and O-Noto sit down by the lantern to take breath, for the work was hard." [35] Hearn dedicated *Out of the East*

To
Nishida Sentaro
In Dear Remembrance of
Izumo Days

In Kobe, after recovering from his eye affliction, and having no longer a day job, Hearn read a great deal. If he had a new idea about an old book, he wrote immediately to his friends who were all out of reach of conversation.

His letters to Chamberlain were indications of what he amused himself with, in his private time. In August 1894 he praised the "old English Bible translators." In October he decried contemporary poetry: "Really, we have no more great poets now." [36] A week later he lectured the professor, "I am sure that if you would read systematically Spencer's first volume of Sociology you would find reasons for agreeing with me." [37] At another time he explained to this friend the importance of Lewis Carroll, at another, the importance of Hans Christian Andersen. In this way Hearn ran on vivaciously in his letters. They were written at top speed and with no revision. Hearn insisted that being careful in personal correspondence spoiled the freedom of communication.

Dr. Toyama of the Imperial University did not long leave Hearn to read and write in peace. On April 2, 1896, he wrote to Hearn offering him, as from the university, a "preliminary contract" to run from September 10, 1896, to July 31, 1899, but he also asked him if his citizenship had yet been changed. Hearn replied that it had, that he was now Koizumi Yakumo. Toyama addressed the envelope of his next letter, on April 10th, to Mr. Yakumo Koizumi—using the English order for the name—but began the letter, as if knowing that Hearn was really still Hearn, "Dear Mr. Hearn." He said that the change of citizenship had after all raised a difficulty. He would let him know when it had been "solved." [38]

Hearn doubted that the matter could be settled as he desired, but he did not waver in his tone. He liked Toyama in his letters, however, and sent him a copy of his third Japanese book, *Kokoro,* just published. If the university should accede to his demand, then he would indeed be bound to a new situation and a new place. He would not be able to board a train or ship or hire a kurumaya and set off freely to some hitherto unseen corner of Japan. Therefore, during the warm months of 1896 he proceeded to sate himself with travel. He had also the excuse and need of recuperation from his recent illness.

At the end of June he went home to Izumo with Setsu and Kazuo. In May 1897 an account of this visit appeared in the *Atlantic Monthly* but was never reprinted in any of his books. In the article it is possible to glimpse some of the emotion he felt upon his return:

"I felt curious in advance as to the nature of the impressions I was going to receive on revisiting, after years of absence, a place known only in the time when I imagined that all Japan was like Izumo." [39] He walked the streets he had known so well, sometimes with his little boy, sometimes alone. Knowledge had inevitably changed his vision. "The white bridge had turned, I fancied, somewhat gray.[40]

"I went to my former home, tenanted now by its owner, where I was welcomed as a friend, and allowed to look at the lotos-pond, the chrysanthemums, and the little shrine of Inari under the dove-haunted hill." [41]

He visited the Middle School and was received by a new director who showed him the rooms where he had taught. All the classes stood up when the head of the school and the strange-looking foreign visitor came into the room. Hearn saw the same youthful faces looking at him as he had seen there five years before, but not one of them was familiar.

One evening a banquet was given in his honor by several of his old friends. "There were recitations of poems by guests, and there were dances by dancing-girls. One of the latter, whom I remembered having seen when a very small child-*maiko,* during an official dinner given at the governor's house in the twenty-third year of Meiji, had grown up into a tall and graceful woman. . . . At my request, the girl danced the dance of Urashima." [42] (It was the old story he had rewritten in his own version one sultry summer in Kumamoto.) She danced first as the handsome youth, then as an old man, wearing the mask of old age to depict Urashima as he became when he opened the forbidden box.

"Afterwards she brought me the mask to look at. I thought its pasteboard features had a faint mocking resemblance to my own; and I suppose that I must have fallen into a reverie, for a friend laughingly handed me a wine-cup, with the wise remark, 'Tonight we must think only of happy things.' . . . But, after all, nobody can revisit with absolute impunity a place once loved and deserted. . . . Was not the lost charm something that had evaporated out of my own life . . ." [43]

Hearn identified his lost idyllic Japan with Urashima's lost kingdom under the sea. It was gone as surely as Urashima's happiness and love were destroyed when he disobeyed the injunction of the beautiful princess and opened the box which he was not to open, on pain of never returning to her father's land beneath the waves.

Seeing Nishida was a pleasure and a distress, for his friend was visibly fading in the grip of tuberculosis.

After Matsue, the Hearns went on to Mionoseki and Sakai, little fishing villages and ports on the Japan Sea. Nishida went down to the dock on the Ohashi River to see them off. Hearn wrote to him later from Sakai:

I felt unhappy at the Ohashi, because you waited so long, and I had no power to coax you to go home. I can still see you sitting there so kindly and patiently—in the great heat of that afternoon. Write soon—if only a line in Japanese—to tell us how you are.

Kaji-*chan* remembers you, and sends his little greeting to Nishida-San no Oji-San. We all hope to have another summer with you next year.

Ever faithfully, with warmest regards of all

LAFCADIO HEARN

I still see you sitting at the wharf to watch us go. I think I shall always see you there.[44]

At some time during the summer the university offered Hearn what he wanted, a teaching job of moderate hours and considerable honor, at a monthly rate of the kind paid foreign teachers. Hearn capitulated. He would teach; he would move to Tokyo.

Later, when he wrote the *Atlantic* article "Notes of a Trip to Izumo," he put into it the significant doubt and anticipation he felt at this change in his life: "For me the New Japan is waiting; the great capital so long dreaded, draws me to her vortex at last. And the question I now keep asking myself is whether in that New Japan I can be fortunate enough at happy moments to meet with something of the Old." [45]

"In Ushigome we are prac-
tically in the country, and observe the seasons." [1]

LH to McDonald

19 ❊ The Cedars of Kobudera

The hill behind the house was dark with cedars. Hidden in the trees
was a temple of one of the Zen sects. Between the hilltop and the house
was a field where pheasants cried. The house itself was not large and had
no beautiful garden of its own. But the hillside field and woods, the
nearness of the temple with its graveyard, its shadowed grounds, its
mossed sculpture, and its cool, worn interior decided Hearn upon the
place. Number 21 Tomihisa-cho, Ichigaya, Ushigome, became his new
address. He had settled at last in the city of Tokyo.

In the dusty street which the house faced were evidences of the city
he feared, a city which was moving, growing, breaking things. Even in
this suburban neighborhood the roadway was torn up. Ditches were
being dug for a new system of waterpipes. When Hearn set off each
morning to the university, three miles away across the hilly landscape of
the scattered city, his kurumaya, Nakamura, had to pick his way carefully among workmen, pipes, and broken places in the road. Yet in this
neighborhood the city trailed away into the country. Within walking
distance were open spaces where children played, farms with rice fields
and groves of bamboo and pine. Hearn could take his regular walks here,
and never, except when he wished, walk on city streets. Nakamura and
his wife were allowed to use land belonging to the temple to grow
vegetables. Kazuo, who was three years old when the family moved to
Tokyo, found a half-wild, spacious place to play. Hearn quickly made

friends with the abbot of Kobudera and came to think of the temple as an annex to his study. Here he could walk in near solitude and enjoy the freshness of the grass, the dark shade of the trees, the suggestions which Buddhist sculpture and architecture made to his imagination.

The religious name of the temple was Ji-sho-in. It had been built in the first half of the seventeenth century by a daimio (prince) as a place of family worship. Its familiar name was Kobudera, Knotty Pine, for the peeled timbers of burled wood of which the curious structure was made. The nearness of Kobudera and its friendly abbot meant something particular to Hearn during the years he lived in the Ushigome district. Although he had dreaded coming to Tokyo, his first years in the city were relatively happy. Kobudera, on the hill behind his house, was a sign of that happiness.

Almost as soon as Hearn arrived in Tokyo he began going to the university to teach. He was shy of the title of Professor to which his new position entitled him. He never signed himself so, and asked his friends not to address him in this manner. The students came to his classes out of curiosity at first. They crowded in pell-mell, in a local system which allowed first-year, second-year, and third-year men to attend the same classes. Hearn complained about the lack of preparation of the students, about a dearth of books, about the absence of gradation. He could not at first teach as he wished, beginning with simpler things and moving on in successive years to more complex matters.

Even in the beginning Hearn gained a hold upon the Tokyo University students who were accustomed to being unruly whenever they liked, who judged teachers harshly, and who deserted when they were bored. Hearn used the books from his own library and arranged through Ellwood Hendrick to procure others directly through an American dealer, paying for them out of his own pocket. He used most effectively his own quiet, incisive imagination to create an interest in a subject for which these young Japanese were totally unprepared technically and emotionally.

His willful students made matters more difficult for themselves than they needed to, and for their new teacher standing quietly, chalk in hand, at the front of the classroom. During one period of his first year Hearn led a class through the difficult, almost inaccessible pages of *Paradise Lost* simply because his students insisted on voting for the book. Another class studied texts in Tennyson, a third read miscellaneous texts from various Victorian authors. Special classes studied a history of early English literature, another modern fiction. Hearn altered his courses considerably in successive years to please himself, yet he was always engaged in leading one group straight through English literature, wearying himself over those periods which he disliked, and confessing wryly to friends that he would have been happier teaching French literature.

However, as a teacher he was always even toned in handling what he did not like. He explained carefully matters which were foreign to his own personality as to his students'. He taught backgrounds as carefully as texts. The simplicity of approach which his students' ignorance required was congenial to Hearn's natural bent. He taught literature as the highest achievement of emotion. The individual shaped the work out of feeling; the age shaped the individual. Thus the age and the individual were lifted together to a climax in the production of a particular work of literature.

One of his colleagues, Ernest Foxwell, recalled in 1908 the impression he gained of Hearn's almost hypnotic effect upon his students when, having business with Hearn, he stepped into his class one day:

I opened the door and went in. His students, the first two or three rows of his students at any rate—and you must remember that Japanese university students are between twenty-two and twenty-seven years of age—were all in tears. I do not know what it was about. It is a rare event for a Japanese to be in tears; even a coolie is ashamed of it, and with men of higher rank it is much more striking than it would be in England. Hearn had been reading some very simple English poem; and there was the effect.[2]

One of his students, Hakucho Masamune, wrote, ". . . His lectures on English literature were revelations to us, at once poignant and lucid." [3] Mock Joya has written about the personal regard his students had for Hearn. "Most of the foreign teachers were proud and indifferent, and it was a great contrast to see Hearn teaching . . ." [4] Other students, more than a generation after he died, remembered and wrote down something of Hearn's method.

He spoke slowly. Many took down his lectures word for word. He talked without fully prepared notes. "He brought with him a tiny memorandum containing only names and dates." [5] He began the day by unwrapping from a purple *furoshiki* (the scarf in which Japanese customarily carry things— books, lunch, purchases) the volumes he would need for the day. During his lecture, ". . . He used to make sketches on the board, should a description of anything exotic or unfamiliar to us occur in quotations." [6] Hearn was reserved, but, "Sometimes a faint, shy smile would lighten up his face when he seemed satisfied." [7] The musical voice exerted such an influence that its effect was almost physical. "It often seemed to us as if we were actually leaning out from the bar of Heaven beside the Blessed Damozel, or walking along the corridors of the Palace of Art, till the bell for the recess broke the spell." [8]

Hearn spoke justly and evenly of his own work as a teacher to his friends. He did not think his lectures worth reprinting. "They are only dictated lectures—dictated out of my head, not from notes even: so the form of them cannot be good. Were I to rewrite each of them ten or fifteen times, I might print them. But that would not be worth while. I am not a scholar, nor a competent critic of the best . . . The lectures are good for Tokyo University, however—because they have been adapted, by long experience, to the Japanese student's way of thinking and feeling, and are put in the simplest possible language." [9]

Hearn's influence was not limited to his official subject. To his students he insisted that their study of English literature was of no use if they did not apply this new knowledge to the creation of a modern Japanese literature. He created enthusiasms, he scattered ambitions. The sight of him was an excitement to the students who saw him walking across the campus. Studying under him was a stimulation. In time Hearn became more than a curiosity. He became a hero. He was adored, not simply admired.

All this came slowly. At first he was helped to endure the frank assessments of curiosity by the renewal of old friendships. His former students claimed him immediately, and did not hesitate to come up to him on the campus, asking for advice or simply for comfort. Hearn went to dinner with a group of students from Kumamoto. He stopped gladly on his nearsighted passage between buildings to talk to some from Matsue and invite them to his house in Ushigome.

Among the students from Matsue was his literary helper Masanobu Otani, who entered Tokyo Imperial University when Hearn began teaching. Hearn in fact made it possible for Otani to attend. He entered into an informal agreement with the young man. Otani was to help him on assigned subjects. Hearn would pay enough to put him through the university. It was a steadily functioning arrangement. Hearn assigned subjects usually a month ahead. Otani gathered information or translated documents in his spare time and brought the results to Hearn's house. Sometimes the writer could use the material, sometimes not. In this relationship Hearn was more than an employer. He reproved Otani, praised and advised him, and encouraged him. He let him off work during examinations and lectured him on caring for his health. Otani, who eventually became a teacher in Hiroshima, wrote in 1920, "I should never have been able to finish the university course had it not been for his extraordinary favours. Words really fail to express my gratitude to him. He is my ever-remembered benefactor." [10]

Hearn helped other students. Adzukizawa and perhaps one or two others assisted in the same way as Otani. And there was a Japanese custom of which Hearn thoroughly approved, allowing university students to live in one's house rent free during their time in school, and asking little in return but chores and help with the children. Houses had customarily a small room or rooms called students' rooms. Hearn had taken in his first student toward the end of his stay in Kumamoto. He continued the custom all the rest of his time in Japan. In Tokyo he had one, sometimes two, of these boys as part of his household. Their names in successive years were: Niimi (there were two of the same name, brothers), Aki, Okumura. The students went on vacation with the family and helped the children learn to swim as well as to trace their first Chinese characters with ink and brush on folds of newspapers. One or another accompanied Hearn on his long walks into the countryside upon the north side of Tokyo, walks which tired or bored Setsu in these later years and from which she often excused herself. Hearn treated the students neither as employees nor servants, but as members of an enlarged family.

Hearn's relations with young people were always good. He had a quick way of touching them in their emotions and intellect. They admired him at once. Then he was pleased and at ease. He was not so clever with his fellow teachers. He was interested in them, amused by them, and studied them as a curious species. The distinguished foreigners on the staff of Tokyo Imperial University occupied an anomalous position. They were not secure. Government policy might turn against them at any time. There was motive for scheming and betrayal among them. Hearn was never a trusting animal in any case, and he was wary of his colleagues.

However, he wrote entertainingly about the odd affinity which had developed among a small group on the staff, "The existing group of professors in the Library college who keep a little together are the Professor of Philosophy (Heidelberg), the Professor of Sanscrit and Philology (Leipsig), the Professor of French Literature (Lyons), and the Professor of English literature—from the devil knows where." [11] He explained the matter to Ellwood Hendrick as "the *Latin* feeling surviving in Catholicism" [12] among the four although only one of them, the Jesuit, had remained a believer. "Horror of horrors—I do believe I like the Jesuit best of all—yet I'm *sure* he would burn me!" [13]

In the scholarly world of Tokyo no name at this time had more luster than Ernest Fenollosa's. He had been honored because he had aroused the government to save its heritage of paintings, its rolls of calligraphy, its porcelains, bronzes, and sculptures at a time when many of these treasures were being carelessly thrown away or sold cheaply because they did not seem to belong to modern times. He had also done well personally by selling

Japanese art objects to Western museums, particularly to the Museum of Fine Arts in Boston. Mr. and Mrs. Fenollosa courted Hearn, but he was embarrassed by their attentions and did not let them come close to him.

Among the Japanese on the staff Hearn best liked Dr. Toyama who reminded him of Senataro Nishida in his helpfulness and kindness. Toyama believed in the foreign professors, and he showed Hearn special consideration.

Among the English-speaking teachers there were two with whom Hearn had particularly pleasant relations. One was Osman Edwards who in 1901 dedicated a book, *Japanese Plays and Playfellows,* to Hearn. The other was Ernest Foxwell, who was to comment upon Hearn's classroom manner.

When Foxwell and Hearn met in the teachers' common room in the spring of 1897, Foxwell was recovering from smallpox and his face was "beetroot colored." [14] He was sensitive and grateful when Hearn paid not the slightest attention to his bizarre appearance. ". . . He had lived too much to be surprised. . . . He had a mind which worked with velvet or gossamer touch." [15]

Yet Foxwell thought that Hearn missed much by excluding himself from the foreign colony. He believed too that Hearn's bad opinion of the missionaries was extreme. He had personally known missionaries sympathetic to the Japanese, and tried vainly to convince Hearn of the fact. However, he recalled missionary distaste for Hearn. "I remember the wife of a missionary, an English missionary, who said to me one day, 'Mr. Foxwell, how can you walk about with that worm?' " [16]

Foxwell sometimes argued genially with Hearn that "It was a sort of slander on the real Japan" [17] to ignore so much its modern bustle, and to write so exclusively about the old Japan. He thought Hearn should have painted a portrait of the Japanese as they ordinarily were. Hearn did not admit the necessity. Only in his last book, *Japan: An Attempt at Interpretation,* did he try to do something of the kind, but even in *Japan* he was interested in essences rather than averages. In all the earlier books he was interested in particular rather than general aspects of the national life.

Hearn and Foxwell, in spite of differences, argued without animus and remained on excellent terms during the years of their association. This endured in daily meetings until 1900 when Foxwell left the university. After that time they corresponded.

His friendship with Basil Hall Chamberlain strangely lapsed when Hearn moved to Tokyo. Something in Hearn had been touched—as if by an ice that froze up intimacy—and he wrote no more to Chamberlain, nor did he see him, although they lived in the same city and taught in different depart-

ments of the same university. Chamberlain did not understand, but accepted
the rejection. (This was after one last act of friendship—a strong recommendation of Hearn's appointment to the university.)

Within the family circle Hearn always spoke well of Chamberlain. After
Hearn's death Chamberlain and the family were friends again. In 1936,
when both Chamberlain and Hearn were dead, Kazuo Hearn edited a
volume of Chamberlain's letters to his father and wrote in the foreword:
"The gentleman fully understood Hearn's disposition and temperament,
and kept him in his favour to the last. He was of fine character; whether
the friendship between him and my father was firm or not, and lasted long
or short, he was among Hearn's truly revered friends." [18]

Yet while the two men lived within visiting distance of each other, perhaps
only narrowly missing each other in university halls and on university walks,
the association was suspended. The small number of difficulties which had
occurred did not account for the end of the intimacy, but contributed to the
break.

In Kumamoto, when Hearn was morassed in a sticky kind of unhappiness,
he had expected more sympathy from Chamberlain than he got. When
Glimpses of Unfamiliar Japan was published in 1894, dedicated in "affection
and gratitude" to Chamberlain as well as to Mitchell McDonald, Hearn
conceived the idea that the professor did not like the book, was embarrassed
by the dedication, and had on occasion declined to review it or to speak
favorably of it. Even in matters of general opinion, where once he would
have enjoyed a combat, Hearn now argued with personal anger. He thought
Chamberlain was willful in refusing to accept Herbert Spencer as fully as
he did. He lost his breath in anger when the professor did not agree with
him that the government was failing to foster patriotism. Chamberlain told
Hearn smartly that in his opinion there was in Japan altogether too much
jingo patriotism.[19]

He was once hurt by a phrase Chamberlain had used as a joke, and showed
the hurt by repeating the phrase to another friend, Page Baker: "As Chamberlain says, 'No, you'll never be a ladies' man.' " [20] Hearn thought Chamberlain was commenting on his appearance.

When the end came Hearn caused it. He was only silent. He did not fight
with Chamberlain, but he did not answer his letters. Hearn's loss was tragic.
It left a large gap in his intellectual life which nothing ever filled. (Whether
Hearn included Chamberlain's friend and colleague Mason in his interdict
is not known. There are no more known letters to Mason after Hearn's
arrival in Tokyo, or references to trips to Yokohama to see him.)

However, Hearn often made the twenty-mile journey to Yokohama in order to visit Mitchell McDonald. He approached McDonald's hotel, the Grand, gingerly, and coaxed the easygoing owner away to Kamakura Beach for steaks and beer, for lazy swimming and talking, for freedom from responsibility, for rest in the company of one who never made any demands upon him.

The friendship was not primarily intellectual, although McDonald had an intense feeling for literature and was ready to burst with pride for Hearn's talking to him about his work. The sailor-businessman knew that he had never had any trouble in making the world come to terms with him. He wanted to put his natural abilities at the service of his friend who seemed always running blindly into trouble. McDonald asked not only the right to praise and defend Hearn, but to be allowed to look after him, his affairs, and his family.

He persuaded Hearn to put some of his savings into one of his business concerns. This investment involved Hearn's coming to semiannual meetings or sending McDonald his proxy—he asked to do the easier thing. "Lo! I am a bloated bondholder. I am 'astonished' and don't know what to say—except that I want to hug you." [21] Hearn profited and was delighted by his venture into capitalism.

The writer had his will drawn up, and named McDonald as an executor. In doing this, he resigned into another's care a little of his worry for the future.

McDonald came regularly to Tokyo on Sundays to spend the day with the family. He brought candy and toys for the boys and swung them up in his arms to greet them. He was ushered by Mrs. Hearn into her husband's study to sit long hours in the rocking chair especially reserved for him. From this room the family heard unrestrained laughter even when McDonald visited Hearn during anxious times. The captain was a relief to the man who had unconsciously disciplined himself to a certain kind of behavior among the Japanese. With McDonald he forgot restraints, sure of a solid bond of understanding of ordinary, unimportant Western facts and fancies for which he had become homesick.

Hearn warned McDonald not to overrate him. "Unless I can manage in the next three years to write something very extraordinary indeed, I fear you will be horribly disappointed some day." But, trusting McDonald, he added, ". . . Don't for a moment imagine me modest in literary matters. I am Satanically proud—not modest at all. If I tell you that much of my work is very bad, I tell you so, not because I am modest, but because, as a professional writer, I can see bad execution where you would not see it unless I pointed it out to you." [22]

McDonald allowed Hearn to lecture him in bookish matters, but he was capable of a brusque lecture to his literary friend on personal matters. When Hearn scolded Kazuo during a lesson he was one day giving him, McDonald protested: "Don't scold so much! He will learn in time. It's good that he knows as much as he does. If an American boy of Kazuo's age knew as much as he did, they would think he was doing fine." Kazuo, who recalled the exchange, remembered that his father said, "But if I don't teach him as much as I can, my life will not wait." And McDonald took him up: "Never mind, I am standing by watching him. I am stronger and younger. McDonald is at hand. Don't worry." [23]

Such friendship lighted a dark space in Hearn's imagination. It warmed his mind as McDonald's coat one day warmed his body. He had come to Yokohama in cold weather, running away from Tokyo without a wrap. When McDonald met him at the station he promptly took off his coat and wrapped it round Hearn's shoulders. Hearn, grateful for more than the coat, wrote his friend after his return: "But what can one do with a man who deliberately takes off his own coat to cover his friend during a nine minutes' drive? I shall remember the *feeling* of that coat—warmth of friendship must also have been electrical in it—until I die." [24]

Having only one friend like McDonald, keeping to surface relations with his university colleagues, intimate with most of his students only in the classroom, he was always hurrying home to write.

His wife saw to it—with some difficulty, for the house was small—that his study was a quiet place. She or the maid answered the door and kept people from him, and managed that Kazuo, three years old, did not make too much noise in his playing.

Late in 1896, at about the time his third Japanese book, *Kokoro,* was being published, his second son, Iwao, was born. Iwao thrived and was a laughing child. Hearn did not extend to this little brown Japanese boy the nervous regard he had always had for his firstborn. It was an attention which had perhaps helped to make Kazuo a nervous, oversensitive, and easily hurt child.

In his new situation in 1896—Kazuo old enough to enjoy playing in the fields behind the house, a new quiet baby sleeping long hours away, Setsu making the house run smoothly, the teaching at the university not too difficult, the writing going well—it must have seemed to Hearn that Tokyo suited him better than he had thought it would.

In the spring of 1897 the new professor completed his first year and submitted a confident, tactful report to the Dean of the College of Literature, suggesting changes in the organization of his classes, pointing out the accomplishments and the deficiencies of the past year.[25] Then he dropped responsibility and took his family for a long vacation to a region of fishing villages on the Pacific coast south of Mount Fuji.

The Hearns tried two prosperous resorts, Hamamatsu and Maisaka, but the head of the family decided characteristically upon a much poorer place. This was the small village of Yaizu on Suruga Bay. It was just off the railroad line, but hidden from it, turning its back upon the busy traffic going from Tokyo to Nagoya and beyond, facing instead the sea out of which the inhabitants drew a living and with which they struggled often for their lives.

The fact that Yaizu had no other summer visitors than the Hearns (Koizumis) was a mark in its favor. Yaizu had a deep harbor, an anchorage into which entered the full swinging force of the ocean, and against which the men of Yaizu had built a strong breakwater. There was not much beach, very little sand, but many small, round stones which moved with the tide and were slippery underfoot. But one could sit on the wall and stare out at the water or watch the activity of the village, the pushing off of boats from the shingle, the difficult pulling of them onto the shore; one could even help on such an occasion when women, children, even a visitor was welcome to add his pair of arms to the straining effort. And from the break-water it was a simple matter to slip into deep water and swim. Such easy swimming as performed by the visitor the people of Yaizu had never seen before.

The fastidious housemaids, the wife, the children, accustomed to the clean, quiet, well run house in Tokyo might wrinkle their noses at the smells, the sights, the sounds of the village street, and shrink back shocked at Hearn's choice of a house, the fish seller's house, of which he rented the entire top floor. But all the family came to love Otokichi Yamaguchi, his family, and his village. It was a place too busy to treat them otherwise than courteously and familiarly, and to judge them simply as fellow human beings.

The journey to Yaizu was to become year after year a familiar excitement: the train's leaving Tokyo, gathering speed after passing through Yokohama, thrusting out into the country where on clear days one saw Fuji, rushing through smoky tunnels, emerging into the flashing nearness of the sea, crossing rivers, arriving at last at the small railway stop that was Yaizu, the conductor calling strongly Y-A-I-D-Z-U, emphasizing the invisible and emphatic *D*. At the station the luggage was shifted from the train platform to two or three kuruma and they were all pulled, excited, toward the sea fringed from their sight by trees and low hills. They entered the village to greetings from the unabashed, frank folk who soon learned to call Hearn "Sensei" (Master) but who were not otherwise ceremonious.

They came to a stop at Otokichi's door beside which was a cooling bench where the men, Hearn among them, sat at night to rest and talk. Beyond the door was a series of cool, high-ceilinged rooms with many shelves where were displayed Otokichi's wares, fish, baskets, sandals, pears, lemonade in rows of bottles. Otokichi sold fish out of a tub in which ice and dead fish floated and on top of which rested his chopping block. Near his work place facing the street door was a god-shelf where sat the large staring image of the legless, armless Daruma (staring sightlessly, with one eye, or with two, depending upon Otokichi's luck; for the god was given an eye only when he gave his owner a piece of luck, and when the god had both eyes, he was replaced by a sightless image).

Otokichi's house had only the virtues of privacy, obscurity, and the good nature of its owner. Hearn's family occupied the rooms upstairs. These rooms were low-ceilinged, hot, smelled sometimes of fish, sometimes had fleas, and although they opened to the east and to the west, they had no view of the sea to the south where other buildings intervened. Yet Hearn valued so highly the particular good he had in Otokichi's house and in Yaizu, that he was willing to endure these disadvantages. There were no foreigners here, no affected new Japanese, only the fishermen, their wives and children, too little used to Westerners to have any prejudices.

When Hearn walked along the curving street of the town, curving to fit the angle of the harbor, the people of Yaizu spoke to him, showed him what they were doing, admired his reputed learning and his swimming. The children of the fishermen called the Sensei's children to play among the nets and boats of the beach or in the pine woods which backed the town. Hearn, returning year after year, brought first only Kazuo, then Iwao, and then Kiyoshi, and at last a daughter, Suzuko.

Otokichi's daughter, O-saki, went back to Tokyo one year with the Hearns to be their maid. In her first loneliness she ran out to the gate at the back of the house and cried, but she came to love the Sensei and his family and to be a valued member of the household. This bond strengthened the ties between Hearn and Otokichi, for in Japan a servant was a member of the family. The fish seller took a protective interest in his guest and watched over him carefully, worrying about his long absences when the Sensei swam too far out to sea, walking upon the sea wall or along the beach to explain local matters to him, acting as his sponsor and helper in any little affair that was to be handled in Yaizu.

Yaizu was good for Hearn in several ways. He rested here. He did no writing on vacations, although he sketched in Chinese ink and water color, and taught Kazuo to do the same. The spectacle of the small, industrious fishing village, its intensely parochial and ingrown ways unselfconsciously spread out before him, intensified his knowledge of Japan. The place gave him matter for several essays and deepened his grasp of the mannerly, orderly, humorous, deeply religious functioning of everyday life in the Empire.

That Hearn was a man of letters caused him to be deeply respected. No one who belonged to Yaizu read his books, but they admired him for his occupation and he gained a local reputation as a storyteller. His childlike Japanese made the fishermen and shopkeepers, gathered around Otokichi's cooling bench, smile, but they lost themselves in enjoyment when his words made a story. After Herun-san stopped, the others were less shy, and the liquor seller, the basketmaker, or the fish seller told of strange things that had happened to him or his neighbors. These tales of work and disaster, wrecks and rescues confirmed in Hearn his belief that the natural and the supernatural lived together without conflict in the villagers' lives. Yaizu gave him a backing of sureness when in winter in Tokyo he sat down to write tales of the people.

In Yaizu there was a presence that was not human. The sea was always there, and Hearn liked its look best on days when it changed from calm to rough. In Otokichi's house, after watching from the wall all day, he lay awake at night and still listened "to the thunder-rolls and crashings." [26] In that impersonal, gigantic menace Hearn relaxed and rested.

At the end of his first summer at Yaizu, and before returning to Tokyo, Hearn gathered his energies for an adventure. He was determined, with some fear of failing, to climb Fuji-san, which was a near neighbor to Yaizu and on clear days seemed to fill the northern sky. Hearn was encouraged by having the support of a young friend. His former student Adzukizawa (who had taken the name Fujisaki, in being adopted into a family more prosperous than his own) had come to Yaizu to visit the Hearns. Fujisaki, handsome in his uniform of a military cadet, had joined the family in its games and songs and stories and now supported Hearn in his ambition to climb the sacred mountain.

The two climbers, accompanied by Mrs. Hearn, her mother, and Kazuo, went first to the mountain town Gotemba, on the south slope of Fuji. Here Hearn hired two guides, a kuruma, and a horse. Hearn and Fujisaki waved goodbye and set off at a rapid pace across the plain at the foot of the steep slope. The way got rougher and put an end to holiday ease. The horse had to be left behind in one of the wayside stations along the route. The two guides began to push and pull Hearn up the slope where the intervals between rest huts seemed to grow longer, where his lungs seemed about to burst, his feet to find no holding place, and the path, marked only by discarded sandals, to go straight up at a nightmare pitch.

Hearn implied in "Fuji-no-yama" that a close look at Fuji was like a close look at Japan, or a scrutiny of life:

Fuji has ceased to be blue of any shade. It is black—charcoal-black—a frightful extinct heap of visible ashes and cinders and slaggy lava.—Most of the green has disappeared. Likewise all of the illusion. The tremendous naked black reality—always becoming more sharply, more grimly, more atrociously defined—is a stupefaction, a nightmare. Above—miles above—the snow patches glare and gleam against that blackness—hideously. I think of a gleam of white teeth I once saw in a skull —a woman's skull—otherwise burnt to a sooty crisp.[27]

The climbers spent the night in a hut not far short of the top. Here they saw the sunrise, and for a moment Hearn was content. Then they struggled on to attain the ugly cusped crater lifted into the sky where pilgrims saluted the sun goddess. After the hard work of the climb it seemed easy to slide down snow and ashes by an easier route to Gotemba and enjoy the smiles of Setsu and the child upon their return.

Hearn returned to Tokyo in the possession of a usable interest in a new place. He was confident of his teaching, and had within reach several new subjects out of which to make stories or essays. Changing publishers again was an exhilaration rather than a sorrow. He thought that the Houghton Mifflin Company had invaded his privacy in printing an advertising biography of him. When they sent him proof, he threw it in the stove and quit them. He had his usual sanguine hopes of a new publisher in taking up relations with Little, Brown and Company. After May 1897 (probably at his request), his articles in the *Atlantic Monthly* ceased appearing. Nothing more of his was published in that or any other magazine until March 1903, when he left Tokyo Imperial University.

His books came out with almost monotonous regularity year after year. Houghton published *Gleanings in Buddha-Fields* in 1897. Little, Brown published *Exotics and Retrospectives* and Hasegawa of Tokyo published his *The Boy Who Drew Cats* in 1898. *In Ghostly Japan* appeared in 1899, *Shadowings* in 1900, and *A Japanese Miscellany* in 1901—all brought out by Little, Brown. The books had a certain sameness like the slow unrolling of a Japanese scroll painting. There was not much variety, only a difference in scene. It was the ambling journey of a thoughtful, sensuous traveler through a delightful landscape where there were occasional tightenings of mood, acute intuitions, and concentrations of feeling. The "little" essays, mild disquisitions on such subjects as "Frogs," "Japanese Female Names," "Dragon-Flies," "Songs of Japanese Children," were now the result of careful research (research disguised), not merely of chance observation. There were listings, compilings, arrangements of facts, designed to give delight and convey knowledge. The naming of things was made to stand for the fundamental qualities of a national life. The stories, into which Hearn poured his most anxious care, were shorter, tighter, more objective.

One contemporary reviewer (of *Shadowings* in the *Athenaeum* of January 5, 1901) complained that Hearn stripped his stories of local glamour and color. This was his purpose. There was not one inessential trapping of frivolous local interest, although each one was firmly rooted in a particular psychology. What was left was the human gesture. Nearly every story of the Tokyo period was durable.

These stories often invoked horror. The quality which perhaps he unconsciously sought out in the Japanese scene was the same that had haunted his childhood. The insistence was a morbidity of Hearn's, yet the writer had learned to use his own fears. The faceless ghost of "Mujina" [28] was very like the aspect which Cousin Jane had turned to him in a dark room on the top floor of the house in Dublin. The various dead lovers haunting live ones were ghostly relatives of the tomb haunters of his New Orleans' "fantastics," yet these ghosts had their own validity of passion, and were not subjective musings. They were actions which the imagination had pushed out into the world, cut away from itself, and left standing in sunlight or moonlight to cast shadows.

The Japanese ghost stories took the haunting of the living by the dead as something granted. The storyteller seemed to say: This is how things are, we understand such things. The greater horror was the intensity of the human emotion which caused the haunting. A typical instance was the icy hate of the woman in "The Corpse Rider," who "had died of grief and anger at having been divorced." [29] This emotion, manifesting itself after death, seemed only excessive, not unnatural.

Because his work went well in Ushigome, Hearn was comfortable in his relations with Tokyo. He abused the place but without much heat. He came to know the city well. "To describe to you the place would be utterly impossible," he wrote to Hendrick "—more easy to describe a province." But then he went right ahead:

Here the quarter of the foreign embassies, looking like a well-painted American suburb;—near by an estate with quaint Chinese gates several centuries old; a little further square miles of indescribable squalor;—then miles of military parade-ground trampled into a waste of dust, and bounded by hideous barracks;—then a great park, full of really weird beauty, the shadows all black as ink;—then square miles of streets of shops, which burn down once a year;—then more squalor;—then rice-fields and bamboo groves;—then more streets. All this not flat, but hilly—a city of undulations. Immense silences—green and romantic—alternate with quarters of turmoil and factories and railroad stations. Miles of telegraph-poles, looking at a distance like enormous fine-tooth combs, make a horrid impression. Miles of water-pipes—miles and miles and miles of them—interrupt the traffic of the principal streets: they have been trying to put them underground for seven years—and what with official trickery, etc., the work makes slow progress. . . . Streets melt under rain, water-pipes sink, water-pipe holes drown spreeing men and swallow up playful children; frogs sing amazing songs in the streets.[30]

He wrote often as if he only hated Tokyo—"this detestable Tokyo" [31]— but he contradicted himself. He told Hendrick how he had gone one night recently into a maze of crooked streets not known by him before and found there the market of the insect sellers. "This is a refinement of sensation, is it not?—only a poetical people could have imagined the luxury of buying summer-voices to make for them the illusion of nature where there is only dust and mud." [32]

The teacher of Ushigome became a member of the community and a part of the life of the dusty streets. A heavy pipe fell upon the back of a workman engaged in digging. The Sensei paid for the man's medical care. An ugly white dog with an unearthly habit of howling at nothing in particular seemed to belong to the house in Ushigome when Hearn and his family moved in. Hearn let the dog stay and observed her in her habits. She was a melancholy bitch who was gentle with all the children of the neighborhood, and who ate indiscriminately at the door of many shopkeepers as well as at the gate of the teacher. When the police threatened to pick her up and destroy her, Hearn and his neighbors joined together in saving the dog. He told the story in his book *In Ghostly Japan,* describing how the smith's wife said, "It stays in the house of the foreigner," and how the policeman answered, "Then let the foreigner's name be put upon the dog." And:

Accordingly I had my name painted on her back in big Japanese characters. But the neighbors did not think that she was sufficiently safeguarded by a single name. So the priest of Kobudera painted the name of the temple on her left side, in beautiful Chinese text; and the smith put the name of his shop on her right side; and the vegetable-seller put on her breast the ideographs for "eight-hundred,"— which represent the customary abbreviation of the word *yaoya* (vegetable-seller),— any yaoya being supposed to sell eight hundred or more different things. Consequently she is now a very curious-looking dog; but she is well protected by all that calligraphy.[33]

Hearn watched the children of the broken street play, Kazuo among them, Iwao when he grew old enough to tumble about, and later, little Kiyoshi.

He took down the words of children's game songs. Among his own children he sang often a local sunset song:

Yu-yake!	Evening-burning!
Ko-yake!	Little-burning!
Ashita wa tenki ni nare.	Weather, be fair tomorrow! [34]

Tokyo was a city of small, clotted centers where each inhabitant knew all about everyone else. The Sensei was a familiar sight to the vegetable seller, the smith and his wife, the workmen digging the ditches for the waterpipes, all the people of the neighborhood. His departure for the university each morning in the kuruma pulled by Nakamura was part of the street's rhythm of the day. He was observed to wear Western clothes when he left his house, but to carry his books, Japanese-style, in a scarf. He was known to hate umbrellas and to be scornful of anyone who carried one.

In his classes he spoke gently each succeeding year to new groups of students about the great writers of the English language. He made these figures seem not so strange or so distant. Of Blake, he said one day: "But like the great teachers of the *Zen* sect, Blake suggests questions without giving answers; you must think of the answers for yourself." [35] Of Keats' "Ode to Autumn" he said, "The picture is not unlike a drawing by Hiroshige or Toyokuni." [36] He never claimed that the writing or the speaking of English was the most important thing they had to do: "You know that I have often expressed the hope that some of you will be among those who make the future literature of Japan . . ." [37] Privately to Otani he wrote, "Except with the sole purpose of making a new *Japanese* literature, I do not sympathize with English or French or German studies." [38]

At the end of each school year Hearn gave money prizes out of his own pocket to the three students in each class who had shown the greatest gain in thinking for themselves in English. Hearn had a certain sense of marking finalities. He liked to emphasize and celebrate accomplishment in a perfectly definite way.

When Massanobu Otani had finished his years in the university, Hearn drew up a semiformal document to mark the satisfactory end of the arrangement between them. And he wrote a characteristic, affectionate, admonishing letter:

Your three years' course at the University is over, and I am glad to be able to present you with the enclosed document. I have gone through somewhat into particulars, only because I want you to *feel* that you have really paid for your own education, like a man, and have no obligations of any sort so far as I am concerned. Of course, it is true that everybody could not have disposed of your work as I did,—

used it in just the same way; but that does not in the least affect the fact that you have really *paid* for your expenses for three years in Tokyo.

I do not pretend that I have been kind to you; and the work must have sometimes been tiresome.[39]

Hearn knew the intolerable weight of obligation which a Japanese could feel for a favor done. This letter relieved Otani forever from this burden. They remained good friends. Only in his last years, when he shut out the world, Hearn shut out Otani too.

At the end of each school day Hearn returned home to take off his hateful Western dress and put on his Japanese kimono, his comfortable uniform for writing. First he smoked. "He used to sit," his wife remembered, "as a Japanese; and when he smoked, he put his left hand mannerly upon his knee, and swayed his body back and forth. And I heard him occasionally murmuring 'No' while he was smoking." [40]

Hearn turned away from his writing regularly to spend time upon his children's English education. He believed in the saying of Herbert Spencer that a father who was able should teach his own children.[41] Hearn invented attractive, ingenious methods to hold the attention of the boys. He repeated to them old English nonsense rhymes, or invented new ones for help in learning letters and words. He retold fairy stories or made up others to teach vocabulary, ideas, and attitudes. He encouraged drawing and painting as a variation. He allowed Kazuo to sit at a small table beside him in his study and encouraged him to work alongside him.

Kazuo remembered the stern way his father had of making him stay with whatever he had begun. The teacher-father was relentless in pushing his eldest son, in making him be punctual and regular, in drilling, exhorting, reproving him—even to the point of tears. The child would lean against the glass shoji of his father's study and weep warm tears of rebellion. Hearn one day found the streaks upon the glass and, wiping them off, muttered (overheard by the little boy hiding outside in the grass), "Don't think me cruel." [42]

If Kazuo remembered his father's hardheartedness to him when he was doing his lessons, he remembered also his extraordinary softheartedness toward all animals, even insects. Once, trying to write, he was bothered again and again by a fly. After several attempts he caught it and said: " 'No one that has had such luck in escaping death ought to be killed, not even a fly.' [Then] he opened the window, and saying 'Sayonara (goodbye), don't come again,' he let it go." [43]

On Thursdays Hearn did not come home at once after school. This was the day when Mrs. Hearn usually went shopping. She joined him for lunch at the Seiyoken Restaurant in Ueno Park, not far from the university. Then, sometimes with the children, they walked about under the trees, looked at the famous bell tower, went to the museums, or to outdoor art shows. Hearn particularly enjoyed buying contemporary prints, choosing what he liked from unknown artists, contemptuous of those who insisted upon signatures by famous men. Buying pictures or visiting shrines, he disregarded set prices. He paid what he thought the object or the experience was worth to him. He often extravagantly increased the amount above the asking price. "It seemed very queer to the people in the temples, and they would ask his name, but naturally we did not give it." [44] So Mrs. Hearn wrote.

At home, after hours of writing, or after an expedition, Hearn was an absent-minded eater of the evening meal. He forgot himself in the act of raising food to his mouth, and often ignored his food altogether. The others reminded him where he was, and he laughed with them, taking up his chopsticks to begin again.

Kazuo also wrote about the family evenings. "To retire soon after supper was not good, father always said. So almost every evening after supper in the dining-room of twelve mats (which served also as the children's play-room), we all gathered, children, servants, maids, and all, and sang songs. While singing war-songs [this was during the war with Russia] we would march around the large dining-table for about an hour." [45] Quiet would fall. ". . . Father often told us goblin stories in his poor ungrammatical Japanese, in a Japanese-like manner, the meaning of which we understood very clearly. Toward dusk, this big-eyed, big-nosed man looked scary as he related these tales, and his face looked so pale that I would frequently cry out for him to stop." [46]

After the children and the servants and the older relatives had gone to bed, Hearn had what was left of the late hours for private work. He wrought himself to a high pitch of effort, forgetting himself, forgetting time. Staying one night in the house, Amenomori noticed the professor's light still on, and heard him coughing. Thinking he might be ill, he ventured to open the sliding door and looked in. Hearn was unconscious of Amenomori's entrance. "I saw my friend intent in writing at his high desk, with his nose almost touching the paper. Leaf after leaf he wrote on. In a while he held up his head, and what did I see! It was not the Hearn I was familiar with; it was another Hearn. His face was mysteriously white; his large eye gleamed. He appeared like one in touch with some unearthly presence." [47]

Away from his desk Hearn was of a changeable and unpredictable temper, a difficult companion. He could be deliciously happy. He could be heavy with despair. "Often I found Hearn very much elated or very sad," wrote

Setsu. "Sometimes he would walk the corridor almost as if he were dancing, and laughing to himself." [48] When letters came from America he was beside himself with joy. On the other hand ". . . He wept when alone by himself, and he was irritated or elated in an abnormal degree." [49] When he was angry he expressed himself with a fierceness that was droll to the family who knew his habitual gentleness. His son remembered that ". . . He would turn pale, and exclaim, 'I'll slap off your head!' or, 'I'll cut off your head!' " [50]

Hearn happy or sad was the center of a warmly attentive world. It was a regard that warmed his bones, chill from so many years of neglect. Yet occasionally he had a moment of rebellion. He recalled how easy it had once been to remove himself from dullness, how pleasant to sail out of responsibility into new places and situations. When the Spanish-American War threatened to take Mitchell McDonald away from Yokohama and send him into excitement as well as danger, Hearn regretted more than his friend's threatened absence. He wrote to McDonald in April 1898: "I am a little anxious lest war take you away from Japan, which would leave me less satisfied with this world than I am now. But I should like indeed to accompany you in a descent on Manila, and to chronicle events picturesquely." [51] He embroidered for McDonald's and his own benefit the picture of himself as a war correspondent, seeing things that others shallowly missed, describing such events keenly, risking death. He had never cared about death, he told McDonald, in the days when he had been without responsibilities—that is, not caring greatly, he had always escaped. Now that he so greatly cared, he would probably not escape. No: he could not go and risk himself. He must stay home and work and only watch others go.

McDonald was still in Yokohama in the summer of 1898. Hearn invited both him and Amenomori to visit him at Kugenuma near Enoshima where he had brought the family for a seaside vacation. If he could not now escape far, he could pretend in the company of such friends that he was without burdens. Amenomori wrote later how one day they had all behaved like children:

It is impossible to forget that afternoon when the "dear Paymaster" and myself went to see Lafcadio at Kugenuma,—near the island, Enoshima,—where he was spending with his family a summer vacation. . . . We strip ourselves and plunge into the surf. We swim. Lafcadio, a good swimmer, makes somersaults in the water to show us his skill. We are in the best of spirits. Coming out of the sea, we play in pure Adamic suit like children on the beach. Terrified are the small crabs, for we chase them; preventing some from getting into their holes, and digging others out of holes. A young white dog of the village comes running to us, and joins us in the chase. We did not kill the crabs, be it said; we simply chased them for fun, only the dog had his own way of disposing of them. It seemed very short, that day; and dusk brought us back to Lafcadio's lodging. There we played with his children. The "dear Paymaster" taught Kazuo, the eldest son, some gymnastic exercises; and Lafcadio and myself performed some acrobatic feats, vying with each other, to the great amusement of his wife, children, the nurses, and the hotel-servants.[52]

Hearn admired the swings and bars of the hotel's gymnastic set. When he returned to Tokyo, he had similar equipment set up behind the house in Ushigome and encouraged Kazuo and Iwao to exercise. He was not so quick and light as he had once been, but he was complacent about the long time he could hang from the bar by his arms, while smoking a cigar.

McDonald's departure was delayed for two years, but in January 1900 Hearn knew that his friend was going at last. He dreaded the absence of McDonald. Having heard recently from Elizabeth Bisland Wetmore after a long silence, he was more than usually moved. "Memories of handwriting must have become strong with me; for I recognized the writing before I opened the letter," he began in answering her. From this time he wrote frequently to her. He continued also to exchange opinions, prejudices, affectionate remonstrances with Ellwood Hendrick. These two were now his only regular American correspondents. He wrote last to Henry Watkin in 1896, and apparently heard no more from him after that time.

In a world made lonely by the departure or the silence of friends, or the ending of relationships, Hearn shut himself more closely in the refuge he had made for himself in Ushigome. It was the whole space of his house, the temple, the graveyard that was his realm. The boys knew that if Papa was not to be found in the house he was to be sought at Kobudera.

Hearn discovered bit by bit that the safety he thought he had found was an illusion. Ushigome could not protect him from bad news. Nor was it an island of peace.

In 1898 Sentaro Nishida died in Matsue. Hearn, who had not seen his friend for two years, could not at first believe in Nishida's death. The back of a passer-by in a street reminded him of Nishida one day, and forgetting, he ran after the man, only to be disappointed. He tried to put into simple English for Setsu the way he felt: "How bad God is! I am angry." [53]

In 1900 Dr. Toyama died. Hearn went to his funeral. The occasion was somber: the death of a friend and perhaps the end of security in the university. Toyama had been his personal advocate and the patron of all the foreign teachers. Now that he was dead another faction would rule.

Toward the end of 1901 the sound of axes biting into live wood destroyed Hearn's private refuge. One day a dead limb of one of the giant cedars of Kobudera fell with a crash and damaged one of the tombs under the tree.

The parishioners voted to cut down the tree and sell the wood. Hearn offered to buy the tree or the ground on which it stood. He was refused. Not one tree, but three, were felled.[54]

At about this same time the friendly abbot of Kobudera was transferred to another Tokyo temple. A younger abbot succeeded. He accelerated the new program of tree cutting. The axes continued to swing to provide needed income for Kobudera. The hill was soon bare. The temple also sold lots on the hillside for the building of houses.

Hearn had no longer his private strolling place beneath the cedars. The hill behind his house was ugly and public. His dwelling place was cramped by the growth of the city. And the nearby prison began to march its manacled line of prisoners past Hearn's front door morning and evening. He could no longer endure Ushigome. Hearn suggested without force to Setsu that they should all move to the Oki Islands. Then, more realistically, he prepared to look for another place in Tokyo to live.

20 ❧ Final Address

A house was found in a part of the city to the west and to the south of Ushigome, a section still precariously open and partly rural. Number 266 Nishi-Okubo was newly built, in the Japanese style. For Hearn's family it was somewhat small but could be enlarged. Hearn asked for himself only a study that faced west, a room that could be made warm in winter. He was well pleased with the large garden which no stranger could destroy.

He gave up to his wife all the business of making alterations in the new house and arranging the family move. "Well, you do as you please. I know how to write, that is all, and you, Mamma-san, know much better." He refused to give advice or even to look in on the work. "When that house is all ready, you might say, 'Papa-san, please come to our new house in Okubo to-day.' Then I will say good-bye to this house, and will go to Okubo just as I would go to the university. That is all." [1]

In the midst of managing shoji makers, carpenters, and cabinetmakers, Setsu called Hearn one day to come to the ceremony of roof raising. His name, Koizumi Yakumo, was written in Chinese characters on the main beam of the new part of the house, and to the accompaniment of the carpenters' singing and clapping hands in a Shinto ceremony, the beam was raised to its final place. Kazuo, eight years old, knew that this was his mother's rather than his father's house. Its refinement and elegance were hers. Hearn would have liked a plainer style, but it did not greatly matter. He did not notice. He was neither elated nor moved by this change to comfort and elegance. He simply transferred his papers from a study in Ushigome to one in Okubo.

Everything in this room had been arranged for the writer's convenience. As he had requested, his desk faced west. He would interrupt his work regularly at sunset to call Setsu and the children to come see the spectacle, often exclaiming that they had arrived just too late. The room was warm in winter, heated by a stove, and it had glass, instead of paper, shoji. These sliding walls could be pushed aside in summer, and then he looked outward into greenness; and insect noises and bird calls and the varied scents of the garden drifted in to him. He could step down upon a flat rock where his sandals waited and step down again to graveled walks which led away from his room through stands of bamboos and pines.

Except for momentary awakenings to natural things, Hearn was almost unconscious of either the newness or the beauty of the house and garden. It was a convenient shell. He lived his last years in an almost unrelieved tension, writing ceaselessly. He withdrew not only from society, but even from his own family into an inner world where only his work mattered.

Hearn did not mix in the practical life of the house, the coming and going of tradesmen, the buying of food or clothes, the cleaning, or the repairing which was done meticulously with the changing of the seasons. But he did sometimes look up and see an individual—a shopkeeper, a workman, a jinrikisha man, a pilgrim, a beggar—who had come into the house on business or for charity and ask him a question which might elicit an anecdote, a story, a point of view.

He sometimes pulled his wife away from her practical cares and asked her help. He sent her to the Kabuki and other popular theaters, and when she came home he required of her a careful relation of the plot of the plays seen. He sent her to the bookstalls of the Kanda section to find old storybooks. He then asked her to read the stories and retell the skeleton story to him. He took hold of such stories and turned them about, subtracting, adding, putting lively and uneasy flesh on old ghosts. He rejected what he could not use or did not want; he combined, rearranged, and largely created again in a new form what had been given him.

He practiced his first versions upon Setsu, finding her a responsive listener. She wrote that when he became absorbed in a tale ". . . His facial expression would change and his eyes would burn intensely." " 'I think it was in this way,' he would say; 'how do you think, yourself?' and so forth,—all of this was not at all in the books,—and he would consult with me about it.

Had any one seen us from the outside we must have appeared like two mad people." [2]

With her, he play-acted the story he was writing:

I went into the adjoining room, and called out in a small voice, "Yoshi-ichi! Yoshi-ichi!"

"Yes," Hearn answered, playing the part, "I am blind. Who are you?" [3]

Some of the stories Hearn retold were very old, belonging to the number every Japanese child knew in one version or another. Others were from the day before yesterday, or out of a contemporary newspaper. "The Legend of Yurei-Daki" in which a mother lost the life of her child to the guardian spirit of a shrine when she tempted vengeance by carrying away the money box began "One icy winter's evening, thirty-five years ago," and it had happened to "the women and girls employed at a certain *asatoriba,* or hemp-factory." [4] The writer pulled the supernatural into modern times and brought the commonness of today into the older stories. Homeliness of detail, ordinariness of feeling—intensified by the piercing oddity of the supernatural—made Hearn's mode.

He had at last found the way to master his own haunting by handling ghosts with objectivity, asperity, and even humor in the midst of the primary terror. The hinge of each story was the fear, hate, love, jealousy, or pity in it. Horror did not exist in a void, nor was it conjured up simply to titillate the nerves (as it had been in the Cincinnati stories of sensation). Horror here illustrated the humanity of those unfortunately involved in ghostly visitations.

In these tales of his later years, Hearn got briefer and briefer. He was less the obvious artist. He used the force of common verbs and nouns. He wrote dialogue that was succinct and direct. He made macabre comments through the country folk or city folk who could not spare their earthy humor even in supernatural vicissitudes. In *Kotto* "Common Sense" and "Story of a Pheasant," in *Kwaidan* "The Story of Mimi-Nashi-Hoichi," "Oshidori," "Diplomacy," and "The Dream of Akinosuke," and in *Japanese Fairy Tales* "The Old Woman Who Lost Her Dumplings" and "The Boy Who Drew Cats" were prime examples of direct, unassuming power. These tales, told in a quiet, even tone, were all of a piece, living, and whole. Not one sentence could be taken away. Nothing could be added.

To write these stories was the hardest work Hearn had ever done. Some irreplaceable part of himself was built into each story. He described the process metaphorically in an essay, "Kusa-Hibari," the seemingly slight narration of the death of a pet cricket.

The mosquito-sized insect whose Japanese name meant "grass lark" sang only at night, filling the shadowy rooms of the house with "a thin, thin silvery rippling and trilling as of tiniest electric bells." [5] One night, missing the grass lark's "song," Hearn looked into the cage and discovered it dead. The cricket had not been fed and was lying "beside a dried-up lump of egg-plant as gray and hard as a stone." [6] Aki, who usually fed the pet cricket, had gone away for a holiday. Hana, the housemaid, had not taken seriously her unfamiliar duty, and had forgotten to feed the insect its tiny slice of fresh eggplant or cucumber. Although the grass lark had starved for several days, it had sung till the night before Hearn found it. The cricket had had "an atrocious end, for he had eaten his own legs! . . . Yet, after all, to devour one's own legs for hunger is not the worst that can happen to a being cursed with the gift of song. There are human crickets who must eat their own hearts in order to sing." [7]

The visible result in 1902 of Hearn's self-devouring work was another book, *Kotto,* his ninth Japanese book, published by The Macmillan Company. Almost half the book was made up of traditional stories, retold. There was also included "A Woman's Diary," one of Hearn's most sensitive translations: the transcript of an obscure life lived exquisitely in poverty-ridden self-respect upon a back street of the city.

In the austere industry which produced one book a year in the time hedged away from teaching, Hearn seemed remote even to his own family. They heard him weep or exclaim for inexplicable reasons when he paced up and down the veranda, and rushed to comfort him, and found no way of doing so. He was oblivious of them at the table. He did not notice the hours, and wrote all night, letting his lamp gutter.

In the stillness of solitude Hearn was able at last to contemplate his own past. He wrote down certain memories of his childhood and his youth and put them away. He wrote again a few pages about Martinique when he learned that his lemon-colored city, St. Pierre, had been completely destroyed by Mont Pelée on May 8, 1902: "But all this was—and is not! . . . Never again will sun or moon shine upon the streets of that city;—never again will its ways be trodden;—never again will its gardens bloom—except in dreams." [8]

He believed that for a writer dreams were indispensable. To a group of university students he said once: ". . . When, as men-of-letters, you have to deal with any form of supernatural subject—whether terrible, or tender, or pathetic, or splendid—you will do well, if you have a good imagination, not to trust to books for your inspiration. Trust to your own dream-life; study it carefully, and draw your inspiration from that. For dreams are the primary source of almost everything that is beautiful in literature which treats of what lies beyond mere daily experience." [9] The Japanese stories which caught his interest were always those which had some correspondence to his own dream life.

The man who wrote the stories and who taught daily at the university became more and more the object of curiosity and the focus of a growing legend. Tales were told about him in Tokyo and were carried in magazine articles in America,[10] stories about his prestige as a teacher, his mastery of Japanese subjects, the admiration with which he was greeted in Tokyo's streets. His reserve was treated as a mystery. Some of this gossip was friendly, but vague. Other talk was malicious. Hearn was hardly touched by it at all. He was unaware of any general interest in his person and was concerned only with holding onto the little corner of security he had gained, so that he could write, so that he could support his family while he lived, and leave them something when he died.

He could not have explained why he felt this anxiety to produce, but the matter was made clear to him privately when in the last weeks of 1902 he tasted blood in his mouth. During an attack of bronchitis he suffered a dangerous hemorrhage from a burst blood vessel in his throat. He went to bed and was forbidden to talk above a whisper. He recovered slowly, and after days of enforced passivity returned to the classroom.

The teacher who came back to his students in the early days of 1903 seemed to have grown old. (He was fifty-two.) He walked slowly. His thick, coarse hair and ragged mustache had become very gray. His clothes fitted his body loosely.

At this time he came up against the gathered forces of those unfriendly to him in the university. His teaching contract was due for a renewal in March 1903. Brusquely it was announced to him that it would be renewed but that henceforth he would be paid as a Japanese citizen; that is, his salary would be sharply reduced. He was also due a sabbatical year. He asked for this free year. He was refused.

Hearn made no public statements and only expressed his bitterness privately in a few cries of anger and pain in letters to friends in America. He repeated what must have been the ugliest remark made to him, that if he could not live upon the reduced salary he should learn, like any other Japanese, to eat rice.

Hearn was unable to beg, even for his family's security. He resigned from the university and went home. He hoped for some change of heart, for some mitigating offer, but the authorities gave no sign. The students, who loved him and wanted to agitate for him, were not encouraged by him to do so. Still, for several days there was much disturbance among them.

Some fragments of the diary of Kaworu Osarai, a university student of that time, have been published. His entries show the furious brief agitation which swept through the student body and which then faded away without any effective action. He wrote on March 2nd: "I went to school in the afternoon; and found many students talking in agitated tones in the corridor, and I soon came to the knowledge that Mr. H—— was going to be dismissed from the school. . . . My heart stirred. . . . We have many professors here, but not one interests us as Mr. Hearn." On March 5th he wrote: "We are saying that we must not give up Mr. H——; we should hold him with our school under any circumstances." There was a meeting of the students to protest Hearn's dismissal. One got up to speak and said that as a girl picks a lover out of a thousand, so ". . . We will choose one beloved teacher from the hundred others." Another jumped up to say: "The existence of the Imperial University of Tokyo is known to foreign countries on account of Lafcadio Hearn, the writer. What has the university to be proud of, if he goes." On March 16th the student wrote: ". . . I am told that Mr. H—— said, when the representative [of the students] saw him, that he would never forget our sympathy; and it is said he even cried." [11]

Others recalled that the delegation of students had to wait upon Hearn more than once for him to receive them at all, and that he did not ask their help. He would not press upon this considerable lever of power. He would not exert himself to gain what he thought was a right.

Hearn was sustained by the knowledge of a superior resource. He had received an offer from Cornell University in November 1902 asking him to deliver a series of lectures on the civilization of Japan. It was because of this offer that he had asked for his sabbatical year. He had been uneasy about his position at the university long before the actual crisis. He had written to Mrs. Wetmore as early as July 1902 asking her to look about for something for him in America. He wanted to take Kazuo to the United States to begin his Western education, and he was restless at the fixity of his Japanese situation. Mrs. Wetmore had interested President Schurman of Cornell in Hearn.

On being asked to deliver a set of formal lectures Hearn had wondered for a moment if he would have the temerity to accept. "I am quite sure that I do *not* know anything about Japanese art, or literature, or ethnology, or politics, or history. . . . At present I have no acquaintance even with the Japanese language. [He exaggerated.] I have held a chair of English literature here for nearly seven years, by setting all canons at defiance, and attempting to teach only the emotional side of literature, in its relations to modern thought;—playing with philosophy, as a child can play with the great sea." [12]

After naming all the things he did not know, he regained his confidence and wrote:

What I could do would be about thus:

I could attempt a series of lectures upon Japanese topics—dealing incidentally with psychological, religious, social, and artistic impressions—so as to produce in the minds of my hearers an idea of Japan different from that which is given in books. Something, perhaps, in the manner of Mr. Lowell's "Soul of the Far East" (incomparably the greatest of all books on Japan, and the deepest)—but from a different point of view.

What I could *not* do would be to put myself forward as an authority upon Japanese history, or any special Japanese subject. The value of my lectures would depend altogether upon suggestiveness—not upon any crystallizations of fact.[13]

He began to daydream about seeing again his friends of 1890, Ellwood Hendrick and Elizabeth Bisland Wetmore, in particular. "Only to see you again—" he wrote to Mrs. Wetmore, "even for a moment—and to hear you speak (in some one of the Myriad Voices), would be such a memory for me. And you would let me 'walk about gently, touching things'?" [14]

Hearn had recently completed a book of stories, *Kwaidan,* and sent the manuscript to America. (It was to appear in 1904, published by Houghton Mifflin Company.) This tenth Japanese book was at the end of the development of his thought that had begun when he finished *Glimpses.* Everything he had learned about Japan had become objective and dramatic in stories that were succinct, sometimes brutal, and always evocative. The most effective stories in the volume were "The Story of Mimi-Nashi-Hoichi," "Oshidori," and "Diplomacy," but there was no waste in the other slightly less effective stories. There was no packing and filling of the volume with self-indulgent "fantastics" or essays about subjects on which he was not expert. Probably without knowing it, he had achieved the one little book of stories of his ambition, his "something very extraordinary" [15] which he had once mentioned in a letter to McDonald.

Having rid himself of *Kwaidan,* he was free to prepare for a visit to America. During the months of unpleasantness at the university in the early spring of 1903, he began the writing of a set of lectures for Cornell University. This was a new kind of mental exercise. He read, studied, organized, forced himself to come to conclusions as he had never done before. All this—at a time when his health and his security were failing.

The teacher who went home from his university classroom one day in

March 1903, his resignation accepted with insulting smoothness, did not have very long a compensatory prop for his pride. Some time in the early part of 1903 Hearn had word from President Schurman of Cornell that the lectures which he had been asked to deliver would have to be canceled. There had been an outbreak of typhoid fever on the campus. All activities and expenditures of Cornell had had to be curtailed.

Hearn was left gazing blankly into his future. He was afraid, but his fears ran ahead of the facts. When he had had time to adjust himself to his two losses, he found that his condition was not desperate. His dread of being without money was always, after he acquired a family, excessive. His income from writing continued in 1903 and 1904, perhaps even with some acceleration. He resolved not to waste the effort he had put into writing the lectures, but to convert this good material into a book. Yet Hearn needed the courage he gathered together. His wife was pregnant again; he and Setsu were to be parents for the fourth time. (A girl, Suzuko, was to be born in the autumn of 1903.) Meantime Hearn bent to his desk and growled, "This book will kill me." [16]

He showed a better humor to Elizabeth Wetmore in August: "I am sorry for my dismal letter of the other day. (After having worked during thirteen years for Japan, I have been only driven out of the service, and practically banished from the country.) [17] . . . I feel to-day much braver, and think that I can fight it out here in Japan. . . . For the present, I think that I shall simply sit down, and work as hard as Zola. . . . You will hear from me in print;—there I can give you pleasure, perhaps: I am not fit to write letters." [18]

He spent the succeeding months living almost entirely in his work. He completed the book *Japan: An Attempt at Interpretation,* the final form of the Cornell lectures. This study, which was his last word upon Japan, was a somber reversal of many of his first conclusions. He had thought the Japanese spontaneous and free. He exhibited them now as disciplined and determined. The determining factor was the organization of instincts and habits which society had accomplished over hundreds, perhaps thousands, of years. The delicate beauty of manners, dress, crafts, the subtle adjustments of individual to individual, of person to society, the seemingly unthinking propriety of civil and religious practices—all these good things were the result not of choice but of pressure. Hearn did justice to the deft management, the color, the subtlety of Japanese living, but he also showed the great price paid for a great good. The book was logical in arrangement and exhilarating in its clarification of a single idea. Yet it was not a polemical or argumentative book. He demonstrated what he had found to be true. He left it to the reader to argue the tragic mixture of good and bad in the pattern.

He worked otherwise upon the writing of a few haunting fairy tales, particularly the stringing together of lyrics into the story of Tanabata, the Weaving Lady, and her lover, Hikoboshi, in "The Romance of the Milky Way." Under pressure his mind gained an edge it had never had before. But he wore his body out. He seemed not to belong to that body but to be outside it, looking down at one who wrote and wrote. He humbly apologized for being late to meals when the impatient boys, Kazuo, Iwao, and Kiyoshi, called to him to come, and Setsu said, "Papa-san, it is about time that I should ask you to wake up from your dream!" [19] These were not easy years for Hearn wife's. Her son, two generations later, wrote vaguely of his mother's "hysteria." [20]

Hearn's great concern for his children, the three boys, and the little girl, was that he could provide some buffer between them and the world which, in his experience, had always been ready to gobble up young victims. Education was the means, he hoped, to safeguard the children. Equipped with some sort of usable knowledge (he hated abstract learning) they would be able to fight, as he had not known how, during his youth.

The father had undertaken Kazuo's education in English from the child's earliest years and enlisted Iwao in these lessons as soon as that merry little boy was able to guide a pencil or a brush. Kiyoshi would be old enough soon to bend his head above a desk in his father's study also and trace the strange shapes of the English alphabet. As for Suzuko, her father could do nothing for her yet but forebode her future. "What pain is in my heart," [21] he said, looking at the little girl.

Of all the children it was the eldest, Kazuo, about whom the father most worried. The others seemed more Japanese and more thoughtlessly able to adjust themselves to life. They would have an easier growing up, it seemed to the father, than this shy, sensitive boy who showed his European ancestry.

He had enrolled Iwao in the Okubo elementary school in the spring of 1903. He could not bring himself to place Kazuo in the public school until April 1904. The father's teaching, supplemented by lessons in Japanese from the "students," had been so excellent that the child was promoted at the end of the second term from the fourth to the fifth year.

At home Hearn still continued to hold Kazuo and Iwao to a rigorous schedule of English lessons. Even on vacation at Yaizu he did not let the boys escape altogether to play. Since 1900 Hearn himself had sat down side by side with his sons to study the writing of Japanese characters under Niimi, Aki, or Okumura.

In studying under his father Iwao was lighthearted, laughing even when punished, slipping away often to play. His father let him go, regarding Iwao indulgently. It was different with Kazuo. The sessions between the father and the eldest son were usually stormy. Hearn often made Kazuo cry. Kazuo took advantage of his father sometimes by slyly suggesting that his eyes were tired. Because Hearn had a horror of eye trouble, he would let the child run away and play if he thought that his eyes were being strained. In pain and trouble himself, he held Kazuo to regular sessions of work in winter and in summer.

Although the hours of English study were a seesaw struggle between father and son, with much emotion mixed with the teaching and learning, Kazuo was quick. He learned to read and write English readily, to keep a diary in English, to enjoy the little stories his father dictated for writing practice.

Sometimes, before the family moved to Okobu, the exercise became a fantasy:

In Tokyo there was a little boy named Koizumi Kazuo. He lived at Number 21 Tomihisacho, in Ushigome. He was a nice lad; but he was very much afraid of lions.

One day, when Kazuo's parents were both out and Kazuo was all alone upstairs, a strange thing happened—a lion came into the house. When the lion came in everybody ran away, except Kazuo, who was upstairs. O-Baba San, O-Hana, and O-Yone, ran to Kobudera, with the baby; Aki ran to Kotsuya with Iwao; and Niimi ran for the police.[22]

Sometimes the exercise was fiercely hortatory, showing more of Papa's state of mind than Kazuo's. From the boy's diary:

Today I was very naughty and disobedient, and so my father set me to taking dictation as follows:—

"Can you write Japanese?" "Only a little." "Can you write a Japanese letter as well as Nakumura?" (a rikisha-man) "No, I cannot." "Can you read a Japanese newspaper?" "No." "Can you read a Japanese letter?" "No." "Can you write or read or speak English well?" "No." "Have you learned any trade?" "No." "When papa is dead, how will you make some money?" "I do not know." 'If you do not know, this house will be taken and sold—you will have no home—and your mamma and grand-mamma will be dead—and you will have no friend. Then you will find how cruel people are in this world." [23]

Part of an English alphabet ran more smoothly:

> I am a very nice little boy. I I
> I am now learning how to swim. I I
> I am staying at Yaizu with my papa.
> J was a jelly-fish J J J Jelly-fish.
> K was a pretty little kitten K K K [24]

The jellyfish and the kitten were real objects in Kazuo's universe. The kitten was found and rescued by Hearn on one of the daily walks he took with the boys along the shore through pine woods and bamboo groves near Yaizu. The learning to swim was a matter of great importance.

When the shorter summer lessons were over, Hearn, with Kazuo and Iwao, and the "students" ran down to the beach—to play together and to swim. Kazuo was afraid of the water, but his father made him persist, and at last the boy learned to handle himself skillfully even in deep water.

Kazuo never forgot a long swim his father made him undertake in the summer of 1901 when he was eight years old. Far out beyond the circle of the little harbor a fishing boat was anchored. Thus far, Hearn told Kazuo, the two of them must swim. Kazuo doubted that he could do so, but encouraged by the father who swam beside him, who told him not to cry when stung by jellyfish, who instructed him when to turn over and float, Kazuo found himself under the shadow of the boat. He and his father grasped a rope lowered to them and talked with the fishermen who admired them. "For Tokyo visitors, you are great swimmers." "How old is the child?" [25] they asked. Then Kazuo and his father turned back, and slowly, slowly, it seemed, and with increasing weariness, they regained Yaizu Harbor.

Kazuo's success meant much more to the father than to the son. Through his tiredness the boy heard his father praising him, "If you can swim that much, you are quite safe. . . . Afterward he repeatedly said, 'Don't ever forget the hard struggle of today!' " [26]

Hearn insisted upon Kazuo's learning to swim because that skill stood to him for all the other skills Kazuo would need to learn to survive in a rough world. It was to equip Kazuo to combat the world that he planned to take him to America or to Europe to study Western languages and sciences. When the lectures at Cornell were canceled, Hearn was forced to give up any immediate plans for Kazuo's Western education.

By the spring of 1904 life seemed easier again. Hearn had accomplished a considerable amount of writing during the previous winter. His health seemed somewhat better. He was once more in demand in academic circles.

The great liberal private university, Waseda University, endowed by one of the leaders of the Meiji generation, Count Okuma, a man whom Hearn greatly admired, had asked him to teach again. In the last weeks of the spring session in 1904, he began lecturing on English literature to classes of would-be writers and journalists. (Waseda attracted the more liberal and more literary among the students, while Tokyo Imperial University drew to itself the future government leaders.) He found himself in a congenial atmosphere on the campus of this new school located not far from his own neighborhood. Here there were open respect and admiration for him, and an anxious desire to please him.

In the same season of hopefulness Hearn opened with some curiosity a letter from P. J. Hartog, the Academic Registrar of London University. Under the date March 26, 1904, the letter began: "I am directed to ask if you will kindly consent to deliver a course of ten lectures for the University of London (under the Martin White Benefaction) on the 'Civilization of Japan' during the coming session, and preferably either in the Lent or Summer terms?" [27]

Hearn was greatly pleased. He did not see how he could transport himself alone as far as London to deliver ten lectures, nor did it seem plain that this was to be his chance to take Kazuo to the West, but he suspected that these possibilities might work out. It was gratifying to learn from the registrar that Mr. Hearn was to be completely free in his choice and management of topics, and that London University anticipated enlightenment from him.

During the summer of 1904 Setsu kept the baby, Suzuko, and the smallest boy, Kiyoshi, in Tokyo while she supervised repairs to the house. Hearn, delighted to be banished from big and little problems, went to Yaizu with Kazuo and Iwao for several weeks. (He had not missed a summer in Yaizu except the year before, when Suzuko was born.)

But even in Yaizu the world intruded. "Yaizu has sent her seventeen soldiers out to Manchuria," [28] Hearn wrote to his wife on August 13th. The enemy of this action was Russia, the aim of the new war, to Hearn, was uncertain. He did not doubt Japan's strength. Yet he doubted the end; it might bring to power the very men of the Empire who would complete the killing of all that was left of the Japan he loved. (In Tokyo, O-saki, the maid, Otokichi's daughter, had opened the professor's door several times recently to former students, dressed in uniform, come to say goodbye before going away to war.) Here in Yaizu the small fishing fleet was almost crippled by the recruiting of men for the army.

Yet in the fine salt air Hearn tried to dismiss the war from his mind, as well as his own private struggle. Life seemed pleasant when a walk along the curving street was interrupted at almost every step by a friendly turning away from the work of mending a net or making a basket, a hailing from the doorways. These sunburned faces were unceremonious, unmalicious, and only briefly curious. The Sensei was a part of the scenery of Yaizu.

Hearn liked the respect he received, and the uncomplicated friendliness. His boys played with the children of the village and shared with them the village cats and dogs. Hearn asked for news of sons and daughters who seemed suddenly to have grown up. The boys were away at war or voyaging along the coasts of the islands in large fishing vessels. The girls had married or gone adventurously to Tokyo as maids.

Hearn kept his own boys busy with their English lessons for short periods in the morning and afternoon. This summer the lessons seemed to go unusually well. "I am giving just a moderate work to Kazuo and he does it well," he wrote to Mrs. Hearn ("Dear Mamma-Sama"). "It is just the reviewing, not the new lessons. When we return to Tokyo, I shall give him new lessons. At present he is diligent in penmanship, letter-writing, writing his diary, and English reading, so I do not press upon him. Nor do I force Iwao, for he does his half an hour's study very well. It is simply lovely to see them learn well." [29] Two days later he wrote another kind of news characteristic of Yaizu: "The boys catch dragonflies and grasshoppers, they laugh, they gather stones, they play cards, they eat much and sleep well. Papa is splendid too." [30]

After August 24th he brought the boys home. Hearn faced a future that did not look bad at all. He was to teach again at Waseda University. He awaited the publication of *Japan: An Attempt at Interpretation*. He had not been able to dismiss it from his mind after sending it to America. He had had so far one word from the publisher, "Good," [31] and imagined in abstracted moments that he heard "the noise of the tick-tack of setting the type . . ." [32]

This moment of anticipation and precarious well-being was a small climax beyond which Hearn would never go in either good or bad fortune.

On September 19, 1904, Setsu found Hearn walking up and down in his study. He clutched his chest as if he held an enemy there. " 'Are you not well?' I asked. 'I have a new kind of sickness.' I inquired, 'What kind?' 'Sickness of heart, I think.' " [33] He would take no advice to rest. He sat down to write a letter—apparently of instructions to a friend for arrangements if he should die. His wife remembered his speaking to her in the following manner: " 'This is a letter to Ume-san. If trouble comes, he will help you. Perhaps, if this pain of mine increases, I may die. If I die, do not weep. Buy a little urn; you can find one for three or four *sen*. Put my bones in it, and bury it near a quiet temple in the country. I shall not like it if you cry. Amuse the children and play cards with them—how much better I shall enjoy that! There will be no need of announcing my death. If any one asks, reply, "Oh, he died some time ago!" That will be quite proper.' " [34]

Suddenly the pain stopped. Hearn had a moment in which he felt that he had cheated his fate, and was triumphant. He took a cold shower. He drank a glass of whisky. He laughed at the doctor who came late, telling him that now there was nothing to treat him for.

Seven days later, when he was walking alone on the veranda after supper, he felt the pain again. He came to find his wife and said to her, " 'Mamma-san, the sickness of the other day has come back again.' " [35] He walked "around the room with his hands on his breast," [36] and then let his wife help him to bed. He died very quickly. What he said last, Kazuo remembered—words spoken as if casting a long look ahead at all that he would not do, would not see, would not know—was only this: " 'Ah, byoki no tame' "—" 'Ah, on account of sickness . . .' " [37]

His family and friends denied to him his wish to slip unnoticed into death. His funeral was conducted in the ceremonies of the Soto school of Zen Buddhism at the Kobudera temple. Hearn's friend, the abbot, came back to the hilltop in Ushigome (where there were no longer any cedars) to officiate. A Tokyo newspaper counted those present: three foreigners, forty professors, one hundred students. Friends, teachers, students, white-robed wife and children listened to the chanting of the sutras.

The students presented a laurel wreath with an inscription which mixed regret with the insistent patriotism of the moment: "In memory of Lafcadio Hearn, whose pen was mightier than the sword of the victorious nation which he loved and lived among, and whose highest honor it shall ever be to have given him citizenship and, alas, a grave!" [38]

Otokichi from Yaizu attended the ceremony. He had heard that the Sensei had died and had come at once by train. He was allowed to take part in the ceremony of the gathering of the bones after the burning of the body at the crematory. Kazuo, ten years old, did not forget the sight:

While muttering Buddhist prayers and picking up father's bones (two persons picking up the same bone with unmated chopsticks), Otokichi suddenly remarked, "Here is something like the cover of *sazae* (top-shell) round and flat. What is it?" he asked of the crematory man. "That is the knee-cap—in common called *hiza kozo*." When Otokichi heard this, "He-he-i, is that so? Then with this Sensei-sama moved his leg and swam in our sea until just a little while ago—eh?" So saying, he wiped his eyes with his blue towel to brush away the tears.[39]

The bones were buried in Zoshigaya Cemetery, a burial site in the northern part of Tokyo, not far from Ushigome, not far from Okubo. It was a green space under tall trees where Hearn had liked to take his family to walk. The dead man's posthumous name, according to Buddhist practice, was placed over the grave, "Believing man similar to undefiled flower blooming like eight rising clouds, who dwells in mansion of right enlightenment." [40]

His name in life, Koizumi Yakumo, and his dates, 1850 to 1904, were also inscribed on a rough stone shaft.

Hearn would have liked better the familiar inscription carved upon a memorial marker set up in Yaizu. "In commemoration of the place where sang Professor Yakumo Koizumi . . ." [41] The people of the village recalled the Sensei joining his children in singing in the sunset each evening, "Yu-yake! Ko-yake! . . . Evening-burning! Little burning! Weather, be fair tomorrow!"

Notes

In the Notes below, I cite each title in full on the first mention in each chapter. I make an exception for convenience of the following title: *The Writings of Lafcadio Hearn,* 16 vols. (Boston, 1922). It will be shown as Hearn, *Writings,* with the appropriate, individual title preceding this identification in each reference. Included in Hearn, *Writings,* as Vols. XIII, XIV, and XV, is the work *Life and Letters of Lafcadio Hearn,* Elizabeth Bisland, ed. (Boston, 1906).

PREFACE

1. Paul Elmer More, *Selected Shelburne Essays* (New York, 1935), 26.

Chapter 1
ENTRANCE

1. Hearn, in a letter to his half sister, Minnie Atkinson. Nina H. Kennard, *Lafcadio Hearn: Containing Some Letters from Lafcadio Hearn to His Half-Sister, Mrs. Atkinson* (New York, 1912), 32.

Chapter 2
PATRICK LAFCADIO

1. Nina H. Kennard, *Lafcadio Hearn: Containing Some Letters from Lafcadio Hearn to His Half-Sister, Mrs. Atkinson* (New York, 1912), 215. 2. O. W. Frost documented the facts about Hearn's parentage and birth in Greece. See his *Young Hearn* (Tokyo, 1958) and "The Birth of Lafcadio Hearn," *American Literature,* Vol. XXIV, No. 3 (Nov. 1952), 372–77. 3. Undated letter, probably late 1889 or early 1890. E. C. Beck, "Letters of Lafcadio Hearn to His Brother," *The English Journal,* Vol. XX (1931), 288. 4. "Dream of a Summer's Day," *Out of the East,*

Hearn, *Writings,* VII, 17–18. **5.** *Letters from the Raven: Being the Correspondence of Lafcadio Hearn with Henry Watkin,* Milton Bronner, ed. (New York, 1907), 135. **6.** Kennard, *op. cit.,* 12. **7.** *Ibid.,* 13–14. **8.** Beck, *op. cit.,* 287–88. **9.** *Ibid.,* 288. **10.** From Susan Maria Hearn's diary, in Frost, *Young Hearn,* 27. **11.** Beck, *op. cit.,* 288, 290. **12.** O. W. Frost says in 1856; Vera McWilliams says earlier. **13.** Beck, *op. cit.,* 288. **14.** *Ibid.* **15.** Frost, *Young Hearn,* 32. **16.** Beck, *op. cit.,* 289–90. **17.** *Ibid.,* 288–89. **18.** Hearn to Minnie Atkinson. Kennard, *op. cit.,* 22. **19.** Frost, *Young Hearn,* 53. **20.** *Ibid.,* 62. **21.** "Nightmare-Touch," *Shadowings,* Hearn, *Writings,* X, 165. **22.** *Ibid.* **23.** *Ibid.,* 167–68. **24.** *Ibid.,* 169. **25.** "Gothic Horror," *Shadowings,* Hearn, *Writings,* X, 149. **26.** Hearn Ms., My Guardian Angel—undated except, "Tokyo, Japan." Barrett Collection, University of Virginia. The document is quoted in Bisland, *Life and Letters,* Hearn, *Writings,* XIII, 17–21. **27.** *Ibid.* **28.** *Ibid.* **29.** *Ibid.* **30.** *Ibid.* **31.** *Ibid.* **32.** *Ibid.* **33.** "Hi-Mawari," *Kwaidan,* Hearn, *Writings,* XI. **34.** Bisland, *Life and Letters,* Hearn, *Writings,* XIV, 259. **35.** *Ibid.,* XIII, 27. **36.** *Ibid.,* 28. **37.** Frost, *Young Hearn,* 48. **38.** O. W. Frost says De Maupassant attended the school, 1863–64 and 1866–67. See *Young Hearn,* 53. **39.** Translated and quoted by Francis Steegmüller, *Maupassant: A Lion in the Path* (New York, 1949). **40.** *Ibid.,* 17. **41.** *Ibid.,* 25. **42.** Said in a lecture on Shelley to Japanese students at the Tokyo Imperial University. See Lafcadio Hearn, *Interpretations of Literature,* I, John Erskine, ed. (New York, 1915), 142. **43.** D. H. Langton, "Lafcadio Hearn, Journalist and Writer on Japan," *Manchester Quarterly,* Vol. 31 (1912), 5. **44.** Ms. Hearn letter to George M. Gould, on microfilm, undated, Stedman Collection, Columbia University. **45.** "Of Moon-Desire," *Exotics and Retrospectives,* Hearn, *Writings,* IX, 129–30. **46.** Kennard, *op. cit.,* 44. **47.** *Ibid.,* 45. **48.** *Ibid.,* 46. **49.** In Michael Monahan, "A Friend of Lafcadio Hearn," *Nemesis* (New York, 1926), 143. **50.** Kazuo Koizumi, *Father and I* (Boston, 1935), 164–65. **51.** Frost, *Young Hearn,* 64–65. **52.** Letter to Minnie Atkinson, quoted in Kennard, *op. cit.,* 31–32. **53.** "A Street Singer," *Kokoro,* Hearn, *Writings,* VII, 298.

Chapter 3
CINCINNATI STREETS

1. Nina H. Kennard, *Lafcadio Hearn: Containing Some Letters from Lafcadio Hearn to His Half-Sister, Mrs. Atkinson* (New York, 1912), 67–68. **2.** *Ibid.* **3.** *Ibid.,* 68. **4.** *Ibid.,* 69. **5.** *Ibid.,* 65. **6.** To Basil Hall Chamberlain, August 21, 1894. *The Japanese Letters of Lafcadio Hearn,* Elizabeth Bisland, ed. (Boston, 1910), 371–72. **7.** Hearn had available at the Cincinnati Public Library all the contemporary French books from which he translated, or which he reviewed, in the Cincinnati newspapers in the 1870's. Conversation, Yeatman Anderson III, Curator of Rare Books, the Public Library of Cincinnati and Hamilton County. **8.** Not after Vickers became Librarian. O. W. Frost, *Young Hearn* (Tokyo, 1958), 71. **9.** Conversation, Lee Allen, who checked this and other names of Hearn's obscure Cincinnati associates against the appropriate yearly city directories. **10.** Lafcadio Hearn, "Some Strange Experience: The Reminiscences of a Ghost-Seer," Cincinnati *Commercial,* Sept. 26, 1875. Collected in Lafcadio Hearn, *An American Miscellany,* I, Albert Mordell, ed. (New York, 1924), 62. **11.** *Ibid.,* 66. **12.** John A. Cockerill,

"Lafcadio Hearn, the Author of *Kokoro*," *Current Literature*, Vol. XIX, No. 6 (June 1896), 476. Cockerill wrote this article after visiting with Hearn in Kobe, Japan, when an interval of almost a generation had passed since the two men were editor and reporter on the Cincinnati *Enquirer*. **13.** In Lafcadio Hearn, *Occidental Gleanings*, I, Albert Mordell, ed. (New York, 1925), 15. **14.** Cincinnati *Enquirer*, Dec. 21, 1873. **15.** Hearn, *Occidental Gleanings*, I, 32.

Chapter 4
SENSATIONAL REPORTER

1. From New Orleans, Aug. 14, 1878. In *Letters from the Raven: Being the Correspondence of Lafcadio Hearn with Henry Watkin*, Milton Bronner, ed. (New York, 1907), 64. **2.** To B. H. Chamberlain, in Bisland, *Life and Letters*, Hearn, *Writings*, XIII, 48. **3.** *Letters from the Raven.* **4.** "The Restless Dead," Cincinnati *Commercial*, Aug. 29, 1875. Collected in Hearn, *An American Miscellany*, I, Albert Mordell, ed. (New York, 1924), 52. **5.** Collected, under the title "Violent Cremation," in *The Selected Writings of Lafcadio Hearn*, Henry Goodman, ed. (New York, 1949), 234. **6.** *Ibid.*, 236. **7.** *Ibid.* **8.** *Ibid.* **9.** *Ibid.*, 237. **10.** In a lecture to students of Tokyo Imperial University. Collected in Hearn, *Talks to Writers*, John Erskine, ed. (New York, 1927), 27–28. **11.** To H. E. Krehbiel. Bisland, *Life and Letters*, Hearn, *Writings*, XIII, 216. **12.** *Ibid.*, 286–87. **13.** *Ibid.*, 301. **14.** Cincinnati *Enquirer*, Oct. 18, 1874. Collected in Hearn, *Occidental Gleanings*, I, 50–51. **15.** *Ibid.*, 54. **16.** The only extant originals of all nine issues are held in the Public Library of Cincinnati and Hamilton County. **17.** "Giglampz!" Oct. 4, 1874. Collected in Hearn, *American Miscellany*, I, 25. **18.** *Ibid.*, 26. **19.** *Ibid.*, 28.

Chapter 5
LOW LIFE AND ROMANTICISM

1. "Notes of a Trip to Kyoto," *Gleanings in Buddha-Fields*, Hearn, *Writings*, VIII, 51. **2.** Collected in Hearn, *Occidental Gleanings*, I, Albert Mordell, ed. (New York, 1925), 67–68. **3.** Cincinnati *Enquirer*, Jan. 10, 1875. **4.** Cincinnati *Enquirer*, March 14, 1875. **5.** Quoted in Oscar Lewis, *Hearn and His Biographers: The Record of a Literary Controversy* (San Francisco, 1930), 110–11. **6.** John A. Cockerill, "Lafcadio Hearn: the Author of *Kokoro*," *Current Literature*, Vol. XIX, No. 6 (June 1896), 476. **7.** Quoted in Bisland, *Life and Letters*, Hearn, *Writings*, XIII, 49. **8.** Cincinnati *Commercial*, Jan. 16, 1876. **9.** Collected in *The Selected Writings of Lafcadio Hearn*, Henry Goodman, ed. (New York, 1949), 214. **10.** Cincinnati *Commercial*, Sept. 5, 1875. Collected in Hearn, *Occidental Gleanings*, I, 92. **11.** Cincinnati *Commercial*, Jan. 7, 1877. Collected in *Selected Writings*, 257. **12.** *Ibid.*, "Gibbeted," 205. **13.** *Ibid.*, "Some Pictures of Poverty," 256. **14.** Cincinnati *Commercial*, March 17, 1876. Collected as "Levee Life," in Hearn, *An American Miscellany*, I, Albert Mordell, ed. (New York, 1924), 147. **15.** "Butler's," Cincinnati *Enquirer*, Nov. 22, 1874. Collected in Lafcadio Hearn, *Children of the Levee*, O. W. Frost, ed. (The University of Kentucky, 1957), 92. **16.** "Ole Man Pickett," Cincinnati *Enquirer*, Feb. 21, 1875. Collected in Hearn, *Children of the Levee*, 54–55. **17.** "Black Varieties," Cincinnati *Commercial*, April 9, 1876. Collected in Hearn, *Occidental Gleanings*, I, 124. Also collected in Hearn, *Children* *of the Levee.* **18.** "The Rising of the Waters," Cincinnati *Commercial,* Jan. 18, 1877. Collected in Hearn, *Children of the Levee,* 103. **19.** "Ole Man Pickett," Cincinnati *Enquirer,* Feb. 21, 1875. Collected in Hearn, *Children of the Levee,* 60. **20.** "Dolly: An Idyl of the Levee," *Selected Writings of Lafcadio Hearn,* 249. Also collected in Hearn, *Children of the Levee,* 21. **21.** "Pariah People," Cincinnati *Commercial,* Aug. 22, 1875. In Hearn, *Occidental Gleanings,* I, 85. Also collected in Hearn, *Children of the Levee,* 48. **22.** "Levee Life," Cincinnati *Commercial,* March 17, 1876. In Hearn, *Selected Writings,* 223. Also collected in Hearn, *Children of the Levee,* 71. **23.** *Ibid., Selected Writings,* 224–25, and *Children of the Levee,* 72. **24.** *Ibid., Selected Writings,* 228–29 and *Children of the Levee,* 76–77. **25.** "A Child of the Levee," Cincinnati *Commercial,* June 27, 1876. Collected in Hearn, *Children of the Levee,* 10. **26.** *Ibid.,* 11. **27.** "Levee Life," Hearn, *Selected Writings,* 232–33, and Hearn, *Children of the Levee,* 82–83. **28.** Bisland, *Life and Letters,* Hearn, *Writings,* XIII, 49–50. **29.** Cincinnati *Enquirer,* April 17, 1921. **30.** The title story from Théophile Gautier, *One of Cleopatra's Nights and Other Fantastic Romances,* Lafcadio Hearn, translator (New York, 1882), 62. **31.** Théophile Gautier, *Nouvelles,* 7th ed., rev. (Paris, 1865), 353. **32.** Hearn, tr., *One of Cleopatra's Nights,* 6. **33.** *Ibid.,* 27. **34.** Gustave Flaubert, *The Temptation of Saint Anthony,* Lafcadio Hearn, translator (New York and Seattle, 1910), 156.

Chapter 6
FLIGHT SOUTHWARD

1. Lafcadio Hearn, *Occidental Gleanings,* I, Albert Mordell, ed. (New York, 1925), 156. **2.** H. E. Krehbiel to Joseph Tunison, quoted in Oscar Lewis, *Hearn and His Biographers: the Record of a Literary Controversy* (San Francisco, 1930), 110. **3.** Entire letter quoted by O. W. Frost in "Two Unpublished Hearn Letters," *Today's Japan,* Vol. 5, No. 1 (1955–60: Fifth Anniversary Issue, Jan. 1960), 43–48. **4.** *Ibid.* **5.** Quoted in Lewis, *op cit.,* 53–54. **6.** Bisland, *Life and Letters,* Hearn, *Writings,* XIII, 59. **7.** Lafcadio Hearn, *Letters from the Raven: Being the Correspondence of Lafcadio Hearn with Henry Watkin,* Milton Bronner, ed. (New York, 1907), 97. **8.** Lecture on Shelley, Lafcadio Hearn, *Interpretations of Literature,* I, John Erskine, ed. (New York, 1915), 145. **9.** Hearn, *Letters from the Raven,* 130. **10.** *Ibid.,* 141. **11.** *Ibid.* **12.** *Ibid.,* 133. **13.** *Ibid.,* 129. **14.** *Ibid.,* 142. **15.** *Ibid.,* 150. **16.** From copies of these passages in the George M. Gould Collection of Hearniana, Library of Congress. **17.** Conversation, Yeatman Anderson III, Curator of Rare Books, Public Library of Cincinnati and Hamilton County. **18.** Hearn, *Letters from the Raven,* 34. **19.** Quoted by Albert Mordell in his Introduction, Lafcadio Hearn, *An American Miscellany,* I (New York, 1924), li. **20.** Hearn, *Letters from the Raven,* 34. **21.** *Ibid.,* 36–37. **22.** Kazuo Koizumi, *Father and I: Memories of Lafcadio Hearn* (Boston, 1935), 11, and Ellwood Hendrick, *Percolator Papers* (New York, 1919), 190–91. **23.** Article dated Nov. 1, 1877, collected in Hearn, *Occidental Gleanings,* I, 145–46. **24.** *Ibid.,* 155. **25.** Wilkie Collins, *Armadale* (New York, 1866), 45. **26.** *Ibid.* **27.** Paraphrase of Hearn's description in his article for the Cincinnati *Commercial* dated Nov. 14, 1877, "Memphis to New Orleans," *Occidental Gleanings,* I. **28.** Hearn, *Letters from the Raven,* 42–43.

Chapter 7
POVERTY IN THE SUNSHINE

1. Lafcadio Hearn, *Letters from the Raven: Being the Correspondence of Lafcadio Hearn with Henry Watkin,* Milton Bronner, ed. (New York, 1907), 42. 2. *Ibid.,* 51–52. 3. "The South," Cincinnati *Commercial,* dated from New Orleans Nov. 29, 1877, collected in Hearn, *Occidental Gleanings,* I, Albert Mordell, ed. (New York, 1925), 187. 4. Facsimile of a postal card, Hearn, *Letters from the Raven,* opposite 40. 5. Hearn, "New Orleans," Cincinnati *Commercial,* dated from New Orleans Dec. 21, 1877. Collected in Hearn, *Occidental Gleanings,* I, 232. 6. "New Orleans in Wet Weather," Cincinnati *Commercial.* Collected in Hearn, *Occidental Gleanings,* I, 219–20. 7. Cincinnati *Commercial,* Dec. 7, 1877. 8. "Some Little Creole Songs," Cincinnati *Commercial,* dated from New Orleans, Jan. 1878. Collected in Hearn, *Occidental Gleanings,* I, 271–72. 9. "New Orleans Letter," dated from New Orleans, Jan. 5, 1878. Collected in Hearn, *Occidental Gleanings,* I, 243–44. 10. Copy of Ms. Hearn letter, George M. Gould Collection of Hearniana, Library of Congress. 11. "New Orleans Letter, *op. cit.,* 238–39. 12. Bisland, *Life and Letters,* Hearn, *Writings,* XIII, 155. 13. O. W. Frost, *Young Hearn* (Tokyo, 1958), 182. 14. John S. Kendall, "Lafcadio Hearn in New Orleans," II, *Double Dealer,* Vol. III, No. 18 (June 1922), 314. 15. Bisland, *Life and Letters,* Hearn, *Writings,* XV, 245. 16. Copy of Ms. Hearn letter, Gould Collection, Library of Congress. 17. *Encyclopædia Britannica,* 57th ed. 18. Hearn, *Letters from the Raven,* 54–55. 19. *Ibid.,* 54. 20. Kendall, I, *op. cit.,* 238. 21. Bisland, *Life and Letters,* Hearn, *Writings,* XIII, 72. 22. Ethel Hutson, "Lafcadio Hearn's Cartoons," Preface, Lafcadio Hearn, *Creole Sketches,* Charles W. Hutson, ed. (Boston, 1924), XIX–XX. 23. Hearn, *Letters from the Raven,* 68. 24. *Ibid.,* 64. 25. Quoted in Edward L. Tinker, *Lafcadio Hearn's American Days,* 2nd ed. (New York, 1924), 105. 26. Hearn, *Letters from the Raven,* 67.

Chapter 8
A CREOLE CITY

1. Bisland, *Life and Letters,* Hearn, *Writings,* XIII, 208. 2. *Ibid.,* 176. 3. Lafcadio Hearn, *Letters from the Raven: Being the Correspondence of Lafcadio Hearn with Henry Watkin,* Milton Bronner, ed. (New York, 1907), 57. 4. *Ibid.,* 71. 5. New Orleans *Item,* June 24, 1878. Collected in Lafcadio Hearn, *Editorials: New Orleans Journalistic Writings,* Charles Woodward Hutson, ed. (Boston, 1926), 2–3. 6. New Orleans *Item,* June 25, 1878. Collected in Hearn, *Editorials,* 4. 7. New Orleans *Item,* July 11, 1878. Collected in Hearn, *Editorials,* 17–18. 8. "Jewish Emigrants for Louisiana," New Orleans *Item,* Sept. 20, 1881. Collected in Lafcadio Hearn, *Barbarous Barbers and Other Stories,* Ichiro Nishizaki, ed. (Tokyo, 1939), 156. 9. H. E. Krehbiel, *Afro-American Folksongs* (New York, 1914), 134. 10. Quoted in Oscar Lewis, *Hearn and His Biographers: the Record of a Literary Controversy* (San Francisco, 1930), 74. 11. Bisland, *Life and Letters,* Hearn, *Writings,* XIII, 223. 12. *Ibid.,* 177. 13. *Ibid.* 14. *Ibid.* 15. *Ibid.,* 181. 16. *Ibid.,* 164. 17. *Ibid.,* 164–65. 18. *Ibid.,* 206–08. 19. Collected in Lafcadio Hearn, *Creole Sketches,* Charles W. Hutson, ed. (Boston, 1924), 129. 20. New Orleans *Item,* Oct. 5, 1879. Collected in *The Selected Writings of Lafcadio Hearn,* Henry Goodman, ed. (New

York, 1949), 266. Also in Hearn, *Creole Sketches.* **21.** Aug. 25, 1880. Collected in Hearn, *Creole Sketches,* 70–71. **22.** New Orleans *Item,* July 22, 1881. Hearn, *Creole Sketches,* 199–200. **23.** Ethel Hutson, "Lafcadio Hearn's Cartoons," Preface, Hearn, *Creole Sketches,* XXII. **24.** March 10, 1879. Collected in Lafcadio Hearn, *Buying Christmas Toys and Other Essays,* Ichiro Nishizaki, ed. (Tokyo, 1939), 45. **25.** July 17, 1879. **26.** Hearn, *Creole Sketches,* 14–21. **27.** Bisland, *Life and Letters,* Hearn, *Writings,* XIII, 161–63. **28.** New Orleans *Item,* Sept. 24, 1879. Collected in Lafcadio Hearn, *Fantastics and Other Fancies,* Charles W. Hutson, ed. (Boston, 1914), 33. **29.** "A Dream of Kites," New Orleans *Item,* June 18, 1880. Collected in Hearn, *Fantastics,* 57–59. **30.** "A Dead Love," New Orleans *Item,* Oct. 21, 1880. Collected in Hearn, *Fantastics,* 120. **31.** Bisland, *Life and Letters,* Hearn, *Writings,* XIII, 211–12. **32.** New Orleans *Item.* Collected in Hearn, *Creole Sketches,* 79–81.

Chapter 9
STEPSON TO NEW ORLEANS

1. "Note on the Influence of Finnish Poetry in English Literature," *Books and Habits: From the Lectures of Lafcadio Hearn,* John Erskine, ed. (New York, 1921), 231. **2.** Quoted in Julia Collier Harris, *The Life and Letters of Joel Chandler Harris* (Boston, 1918), 61. **3.** *Ibid.* **4.** Letter to Minnie Atkinson, quoted in Nina H. Kennard, *Lafcadio Hearn: Containing Some Letters from Lafcadio Hearn to His Half-Sister, Mrs. Atkinson* (New York, 1912), 224. **5.** Grace King, *Memories of a Southern Woman of Letters* (New York, 1932), 58. **6.** "The Art of Fiction," in Henry James, *Partial Portraits* (London, 1888), 398. **7.** Letter to H. E. Krehbiel, Bisland, *Life and Letters,* Hearn, *Writings,* XIII, 186. **8.** "Some Fancies About Fancy," March 28, 1881. Collected in Lafcadio Hearn, *Editorials: New Orleans Journalistic Writings,* Charles W. Hutson, ed. (Boston, 1926), 133–34. **9.** *Ibid.,* 135. **10.** "The Sexual Idea in French Literature," June 17, 1881. Collected in Hearn, *Editorials,* 143–44. **11.** "Recent American Novels," June 18, 1881. Collected in Hearn, *Editorials,* 149. **12.** Names and functions from Edward L. Tinker, *Lafcadio Hearn's American Days* (New York, 1924), 148. **13.** Bisland, *Life and Letters,* Hearn, *Writings,* XV, 14. **14.** *Newly Discovered Letters from Lafcadio Hearn to Dr. Rudolph Matas,* Ichiro Nishizaki, ed. (Tokyo, 1956), 113. The item in question is not a word, but a drawing, in Hearn's letter. **15.** In Hearn's introduction to a translation of Alfred de Musset, under "The Foreign Press" in the New Orleans *Times-Democrat,* Oct. 1, 1882. **16.** New Orleans *Times-Democrat.* Collected in Hearn, *Editorials,* 229. **17.** Aug. 27, 1882. Collected in Lafcadio Hearn, *Occidental Gleanings,* II, Albert Mordell, ed. (New York, 1925), 51–52. **18.** Sept. 25, 1882. In Hearn, *Editorials,* 189. **19.** "An Atmosphere About the Moon," Nov. 14, 1882. **20.** "The New Radiance," Sept. 16, 1881. Collected in Lafcadio Hearn, *The New Radiance and Other Scientific Sketches,* Ichiro Nishizaki, ed. (Tokyo, 1939), 1. **21.** June 25, 1882, New Orleans *Times-Democrat.* Collected in Lafcadio Hearn, *Fantastics and Other Fancies,* Charles W. Hutson, ed. (Boston, 1914), 370. **22.** Jan. 10, 1884. Collected in Lafcadio Hearn, *Oriental Articles,* Ichiro Nishizaki, ed. (Tokyo, 1939), 79. **23.** "Letters of a Poet to a Musician: Letters from Hearn to H. E. Krehbiel," *The Critic,* Vol. 48–49 (April 1906), 312. **24.** In Edward L. Tinker, *op. cit.,* 226. Tinker gives very fully the everyday background of Hearn's life at this time. **25.** Lafcadio Hearn, tr., *One of*

Cleopatra's Nights and Other Fantastic Romances, by Théophile Gautier (New York, 1882), XV–XVI. **26.** "The Brahman and His Brahmani," *Stray Leaves from Strange Literature,* Hearn, *Writings,* II, 44. **27.** "The Corpse-Demon," *Stray Leaves,* Hearn, *Writings,* II, 64. **28.** Sept. 1883. Bisland, *Life and Letters,* Hearn, *Writings,* XIII, 271–72. **29.** New Orleans *Times-Democrat.* Collected in Hearn, *Occidental Gleanings,* II, 275–77. **30.** In March 1894. Kennard, *op. cit.,* 222. **31.** Collected in Hearn, *Fantastics,* 150. **32.** Quoted in Tinker, *op. cit.,* 175. **33.** Bisland, *Life and Letters,* Hearn, *Writings,* XV, 196. **34.** *Ibid.,* XIII, 263. **35.** *Ibid.,* 284. **36.** *Ibid.,* 308–10. **37.** *Ibid.,* 312. **38.** *Ibid.,* 322. **39.** The count of his subhuman friends is from Tinker. **40.** Collected in Lafcadio Hearn, *An American Miscellany,* II, Albert Mordell, ed. (New York, 1924), 92–93. **41.** Oct. 26, 1882. Copy of Ms. Hearn letter, George M. Gould Collection of Hearniana, Library of Congress. **42.** Bisland, *Life and Letters,* Hearn, *Writings,* XIII, 301. **43.** *Ibid.,* 307. **44.** From a talk by Rudolph Matas, included in *Lafcadio Hearn in New Orleans: the Dedication of the Lafcadio Hearn Room of the Howard-Tilton Memorial Library* (New Orleans, 1941), 13. **45.** Ms. Hearn letter, Stedman Collection, Columbia University. **46.** From a talk by Rudolph Matas, *op. cit.,* 18. **47.** Oct. 26, 1882. Lafcadio Hearn, *Letters from the Raven: Being the Correspondence of Lafcadio Hearn with Henry Watkin,* Milton Bronner, ed. (New York, 1907), 79.

Chapter 10
THE BEACH AT GRAND ISLE

1. *Chita,* Hearn, *Writings,* IV, 155. **2.** "The Post Office," New Orleans *Times-Democrat,* Oct. 19, 1884. Collected in Hearn, *Fantastics and Other Fancies,* Charles W. Hutson, ed. (Boston, 1914), 229. **3.** Bisland, *Life and Letters,* Hearn, *Writings,* XIII, 81–82. **4.** Copy of Ms. Hearn letter, George M. Gould Collection of Hearniana, Library of Congress. **5.** Quoted in Edward L. Tinker, *Lafcadio Hearn's American Days* (New York, 1924), 217. **6.** *Ibid.,* 218. **7.** *Ibid.* **8.** *Ibid.,* 222. **9.** *Ibid.,* 218. **10.** *Ibid.,* 221. **11.** "Selections from Baudelaire, the Edgar Poe of France," New Orleans *Times-Democrat,* Dec. 31, 1882. **12.** "Torn Letters," New Orleans *Times-Democrat,* Sept. 14, 1884. Collected in Hearn, *An American Miscellany,* II, Albert Mordell, ed. (New York, 1924), 56–57. **13.** Bisland, *Life and Letters,* Hearn, *Writings,* XIII, 81. **14.** Quoted in Tinker, *op. cit.,* 255. **15.** Copy of Ms. Hearn letter to Page Baker, George M. Gould Collection of Hearniana, Library of Congress.

Chapter 11
INTENSIFICATIONS

1. Bisland, *Life and Letters,* Hearn, *Writings,* XIV, 12. **2.** Probably 1881. "Letters of a Poet to a Musician, Letters from Hearn to H. E. Krehbiel," *The Critic,* Vol. 48–49 (April 1906), 313. **3.** Bisland, *Life and Letters,* Hearn, *Writings,* XIII, 282. **4.** *Ibid.,* 332. Jan. 1885. **5.** "The Government Exhibit at New Orleans," *Harper's Weekly,* April 11, 1885. Collected in Hearn, *Occidental Gleanings,* II, Albert Mordell, ed. (New York, 1925), 240. **6.** Collected in *The Selected Writings of Lafcadio Hearn,* Henry Goodman, ed. (New York, 1949), 271. **7.** *Some Chinese Ghosts,* Hearn, *Writings,* I, 287. **8.** *Ibid.,* 215–16. **9.** Letter to Mitchell McDonald from Tokyo, 1898. Bisland, *Life and Letters,* Hearn, *Writings,* XV, 100. **10.** Phrases

25, 26, 126, 177 in Lafcadio Hearn, *Gombo Zhèbes: A Little Dictionary of Creole Proverbs* (New York, 1885). **11.** "The New Orleans Exposition: The Japanese Exhibit," *Harper's Weekly*, Jan. 31, 1885. Collected in Hearn, *Occidental Gleanings*, II, 211. **12.** *Ibid.*, 212. **13.** "To the Fountain of Youth," Collected in *Leaves from the Diary of an Impressionist*, Hearn, *Writings*, I, 3. **14.** *Ibid.*, 17. **15.** Bisland, *Life and Letters*, Hearn, *Writings*, XIII, 339. **16.** New Orleans *Times-Democrat*, Nov. 22, 1885. **17.** Bisland, *Life and Letters*, Hearn, *Writings*, XIII, 371. **18.** *Ibid.*, 230. **19.** *Ibid.*, 374. **20.** "The Market of Guet-N'Dar, Senegal," from *Le Roman d'un Spahi* by Pierre Loti, New Orleans *Democrat*, Nov. 20, 1881. Collected in *Stories from Pierre Loti*, Lafcadio Hearn, translator, Albert Mordell, ed. (Tokyo, 1933), 57. **21.** "Water Colors from Indo-Chinese Seas: Pierre Loti's Sketches," New Orleans *Times-Democrat*, Oct. 12, 1884. **22.** "The Market of Guet-N'Dar, Senegal," *op. cit.*, 55. **23.** "In Algeria," New Orleans *Times-Democrat*, April 1, 1883. Collected in *Stories from Pierre Loti*, 73–74. **24.** Letter to B. H. Chamberlain, Feb. 18, 1893, in *The Japanese Letters of Lafcadio Hearn*, Elizabeth Bisland, ed. (Boston, 1910), 61. **25.** In Lafcadio Hearn, *Editorials: New Orleans Journalistic Writings*, Charles W. Hutson, ed. (Boston, 1926), 324. **26.** New Orleans *Democrat*, Sept. 18, 1881. Collected in Guy de Maupassant, *Saint Anthony and Other Stories*, Lafcadio Hearn, translator, Albert Mordell, ed. (New York, 1924), 20. **27.** To Henry Watkin on Nov. 24, 1882. Lafcadio Hearn, *Letters from the Raven*, Milton Bronner, ed. (New York, 1907), 81. **28.** "Letters of a Poet to a Musician," 314. **29.** Letter of April 7–14, 1887. Bisland, *Life and Letters*, Hearn, *Writings*, XIV, 12. **30.** July 8, 1886. *Newly Discovered Letters from Lafcadio Hearn to Dr. Rudolph Matas*, Ichiro Nishizaki, ed. (Tokyo, 1956), 87. **31.** *Ibid.*, 88. **32.** Bisland, *Life and Letters*, Hearn, *Writings*, XIV, 3. **33.** Review of Hearn's *Some Chinese Ghosts*, *The Nation*, Vol. 44 (May 26, 1887), 456. **34.** Bisland, *Life and Letters*, Hearn, *Writings*, XIV, 4. **35.** *Ibid.*, 5. **36.** Leona Q. Barel, *The Idyl: My Personal Reminiscences of Lafcadio Hearn* (Tokyo, 1933), 24. **37.** July 1, 1887. *Newly Discovered Letters from Lafcadio Hearn to Dr. Rudolph Matas*, 90–91. **38.** Barel, *op. cit.*, 31.

Chapter 12

UNDERNEATH PELÉE

1. June 1888. Bisland, *Life and Letters*, Hearn, *Writings*, XIV, 48. **2.** Lafcadio Hearn, *Letters from the Raven*, Milton Bronner, ed. (New York, 1907), 85. **3.** *Newly Discovered Letters from Lafcadio Hearn to Dr. Rudolph Matas*, Ichiro Nishizaki, ed. (Tokyo, 1956), 90. **4.** Bisland, *Life and Letters*, Hearn, *Writings*, XIV, 32–33. **5.** *Newly Discovered Letters*, 90. **6.** "A Midsummer Trip to the Tropics," *Two Years in the French West Indies*, Hearn, *Writings*, III, 3. **7.** *Ibid.*, 8–9. **8.** *Ibid.*, 15. **9.** *Ibid.*, 16. **10.** *Newly Discovered Letters*, 91. **11.** *Ibid.*, 87. **12.** *Ibid.*, 92. **13.** Bisland, *Life and Letters*, Hearn, *Writings*, XIV, 36–37. **14.** Ms. Hearn letter on microfilm, April 27, 1888. Hearn Collection, Henry E. Huntington Library and Art Gallery, San Marino, California. This collection is used with the permission of Professor Ichiro Nishizaki, Tokyo, Japan. From this collection is derived *New Hearn Letters from the French West Indies*, by Ichiro Nishizaki (Tokyo, 1959). **15.** Ms. Page Baker letter to George M. Gould. Gould Collection of Hearniana, Library of Congress. **16.** *Ibid.* **17.** Sept. 28, 1887. *Newly Discovered Letters*, 108.

18. Bisland, *Life and Letters,* Hearn, *Writings,* XIV, 45.   19. Undated, from St. Pierre. Ms. Hearn letter on microfilm. Hearn Collection, Huntington Library. 20. *Ibid.,* undated, probably Dec. 1887.   21. *Ibid.,* undated.   22. *Ibid.,* from Morne Rouge, Jan. 8, 1888.   23. *Ibid.,* undated, from St. Pierre.   24. *Ibid.*   25. "La Guiablesse," *Two Years in the French West Indies,* Hearn, *Writings,* III, 225. 26. Ms. Hearn letter on microfilm. Hearn Collection, Huntington Library. From St. Pierre, Feb. 8, 1888.   27. *Ibid.,* Aug. 8 and 16, 1888.   28. *Ibid.,* undated. 29. *Two Years in the French West Indies,* Hearn, *Writings,* III, 245.   30. *Ibid.,* 268–69.   31. *Ibid.,* 269.   32. *Ibid.,* 250.   33. *Ibid.,* 259–60.   34. *Ibid.,* 249–50. 35. *Ibid.,* 291.   36. *Ibid.,* 293.   37. An assumption. He does not say typhoid in his own case.   38. Ms. Hearn letter on microfilm. Hearn Collection, Huntington Library.   39. *Ibid.*   40. *Ibid.,* Sept. 13, 1888.   41. *Two Years in the French West Indies,* Hearn, *Writings,* III, 359–60.   42. Ms. Hearn letter on microfilm. Hearn Collection, Huntington Library. From St. Pierre, Aug. 8, 1888.   43. *Two Years in the French West Indies,* Hearn, *Writings,* III, 299.   44. April 30, 1888. *Newly Discovered Letters.* Also copy in Gould Collection of Hearniana, Library of Congress.   45. *Two Years in the French West Indies,* Hearn, *Writings,* IV, 69–70. 46. *Ibid.,* 71–72.   47. *Ibid.,* 110.   48. Ms. Hearn letter on microfilm. Hearn Collection, Huntington Library. Undated, probably fall, 1888.   49. *Newly Discovered Letters,* 117.

Chapter 13
CYCLOPEAN STREETS

1. *Kokoro,* Hearn, *Writings,* VII, 277.   2. Bisland, *Life and Letters,* Hearn, *Writings,* XIV, 70–71.   3. *Ibid.,* 54.   4. *Ibid.,* 20.   5. *Ibid.,* 60.   6. *Ibid.,* 61.   7. Ms. Hearn letter on microfilm. E. C. Stedman Collection, Columbia University.   8. April 1889. Bisland, *Life and Letters,* Hearn, *Writings,* XIV, 69.   9. *Ibid.,* 75.   10. *Ibid.,* 74. 11. Ms. Hearn letter on microfilm. Stedman Collection, Columbia University. 12. *Ibid.*   13. July 3, 1889. Ms. Hearn letter on microfilm. Hearn Collection, Henry E. Huntington Library and Art Gallery, San Marino, California.   14. Ms. Hearn letter on microfilm. Stedman Collection, Columbia University.   15. George M. Gould, "Lafcadio Hearn," Chapter VI, *Biographic Clinics,* IV (Philadelphia, 1906), 223.   16. Ms. Hearn letter on microfilm. Stedman Collection, Columbia University. 17. Oct. 17, 1889. *Ibid.*   18. Ms. Joseph Tunison letter. Gould Collection, Library of Congress.   19. J. Henry Harper, *I Remember* (New York, 1934), 175. Harper misdated the occasion as January 1889. It was January 1890.   20. *Ibid.,* 175–76. 21. [William Dean Howells], Review of *Youma,* in "Editor's Study," *Harper's Magazine,* Vol. 81 (Sept. 1890), 642.   22. Ms. Hearn letter on microfilm. Stedman Collection, Columbia University.   23. *Ibid.*   24. Nov. 1889. *Ibid.*   25. *Ibid.*   26. Bisland, *Life and Letters,* Hearn, *Writings,* XIV, 97. Elizabeth Bisland printed the letter as To ———.   27. October 17, 1889. Ms. Hearn letter on microfilm. Stedman Collection, Columbia University.   28. *Ibid.* Nov. 1889.   29. *Ibid.,* undated, from W. Tenth St., New York City.   30. Ellwood Hendrick, "Lafcadio Hearn," *The Nation,* Vol. 116 (April 11, 1923), 432.   31. Ellwood Hendrick, *Percolator Papers* (New York, 1919), 190.   32. *Ibid.*   33. Ellwood Hendrick, "Lafcadio Hearn as a Blue Ghost," *Boston Evening Transcript,* Book Section, Feb. 7, 1931.   34. Henry Tracy Kneeland, "Lafcadio Hearn's Brother," *Atlantic Monthly,* Vol. 131, No. 1 (Jan.

1923), 22. **35.** *Ibid.* **36.** E. C. Beck, "Letters of Lafcadio Hearn to His Brother," *The English Journal,* Vol. 20 (1931), 289. **37.** *Ibid.,* 290–91. **38.** *Ibid.,* 292. **39.** Kneeland, *op. cit.* **40.** Quoted in Edward L. Tinker, *Lafcadio Hearn's American Days* (New York, 1924), 328–29. **41.** *Ibid.,* 334–35. **42.** Quoted in Vera McWilliams, *Lafcadio Hearn* (Boston, 1946), 257. **43.** Jan. 1899. Bisland, *Life and Letters,* Hearn, *Writings,* XV, 159–60. **44.** Bisland, *Life and Letters,* Hearn, *Writings,* XIV, 98. Elizabeth Bisland identified this letter only as To ——. **45.** *Ibid.,* 101. Letter of March 7–Sept. 9, 1890. Again identified by the editor and recipient, Elizabeth Bisland, as To ——. **46.** Lafcadio Hearn, "A Ghost," *Harper's Magazine,* Dec. 1889, 61. **47.** *Ibid.,* 59.

Chapter 14
YOKOHAMA: ANTEROOM TO JAPAN

1. *The Japanese Letters of Lafcadio Hearn,* Elizabeth Bisland, ed. (Boston, 1910), 5. **2.** *Glimpses of Unfamiliar Japan,* Hearn, *Writings,* V, 4–10. **3.** *Ibid.,* 10–11. **4.** *Ibid.,* 19–20. **5.** *Ibid.,* 6. **6.** *Ibid.,* 34. **7.** *Ibid.,* 77. **8.** *Ibid.,* 88. **9.** *Ibid.,* 91. **10.** *Ibid.,* 88. **11.** May 25, 1894. *Japanese Letters,* 313. **12.** *Letters from the Raven: Being the Correspondence of Lafcadio Hearn with Henry Watkin,* Milton Bronner, ed. (New York, 1907), 94. **13.** *Japanese Letters,* 311. **14.** *Ibid.* **15.** *Ibid.* **16.** Typewritten, signed letter, dated Oct. 27, 1890, in Hearn Collection, Tenri College Library, Tenri, Japan. Addressed only to "Mr. McNicoll," evidently an employee of the Canadian Pacific Railway. **17.** Ms. Hearn letter on microfilm, undated. Hearn Collection, Henry E. Huntington Library and Art Gallery, San Marino, California. **18.** *Ibid.* **19.** Ms. Hearn letter, Harper Collection, The Pierpont Morgan Library, New York City. **20.** Ms. Alden letter. George M. Gould Collection of Hearniana, Library of Congress. **21.** Ms. Hearn letter on microfilm. E. C. Stedman Collection, Columbia University. **22.** Quoted in Oscar Lewis, *Hearn and His Biographers* (San Francisco, 1930), 9–12. **23.** *Japanese Letters,* 4. **24.** Edward B. Clarke, *Stray Leaves: Essays and Sketches* (Tokyo, 1936), 4. **25.** *Ibid.,* 5. **26.** *Ibid.,* 8. **27.** *Ibid.,* 9. **28.** *Japanese Letters,* 6. June 9, 1890. **29.** *Ibid.* **30.** Bisland, *Life and Letters,* Hearn, *Writings,* XIV, 102–05. Parts of two letters. **31.** Conversation, Professor Yasuyuki Kajitani, adviser to the Lafcadio Hearn Museum, Matsue, Shimane Prefecture, Japan. **32.** "Bon-Odori," *Glimpses,* Hearn, *Writings,* V, 139. **33.** *Ibid.,* 154. **34.** *Ibid.,* 138.

Chapter 15
LAND OF THE GODS

1. Bisland, *Life and Letters,* Hearn, *Writings,* XIV, 147. **2.** Conversation, Mrs. O-tani (Yasuda) Uya, in Kitzuki, Japan, Oct. 1959. **3.** *Glimpses of Unfamiliar Japan,* Hearn, *Writings,* V, 242–43. **4.** May 22, 1891. *The Japanese Letters of Lafcadio Hearn,* Elizabeth Bisland, ed. (Boston, 1910), 10–11. **5.** Bisland, *Life and Letters,* Hearn, *Writings,* XIV, 114. **6.** "In a Japanese Garden," *Glimpses,* Hearn, *Writings,* VI, 3. **7.** *Glimpses,* Hearn, *Writings,* V, 140. **8.** Bisland, *Life and Letters,* Hearn, *Writings,* XIV, 125–26. **9.** Setsuko Koizumi, *Reminiscences of Lafcadio Hearn,* Paul Kiyoshi Hisada and Frederick Johnson, translators (Boston, 1918), 6. **10.** *Ibid.,* 8–9. **11.** *Ibid.,* 9–10. **12.** Hearn Ms. letter, 1891. Hearn Collection, New York Public Library. Ellwood Hendrick divided his letters from Hearn and gave

some to the NYPL and some to the Century Association, New York City. **13.**
Hearn Ms. letter, dated Nov. 17, 1892. Hearn Collection, The Century Association,
New York City. **14.** Bisland, *Life and Letters,* Hearn, *Writings,* XIV, 137. **15.**
Setsuko Koizumi, *op. cit.,* 12–13.

Chapter 16
KITABORI

1. *Glimpses of Unfamiliar Japan,* Hearn, *Writings,* VI, 48. **2.** Setsuko Koizumi,
Reminiscences of Lafcadio Hearn, Paul Kiyoshi Hisada and Frederick Johnson,
translators (Boston, 1918), 11. **3.** *Ibid.* **4.** *Ibid.,* 11–12. **5.** *Glimpses,* Hearn,
Writings, VI, 149–50. **6.** *Ibid.,* 150–52. **7.** Not in collected *Writings.* See appendix
to original edition, Lafcadio Hearn, *Kokoro* (Houghton, 1896), 327–31. **8.**
Glimpses, Hearn, *Writings,* V, 359–60. **9.** *Ibid.,* 249–50. **10.** *Ibid.,* 262–63. **11.**
Ibid., 221. **12.** Bisland, *Life and Letters,* Hearn, *Writings,* XIV, 128. **13.** Setsuko
Koizumi, *op. cit.,* 15. **14.** *Ibid.,* 17. **15.** Ms. Hearn letter, dated Oct. 7, 1891. Hearn
Collection, New York Public Library. **16.** *Glimpses,* Hearn, *Writings,* VI, 394–96.

Chapter 17
BUDDHA ON A HILLSIDE

1. *The Japanese Letters of Lafcadio Hearn,* Elizabeth Bisland, ed. (Boston, 1910),
185. **2.** Masujiro Honda, review of *The Japanese Letters of Lafcadio Hearn, The
Oriental Economic Review,* Vol. 1, No. 3 (Dec. 10, 1910), 43–44. **3.** *Some New
Letters and Writings of Lafcadio Hearn,* Sanki Ichikawa, ed. (Tokyo, 1925), 34. **4.**
The complete working out of this train of thought I owe to Professor Masayuki
Kawarabata, of the Faculty of Law and Literature, Kumamoto University, Kuma-
moto, Kyushu, Japan, in a letter written to me on Nov. 23, 1959. The letter sum-
marizes his ideas more fully expressed in an article in Japanese, published as a
monograph in Japan, with the English subtitle "Three Years' Experience of Dis-
comfort," a quotation from one of Hearn's letters. **5.** *Some New Letters,* 21. **6.**
Ms. Hearn letter undated, probably 1891. Barrett Collection, University of Virginia.
Also in *Some New Letters,* 22. **7.** *Some New Letters,* 23. **8.** Ms. Hearn letter.
Barrett Collection, University of Virginia. **9.** Bisland, *Life and Letters,* Hearn,
Writings, XIV, 171. **10.** *Ibid.* **11.** *Ibid.,* 175. **12.** Ms. Hearn letter. Fujisaki Col-
lection. Houghton Library, Harvard University. **13.** *Ibid.,* Feb. 27, 1892. **14.** *Ibid.,*
Jan. 29, 1892, and March 16, 1892. **15.** Ms. copy of Hearn letters to Otani, letter No.
10, undated. Hearn Collection, Tokyo University. **16.** Honda, *op. cit.,* 45. **17.**
"With Kyushu Students," *Out of the East,* Hearn, *Writings,* VII, 31. **18.** To
Nishida in 1891. Bisland, *Life and Letters,* Hearn, *Writings,* XIV, 169. **19.** Ms.
Hearn letter to Adzukizawa, March 7, 1892. Fujisaki Collection. Houghton Library,
Harvard University. **20.** *Out of the East,* Hearn, *Writings,* VII, 26. **21.** Ms. Hearn
letter. Barrett Collection, University of Virginia. **22.** *Out of the East,* Hearn,
Writings, VII, 3. **23.** *Japanese Letters,* 97–98. **24.** Bisland, *Life and Letters,*
Hearn, *Writings,* XIV, 216. **25.** Ms. Hearn letter. Barrett Collection, University
of Virginia. **26.** Copy of Hearn letter, dated June 2, 1892. Gould Collection of
Hearniana, Library of Congress. **27.** Quoted in Oscar Lewis, *Hearn and His
Biographers, The Record of a Literary Controversy with a Group of Letters from
Lafcadio Hearn to Joseph Tunison Now First Published* (San Francisco, 1930),

13–15. **28.** Quoted in Nina H. Kennard, *Lafcadio Hearn, Containing Some Letters from Lafcadio Hearn to His Half-Sister, Mrs. Atkinson* (New York, 1912), 205. **29.** *Ibid.,* 212. **30.** *Ibid.,* 214–15. **31.** On May 12, 1893. *Japanese Letters,* 97. **32.** *Ibid.,* 406. July 30, 1892. **33.** *Ibid.,* 407. **34.** In the Lafcadio Hearn Museum, Matsue, Shimane Prefecture, Japan. Others have survived and are preserved in the Barrett Collection, University of Virginia. **35.** *Japanese Letters,* 408. **36.** *Ibid.,* 202. **37.** *Ibid.,* 411–13. To Mason, Aug. 6, 1892. **38.** Setsuko Koizumi, *Reminiscences of Lafcadio Hearn,* Paul Kiyoshi Hisada and Frederick Johnson, translators (Boston, 1918), 21–23. Mrs. Hearn thought the journey took place in 1893, but it was the trip of 1892. She did not travel in 1893 owing to her first pregnancy. **39.** Bisland, *Life and Letters,* Hearn, *Writings,* XIV, 216, 236. **40.** *Japanese Letters,* 433–34. **41.** Ms. Hearn letter dated Aug. 26, 1893. Barrett Collection, University of Virginia. **42.** "At a Railway Station," *Kokoro,* Hearn, *Writings,* VII. **43.** "On a Bridge," *A Japanese Miscellany,* Hearn, *Writings,* X, 350–51. **44.** *Japanese Letters,* 62. **45.** *Some New Letters,* 71. **46.** *Japanese Letters,* 35–37. **47.** Bisland, *Life and Letters,* Hearn, *Writings,* XIV, 206. **48.** *Ibid.,* 213. **49.** Ms. Hearn letter, Hearn Collection, New York Public Library. **50.** Ms. Hearn letter, Hearn Collection. The Century Association, New York City. **51.** *Ibid.* **52.** *Out of the East,* Hearn, *Writings,* VII, 5. **53.** Setsuko Koizumi, *op. cit.,* 8. **54.** Bisland, *Life and Letters,* Hearn, *Writings,* XIV, 257–61. **55.** *Ibid.,* 285. **56.** *Japanese Letters,* 340. **57.** *Ibid.* **58.** *Ibid.,* 350. **59.** Ms. Hearn letter. Hearn Collection, New York Public Library. **60.** *Japanese Letters,* 342. **61.** *Ibid.,* 347. **62.** *Ibid.,* 349. **63.** *Ibid.,* 353. **64.** *Ibid.* **65.** *Ibid.,* 354. **66.** *Ibid.,* 358–59. **67.** *Ibid.,* 359. **68.** Ms. Hearn letter, dated May 15, 1896. Hearn Collection, New York Public Library. **69.** *Japanese Letters,* 388. **70.** *Ibid.,* 384. **71.** *Ibid.,* 331. Letter dated June 24, 1894.

Chapter 18
A KOBE VIEW

1. Bisland, *Life and Letters,* Hearn, *Writings,* XIV, 311. **2.** *Some New Letters and Writings of Lafcadio Hearn,* Sanki Ichikawa, ed. (Tokyo, 1925), 132. **3.** *Ibid.,* 133–34. Oct. 23, 1894. **4.** Robert Young, "Lafcadio Hearn," *The Living Age,* Vol. 252 (March 23, 1907), 760. **5.** *The Japanese Letters of Lafcadio Hearn,* Elizabeth Bisland, ed. (Boston, 1910), 391. **6.** Young, *op. cit.,* 761. **7.** *Ibid.* **8.** Bisland, *Life and Letters,* Hearn, *Writings,* XIV, 298. **9.** *Ibid.,* 307–08. **10.** *Ibid.,* 331. **11.** *Japanese Letters,* 340–41. **12.** Bisland, *Life and Letters,* Hearn, *Writings,* XIV, 319. **13.** *Ibid.,* 321. **14.** *Ibid.,* 326. **15.** *Ibid.,* 331. **16.** *Ibid.,* 331–32. **17.** *Japanese Letters,* 232. To Chamberlain, Jan. 27, 1894. **18.** Bisland, *Life and Letters,* Hearn, *Writings,* XIV, 359–60. **19.** *Ibid.,* 310. **20.** Ms. Hearn letter to Ellwood Hendrick, dated Sept. 30, 1894. Hearn Collection, New York Public Library. **21.** *Japanese Letters,* 41. **22.** *Ibid.,* 62. **23.** Ms. Hearn letter. Hearn Collection, New York Public Library. **24.** *Ibid.* **25.** *Ibid.* **26.** Bisland, *Life and Letters,* Hearn, *Writings,* XV, 5–6. **27.** *Ibid.,* 6. **28.** Ms. Toyama letter. Barrett Collection, University of Virginia. **29.** *Ibid.* **30.** *Japanese Letters,* 225. **31.** Nobushige Amenomori, "Lafcadio Hearn, the Man," the *Atlantic Monthly,* Vol. 96 (July 1905), 517. **32.** *Japanese Letters,* 232–33. **33.** Bisland, *Life and Letters,* Hearn, *Writings,* XIV, 384–85. **34.** "Recent Books on Japan," the *Atlantic Monthly,* Vol. 75 (June 1895), 830. **35.** *Out* of the East, Hearn, *Writings*, VII, 111. **36.** *Japanese Letters*, 387. **37.** *Ibid.*, 391. **38.** Ms. Toyama letter. Barrett Collection, University of Virginia. **39.** Lafcadio Hearn, "Notes of a Trip to Izumo," the *Atlantic Monthly*, Vol. 79 (May 1897), 678. **40.** *Ibid.*, 679. **41.** *Ibid.* **42.** *Ibid.*, 680. **43.** *Ibid.*, 680–81. **44.** Bisland, *Life and Letters*, Hearn, *Writings*, XV, 34. Aug. 1896. **45.** Hearn, "Notes of a Trip to Izumo," 687.

Chapter 19

THE CEDARS OF KOBUDERA

1. March 1898. Bisland, *Life and Letters*, Hearn, *Writings*, XV, 99. **2.** Ernest Foxwell, "Reminiscences of Lafcadio Hearn," Japan Society, *Transactions and Proceedings*, Session 17, Vol. 8 (London 1908), 84. **3.** Hakucho Masamune, "New Light on Lafcadio Hearn," *Contemporary Japan*, Vol. 2 (Tokyo, 1933), 280. **4.** Mock Joya, "Hearn Sen-Sei, Memories of Lafcadio Hearn," *Bookman*, Vol. 39, No. 2 (April 1914), 176. **5.** Preface, Lafcadio Hearn, *On Poets*, R. Tanabe and others, eds. (Tokyo, 1934), IV. **6.** *Ibid.* **7.** *Ibid.*, IV–V. **8.** *Ibid.*, V. **9.** To Mitchell McDonald, Feb. 1899. Bisland, *Life and Letters*, Hearn, *Writings*, XV, 165–66. **10.** Foreword, dated Aug. 1920, Lafcadio Hearn, *Letters from Tokyo*, M. Otani, ed. (Tokyo, 1920), 6–7. **11.** To Ellwood Hendrick, Oct. 1896. Bisland, *Life and Letters*, Hearn, *Writings*, XV, 41. **12.** Jan. 10, 1897. Ms. Hearn letter. Hearn Collection, New York Public Library. **13.** *Ibid.* **14.** Ernest Foxwell, *op. cit.*, 68. **15.** *Ibid.*, 69–70. **16.** *Ibid.*, 75. **17.** *Ibid.*, 76. **18.** Foreword, *Letters from B. H. Chamberlain to Lafcadio Hearn*, Kazuo Koizumi, comp. (Tokyo, 1936), i. **19.** *More Letters from Basil Hall Chamberlain*, Kazuo Koizumi, ed. (Tokyo, 1937), 108. **20.** Bisland, *Life and Letters*, Hearn, *Writings*, XIV, 379. **21.** *Ibid.*, XV, 181. **22.** *Ibid.*, 108–09. **23.** Kazuo Koizumi, *Father and I, Memories of Lafcadio Hearn* (Boston, 1935), 155. **24.** March 1898. Bisland, *Life and Letters*, Hearn, *Writings*, XV, 97–98. **25.** The report is held in the Barrett Collection, University of Virginia. **26.** *In Ghostly Japan*, Hearn, *Writings*, IX, 367. **27.** *Exotics and Retrospectives*, Hearn, *Writings*, IX, 11–12. **28.** *Kwaidan*, Hearn, *Writings*, XI. **29.** *Shadowings*, Hearn, *Writings*, X, 19. **30.** Aug. 1897. Bisland, *Life and Letters*, Hearn, *Writings*, XV, 64–66. **31.** *Ibid.*, 64. **32.** *Ibid.*, 66. **33.** "Ululation," *In Ghostly Japan*, Hearn, *Writings*, IX, 300. **34.** "Songs of Japanese Children," *A Japanese Miscellany*, Hearn, *Writings*, X, 284. **35.** Lafcadio Hearn, *Interpretations of Literature*, I, John Erskine, ed. (New York, 1915), 65–66. **36.** *Ibid.*, 190. **37.** Lafcadio Hearn, *Talks to Writers*, John Erskine, ed. (New York, 1927), 215. **38.** Jan. 1900. Bisland, *Life and Letters*, Hearn, *Writings*, XV, 202. **39.** June 30, 1899. *Some New Letters and Writings of Lafcadio Hearn*, Sanki Ichikawa, ed. (Tokyo, 1925), 253. **40.** Yone Noguchi, *Lafcadio Hearn in Japan . . . With Mrs. Hearn's Reminiscences* (London and Yokohama, 1910), 39. **41.** Hearn, *Interpretations of Literature*, I, 43. **42.** Kazuo Koizumi, *op. cit.*, 144. **43.** *Ibid.*, 69. **44.** Setsuko Koizumi, *Reminiscences of Lafcadio Hearn*, Paul Kiyoshi Hisada and Frederick Johnson, translators (Boston, 1918), 51. **45.** Kazuo Koizumi, *op. cit.*, 61. **46.** *Ibid.*, 75. **47.** Nobushige Amenomori, "Lafcadio Hearn, the Man," the *Atlantic Monthly*, Vol. 96 (July 1905), 524. **48.** Setsuko Koizumi, *op. cit.*, 47. **49.** *Ibid.*, 33. **50.** Kazuo Koizumi, *op. cit.*, 11. **51.** Bisland, *Life and Letters*, Hearn,

Writings, XV, 106. **52.** Amenomori, *op. cit.,* 518. **53.** Setsuko Koizumi, *op. cit.,* **3. 54.** Varying versions in Setsuko Koizumi, *Reminiscences,* 28–29, and in Nobushige Amenomori, "Lafcadio Hearn, the Man," 519.

Chapter 20
FINAL ADDRESS

1. Setsuko Koizumi, *Reminiscences of Lafcadio Hearn,* Paul Kiyoshi Hisada and Frederick Johnson, translators (Boston, 1918), 31. **2.** *Ibid.,* 37–38. **3.** *Ibid.,* 38–39. **4.** *Kotto,* Hearn, *Writings,* XI, 3. **5.** *Ibid.,* 145. **6.** *Ibid.,* 147. **7.** *Ibid.,* 148–49. **8.** Hearn Ms. Barrett Collection, University of Virginia. **9.** Lafcadio Hearn, *Talks to Writers,* John Erskine, ed. (New York, 1927), 149. **10.** As in "General Gossip of Authors and Writers," *Current Literature,* Vol. 26 (Oct. 1899), 310. **11.** In Yone Noguchi, *Lafcadio Hearn in Japan* (London and Yokohama, 1910), 137–44. **12.** To Elizabeth Bisland, Nov. 1902. Bisland, *Life and Letters,* Hearn, *Writings,* XV, 225–26. **13.** *Ibid.,* 227. **14.** *Ibid.,* 228. **15.** *Ibid.,* 108. **16.** Setsuko Koizumi, *op. cit.,* 40. **17.** Bisland, *Life and Letters,* Hearn, *Writings,* XV, 233. **18.** *Ibid.,* 243–44. **19.** Setsuko Koizumi, *op. cit.,* 46. **20.** Kazuo Koizumi, *Father and I, Memories of Lafcadio Hearn* (Boston, 1935), 165. **21.** Setsuko Koizumi, *op. cit.,* 67. **22.** Kazuo Koizumi, *Re-Echo* (Caldwell, Idaho, 1957), 114. **23.** *Ibid.,* 126. **24.** *Ibid.,* 83. **25.** Kazuo Koizumi, *Father and I,* 99–100. **26.** *Ibid.,* 100–01. **27.** Autograph Hartog letter. Barrett Collection, University of Virginia. **28.** *The Japanese Letters of Lafcadio Hearn,* Elizabeth Bisland, ed. (Boston, 1910), 323. The letters to Mrs. Hearn were written first in simple Japanese by Lafcadio Hearn. For inclusion in the book, they were translated into English. **29.** *Ibid.,* 328. **30.** *Ibid.,* 329. **31.** Setsuko Koizumi, *op. cit.,* 41. **32.** *Ibid.,* 42. Mrs. Hearn mistakenly identified the work in process as *In Ghostly Japan.* It was Hearn's last book, *Japan, An . . . Interpretation.* **33.** *Ibid.,* 73. **34.** *Ibid.,* 74. **35.** *Ibid.,* 82. **36.** *Ibid.* **37.** Kazuo Koizumi, *Father and I,* 208. **38.** Clipping from a Tokyo English-language newspaper the week of Hearn's death. Barrett Collection, University of Virginia. **39.** Kazuo Koizumi, *Father and I,* 126. **40.** Nobushige Amenomori, "Lafcadio Hearn, the Man," the *Atlantic Monthly,* Vol. 96 (July 1905), 523. **41.** Makoto Sangu, "Lafcadio Hearn in Japan," *Today's Japan,* Vol. 4, No. 1 (Jan. 1959), 70.

Selective Bibliography

1. LAFCADIO HEARN COLLECTIONS

In the United States

Fujisaki Collection, Houghton Library, Harvard University. Twenty-three Ms. letters of Hearn to Adzukizawa (later Fujisaki), also miscellaneous letters, autographs, articles, books pertaining to Hearn.

Hearn Collection, a part of the C. Waller Barrett Collection, Alderman Library, University of Virginia. Ms. letters of Hearn to Chamberlain, Mason, Nishida, Ochiai, Toyama, University of London, etc., as well as a number of Hearn's pencil notebooks, photographs, clippings, books by and on Hearn.

Hearn Collection, Rare Book Room, the Public Library of Cincinnati and Hamilton County. The only complete edition of *Ye Giglampz*, also catalogues of Hearn's writings, books and articles on Hearn and by him. The library holds the files of the Cincinnati *Enquirer* and the Cincinnati *Commercial* during the 1870's.

Lafcadio Hearn Room and Hearn Collection, Howard-Tilton Memorial Library, Tulane University. Photographs, Mss. of Hearn books, books by and on Hearn. The library holds some of the surviving files of the New Orleans *Item* and a more complete file of the New Orleans *Democrat* and New Orleans *Times-Democrat* of Hearn's period.

Hearn Collection, the Century Association, New York City. Ms. Hearn letters to Ellwood Hendrick. Hendrick divided his Hearn letters between the Century Association and the New York Public Library.

Hearn Collection, New York Public Library. Forty Ms. Hearn letters to Ellwood Hendrick.

Edmund Clarence Stedman Collection, Columbia University. Forty Ms. Hearn letters and notes, chiefly addressed to Dr. George M. Gould.

Harper Collection, Pierpont Morgan Library. Four Ms. Hearn letters or notes to Harper & Brothers and a memo of sales, March 5, to Sept. 10, 1890.

Hearn Collection, Henry E. Huntington Library and Art Gallery. Approximately forty Ms. Hearn letters, mostly to Henry M. Alden.

Harper & Brothers papers, Library of Congress. Autograph letter from Henry M. Alden to Hearn, dated June 3, 1890.

Ticknor papers, Library of Congress. Ms. Hearn letter to Benjamin H. Ticknor, dated June 13, 1885.

George M. Gould Collection of Hearniana (11 boxes), Library of Congress. Some Ms. Hearn letters and scraps of letters as well as copies Gould made of Ms. Hearn letters he had examined, and letters to Gould from Hearn's friends and enemies, clippings, reviews, much miscellaneous matter connected with the struggle for Hearn's books after his death.

In Japan

Lafcadio Hearn Museum, Matsue, Shimane Prefecture. Contains personal relics and Mss. as well as books by and on Hearn. Adjoining is the Hearn house and garden, Kitabori, preserved as a National Historic Shrine.

Hearn materials owned by Professor Yasuyuki Kajitani, Matsue, adviser to the Lafcadio Hearn Museum. Photographs, teaching contract, photostat of Hearn letter, pamphlets on Hearn.

Hearn Collection, Tenri Central Library, Tenri College, Tenri City, Nara Prefecture. Books by and on Hearn, P. D. Perkins' exhaustive correspondence concerning Hearn with many of the writer's contemporaries and Hearn scholars, clippings, and other miscellaneous material.

Hearn Collection, Department of Literature Building, Tokyo University. Bound volume of mostly unpublished Hearn letters in manuscript (not Hearn's writing) to M. Otani, books in English and Japanese on Hearn and by him. Portrait of Hearn.

2. BIBLIOGRAPHIES

Frost, O. W., comp., *The Early Writings of Lafcadio Hearn, A Bibliography*. Typewritten list compiled by O. W. Frost for the Public Library of Cincinnati and Hamilton County. Champaign, Ill., 1953.

Lafcadio Hearn, 1850–1904 (bibliographical article). *Literary History of the United States: Bibliography*, Robert E. Spiller and others, eds. New York, The Macmillan Co., 1948, pp. 556–59.

Perkins, P. D., *Lafcadio Hearn: A Bibliography of His Writings*. Boston, Houghton Mifflin Co., 1934.

Stedman, Laura, bibliography appended to Gould, George M., *Concerning Lafcadio Hearn*. Philadelphia, G. W. Jacobs & Co., 1908.

Toyama High School, Toyama, Japan (now Toyama University), *Catalogue of the Lafcadio Hearn Library in the Toyama High School, Toyama, Japan, 1927*. Toyama, Toyama High School, 1927.

Descriptive Catalogue of Hearniana in the Hearn Library of the Toyama University. Toyama, Japan, Toyama University Library, 1959 (in Japanese and English).

3. PERIODICALS CONTAINING HEARN'S MAJOR JOURNALISTIC WRITINGS

Atlantic Monthly: 1891–97, 1903–06.
Century Magazine: 1883 (one article only)
Cincinnati *Enquirer:* 1872–75
Cincinnati *Commercial:* 1875–77
Cosmopolitan Magazine: 1890 (two articles)
Harper's Bazar: 1885 (two articles)
Harper's Magazine: 1888–90
Harper's Weekly: 1883–86
Kobe *Chronicle:* 1894–95
Lippincott's Magazine: 1890 (one article only)
New Orleans *Item:* 1878–81
New Orleans *Democrat:* 1880–81
New Orleans *Times-Democrat:* 1881–87
New York *Tribune:* 1886 (one article only)
Southern Bivouac: 1886 (one article only)
Ye Giglampz: June–August, 1874

4. BOOKS AND ARTICLES PERTAINING TO LAFCADIO HEARN

Primary

Amenomori, Nobushige, "Lafcadio Hearn, the Man." *Atlantic Monthly,* Vol. 96 (July 1905), 510–25.

Barel, Leona Q., *The Idyl: My Personal Reminiscences of Lafcadio Hearn.* Tokyo, Hokuseido Press, 1933.

Beck, E. C., "Letters of Lafcadio Hearn to His Brother." *The English Journal,* Vol. 20 (1931), 287–92.

Black, Alexander, "The Camera," *The Latest Thing and Other Things.* New York, Harper & Brothers, 1922, 171–76.

Chamberlain, B. H., *Letters from Basil Hall Chamberlain,* Kazuo Koizumi, ed. Tokyo, Hokuseido Press, 1936.

———, *More Letters from Basil Hall Chamberlain,* Kazuo Koizumi, ed. Tokyo, Hokuseido Press, 1937.

Clarke, Edward B., *Stray Leaves: Essays and Sketches.* Tokyo, Kenkyusha Co., 1936.

Cockerill, John A., "Lafcadio Hearn: the Author of *Kokoro.*" *Current Literature,* Vol. XIX, No. 6 (June 1896), 476.

Edwards, Osman, "Lafcadio Hearn on the Decadent School." *Craftsman,* Vol. 13 (Oct. and Nov. 1907), 14–21.

———, "Some Unpublished Letters of Lafcadio Hearn." Japan Society *Transactions and Proceedings,* Vols. 16–17 (1920), 16–35.

Emerson, Margaret, "Lafcadio Hearn's Funeral." *Critic,* Vol. 46 (Jan. 1905).

Forman, Benjamin, "Recollections of Lafcadio Hearn." *The Stylus.* Austin, Tex., March 1912.

Foxwell, Ernest, "Reminiscences of Lafcadio Hearn." Japan Society *Transactions and Proceedings,* Vol. 8 (1908), 68–94.

"A Glimpse of Lafcadio Hearn—General Gossip of Authors and Writers." *Current Literature,* Vol. 26 (Oct. 1899), 310.

Gould, George M., "Lafcadio Hearn," *Biographic Clinics,* IV. Philadelphia, Blakiston Co., 1906, 209–37.

———, *Concerning Lafcadio Hearn.* Philadelphia, George W. Jacobs & Co., 1908.

———, "Lafcadio Hearn: A Study of His Personality and Art." *Fortnightly Review,* Vol. 86 (n.s. Vol. 80) (July–Dec. 1906), 685–95, 881–92.

Greenslet, Ferris, *Under the Bridge.* Boston, Houghton, 1943.

Harper, J. Henry, *The House of Harper.* New York, Harper & Brothers, 1912.

———, *I Remember.* New York, Harper & Brothers, 1934.

Harris, Julia C., *The Life and Letters of Joel Chandler Harris.* Boston, Houghton Mifflin Co. 1918.

Hendrick, Ellwood, "Lafcadio Hearn." *Nation,* Vol. 116 (April 11, 1923), 432–33.

———, *Lafcadio Hearn* (reprint from *Bulletin* of the New York Public Library). New York, the New York Public Library, 1929.

———, "Lafcadio Hearn as a Blue Ghost." *Boston Evening Transcript,* Book Section, Feb. 7, 1931, 1.

———, "Lafcadio Hearn Traduced." *New York Times,* May 14, 1908.

———, *Percolator Papers.* New York, Harper & Brothers, 1919.

Honda, Masujiro, review, *The Japanese Letters of Lafcadio Hearn. The Oriental Economic Review,* Vol. 1, No. 3 (Dec. 10, 1910), 43–45.

Ichikawa, Sanki, "New Lafcadio Hearn Letters." *Living Age,* Vol. 330 (1926), 366–72.

Joya, Mock, "Days with Lafcadio Hearn." *Lippincott's Magazine,* Vol. XCV, No. 567 (March 1915), 85–91.

———, "Hearn Sen-Sei: Memories of Lafcadio Hearn." *Bookman,* Vol. XXXIX, No. 2 (April 1914), 172–78.

Kendall, John S., "Lafcadio Hearn in New Orleans, I, On the *Item." Double Dealer,* Vol. III, No. 17 (May 1922), 234–42.

———, "Lafcadio Hearn in New Orleans, II, On the *Times-Democrat." Double Dealer,* Vol. III, No. 18 (June 1922), 313–23.

Kennard, Nina H., *Lafcadio Hearn: Containing Some Letters from Lafcadio Hearn to His Half-Sister, Mrs. Atkinson.* New York, D. Appleton & Co., 1912.

Kneeland, Henry T., "Lafcadio Hearn's Brother." *Atlantic Monthly,* Vol. 131, No. 1 (Jan. 1923), 20–27.

Koizumi, Kazuo, *Father and I: Memories of Lafcadio Hearn.* Boston, Houghton Mifflin Co., 1935.

———, *Re-Echo.* Caldwell, Idaho, The Caxton Printers, 1957.

Koizumi, Setsuko, *Reminiscences of Lafcadio Hearn,* Paul Kiyoshi Hisada and Frederick Johnson, translators. Boston, Houghton Mifflin Co., 1918.

Krehbiel, H. E., *Afro-American Folk-Songs.* New York, G. Schirmer, 1914.

Kurihara, Motoi, "My Teacher, Lafcadio Hearn." *Today's Japan,* Vol. 4, No. 1 (Jan. 1959).

"Lafcadio Hearn, A Death-Day Gathering in Japan." *Bookman,* Vols. 50–51 (June 1916), 73–74.

Lafcadio Hearn Society, New Orleans, *Lafcadio Hearn in New Orleans: The Dedication of the Lafcadio Hearn Room of the Howard-Tilton Memorial Library.* The Lafcadio Hearn Society, 1941.

Lawless, R. M., "A Note on Lafcadio Hearn's Brother: with Text of Letter from Japan." *American Literature,* Vol. 10 (March 1938), 80–83.

Lewis, Oscar, *Hearn and His Biographers: the Record of a Literary Controversy, Together with a Group of Letters from Lafcadio Hearn to Joseph Tunison, Now First Published.* San Francisco, The Westgate Press, 1930.

Masamune, Hakucho, "New Light on Lafcadio Hearn." *Contemporary Japan,* Vol. 2 (1933), 270–80.

Tunison, Joseph S., "Lafcadio Hearn." *Book Buyer,* Vol. XIII, No. 4 (May 1896), 209–11.

[Tunison, Joseph S.,] "Lafcadio Hearn." *Montgomery County Reporter,* Dayton, Ohio, May 1, 1908.

Young, Robert, "Lafcadio Hearn." *Living Age,* Vol. 252 (March 23, 1907), 760.

Secondary

Allen, Lee, "Cincinnati's Tanyard Horror." Cincinnati *Times-Star,* July 6, 1957.

———, "Strange Gnome of a Genius." Cincinnati *Enquirer,* July 19, 1959.

Bikle, Lucy L., *George W. Cable: His Life and Letters.* New York, Charles Scribner's Sons, 1928.

Binyon, Laurence, "Lafcadio Hearn on Victorian Poets." *Living Age,* Vol. 303, No. 3935 (Dec. 1919), 601–03.

Blunden, Edmund, "Lafcadio Hearn." *Bookman,* Vol. LXXVII, No. 461 (Feb. 1930), 281–82.

———, "Lafcadio Hearn, Teacher." *Today's Japan,* Vol. 4, No. 1 (Jan. 1959).

Boynton, P. H., "Lafcadio Hearn." *Virginia Quarterly Review,* Vol. 3 (July 1927), 418–34.

———, "Lafcadio Hearn," *More Contemporary Americans.* Chicago, University of Chicago Press, 1927, 51–74.

Brooks, Van Wyck, *The Confident Years: 1885–1915.* New York, E. P. Dutton & Co., Inc., 1952.

Bush, Lewis, "Idzumo." *Today's Japan,* Vol. 4, No. 1 (Jan. 1959).

Coleman, Charles W., Jr., "The Recent Movement in Southern Literature." *Harper's Magazine,* Vol. 74, No. 444 (May 1887), 837–55.

Cowley, Malcolm, "Lafcadio Hearn." Introduction to Henry Goodman, ed., *The Selected Writings of Lafcadio Hearn.* New York, The Citadel Press, 1949.

———, "Lafcadio Herun-san." *New Republic,* Vol. 120 (April 18, 1949), 22–24.

De Smet, Joseph, *Lafcadio Hearn, l'homme et l'œuvre.* 2nd ed., Paris, Mercure de France, 1911.

Erskine, John, "Lafcadio Hearn," *The Memory of Certain Persons.* Philadelphia, J. B. Lippincott Co., 1947, 235–39.

Espey, John J., "Two Japans of Lafcadio Hearn." *Pacific Spectator,* Vol. 4, No. 3 (1950), 342–51.

Ficke, Arthur Davison, "Hearn in the Schoolroom." *Dial,* Vol. LXII, No. 733 (Jan. 11, 1917), 23–24.

Foerster, Norman, "Interpretations of Literature." *Dial,* Vol. LX, No. 711 (Feb. 3, 1916), 112–14.

Frost, O. W., "The Birth of Lafcadio Hearn." *American Literature,* Vol. XXIV, No. 3 (Nov. 1952), 372–77.

Frost, O. W., *Young Hearn*. Tokyo, Hokuseido Press, 1958.

Fukuhara, Shinzo, *The Old Town of Matsue*. Tokyo, Japan Photographic Society, 1935.

Gorman, Herbert S., "Lafcadio Hearn," *The Procession of Masks*. Boston, B. J. Brimmer Co., 1923, 125–35.

Greenslet, Ferris, "Lafcadio Hearn." *Atlantic Monthly*, Vol. 99 (Feb. 1907), 261–72.

Gregory, Alyse, "A Definitive Hearn." *Dial*, Vol. LXXIV, No. 3 (March 1923), 289–92.

[Howells, W. D.,] Rev. *Youma. Harper's Magazine*, Vol. 81 (Sept. 1890), 642. "A Japanese Poet's Defense of Lafcadio Hearn." *Current Literature*, Vol. 50 (Jan. 1911), 90–93.

Josephson, Matthew, "An Enemy of the West: Lafcadio Hearn," *Portrait of the Artist as an American*. New York, Harcourt, Brace and Co., Inc., 1930.

Katsube, Mitake, "Hearn and Japanese Thought." *Today's Japan*, Vol. 4, No. 1 (Jan. 1959).

Keagy, Walter R., *Lafcadio Hearn*. Cincinnati, the author, 1943.

Kennard, Nina H., "Lafcadio Hearn." *Nineteenth Century and After*, Vol. 59 (Jan. 1906), 135–50.

King, Grace, *Memories of a Southern Woman of Letters*. New York, The Macmillan Co., 1932.

Kitzinger, Angela, "Lafcadio Hearn, Translator." *Today's Japan*, Vol. 4, No. 1 (Jan. 1959).

"Lafcadio Hearn Centenary To Be Observed in Japan." *Publishers' Weekly*, Vol. 157 (June 3, 1950), 2455.

Langton, D. H., "Lafcadio Hearn, Journalist and Writer on Japan." *Manchester Quarterly*, Vol. 31 (1912), 1–23.

"The Late Lafcadio Hearn." *Bookman*, Vol. XX (Nov. 1904), 190.

Levin, Harry T., "Civilized Nomad." *New Republic*, Vol. 114 (April 22, 1946), 588–89.

———, "Lafcadio Hearn," *Literary History of the United States*, II. New York, The Macmillan Co., 1948, 1070–72.

Lewisohn Ludwig, *The Story of American Literature*. New York, The Modern Library, 1932, 347–50.

McWilliams, Vera S., *Lafcadio Hearn*. Boston, Houghton Mifflin Co., 1946.

Mais, S. P. B., "Lafcadio Hearn," *Books and their Writers*. London, Grant Richards, Ltd., 1920, 242–76.

Martyr, Graham, "Lafcadio Hearn," *Gokosei of Ryunan*. No publisher, no date (held in Tokyo University Hearn Collection), 61–67.

Miner, Earl, *Japanese Tradition in British and American Literature*. Princeton, N.J., Princeton University Press, 1958.

Monahan, Michael, "Lafcadio Hearn: A French Estimate." *Forum*, Vol. XLIX (March 1913), 356–66.

———, "A Friend of Lafcadio Hearn," *Nemesis*. New York, Frank-Maurice, Inc., 1926, 131–44.

Mordell, Albert, "A Discovery of Early Hearn Essays." *Today's Japan*, Vol. 4, No. 1 (Jan. 1959).

——, " 'Letters to a Pagan' Not by Hearn." *Today's Japan,* Vol. 5, No. 1 (1955–60, 5th anniversary ed.), 89–98.

More, Paul Elmer, "Lafcadio Hearn." *Atlantic Monthly,* Vol. 91 (Feb. 1903), 204–11.

——, "Lafcadio Hearn: the Meeting of Three Ways." *Atlantic Monthly,* Vol. 91 (Feb. 1903), 204.

Noguchi, Yone, "Lafcadio Hearn: A Dreamer." *Current Literature,* Vol. XXXVIII, No. 6 (June 1905), 521–23.

——, *Lafcadio Hearn in Japan, With Mrs. Hearn's Reminiscences.* London, Elkin Mathews, and Yokohama, Kelly & Walsh, 1910.

——, "Lafcadio Hearn's 'Kwaidan.' " *Bookman,* Vol. XX, No. 2 (Oct. 1904), 159–60.

Perkins, P. D., "Lafcadio Hearn . . ." *Japan News-Week,* May 18, 1940.

——, *Reminiscences of a Bibliographer.* Reprint from *Biblia,* No. 13, 1958.

Robert, Marcel, *Lafcadio Hearn,* 2 vols. Tokyo, Hokuseido Press, 1950–51.

Sangu, Makoto, "Lafcadio Hearn in Japan." *Today's Japan,* Vol. 4, No. 1 (Jan. 1959).

Scott-James, R. A., "The Fugitives," *Modernism and Romance.* London, John Lane, The Bodley Head, 1908, 156–61.

Stempel, Daniel, "Lafcadio Hearn: Interpreter of Japan." *American Literature,* Vol. 20 (March 1948), 1–19.

Thomas, Edward, *Lafcadio Hearn.* Boston, Houghton Mifflin Co., 1912.

Ticknor, Caroline, "Lafcadio Hearn," *Glimpses of Authors.* Boston, Houghton Mifflin Co., 1922, 122–31.

Tinker, Edward L., "Lafcadio Hearn, Restaurateur . . ." *New York Times,* Aug. 3, 1924.

——, *Lafcadio Hearn's American Days,* 2nd ed. New York, Dodd, Mead and Co., Inc., 1924.

Watanabe, Shoko, "Hearn's View of Japanese Buddhism." *Today's Japan,* Vol. 4, No. 1 (Jan. 1959).

Wilson, Edmund, "The Ordeal of George Washington Cable." *New Yorker,* Nov. 9, 1957.

Yano, Kazumi, "Lafcadio Hearn as a Critic." *Today's Japan,* Vol. 4, No. 1 (Jan. 1959).

5. CHRONOLOGY OF IMPORTANT LAFCADIO HEARN WRITINGS, PUBLISHED DURING HIS LIFE AND AFTER

Hearn wrote many of his stories and essays first for periodicals, and then selected and arranged them for his books. Much that he did not collect in his lifetime was rescued by various editors and published in book form after his death. This large part of his work is included below only under the book titles:

One of Cleopatra's Nights and Other Fantastic Romances, by Théophile Gautier, Lafcadio Hearn, translator. New York, R. Worthington, 1882.

Stray Leaves from Strange Literature. Boston, J. R. Osgood and Co., 1884.

La Cuisine Créole: a Collection of Culinary Recipes. New York, Will H. Coleman, n.d. [1885.]

"Gombo Zhèbes": A Little Dictionary of Creole Proverbs, Selected from Six Creole Dialects. New York, W. H. Coleman, 1885.

Historical Sketch Book and Guide to New Orleans, ed. and compiled by several leading writers of the New Orleans press. New York, Will H. Coleman, 1885. (Only in part by L. H.)

Some Chinese Ghosts. Boston, Roberts Brothers, 1887.

Chita: A Memory of Last Island. New York, Harper & Brothers, 1889.

The Crime of Sylvestre Bonnard, by Anatole France, Lafcadio Hearn, translator. New York, Harper & Brothers, 1890.

Two Years in the French West Indies. New York, Harper & Brothers, 1890.

Youma. New York, Harper & Brothers, 1890.

Glimpses of Unfamiliar Japan, 2 vols. Boston, Houghton Mifflin Co., 1894.

Out of the East: Reveries and Studies in New Japan. Boston, Houghton Mifflin Co., 1895.

Kokoro: Hints and Echoes of Japanese Inner Life. Boston, Houghton Mifflin Co., 1896.

Gleanings in Buddha-Fields: Studies of Hand and Soul in the Far East. Boston, Houghton Mifflin Co., 1897.

Exotics and Retrospectives. Boston, Little, Brown and Co., 1898.

Japanese Fairy Tales, printed in color by hand from Japanese wood blocks, 5 vols. Tokyo, Hasegawa, 1898–1922.

In Ghostly Japan. Boston, Little, Brown and Co., 1899.

Shadowings. Boston, Little, Brown and Co., 1900.

A Japanese Miscellany. Boston, Little, Brown and Co., 1901.

Kotto: Being Japanese Curios, With Sundry Cobwebs. New York, The Macmillan Co., 1902.

Kwaidan: Stories and Studies of Strange Things. Boston, Houghton Mifflin Co., 1904.

Japan: An Attempt at Interpretation. New York, The Macmillan Co., 1904.

Romance of the Milky Way, and Other Studies and Stories. Boston, Houghton Mifflin Co., 1905.

"Letters of a Poet to a Musician: Letters from Hearn to H. E. Krehbiel." *Critic,* Vols. 48–49 (April 1906), 309–18.

Life and Letters of Lafcadio Hearn, 2 vols., by Elizabeth Bisland. Boston, Houghton Mifflin Co., 1906.

Letters from the Raven: Being the Correspondence of Lafcadio Hearn with Henry Watkin, Milton Bronner, ed. New York, Brentano's, 1907.

Japanese Letters of Lafcadio Hearn, Elizabeth Bisland, ed. Boston, Houghton Mifflin Co., 1910.

The Temptation of St. Anthony, by Gustave Flaubert, Lafcadio Hearn, translator. New York and Seattle, Alice Harriman Co., 1910.

Leaves from the Diary of an Impressionist, Ferris Greenslet, ed. Boston, Houghton Mifflin Co., 1911.

Editorials from the "Kobe Chronicle," Japanese Editorial Writings. New York, privately printed, 1913.

Fantastics and Other Fancies, Charles Woodward Hutson, ed. Boston, Houghton Mifflin Co., 1914.

Japanese Lyrics. Boston, Houghton Mifflin Co., 1915.

Appreciations of Poetry, John Erskine, ed. New York, Dodd, Mead and Co., Inc., 1916.

Life and Literature, John Erskine, ed. Dodd, Mead and Co., Inc., 1917.

Karma. New York, Boni and Liveright, 1918.

Hearn Memorial Translations (in Japanese), 9 vols. Tokyo, Hokuseido Press, 1920–23.

"Some Martinique Letters of Lafcadio Hearn." *Harper's Magazine,* Vol. 142 (March 1921).

Books and Habits, From the Lectures of Lafcadio Hearn. New York, Dodd, Mead and Co., Inc., 1921.

The Writings of Lafcadio Hearn, 16 vols. Boston, Houghton Mifflin Co., 1922.

An American Miscellany, Articles and Stories Now First Collected, 2 vols., Albert Mordell, ed. New York, Dodd, Mead and Co., Inc., 1924.

Creole Sketches, Charles Woodward Hutson, ed. Boston, Houghton Mifflin Co., 1924.

Saint Anthony, and Other Stories, by Guy de Maupassant, Lafcadio Hearn, translator. Albert Mordell, ed. New York, Albert and Charles Boni, 1924.

Occidental Gleanings: Sketches and Essays Now First Collected, 2 vols., Albert Mordell, ed. New York, Dodd, Mead and Co., Inc., 1925.

Some New Letters and Writings of Lafcadio Hearn, Sanki Ichikawa, ed. Tokyo, Kenkyusha, Ltd., 1925.

Complete Lectures on Art, Literature, and Philosophy, R. Tanabe and others, eds. Tokyo, Hokuseido Press, 1925–34.

Editorials: New Orleans Journalistic Writings, Charles Woodward Hutson, ed. Boston, Houghton Mifflin Co., 1926.

Interpretations of Literature, 2 vols., John Erskine, ed. New York, Dodd, Mead and Co., Inc., 1926.

Talks to Writers, John Erskine, ed. New York, Dodd, Mead and Co., Inc., 1927.

Adventures of Walter Schnaffs, by Guy de Maupassant, Lafcadio Hearn, translator. Albert Mordell, ed. Tokyo, Hokuseido Press, 1931.

"Letters of Lafcadio Hearn to His Brother," E. C. Beck, ed. *English Journal,* Vol. XX (1931), 287–92, and *American Literature,* Vol. IV (1932), 167–73.

Stories from Pierre Loti, Lafcadio Hearn, translator. Albert Mordell, ed. Tokyo, Hokuseido Press, 1933.

Stories from Emile Zola, Lafcadio Hearn, translator. Albert Mordell, ed. Tokyo, Hokuseido Press, 1935.

Sketches and Tales from the French, Lafcadio Hearn, translator. Albert Mordell, ed. Tokyo, Hokuseido Press, 1935.

Barbarous Barbers and Other Stories, Ichiro Nishizaki, ed. Tokyo, Hokuseido Press, 1939.

Buying Christmas Toys, and Other Essays, Ichiro Nishizaki, ed. Tokyo, Hokuseido Press, 1939.

Literary Essays, Ichiro Nishizaki, ed. Tokyo, Hokuseido Press, 1939.

The New Radiance and Other Scientific Sketches, Ichiro Nishizaki, ed. Tokyo, Hokuseido Press, 1939.

Oriental Articles, Ichiro Nishizaki, ed. Tokyo, Hokuseido Press, 1939.

Selected Writings of Lafcadio Hearn, Henry Goodman, ed. New York, The Citadel Press, 1949.

Selected Writings of Lafcadio Hearn, The Hearn Centennial Committee, ed. Tokyo, published for the English Literary Society of Japan by Kenkyusha, Ltd., 1953.

"Newly Discovered Letters from Lafcadio Hearn to Dr. Rudolph Matas," Ichiro Nishizaki, ed. Ochanomizu University, Tokyo, *Studies in Arts and Cultures,* Vol. 8 (March 1956), 85–118.

Children of the Levee, O. W. Frost, ed. University of Kentucky Press, 1957.

New Hearn Letters from the French West Indies, by Ichiro Nishizaki. (Reprinted from Ochanomizu University *Studies in Arts and Culture,* Vol. 12) Tokyo, June, 1959.

Lafcadio Hearn: From Hoki to Oki—The Development from His Notes to the Final Version—Appendix: The Contents of Hearn's Note, by Hisashi Kajitani. (Reprinted from the Collection of Essays in Commemoration of the Tenth Anniversary [1959] of Shimane University.) (Human Science) February, 1960.

"Two Unpublished Hearn Letters," O. W. Frost, ed. *Today's Japan,* Vol. 5, No. 1 (1955–60: Fifth Anniversary issue), 43–48.

Index